How Institutions Change

Heiko Breit
Anita Engels
Timothy Moss
Markus Troja (eds.)

How Institutions Change
Perspectives on Social Learning
in Global and Local
Environmental Contexts

Leske + Budrich, Opladen 2003

Gedruckt auf säurefreiem und alterungsbeständigem Papier.

Die Deutsche Bibliothek – CIP-Einheitsaufnahme
Ein Titeldatensatz für die Publikation ist bei Der Deutschen Bibliothek erhältlich

ISBN 3-8100-3858-X

© 2003 Leske + Budrich, Opladen

Das Werk einschließlich aller seiner Teile ist urheberrechtlich geschützt. Jede Verwertung außerhalb der engen Grenzen des Urheberrechtsgesetzes ist ohne Zustimmung des Verlages unzulässig und strafbar. Das gilt insbesondere für Vervielfältigungen, Übersetzungen, Mikroverfilmungen und die Einspeicherung und Verarbeitung in elektronischen Systemen.

Druck: DruckPartner Rübelmann, Hemsbach
Printed in Germany

Contents

Preface
Heiko Breit, Anita Engels, Timothy Moss, Markus Troja...... 7

Foreword
Oran Young...... 9

Introduction
Institutional Change and Social Learning in Environmental Contexts: An Introduction
Heiko Breit and Markus Troja...... 13

Part I: Reshaping Institutions
Introduction: Timothy Moss...... 31

Of Course International Institutions Matter: But When and How?
Ronald B. Mitchell...... 35

Learning in International Public Policy Networks. Managing Institutional Interplay between National and International Forest Programmes
Andreas Obser...... 53

Solving Problems of 'Fit' at the Expense of Problems of 'Interplay'? The Spatial Reorganisation of Water Management Following the EU Water Framework Directive
Timothy Moss...... 85

Using Market Institutions for Sustainability: Environmental Production Standards in the Coffee Trade
Florian Dünckmann and Claudia Mayer...... 123

Part II: Linking Institutional Change to Social Practice
Introduction: Heiko Breit...... 151

Institutionalisation of Ecological Risk Perceptions: The Role of Climate Change Discourses in Germany
Anita Engels...... 155

Politics, Law and Citizens' Responsibility. Justice Judgements in the Everday Reconstruction of Environmental Conflicts
Heiko Breit, Thomas Döring and Lutz H. Eckensberger...... 179

Institutional Dynamics of Changing Land Care Practices
in the Central Namib Desert
Thomas Widlok... 205

Part III: Institutionalising Social Learning
Introduction: Anita Engels.. 229

Resolving Environmental Conflicts. Mediation and Negotiation
as Institutional Capacities for Social Learning
Markus Troja... 233

Myths and Laws: Changing Institutions of Indigenous
Marine Resource Management in Central America
Verena Sandner... 269

Lessons Drawn from Burden Sharing Exercises.
The EC Acidification and Climate Change Policies
Michael Huber.. 301

Social Learning at the Science-Policy Interface – A Comparison
of the IPCC and the Scientific Assessments LRTAP Convention
Bernd Siebenhüner.. 325

Conclusions
Institutional Change in Environmental Contexts
Anita Engels and Timothy Moss.. 355

About the Authors... 377

Preface

In April 1997 a group of social scientists in Germany came together to form a task force on institutional dimensions of global environmental change. At the time they were all engaged in research projects funded by the German Research Council (DFG) within its Priority Programme "Global Environmental Change – Social and Behavioural Dimensions". Coming initially from the fields of political science and sociology they were motivated by a common interest in advancing knowledge on processes of institutional change relevant to major environmental problems. By exploring the capacity of diverse disciplinary approaches to explain institutional change and by exchanging knowledge on environmental institutions in various social, cultural and political settings they aimed to shed fresh light on the complex dynamics of institutions. By 1999 the task force had grown in numbers and scope to include geographers, cultural anthropologists and cultural psychologists, reflecting a unique and broad spectrum of social science research into institutions and the environment. The new members brought not only new disciplinary perspectives to the group, but also an interest in a wider range of institutions functioning at different societal levels and in new cultural settings, including developing countries.

This book is the principal product of the task force. It presents a broad range of state-of-the-art research into different types of institutions shaping resource use, the diverse ways in which they can change or be redesigned and the conditions that can help or hinder the emergence of institutions favourable to sustainable development. Three papers from external authors have been included to complement the expertise of the task force (Mitchell, Huber and Siebenhüner). Intensive exchange within the task force has enabled the individual contributions to be embedded in a common rationale for the book as a whole. A line of argument is developed through the book, looking first at policy-driven examples of institutional change, then broadening the perspective to examine the relationship between institutions and social practice, and subsequently demonstrating how environmentally beneficial processes of social learning can be encouraged. A general introduction and introductory chapters to each section help to guide the reader along the line of argument; the main findings are analysed in a concluding chapter. Altogether this has ensured an unusually cohesive approach for an edited collection.

The editors would like to take this opportunity to express their thanks to the German Research Council for all its help in funding the individual projects and meetings of the task force. They are very grateful also to the coordinators of the Priority Programme, Hans Spada and Michael Scheuermann, for their tireless and professional leadership of the programme. We are indebted above all to other members of the task force – Thomas Döring, Florian Dünckmann, Claudia Mayer, Andreas Obser, Verena Sandner and Thomas Widlok – for their insight and support throughout the long process of creating this book. We also thank Kerstin Rosenow and Tanja John for their valuable support in finalising the book's layout.

Heiko Breit, Frankfurt am Main
Anita Engels, Bielefeld
Timothy Moss, Erkner
Markus Troja, Oldenburg

April 2003

Foreword

All social institutions are dynamic. Whether these systems of rights, rules and decision-making procedures are formal or informal in character, broad or narrow in terms of their functional scope, global or local with respect to their spatial domain, they change continually in response both to endogenous pressures and to exogenous forces. It follows that the study of institutional change should loom large on the research agenda of analysts seeking to improve our understanding of social institutions.

Among those who focus on environmental institutions, however, institutional change has not emerged as a priority theme on the research agenda. It is relatively easy to account for this gap. Research on environmental institutions began by asking how these arrangements form and why institutions emerge to address some environmental problems but not others. But critics were quick to raise questions about the significance of institutions and especially about the role these arrangements play as determinants of the course of human/environment interactions. It seemed natural, under the circumstances, to move directly to a sustained effort to assess the effectiveness of institutions or, in other words, the conditions that determine whether and how institutions matter. Even so, the relative lack of attention to issues of institutional dynamics clearly constitutes a weakness in the rapidly growing literature dealing with environmental institutions. That makes this collection of essays on institutional change a particularly welcome addition to this field of study. For the most part, these essays are exploratory in nature; they open up an important line of enquiry rather than providing definitive answers to the central questions regarding institutional change. This is not a defect. The ideas that the contributors to this book articulate will go far toward defining the research agenda for scholars dealing with the dynamics of environmental institutions during the foreseeable future.

What are the sources of institutional change or, in other words, the driving forces that produce significant alterations in environmental institutions once they are put in place? There are many ways to respond to this question. Yet a few simple distinctions will help to put the contributions of this book into perspective. Changes may be intended in the sense that they arise from conscious efforts to address identifiable concerns or unintended in the sense that they are de facto consequences of actions motivated by other concerns. The amendments to the ozone regime introduced in the wake of the growth of knowledge about the threat of stratospheric ozone depletion following the adoption of the 1987 Montreal Protocol exemplify the case of intended change. De facto shifts in the operation of resource regimes arising from the introduction of new harvesting technologies (e.g. high endurance stern trawlers in marine fisheries) illustrate the case of unintended change.

Similarly, institutional changes can be actor-specific in the sense that they arise from the actions of individuals or interest groups seeking to promote their own interests or collective in the sense that they emerge from coordinated efforts on the part of all (or most) of those subject to the rights and rules of an institution to improve the arrangement's performance. Actor-specific changes (e.g. efforts on the part of energy producers to water down the operational content of key regulations) are pervasive; self-interested actors can be counted on to seize every opportunity to change prevailing institutional arrangements to serve their own ends. Collective changes, by contrast, commonly occur when those subject to an institution's rights and rules recognize that the arrangement is performing poorly from a societal perspective and endeavour to initiate reforms to address the problem. The protracted effort to restructure the law of the sea during the 1970s and 1980s exemplifies this case.

Combining these distinctions produces a 2x2 table that identifies four major types of institutional change. Each of these categories is important and deserves systematic attention. Yet it is fair to say that the authors of the essays included in this book are particularly interested in those institutional changes that are both collective and intended. These are changes featuring a deliberate restructuring of existing arrangements in the interests of improving their performance with regard to social goals like efficiency, equity or sustainability. This is where the idea of social learning, a central theme of the book, comes into play. Social learning occurs in many situations having nothing to do with institutions. But as applied to the analysis of institutional dynamics, social learning refers – first and foremost – to processes in which those operating under the provisions of an institution seek to assess the performance of existing arrangements in terms of one or more common standards and to adjust or adapt these arrangements in the interests of enhancing their performance in subsequent time periods.

There is no guarantee that such processes will yield positive results. Adjustments introduced in the wake of negative performance reviews can prove detrimental rather than constructive. As the authors of this book observe, such problems often involve matters of fit, interplay and scale, the principal analytic concerns of the international project on the Institutional Dimensions of Global Environmental Change (IDGEC). Changes in environmental institutions may yield arrangements that are less rather than more compatible with the major properties of the biophysical systems with which they interact. Adjustments to existing institutions can lead to conflicts with other institutions dealing with issues like trade and finance. Specific alterations may reflect efforts to apply findings pertaining to institutions operating at other levels of social organisation that ultimately prove inappropriate.

As is the case in other areas of human endeavour, then, we can "learn" things about environmental institutions that actually detract from performance rather than enhancing it. Yet this sobering observation should not divert our attention from the importance of social learning as a form of institutional change that can produce constructive results. When it works well, social learning features a feedback process in which initial changes trigger performance reviews, the results of these reviews determine the character and content of the next round of changes, and the process continues as long as it yields socially desirable alterations. So long as we approach these processes with a critical attitude, social learning can serve us well not only as a guide to thinking about an important form of institutional change but also as a means of changing institutions to maximize success in dealing with a variety of environmental concerns ranging from problems of land degradation at the local level to the problem of climate change at the global level.

What makes the essays included in this book particularly attractive is the fact that they provide an array of perspectives that help us to understand the prospects and problems of social learning in a number of settings. The authors of these essays do not offer the sort of uncritical endorsement of social learning that is characteristic of some of the more enthusiastic accounts of adaptive management. Nor do they seek to throw cold water on rising expectations regarding the virtues of social learning. Rather, they endeavour to assess both the nature of social learning as a process of institutional change operating in a range of environmental contexts and the factors that determine the extent to which we can rely on social learning as a mechanism to maximise the performance of environmental institutions through intentional and collective changes.

For these reasons, I am delighted to endorse this book as a substantial contribution to the IDGEC science agenda and to recommend it as a significant contribution to the study of institutional change more generally. These essays can and will serve as a springboard for an important growth area in research dealing with environmental institutions during the years to come.

Oran R. Young
Chair, IDGEC Scientific Steering Committee

Heiko Breit and Markus Troja

Institutional Change and Social Learning in Environmental Contexts: An Introduction

1 The Conceptual and Interdisciplinary Approach of the Book

This book is about institutions through which human beings interact with their environment. Solving growing global environmental problems appears to be beyond the reach of individuals: it requires institutional changes. Individual action is of course needed to attain the objectives of a more sustainable world. However, individual action without institutional support remains powerless in the face of the multiple barriers that render unsustainable so many aspects of human life. Individual actions and institutions are, therefore, inextricably interwoven; they can mutually reinforce as well as block one another.

Changes in the complex web of actions and institutions are the focus of this book that seeks to contribute to a better understanding of environmental issues. To some degree this is done in an exploratory way, which leads to new questions and not to definite answers. Many different fields in the social sciences deal with changing environmental policies and examples of institutional reform (van Tatenhove/Leroy 2000, Berndt 1999, Young et al. 1999, Minsch et al. 1998, Jordan/O'Riordan 1995, 1997). We seek to build on these contributions and to develop a more comprehensive perspective on much needed institutional changes. But we also try to enlarge the viewpoint on institutions and their relations to social action and social learning embodying economic, cultural, social and psychological factors which motivate social actors to undertake ecological remedial action.

For these reasons the book brings together a broad range of studies which

— address different types of institutionalised problems, from environmentally exploitative property regimes to subjective barriers and responsibilities to sustainable practices,
— investigate these problems in different political-cultural settings, from industrialised countries in Europe and the USA to developing countries in Africa and Central America, as well as at different levels of governance (international, national, regional and local),
— explore different forms of institutional change, ranging from the reform of legal frameworks and the introduction of new market institutions to a

process of social learning involving the institutionalisation of new participation procedures that are based on systems of formal rules and informal values within a society, and
— apply different disciplinary approaches to explaining institutional change, from political science, sociology and human geography to cultural psychology and cultural anthropology.

Two distinctive features characterise the innovative nature of the book. The first strength lies in its *interdisciplinary background.* It combines and reflects on the specific contributions of many different fields of research, ranging from political science to sociology, geography, ethnology and developmental and cultural psychology. Each of these different perspectives provides additional insights about institutions and institutional changes and enriches the overall picture we generate throughout the course of the book. An important interdisciplinary feature of the book is that the individual contributions do not restrict themselves to those terminologies and analytical approaches which are at the core of their own discipline. The authors have applied various tools of institutional analysis and, in doing so, have highlighted the boundaries of their respective scientific paradigms as well as areas of significant complementarity. This is illustrated in numerous case studies with complex empirical realities that often escape the narrow boundaries of strictly disciplinary science.

Furthermore, the mono-disciplinary studies are embedded in a common rationale for the book as a whole which developed out of discussions in an interdisciplinary task force on institutional dimensions to global environmental change in which most of the authors were involved over a period of several years. This has ensured an unusually cohesive approach for an edited collection which is reflected in the book's structure (see below). A further interdisciplinary dimension to the book lies in identifying the capacity of each disciplinary approach to explain specific aspects of institutional change and exploring the linkages between the different scientific perspectives – that is to say, how questions raised by one chapter are taken up and explored further by others. In this way it has been possible to build up a story of how institutions change, using the individual studies to explain those chapters of the story for which they are particularly suited.

We see the book's second strength in the *framework of social learning* that we apply to our respective fields of research. Social scientists are just beginning to use social learning as a theoretical frame of understanding in the field of global environmental change (The Social Learning Group 2001a, b), whereas research for instance on organizational learning is already well established (Dierkes/Berthoin/Antal/Child/Nonaka 2001). Analysing the potential and capacity for social learning – as well as aspects of social life that act as barriers to learning processes – is fundamental to understanding how institutions change in environmental contexts.

2 The Understanding of Institutions in Social Science

The authors developed a common (social science) understanding of institutions which is drawn from the science plan of the international project on Institutional Dimensions of Global Environmental Change (IDGEC) in the International Human Dimensions Programme (IHDP) (Young et al. 1999).

Analysing these questions we speak of institutions in the sense of generally accepted and relatively stable patterns, or rules, of conduct and social interaction. This understanding of institutions differs from the everyday meaning of the term as well as from other scientific approaches which often confuse institutions and organisations (Scott 2001, Göhler 1997, Koelbe 1995). In social science the term institution refers to social norms, legal regulations and distributional systems (for power and/or resources), established procedures and routine patterns of individual and social behaviour (Mayntz/Scharpf 1995: 40). Institutions in this sense can be understood as relatively constant structures of control. Organisations in a more material sense are, on the other hand, social entities and corporate actors, usually with a formalised membership, staff, a budget and a specific legal status. Organisations resemble players acting within the framework of institutional settings (Häder 1997: 62). Their moves or actions can be strategic, based on an individual's desire for success. The focus on strategic action is one possible way for analysing institutional change. However, action orientation towards communication and mutual comprehension is another, equally important, theoretical and empirical concept (Habermas 1987).

Institutions, as they appear in the chapters of this book, both enable and constrain human interactions. They form a framework of appropriate and accepted actions and thus reduce uncertainty about the behaviour of individual actors (Dietl 1993: 88ff; Göhler 1997: 28). They do so by building up and stabilising *expectations* about the behaviour of other actors. The existence of institutions is first and foremost an indicator of the *factual acceptance* of a certain mode of behaviour by others, but their effectiveness can also be *normatively* based. Institutions generate a common orientation and serve to co-ordinate different strategies for the allocation of goods or resources. This co-ordination needs argumentation and legitimatisation which – ideally – emerge from public debate or democratic decision-making processes; in other words from discourses and procedures of a civil society.

In real life, existing institutions cannot be understood as the outcome of an actual consensus of citizens but are rather the evolutionary product of social needs and societal functions. Actors do not have to know in detail the intentions and convictions of those with whom they interact. Nor do they have to agree with them. The efficiency of institutions is based on a reduction of transaction costs and the effectiveness of sanctions, whether social, economic and legal sanctions or more internalised sanctions such as feelings of guilt or notions of justice.

This understanding of institutions emphasizes their capacity for explaining human behaviour as a reaction to institutionalised incentives – institutions as the *independent variable*. In this sense, institutions can affect anthropogenic use of natural resources both negatively and positively. Institutions appear as a problem for sustainable development if they serve to stabilise patterns of unsustainable behaviour, but can be turned into a solution if they promote environmentally sound forms of production and consumption. This hints at the potential for institutional change. To varying degrees, institutions involve and allow public discourses and open decision processes, and are thus a platform for social learning. These processes can generate new perspectives, reveal blind spots and blockages and open up innovative options for human behaviour. In other words, institutions can also be treated as a *dependent variable*. The recursive relation of individual action and institutional change is at the heart of processes of social learning. The following section will deal with the emergence of new institutions, induced changes and the active shaping of existing institutions through human action.

3 Social Learning in Environmental Contexts: Looking at the Interaction between Formal and Informal Institutions

When examining induced changes and the active shaping of existing institutions we use as a point of departure the distinction between formal and informal institutions (North 1990). A "sense of justice" and "environmental concern" are examples of types of *informal institutions*, which can be described in terms of traditions, cultural values and non-codified norms. The set of informal institutions form the "ethos" of a society which entails what we call "culture" including the community's prevailing perceptions about the world, the accumulated wisdom of the past and a current set of values (North 1990: 37). By contrast, constitutions, common law, regulations and statutes are examples of *formal institutions*.

The explicit consideration of informal institutions in this book broadens the perspective on institutional change. This takes into account that institutions are also based on communicative actions and need to be analysed as variables which strongly depend on culture. Institutional change, therefore, is not only understood as a result of policies of the political or economic system, but also of common social practice with its specific cognitive and normative rule systems. The interpretation of reality, i.e. the perception, evaluation and management of environmental risks, depends to a large extent on social interaction with embodied practical knowledge and intersubjective shared norms (Schütz 1970). Formal institutions are the driving force of changes but its initiations and outcomes are a result of changes to both formal and informal rules. Looking at informal institutions in the context of environmental problems means looking at the social construction of problems and problem solving with its typical beliefs about cause and effect and attributions of responsibility (Douglas 1985).

However, an interdisciplinary perspective also blurs the strict boundaries between formal and informal institutions *because* it takes into consideration the cultural and social embeddedness of institutions in different contexts of everyday practices. In some cases formal institutions comprise not only those which are documented in some written form and have explicit rules of conduct, but also taboos and rituals which experience continuation by oral transmission only. Therefore, the book does not exclusively focus on defining the boundaries between formal and informal institutions but rather emphasises the insight that formal institutions depend to some degree on the embeddedness in a web of shared beliefs and meanings, and that the normative control of formal institutions is inextricably intertwined with informal institutions (Münch 1984: 13). This is also the case for those types of highly formal institutions which seem to be "isolated" from day-to-day interaction: the formal institutions of functional differentiation in Western industrialised countries. Functional differentiation led here to the emergence of relatively autonomous subsystems and fields of action such as the economy, jurisdiction, bureaucracy and public administration, which seem to be open to rationalisation, planning and reform (Weber 1975; Luhmann 1985), but not embedded in communication and interaction processes based on informal institutions.

Therefore, analytically it makes sense to distinguish formal from informal institutions to understand the significance of each of these spheres for environmentally sound behaviour and the goal of sustainable development. Empirically, both types of institutions have to be compatible with one another, as too excessive discrepancies could lead to a split culture. A lack of compatibility can have destabilising effects in the long run. A specific law that runs counter to a general sense of justice, for example, is difficult to implement and maintain.

If we assume interdependencies between formal and informal institutions, and the embeddedness of one type of institution in the other, the interplay between the two types of institutions in a complex process of institutionalisation moves centre stage. Because problem solving needs theoretical-scientific, political-administrative *and* practical knowledge as well as formal legislation *and* informal norms and values, the *relationship* between formal and informal institutions is very important for policy design (Nee/Ingram 1998).

How do changes to informal and formal institutions and the way they interact emerge, how do they become stabilised, how can they be induced? Changes depend on processes of *social learning* that occur at the interface between administrative, political and economic imperatives on the one hand and processes of communication and comprehension in the world of everyday life on the other. Social learning processes create knowledge about solutions to problems and change normative rules e.g. about the commitment to act. The central medium of social learning are communication processes on different societal levels as they are described in this book: face-to-face interaction, mass-media, scientific and public discourse. It is the respective communication process that leads to understanding the environmental problem as well as to developing and testing new rules (Ostrom 1998: 12-14).

Understanding institutional change as a potential outcome of processes of social learning, we speak of social learning if institutional changes cause a *successful* readjustment of the relations of human beings and their environment. Success in this context is bound to the *sustainability of these relations*, i.e. the compatibility of the use of resources and the carrying capacity of the environment. Social learning implies changes in perspectives and judgements through a discourse that emerges within specific institutional conditions and through exchanges with other institutional settings. These settings could include different cultural views and discourses.

The importance of social learning derives from the fact that sustainability not only depends on the "instrumental" rationality of natural and technical sciences. Successful reactions to global environmental changes need *human capacities* for social learning both in terms of formal institutions and the informal processes in the public domain. It has been shown that these capacities also depend on world views and the way in which they represent and interpret risks, problems and solutions (Boehm/McDaniels/Nerb/Spada 2001; Thompson/Rayner 1998). In the current situation sustainable development is a new challenge for human capacities for social learning, as the required institutional change has to deal with

— problems of fit: the match or congruence between institutional arrangements and bio-geophysical systems,
— problems of interplay: the linkages among distinct institutional arrangements both at the same level of social organisation and across levels of social organisation,
— problems of scale: the extent to which the causal mechanisms through which institutions affect behaviour can be generalised across space and time (Young et al. 1999).

Dealing with environmental problems involves the integration of economic, social and developmental as well as environmental interests and brings together actors in different cultural settings representing these diverse interests.

This indicates the need for social learning in formal and informal institutional contexts if the economy and society are to readjust to fit better to new global environmental conditions. Social learning is thus both a source and a result of institutional changes. Processes of social learning require certain institutional capacities but also lead to an expansion of these capacities (Healey 1998). Institutional capacities comprise the availability of knowledge resources and the use of reflexive strategies, new networks and alliances, the capacity to mobilise stakeholders and organise public participation, and mechanisms of conflict management. These different institutional capacities can mutually reinforce one another.

As a consequence of this argumentation knowledge as a tool for social learning refers not only to expert knowledge or political-administrative knowledge in organisations, but also to the local knowledge of so-called lay people which is embedded in informal institutions. This is important in another respect as well. All expert knowledge only refers to a limited area of reality and is therefore also a kind of local knowledge (Giddens 1990). Experts are lay people with regard to expert systems other than their own field of expertise. Knowledge relevant to the solution of problems is often communicated in more or less isolated discourses with a distinct logic or rationality. New rules of validity and new forms of argumentation emerge if these diverse discourses are brought together. Knowledge differences are exemplified in contradictory definitions of risk, models and concepts of society and notions of justice and fairness. Examples for bearers of different types of knowledge are representatives of states with different levels of economic development, politicians, scientific experts, organisations, traditional bearers of indigenous knowledge, or people affected by a specific local environmental problem or by the regulation of this problem. The divergent views on problems and solutions that emerge from these differences can at least in part be overcome in processes of social learning.

The chapters of this book deal with the question of how far exchanges and confrontation can lead to new constellations of actors and the emergence of new relations and networks. The face-to-face contact of relevant actors from different social spheres can ease the way for new alliances and create an improved exchange of information and knowledge. Similarly, however, barriers and blockades can emerge and hinder the process of institutional change. Direct contacts can also help build up trust and stable social relations which increase the capacities to deal with future problems and complement formal institutions. Here, too, there is no guarantee: the new relations can also prove too weak in the face of the complex required changes. Furthermore, the importance of non-intended and hidden effects of formal institutions is often overlooked. In spite of these difficulties, it seems that public participation and the involvement of stakeholders are of growing importance for successful institutional changes in a world characterised by specialised expert knowledge in a multitude of knowledge communities, uncertainties about the objective properties of risks (Beck 1992) and the necessity of public acceptance for the implementation of new regulations. This is true for the definition of risks as well as for their management.

Urgent environmental problems call for the active and intentional shaping of institutions. The EU provides several examples of initiatives to stimulate institutional change at the national and regional levels, such as the new Water Framework Directive designed at re-organising water resource management in the EU around the ecological unit of the river basin or the EU directive on ecological agriculture aiming at protecting producers and consumers against unfair competition through the formalisation of standards and procedures of control. Such attempts at institutional reform, however, often collide with existing institutional arrangements and cause problems of interplay. Institutional persistence sometimes hinders rational ways of solving these conflicts, because institutions gain momentum and stability with the help of actors who have learned to use the existing institutions to their own ends. Incomplete information about the relevant field of action and the effectiveness of institutions can also create barriers to change, leading to an increased role of prejudices and ideologies in the evaluation of institutions through actors (Häder 1997: 200-208; Karpe 1997: 73-75; North 1990). Knowledge, networks and participation are thus not automatically a positive source for increasing institutional capacities; they can also be used as resources to block processes of social learning. Likewise, broad public participation can in some cases result in substantial transaction costs.

Conflicts are the normal form of communicating problems in environmental discourses. But conflicts between attempts to reform and attempts to protect existing institutions are not insurmountable barriers to the shaping of new institutions for environmental protection. On the contrary, conflicts also indicate the potential for a learning process. This potential can be tapped if social conflicts over the why, when and how of institutional changes are dealt with in a constructive way. Here, constructive means actors learning to change patterns of behaviour that are environmentally problematic. The capacity to change perspectives helps coordinate legitimate claims and demands of one's own with those of others. This is possible through open information and communication. Capacities for participation and capacities for conflict management are therefore directly intertwined.

At this point, the question of the relationship between informal and formal institutions re-emerges in a different guise. The aim is not only to use this distinction to describe their mutual (non-intended) dependencies but also to explain how they interact efficiently. Neither norms and values nor legislation or political administration alone give rise to institutional change. Change towards sustainable development in particular needs an adequate integration and coupling of formal and informal institutions. One example is the necessity of legal regulations as a facilitating formal institutional context for many discursive, communicative and exchange processes to take place at different levels of society. These formal institutions provide space for action, but this space needs to be filled substantively by a commitment of social actors to make use of, and protect, the space and accept personal responsibility for it. The fruitful interactions of local individual and collective values and goals, as they are embodied in informal institutions, and formal systems of control at the macro-societal level are a precondition for changes which can be rightfully called processes of social learning. Institutional change depends on seeking and creating links between the social learning processes of actors and the capacity of institutions to reflect on these processes. Institutions are expected to serve as the formal framework for change, open for processes of social learning and even promoting and enforcing these learning processes. Actors, on the other hand, are expected to understand and accept institutional changes, to be open for communicative risk definitions and to take responsibility for sustainable actions, but also for the national or global consequences of decisions.

The purpose of the inclusion of actors in the analysis of institutional change is to deliberately broaden the perspective of institutional change to social practice. The participation of responsible actors depends on the perceived potential for changes to patterns of behaviour and interpretation. A public discourse gives room for conflicts between different models of society and notions of social relations, justice and fairness. They can be mutually exclusive or open to mutual influences, in the latter case they can be brought together in a process of social learning and be institutionalised.

4 Structure and Contents of the Book

The conceptual framework which has been developed in the preceding pages leads to a set of broader questions which will be addressed by the chapters of this book:

(1) How do formal and informal institutions interact? How important is the compatibility between these two types of institutions in practice? What kinds of incompatibilities prove particularly obstructive? These questions will be discussed in light of the different disciplinary perspectives brought together in this volume, the essence of which will be integrated into new insights in the concluding chapter.

(2) A second set of questions relate to the distinction between intended and unintended institutional change. How far can institutions be effectively designed? How can we take better account of the unintended effects of

deliberate institutional change? Does social learning in environmental contexts require more regulatory control than hitherto believed, or less?
(3) How are institutions affected by social practice? Changes to institutions reflect experiences with existing institutional arrangements and the way these experiences are perceived. The impact of institutions on social practice in the past has a substantial bearing on how these institutions change, or are changed. How, though, do institutions and social practice influence one another? In what ways, in particular, does social practice contribute to institutional change in environmental contexts?
(4) What levels of social practice are particularly pertinent to processes of institutional change? Institutional change flows through different scales of social organisation, from international regimes, nation states, local communities down to individuals. At each level distinct forms of social practice manifest themselves. What can these different forms of social practice teach us about processes of institutional change at different societal levels? What are the implications of the diversity of cultural contexts for finding new ways in environmental policy?
(5) And finally: What do the answers to these four questions tell us about pathways of social learning towards more environmentally sustainable development? Can we identify certain types of social learning particularly conducive to solving environmental conflicts? How can these types of social learning be encouraged?

Accordingly, the book is structured around three perspectives on institutional change: I: Reshaping Institutions; II: Linking Institutions to Social Practice; and III: Institutionalising Social Learning. Each of the three sections begins with an introductory chapter, outlining the key issues and how the authors contribute to investigating them. In the following we will give a short overview of the chapters.

Part I: Reshaping Institutions

The studies in this section focus on *formal* environmental institutions: their design, implementation and enforcement. Institutional change investigated here is deliberate and policy-driven, with the aim of addressing specific environmental problems. The papers examine cases of institutional reform directed at rearranging the rights and obligations of addressees:

In the first paper, Ronald Mitchell summarises the extensive literature on international environmental institutions (IEIs). Mitchell begins by identifying the empirical and theoretical challenges inherent in trying to demonstrate that IEIs have caused significant changes in policies, behaviour and environmental quality and how different scholars have sought to overcome those challenges.

He then delineates the factors thought to explain variation in the amount or degree of influence that IEIs have, focusing initially on how the components of IEIs influence their effects but then delineating the features of the problem being addressed and the international context, as well as the characteristics of individual countries that create conditions that cause IEIs to have more or less influence. These variables that help identify what type of IEIs have influence under what conditions can operate through rationalist mechanisms involving a "logic of consequences" in which policies and behaviour change in response to re-calculations of material interests manipulated by or through the IEI. However, IEIs can also operate through constructivist mechanisms involving a "logic of appropriateness" in which behaviour and policies are decided based on what is the "right" thing to do in a given social setting given the preferred identity of the actor deciding. Mitchell concludes by identifying the need for new research into questions of how much IEIs influence policies and behaviour relative to other IEIs and relative to other sources of social change, as well as what influence IEIs have in terms of efficiency, cost-effectiveness, equity and other important criteria.

The article by Andreas Obser briefly reviews a variety of analytic tools that are available to explore the complex and contingent interdependencies in global environmental policy making. A major objective is to pursue a governance- and learning-oriented style of explanatory research that creates openings for the integration of analytical methods, which are conventionally employed in international relations, comparative politics, network analysis and public management research. This approach is then applied to explore how the management of international institutions influences social learning in the field of international forest policy. It is argued that the form and processes of international forest institutions significantly affect their role in and effectiveness for social learning. Multi-level governance has emerged as an important analytical framework and linking strategy in the International Arrangement on Forests (IAF), recently established at the United Nations. Focusing on National Forest Programmes (nfp), the article analyses the current allocation of forest policy functions across multiple levels of governance. The growing popularity of decentralization and multi-stakeholder dialogues in many countries has further accentuated the shift to a more multi-levelled governance logic of nfps. Thus far, the often ad hoc and incremental process through which forest policy tasks disperse across different levels of governance has created a confusing pattern of overlapping responsibilities. It is argued that nfps – if networked and results-based – could and should serve as learning-oriented transmission belts in international multi-level arrangements.

The paper by Timothy Moss deals with a particular type of institutional change: the policy-driven reform of supranational environmental legislation and its anticipated impact on existing national, regional and local institutions of resource management. It takes as an example the EU Water Framework

Directive, which came into force in December 2000, and investigates how the future introduction of river basin management across the EU is likely to affect the spatial organisation of water management within Member States. The paper examines how the institutionalisation of river basin management by the Water Framework Directive represents a classic case of trying to solve problems of spatial 'fit' arising from organising a biophysical system along political-administrative territories. It then queries whether, in overcoming this dilemma, problems of 'interplay' between water and other relevant institutions, such as for land use or spatial planning, may be exacerbated in those Member States where water is currently managed by bodies of local and regional government. Moss analyses how problems of institutional 'fit' and 'interplay' are addressed in the scientific community of water specialists, how far the Water Framework Directive and recent EU water policy reflect and build on this knowledge, potential difficulties and opportunities in adapting existing institutions to meet the requirements for river basin management, and the adaptability of old – and the emergence of new – forms of regional environmental governance in the field of water management.

Florian Dünckmann and Claudia Mayer deal with environmental institutions in free markets. Using the analytical distinction between "problem of fit" and "problem of interplay" the paper raises questions that arise from the formulation, supervision and implementation of environmental production standards in the coffee sector. The authors analyse problems of fit in the coffee sector characterised by a multidimensional system consisting of both physical and social elements. Problems of internal interplay arise because in the free market environmental standards are forced to compete with each other. Behind every standard there are different actors which pursue their own interests using their individual resources of power. Consequently, not always the best standard prevails in the market and environmental standards do not prove to be more efficient in steering global trade than environmental policy. Finally, the paper describes problems of external interplay. Legislation and international frameworks are important institutional systems because they define and limit the arena of the free market. The paper draws the conclusion that with the introduction of market mechanisms in environmental regulation the responsibilities of national and international policy are not replaced. Rather a new and complex field for political measures has evolved.

All studies examine the creation or modification of institutions in terms of how they resolve problems of fit, interplay and scale identified as central to institutional effectiveness in the Science Plan of the IDGEC project (Young et al. 1999).

The case studies show examples of highly innovative institutional arrangements that result from processes of learning on the level of formal institutions. But the findings of the papers in this section also indicate how far the success of formal institutions depends ultimately on the motives of individuals and organisations to cooperate within a specific contextual framework. What motivates actors to aspire to change existing institutions at all? This central question – raised by the studies in Part I on reshaping formal institutions – is taken up by the contributions in Part II which examine the dependence of institutional change on social practices.

Part II: Linking Institutions to Social Practice

The contributions to this section deal with the cultural embeddedness of processes of institutionalisation and underline the role of *informal* institutions in institutional change. The three papers study different ways of perceiving and dealing with environmental change and how these shape institutions. They show that processes of social learning and institutional change always take place in a particular social world with its particular practices and discourses. In this way the contributions help elucidate the dynamics of the interplay between informal and formal institutions and the interaction between local contexts of social practice and global processes of change.

The contribution by Anita Engels discusses an example where successful social learning means the institutionalisation of a specific risk perception in a national institutional setting. The case study is about climate change discourses in Germany. By analysing discourses on climate change in science, politics and the mass media over a period of two decades a more evolutionary type of change is highlighted. The paper asks how informal institutions such as risk perceptions form and define legitimate ways of acting on behalf of the environment. In contrast to Part I of the book, this kind of discourse analysis brings unintentional change to the fore, both by showing the uncontrollable dynamics of societal discourses and by demonstrating the heterogeneity of multiple 'local' or 'national' solutions to global environmental problems. This heterogeneity often calls for processes of conflict management, negotiation and decision-making at a higher level of political representation.

The article by Heiko Breit, Thomas Döring and Lutz Eckensberger deals with citizens' understanding of formal institutions such as law and politics and describes public discourse as the centre stage on which informal and formal institutions meet and interact. On the basis of 180 semi-structured interviews on environmental conflicts and a theoretical framework four ideal types can be identified. They entail justice judgements of varying complexity on civil responsibility, and represent different ways of integrating various perspectives and ideas of conflict solution. The authors draw the conclusion that on the one hand institutional change and social learning need complex justice judgements, because only they allow participation, negotiation and mediation procedures which are vital in civil society. On the other hand these procedures only emerge if *open* formal institutions allow co-operation and communication between social actors of different competence embedded in formal *and* informal institutions.

Increasing awareness about the complexity of social institutions implicated in environmental change suggests that institutional arrangements are not easily transferable from their original setting into any other context. This is true for attempts to import local knowledge and practices into more general environmentalist strategies but also, conversely, for attempts to generalise institutional designs (for instance property regimes) so that they cover a wide spectrum of specific local institutional settings. The contribution by Thomas Widlok focuses on the latter issue by investigating how the complexity of particular institutions can be usefully reduced by allowing a more differentiated view of the dynamics of institutional change. The strategy is one of dissecting a particular social institution, namely a property regime for the management of access to wild plant resources in the coastal region of Namibia, into separate analytical layers. Social learning is here described and analysed not in terms of a wholesale import or export of institutional systems. Rather, this case study suggests that in practice institutional change is a product of piecemeal changes taking place at different interconnected institutional layers in a way that generates a particular dynamic. While the approach of dissecting institutions into connected layers that can be represented graphically can be used as a general analytical tool for understanding institutions across diverse cases it also allows for the fact that every particular setting generates its distinctive dynamic.

All three papers in Part II tell us a great deal about the relevance of social practices and perceptions for institutional change but relatively little about how environmentally beneficial processes of social learning can be actively encouraged. As with the studies under Part I the papers here, in answering the questions they are designed to address, have helped raised new questions: in this case on ways of promoting processes of social learning. This is the subject of the contributions in the following section.

Part III: Institutionalising Social Learning

The papers in Part III address *procedures and mechanisms* designed to stimulate or support processes of social learning of potential benefit to the environment. In many ways they build bridges between the two previous sections by demonstrating what practical steps can be taken to encourage learning processes. If informal institutions evolve gradually and do not respond so readily to the kind of deliberate engineering applicable to formal institutions – it is asked – how at least can conditions be created within which this gradual process of institutional change can take place?

Markus Troja provides theoretical and practical insight into resolving public conflicts through environmental mediation and negotiated rulemaking. He describes the innovative character of these approaches in the field of public policy and planning. Following the theoretical concept of transformative mediation, Troja analyses how procedures of cooperative conflict management create an institutional frame for social learning, both on the level of individual conflicting parties and on the level of a policy issue. The interaction between this institutional innovation within the political decision-making process and the existing formal and informal institutions in public policy and planning prove to be one of the main challenges. Troja suggests forms of loose coupling between new and established institutions to cope with this problem of institutional interplay.

Verena Sandner addresses a specific case of institution building: the case of a local resource management system in an indigenous group in Central America. The Kuna people of Panama serve as an example for a traditional society responding to increasing pressure on resources by creating their own, formal institutions following western examples such as closed fishing seasons. The social learning process leading to the creation of these institutions is based on a characteristic feature of Kuna culture: the strong aim to preserve the traditional culture with its specific man-environment relation on the one hand and the openness to innovations such as international paradigms of resource protection (sustainability) and new forms of institutional design (formal laws including financial sanctions) on the other. This duality of old and new paradigms is reflected in the formal institutions which are referring to the indigenous principle of respect for "mother earth" that is now fixed as an obligation for policy in a formal law. The Kuna example shows that social capital (Ostrom) in an indigenous society can be strong enough for local institutions to be created even without outside help, as is postulated in so-called co-management approaches.

In his chapter, Michael Huber outlines the co-evolution of environmental policy tools and the institutional setting of the European Community. Using the example of EC acid rain and climate change policies he outlines how agreements on burden sharing are negotiated, taxes and emission permits are utilised as mechanisms and how they have been developed over a period of twenty years. Furthermore, Huber demonstrates how fairness, legitimacy, efficiency or effectiveness alternatively dominate the policies at stake. This domination is linked to the current state of institutional development. For instance, in the 1970s and 1980s the EC Commission was engaged in early environmental policies without formal competence. Burden sharing was to provide legitimacy by engaging reluctant Member States. Subsequently, it was aspects of fairness or, later on, efficiency that shaped the choice of burden-sharing tools. The notion of burden sharing was adapted to these institutional expectations at each stage: the discussion of taxes or "regulatory bubbles" can thus be linked to a particular stage of policy development and coevolution indicates an overall learning process in EC environmental policy making.

Bernd Siebenhüner focuses on scientific assessments as institutions of social learning at the interface between science and political decision making. He looks at two case studies of international environmental assessments with a perspective on social learning processes, namely the Intergovernmental Panel on Climate Change (IPCC) and the scientific assessments under the Convention on Long-Range Transboundary Air Pollution (LRTAP). Both cases are iterative processes with significant changes of the assessment institutions over time, but they differ in their basic structures and in their effectiveness with regard to political outcomes, permitting their comparison in order to draw some general conclusions. Under the perspective on social learning, Siebenhüner investigates how basic institutional settings of these assessments have changed over time and which factors might have been influential in these processes. He pays particular attention to procedures and mechanisms relevant for internal learning processes such as informal communication networks or highly formalised committees with a distinct set of rules of procedure. Finally, learning processes and these mechanisms are compared across both case studies to draw some general conclusions.

References

Beck, Ulrich (1992): Risk Society, Towards a New Modernity. Thousand Oaks, CA; Sage
Berndt, Christian (1999): Institutionen, Regulation und Geographie. In: Erdkunde, Vol 53; pp. 302-316
Boehm, Gisela/McDaniels, Timothy/Nerb, Josef/Spada, Hans (eds.) (2001): Environmental Risks: Perception, Evaluation and Management, Special Issue of "Research in social problems and public policy", Vol. 9, Oxford: Elsevier
Dierkes, Meinolf/Berthoin Antal, Ariane/Child, John/Nonaka, Ikurio (eds.) (2001): Handbook of Organizational Learning and Knowledge. Oxford; Oxford University Press
Douglas, Mary (1985): Risk Acceptibility According to Social Sciences. New York; Russell Sage Foundation
Dietl, Helmut (1993): Institutionen und Zeit. Tübingen; Mohr
Giddens, Anthony (1990): The Consequences of Modernity. Stanford, CA; Stanford University Press
Göhler, Gerhard (1997): Wie verändern sich Institutionen? Revolutionärer und schleichender Institutionenwandel. In: Göhler, Gerhard (ed.). Institutionenwandel. Leviathan; Special Issue 16. Opladen; pp. 21-56
Habermas, Jürgen (1996): Between Facts and Norms: Contributions to a Discourse Theory of Law and Democracy. Oxford; Polity

Habermas, Jürgen (1984): The Theory of Communicative Action; Vol. 1; London; Heinemann Education

Habermas, Jürgen (1987): The Theory of Communicative Action. Vol. 2; Boston: Beacon/Cambridge; Polity

Häder, Michael (1997): Umweltpolitische Instrumente und Neue Institutionenökonomik; Wiesbaden

Healey, Patsy (1998): Building Institutional Capacity through Collaborative Approaches in Urban Planning. In: Environment and Planning. Vol. 30; pp. 1531-1546

Jordan, Andrew/O'Riordan, Tim (1995): Institutional Adaptation to Global Environmental Change (II): Core Elements of an ‚Institutional' Theory. CSERGE Working Paper GEC 95-21; Norwich, London

Jordan, Andrew/O'Riordan, Tim (1997): Social Institutions and Climate Change: Applying Cultural Theory to Practice. CSERGE Working Paper GEC 97-15; Norwich, London

Koelbe, T,A, (1995): The New Institutionalism in Political Science and Sociology. In: Comparative Politics; Vol. 37; pp. 231-243

Karpe, Jan (1997): Institutionen und Freiheit. Grundlegende Elemente moderner Ökonomik. Münster

Luhmann, Niklas (1985): Social Systems. Stanford CA; Stanford University Press

Mayntz, Renate/Scharpf, Fritz W. (1995): Der Ansatz des akteurzentrierten Institutionalismus. In: Mayntz, Renate/Scharpf, Fritz W. (eds.), Gesellschaftliche Selbstregelung und politische Steuerung. Frankfurt a.M./New York; pp. 39-72

Minsch, Jürgen et al, (1998): Institutionelle Reformen für eine Politik der Nachhaltigkeit. Bericht and die Enquete-Kommission des Deutschen Bundestages Berlin.

Münch, Richard (1984): Die Struktur der Moderne, Grundmuster und differentielle Gestaltung des institutionellen Aufbaus der modernen Gesellschaften. Frankfurt a.M.; Suhrkamp

Nee, Victor/Ingram, Paul (1998): Embeddedness and Beyond: Institutions, Exchange, and Social Structure. In: Nee/Brinton (eds.): The New Institutionalism in Sociology. New York; Russell Sage Foundation; pp. 19-45

North, Douglass C, (1990): Institutions. Institutional Change and Economic Performance. Cambridge; Cambridge University Press

Ostrom, Eleonore (1998): A Behavioural Approach to the Rational Choice Theory of Collective Action. American Political Science Review 92 (Vol. 1); pp 1-22

Scheuermann, Michael/Spada, Hans (1998/2000) (eds.): 3./4. Documentation of the Priority Programme of the DFG "Global Environmental Change – Social and Behavioural Dimensions". Freiburg; Psychologisches Institut

Schütz, Alfred (1970): On Phenomenology and Social Relations. Selected writings. Edited and with an introduction by Helmut R, Wagner. Chicago, London; University of Chicago Press

Scott, W, Richard (2001): Institutions and Organizations. Thousand Oaks, London, New Delhi; Sage

The Social Learning Group (2001 a): Learning to Manage Global Environmental Risks. A Functional Analysis of Social Responses to Climate Change, Ozone Depletion and Acid Rain. Vol. 1; Cambridge, Ma.; MIT Press

The Social Learning Group (2001 b): Learning to Manage Global Environmental Risks. A Functional Analysis of Social Responses to Climate Change, Ozone Depletion and Acid Rain. Vol. 2; Cambridge, Ma.; MIT Press

Thompson, Michael/Rayner, Steve (1998): Cultural Discourses. In: Rayner/Malone (eds,), Human Choice/Climate Change, Vol. 1; The Societal Framework; Columbus, Ohio; Battelle Press, pp. 265-344

van Tatenhove, Jan/Leroy, Peter (2000): The Institutionalisation of Environmental Politics. In: Environment and Policy; Vol. 24; pp. 17-34

Weber, Max (1975): The Protestant Ethic and the Spirit of Capitalism. London; Allen and Unwin

Young, Oran et al (1999): Institutional Dimensions of Global Environmental Change. Science Plan; IHDP Report No.9; Bonn

Part I: Reshaping Institutions

Timothy Moss

Introduction

This first section of the book addresses changes to those institutions most readily associated with the political arena: the regulations, codified norms and written agreements which are commonly termed formal institutions. The reform of a law or the ratification of an international protocol is a very obvious expression of institutional change. A new set of rules is created, supplanting or complementing those already in existence. The enactment of a new formal institution is, of course, only the culmination of a debate over the merits of reform and the specific design of the institution. It is merely an interim product of a continual process aimed at improving the effectiveness of institutional arrangements in providing or securing the public goods for which they are deemed necessary. As experience with existing institutions is gathered and assessed, as new frameworks and logics of action create or block off particular avenues of reform and as notions of what public goods are worth protecting shift over time, pressures emerge for the design of better formal institutions. Since most public goods are regulated at least to some extent by available institutions this process of institutional design is largely directed at reshaping existing institutional arrangements rather than creating a completely new model.

The very nature of environmental problems – with their multiple negative effects across space and time and very varied perception in the public domain – calls for highly complex institutional arrangements. The (re) design of formal environmental institutions is the subject of intense reflection in the scientific communities of international relations, political science, environmental studies and urban and regional studies as well as in policy-making communities at international, supranational, national, regional and local levels. Notwithstanding the diversity of the problems addressed and institutional arrangements available, researchers and practitioners are engaged in a common search to identify what makes a 'good' environmental institution. Do effective environmental institutions possess certain common characteristics? Can we identify general principles for the design and implementation of effective formal institutions? More critically, what effect do formal institutions have at all on the behaviour of actor groups and states?

Generic issues of this kind are central to the first paper in this section, by Ron Mitchell. Mitchell provides a commanding overview of the current state of knowledge on the importance and effectiveness of international environmental institutions. As he emphasises, we know a great deal already about individual institutions but have as yet been unable to draw from the selective case studies convincing general conclusions on the performance of certain types of international institution. On the basis of existing empirical studies Mitchell sets out to provide some broad-brush answers to the central question: What makes international environmental institutions matter, and when? He explores how far the effectiveness of environmental institutions is determined by the features of the environmental problem, the international context and country-specific characteristics.

The other three papers in this section present case studies of innovative attempts to make existing institutional arrangements better. Andreas Obser asks how the Intergovernmental Forum on Forests (IFF) can contribute to the creation of an international policy on the sustainable management of forests in the absence of a legally-binding forest convention. Tim Moss appraises an attempt to institutionalise river basin management across the EU with the new Water Framework Directive. Florian Dünckmann and Claudia Mayer explore the difficulties involved in establishing environmental production standards in coffee production. Each of the three policy/market reforms is an expression of a learning process based on experiences with past institutions. At the same time they each reflect state-of-the-art thinking in their respective policy fields on the design of more effective institutions. This makes them particularly valuable for advancing knowledge on the redesign of formal environmental institutions.

Distinctive to all three papers is that they draw on a common analytical framework for identifying and investigating particular problems of institutional effectiveness as provided by the Science Plan of the Institutional Dimensions to Global Environmental Change (IDGEC) project, a part of the international Human Dimensions to Global Change Programme (HDP) (Young 1999). Two of the most common and persistent limitations to the effectiveness of environmental institutions are problems of fit and problems of interplay. Problems of fit occur when the characteristics of an institution do not match the characteristics of the biophysical system it addresses (Young 2002). Problems of spatial fit, where the spatial remit of a resource regime fails to cover the full territorial area of distribution of an environmental good, have a particularly detrimental effect on the performance of an institution. This is the case, for instance, where water resources are managed without respect for the river basin (Moss), where the international trade in timber is regulated by national institutions only (Obser) or where market institutions to promote environmental standards in coffee production do not cover all those involved between producer and end-consumer (Dünckmann/Mayer). How can environmental institutions be brought more in line with the territorial distribution of the natural resources that they regulate? The three papers illustrate the difficulties encountered in improving spatial fit and, from the perspective of their own policy field, reflect critically on efforts to attain perfect spatial fit between institution and environmental resource.

Problems of interplay also involve boundary issues, but of a different kind. The boundaries here are not territorial but jurisdictional, between different institutions or hierarchies of institutions. The underlying assumption here is that an institution's effectiveness depends not only on its inner qualities but also on the degree of positive interaction with other relevant institutions (Young 2002). It is generally distinguished between vertical and horizontal interplay. Problems of vertical interplay relate to the interaction between different levels of institution, ranging from international agreements to local government statutes. The paper by Moss addresses a central question in this respect: How far can institutional change 'from above' – in the form of the EU Water Framework Directive – induce the desired adaptation of existing institutions at subordinate levels? Obser asks rather how an international forest programme can effectively integrate or reconcile diverse national programmes.

Horizontal interplay refers generally to cross-sectoral cooperation beyond the remit of the institution immediately responsible for the resource in question. Problems of horizontal interplay result from instances where the objectives of one institution are undermined by the impacts of others. How can this be avoided in the design of institutions? In his paper Moss asks what implications the Water Framework Directive will have for policy integration between water management and other water-relevant policy fields, and whether new forms of cross-sectoral governance are likely to emerge. Dünckmann and Mayer study a different kind of horizontal interplay: between the market and government regulation. Are there circumstances, they ask, where market-based production standards require some form of government intervention to become effective?

These issues of institutional design are studied not only in different policy contexts but in different territorial arenas and from varied disciplinary perspectives. The papers together cover a wide range of spatial settings, from international agreements (Mitchell) and their relationship to national programmes (Obser), via the impact of supranational reform on national and subnational institutions in the EU (Moss) to the interrelationship between coffee-producing regions and industrialised countries (Dünckmann/Mayer). There is – in contrast to later sections of this book – a clear emphasis on international or supranational institutions and their impact on lower levels of hierarchy. This is no coincidence: it is here that we find many exciting examples of innovative reform to formal environmental institutions. Similarly, the disciplinary roots of the authors – in political science, international relations, regional studies and economic geography – are varied, but they are all well suited to uncovering the dynamics of policy-driven initiatives to deliberately alter, or reshape, existing institutional arrangements.

References

Young, Oran (1999): Institutional Dimensions of Global Environmental Change. Science Plan. IHDP Report No. 9; Bonn; IHDP

Young, Oran (2002): The Institutional Dimensions of Environmental Change. Fit, Interplay, and Scale. Cambridge (MA); MIT Press

Ronald B. Mitchell

Of Course International Institutions Matter: But When and How?[1]

1 Overview

Research over the last decade by scholars of international relations and comparative politics has clearly demonstrated that international environmental institutions can produce quite dramatic changes in the behaviour of the states and nonstate actors that they seek to influence. Taken as a whole, that body of research has also demonstrated several other important points. First, it has shown that determining whether observed changes in behaviour were driven by the institution or by other, exogenous, factors is not a trivial problem. Second, it has shown that although there are many international environmental institutions (IEIs) that have been quite effective, others have wielded little if any influence. Third, it has begun to identify features of an IEI that promote effectiveness and features that tend to undercut it. Fourth, it has also begun to show how effectiveness depends not only on the features of the IEI but also on features of the problem being addressed, the broader international context and the countries whose behaviour the IEI seeks to influence. The research conducted to date has also demonstrated that IEIs wield influence both through rationalist mechanisms in which states engage in self-conscious processes of identifying and responding to material incentives and through constructivist mechanisms in which norms, identities and ideas play far more important roles than interests and power. One question that has yet to receive attention is how IEIs compare to other social efforts in their ability to induce positive environmental change, including through state policies outside of the IEI realm, through private corporate regimes, through the activities of non-governmental organisations and civil society more generally and through epistemic communities.

---

[1] This chapter was originally presented as a paper at the 2001 Berlin Conference on the Human Dimensions of Global Environmental Change on "Global Environmental Change and the Nation State" organised by the Environmental Policy and Global Change Working Group of the German Political Science Association Berlin, 7–8 December 2001. Completion of this chapter was supported by a generous Sabbatical Fellowship in the Humanities and Social Sciences from the American Philosophical Society and a 2002 Summer Research Award from the University of Oregon.

2 Of Course International Environmental Institutions "Matter"

During the late 1980s and early 1990s, scholars working on international environmental politics spent considerable time and effort engaging in the realist-institutionalist debate over whether institutions matter. The issue at the time was whether international environmental institutions, or "regimes," defined as "norms, principles, rules, and decision-making procedures around which actors expectations converged" ever influenced state behaviour (Krasner 1983, p. 1). Considerable theoretical and empirical research at the time focused on evaluating whether (or demonstrating that) international environmental institutions influenced behaviour at least in some instances. Early in the 1990s, several scholars developed case studies clearly demonstrating states and substate actors taking actions that could not be explained by reference to their pre-institutional power and interests (Haas 1989; Haas/Keohane/Levy 1993; Mitchell 1994b). These efforts soon developed into a research programme focused initially on explaining compliance with international law which then developed further into what has come to be known as regime or institutional effectiveness research (Keohane/Levy 1996; Hasenclever/Mayer/Rittberger 1997; Brown Weiss/Jacobson 1998; Victor/Raustiala/Skolnikoff 1998).

Scholars working within this research programme have produced an array of studies demonstrating that international institutions sometimes lead states and nonstate actors to reduce their harmful behaviour; that sometimes these reductions lead, in turn, to improvements in environmental quality, and, in rare cases, to the elimination of the original problem; that sometimes such institutions can also exacerbate environmental problems; and that, not surprisingly, sometimes they have no influence at all.

Careful studies of the Mediterranean Action Plan, the Convention on Long-Range Transboundary Air Pollution (LRTAP), the Montreal Protocol on stratospheric ozone depletion, and oil regulations under marine pollution treaties have shown both that IEIs have influenced state behaviour and have provided considerable insight into the mechanisms by which they do so (Haas 1990; Levy 1993; Haas 1992; Parson 1993; Parson/Greene 1995; Mitchell 1994a). Other studies have highlighted cases where IEIs made little, if any, difference in state behaviour or even exacerbated the problems they were seeking to remedy, including treaties addressing whaling, many fisheries, whaling, tropical timber, and the Rhine river (Peterson 1992; Andresen 1997; Peterson 1993; Wilder 1995; Bernauer/Moser 1996). Many of these and other studies have produced more nuanced findings demonstrating that IEIs that influence the behaviour of some set of states may have little influence on others, as evident in the Convention on International Trade in Endangered

Species ivory ban, or may initially have little influence but become more influential later in time, as evident in the international wetlands convention (Brown Weiss/Jacobson 1998; Victor/Raustiala/Skolnikoff 1998; Mofson 1996; Matthews 1993). As several commentators have noted, however, the field is plagued by the problem of selection bias, with only a small and undoubtedly unsystematic sampling of the IEIs that exist having been evaluated (Downs/Rocke/Barsoom 1996). For most of the more than 500 multilateral environmental legal instruments currently in existence, we simply have no evidence or analyses relevant to the question of whether they were influential or not.

3 How Do We Know Whether IEIs Matter?

Before engaging the question of whether IEIs "matter", we must clarify what we mean when we ask whether a regime "mattered"? That is, we must define what we mean when we say an IEI or environmental regime (I will use the terms interchangeably here) is effective or influential. In the environmental realm, most scholars have thought of regime effectiveness in terms of how outputs of interest are different than they would have been had the institution not existed. At the institutional level of analysis, research in this tradition attempts to determine whether and in what ways behaviour and/or environmental quality are different than they would have been had the institution not existed. At the state level of analysis, the same question can be framed in terms of how a state whose behaviour is regulated by a regime or institution would behave differently if this behaviour were not regulated, either because it was not a member of the regime or because the regime did not regulate that behaviour. The ultimate objective is to determine whether the energies of the state are directed differently in the presence of the treaty, regime, or institution than they would be otherwise. Initial tendencies to frame questions in terms of regime compliance have more recently been rejected in favor of thinking in terms of regime effectiveness as theoretical logic and empirical evidence demonstrated that compliance was neither necessary nor sufficient for effectiveness. Compliance was not necessary since a demanding treaty might induce considerable behavioural change (and even environmental improvement) even as the behaviour fell short of the legal requirements of compliance. Compliance was not sufficient since a non-demanding treaty (at the extreme, one which merely codified existing behaviours) might be marked by high levels of compliance that resulted from few if any changes in behaviour (and produced no environmental improvement). Much, though not all, research to date on international environmental institutional effectiveness has focused on the influence of regulatory regimes. Young has noted that regimes are not always regulatory, but can also be procedural (facilitating recurring collective choice), programmatic (facilitating the pooling of resources toward collective goals) or generative (helping develop new norms and social practices) (Young 1999b, p. 24ff; Young 1998a, p. 145).

Effectiveness should be distinguished from performance as well as compliance. The performance of an environmental treaty can be thought of as some measurement of the behaviours or environmental quality (the "outputs") observed under a treaty. Effectiveness, by contrast, is better thought of as performance relative to some baseline. The question, of course, is what baseline. Although using different terms, recent scholarship has suggested that effectiveness can be evaluated along two different scales and, in both cases, against two different standards. Effectiveness can be evaluated along scales that measure either changes in the behaviour being regulated or changes in the environmental indicator that is the ultimate concern of the institution. As one might expect, which of these scales is used has important analytic as well as political effects. Making progress in terms of environmental quality often proves more difficult than making progress in terms of behaviour, if only because behavioural change in any given arena is necessary but not sufficient for environmental quality change. Even perfectly successful efforts to alter a given behaviour may not produce corresponding environmental improvements if the environmental degradation at issue, as with many types of environmental degradation, results from a suite of human behaviours rather than simply from one.

Besides distinguishing among scales of effectiveness, we also must distinguish among standards of effectiveness. The two major standards currently being used by scholars are those involving counterfactuals and goal achievement. That is, regardless of the scale being used, one can evaluate progress relative to what would have happened otherwise, asking "how much did the institution contribute to making things better, whether behaviourally or environmentally?" or relative to the intended goal, asking "how much did the institution contribute to achieving the objectives that motivated its creation?" (Young 1998b; Young 1999a).

No small fraction of the debate over the influence and effectiveness of international environmental institutions arises from the simultaneous and often implicit use of very different definitions. Many environmentalists, concerned with motivating institutional progress, focus on how far short most environmental institutions fall from the environmental quality goals established in international agreements, let alone those held by the environmentalists themselves. Not surprisingly, many negotiators and diplomats, concerned with both justifying the existence of such institutions and looking for ways to improve them, focus on how much progress many IEIs make in inducing behaviours that would not have occurred absent the institution.

The preceding discussion makes clear that any attempt to evaluate effectiveness must identify ways of convincingly identifying appropriate and plausible counterfactuals. Any claim that an institution was effective, whether in terms of behaviour or environmental quality and in terms of the goal or some prior baseline, implies that, without the institution, outcomes would have been different. Creating convincing counterfactuals is certainly easier when seeking to evaluate behaviour rather than environmental quality, simply because the number of non-regime influences on behavioural change, however large, is always smaller than the number of non-human influences on environmental quality. Put differently, even a complete model that could exactly predict aggregate human behaviours based on the influence of IEIs and all other factors (an obviously unachievable model) would still be incapable of predicting environmental quality without adding yet more factors into the model, including in most cases a large stochastic component.

Despite the standard obstacles to creating convincing counterfactuals, environmental problems provide interesting options for doing so (Fearon 1991; Biersteker 1993; Tetlock/Belkin 1996; Sylvan/Majeski 1998). We can estimate what a state that was a member of a regulatory treaty would have done otherwise (and hence estimate the effect of the treaty on that state's behaviour) by examining a) the behaviour of that state prior to the treaty's entry into force for that country, b) similar behaviours of that state in areas not regulated by the treaty, and c) the behaviour of states who were not party to the treaty after its entry into force. Since we cannot observe the true counterfactual situation (in what is known as the "fundamental problem of causal inference"), examining these and related observable phenomena provide us with some basis for making educated guesses or informed conjectures about what the member state would have done had it not been a member (King/Keohane/Verba 1994).

4 Why Do IEIs Matter and When?

Evidence demonstrating that some IEIs matter and others do not poses the question of what explains this variance across IEIs. Brown Weiss and Jacobson (1998) have identified four categories of factors. First, negotiators and others concerned with international environmental policy certainly hope that at least some of the variance in effectiveness is due to differences in institutional features. That is, efforts to incorporate different design features may explain the differences in institution effectiveness. That need not be the case, however. Work to date suggests that problem features, context features and features of the country the IEI seeks to influence also help explain variation in the effectiveness of different IEIs. These three sets of factors may produce variation in performance or in effectiveness. That is, they may lead to differences in outcomes in which institutional features play no part. However, it may also be the case that these factors are "permissive", conditioning, or interacting sources of influence, with an IEI having influence on states when these variables have certain values and that same IEI having no influence when these variables have other values.

4.1 What Parts of IEIs Matter? Important Institutional Features

Scholars have identified a range of IEI features that, at least in some cases, appear to determine whether an IEI is influential or not. The rules of the regime, both on paper and in use, certainly may play a part in their influence. These rules can be categorised as the IEI's primary rule system, the information system and the response system (Mitchell 1996). The primary rule system consists of the rules that delineate the behavioural requirements of the regime. The influence of an IEI has been posited as depending on the ambitiousness or "depth" of these rules, whether they consist of negative proscriptions or positive prescriptions, whether they were adopted by a legitimate processes and a range of other features (Downs/Rocke/Barsoom 1996; Princen 1996; Franck 1990; Brown Weiss/Jacobson 1998). An IEI's information system also may determine its ability to alter behaviour. The transparency of the regime and the design of systems for implementation review as well as rules for improving both scientific knowledge of the problem and technical understanding of possible solutions can all have significant impacts on an IEI's effectiveness (Victor/Raustiala/Skolnikoff 1998; Mitchell 1998). An IEI's effectiveness does not depend solely on whether these systems identify violations or compliance, or more broadly identify behaviours that either support or undercut the IEI's goals, without such identification also leading to some form of response, however diffuse and non-material. An IEI's response system can be based in the traditional distinction between sanctions and rewards but much research has also noted the important role that capacity-building, violation prevention, norm generation and labelling and information exchange can play in leading states to adopt new behaviours (Downs/Rocke/Barsoom 1996; Chayes/Chayes/Mitchell 1995; Haas/Keohane/Levy 1993; Mitchell 1994b; Clapp 1994; Parker 1997; see also contributions by Troja, Dünckmann/Mayer and Sandner in this volume).

Besides these elements of, or directly related to, the behavioural requirements of the IEI several other features may also prove influential. Membership rules seem likely to be important determinants of an IEIs influence, although at a theoretical level it remains unclear whether a regime consisting of a smaller but more committed set of states is likely to prove more or less effective (in terms of aggregate behavioural change or environmental improvement) than one with a more universal membership but less aggressive primary rules (Koremenos/Lipson/Snidal 2001). Likewise, and especially in terms of long run dynamic effectiveness or robustness, an IEI's ability to "learn" by responsively revising primary rules, information systems and response systems as things change can be important, reflected in research on questions such as whether frameworks and protocols are more effective than conventions that require amendment (Young 1998b). Of course, the resources that the IEI itself and the member states – as well as supporting non-governmental organisations (NGOs) and multinational corporations – bring to bear in attempting to implement an IEI's provisions will be crucial to converting requirements that may look good on paper into reality.

4.2 When do IEIs matter? The Conditions for Influence

Beyond such institutional features, the performance and effectiveness of IEIs depend on features of the problem, the context and the countries that are their members.

Problem Features

IEIs attempt to remedy a range of environmental problems that do not all share the same characteristics. Recent scholarship has suggested that problems vary in several important ways that influence the ease or difficulty with which they can be remedied (Rittberger/Zürn 1991; Young 1999a; Miles et al. 2002). Thus, environmental problems involving coordination problems have far fewer concerns regarding noncompliance than those involving collaboration or Tragedy of the Commons type problems, which in turn face an easier, if not easy, task than those involving upstream/downstream problems or asymmetric externalities (Stein 1983; Mitchell/Keilbach 2001). The distribution of power among states and the corresponding distribution of interests that states perceive themselves as having in remedying, or ignoring the problem are also important determinants of the ease of remedy. Interests can include both visible and material concerns as well as less obvious but nonetheless potent concerns with underlying values and identities.

Problems may pose greater or lesser challenges to an IEI due to variation in how many actors are causing the problem and in how susceptible those actors are to regulation. Thus, the more concentrated the actors who must be regulated, the easier the process of monitoring their behaviour as evident in the regulation of the relatively few producers of chlorofluorocarbons rather than the myriad consumers under the Montreal Protocol. The activity causing the environmental problem may also be more or less susceptible to monitoring. Thus, destruction of a wetland or other habitat leaves long lasting traces that often can be readily linked to their perpetrators whereas marine or river pollution often is difficult to observe and even more difficult to link back to the perpetrators. Problems vary considerably in how embedded they are in the social, economic and political structures of the societies that perpetrate them, as well. For example, reducing fossil fuel use under the Framework Convention on Climate Change is likely to prove far more difficult than did reducing chlorofluorocarbon use under the Montreal Protocol. The extent of scientific knowledge about the problem is also likely to prove influential in how readily states respond to IEI demands, and this knowledge as well as technical knowledge about solutions is likely to be a function not only of the institution itself (as noted above) but also exogenous factors that may well be uninfluencable.

Context Features

The international context also will condition the ease or difficulty an IEI will have in inducing behavioural change among member states. The level of economic interdependence among member states, whether in the extensiveness of trade relations or the existence of regional economic integration groups like the European Union, seems likely to influence the ease of inducing environmental change as does the level of institutional interdependence, such as that captured by the increasing degree of overlap of membership in a broad array of IEIs. In both cases, these interdependencies are likely to give states a sense, whether accurate or not, that their behaviour within a given IEI will influence the cooperativeness of other states in other realms that may be of more policy importance while simultaneously allowing states who seek to induce environmental cooperation more mechanisms for rewarding or punishing others in their attempt to do so.

The general level of environmental concern in civil society is likely to play an important background role in the responsiveness to IEIs as well. Increases in the general level of environmental awareness and concern may help a wide range of environmental regimes become more effective. Equally important, variation in concern across environmental problems and over time can help explain variation in the effectiveness of corresponding IEIs. Governments are likely to be more responsive to IEIs addressing problems that have higher levels of salience with their publics. Likewise, IEI effectiveness is likely to ebb and flow in tandem with the ebb and flow in the salience of a given problem due to educational efforts by NGOs and the media. Broader themes running through international relations may also influence the willingness of states to fulfill their environmental commitments. Evidence suggests that the Soviet Union was more willing to cooperate under the Convention on Long-Range Transboundary Air Pollution because of concerns related to détente than they would have been otherwise, and the end of the Cold War seems likely to have facilitated cooperation among states that previously were on different sides of the previous East-West divide (Levy 1993). Likewise, the dramatic changes relating to terrorism in 2001 are likely to have significant, if difficult to predict, influences on the effectiveness of IEIs.

Country Characteristics

The influence of an IEI varies across member states as well as across IEIs. To explain these variations, it is necessary to also look at the country level characteristics that influence whether states fulfill their environmental commitments. One of the earliest set of factors identified as crucial in explaining differentials in environmental responsiveness are those related to state capacity. States vary considerably in their financial, technical, and administrative capacities to fulfill their obligations under various IEIs and to induce substate national actors to make required behavioural changes. Noncompliance with IEI requirements can often be attributed to an inability to comply as well as the desire to violate (Haas/Keohane/Levy 1993; Chayes/Chayes 1995; Brown Weiss/Jacobson 1998). The economic, political, and social structures of states also vary widely and alter how responsive governments are to the views of their publics and how responsive their publics are to the policies of their governments.

States vary in the general level of environmental concern as well as in the relative importance given to particular environmental issues. Developed states have a quite different set of environmental concerns than developing states, and it is not surprising to see the former states taking much more concerted action to fulfill the requirements of IEIs that, not surprisingly, reflect their environmental interests more than the environmental interests of developing states. States vary considerably in the number of NGOs, multinational corporations, elites, and publics and in how much influence these various groups wield both in the development and implementation of policy. There are considerable differentials in both the ability and desire of states to take leadership roles in the international community (Young 1991) and in the roles states see themselves playing in that community, as evident in the frequent efforts by Scandinavian states to take strong environmental positions earlier than other states (Levy 1993). Leadership also plays an important role at the domestic level, as the willingness of states to respond to international environmental requirements may change when leaders less committed to environmental action replace those more committed to such actions as evident in the changes in US climate policy during the 1990s. Finally, the level of knowledge and expertise on any given problem, and in particular the level of indigenous knowledge and expertise, varies considerably across countries and is also likely to influence both how willing and able states are to alter those behaviours that influence environmental quality.

5 How Do IEIs Matter? The Mechanisms of Influence

Identifying the factors that determine whether and when an IEI is effective entrains the additional question of how those factors influence behaviour. In line with the recent debate in international relations more generally, we can think of the mechanisms by which IEIs influence behaviour as breaking into rationalist and constructivist categories (March/Olsen 1998; Young 1999a).

5.1 Rationalist Mechanisms

One strain of thinking is that IEIs influence behaviour through a "logic of consequences" in which states alter their behaviour in response to changes in the way in which they calculate what behaviours are in their best interests. In this model, IEIs alter behaviour by providing essentially instrumental changes to the world in which states make decisions, shifting the incentives and opportunities they have to engage in the behaviours the IEI seeks to promote. IEIs can help states overcome collective action problems by altering a variety of the elements of that decision context in which states operate. They can help initiate and sustain a focus on certain environmental problems (and away from others) in a process of agenda setting. They also can increase certain behaviours simply by creating standards (with little if any enforcement), where the standards simply categorize behaviours as desirable or undesirable ("green" or "brown") which provides the foundation for concerns about, and perhaps the reality of, shaming states who do not engage in the behaviours required or encouraged by the IEI.

Obviously, IEIs also can operate much more instrumentally and directly, however. IEIs can incorporate sanctions against states that fail to fulfill their requirements or offer rewards to those that do so. Thus, the Montreal Protocol threatens sanctions for developed states that fail to reduce CFCs according to the targets and timetables laid out while offering assistance as an incentive to developing states that expect to have difficulty in that regard. Both the Rhine river regime and a 1911 fur seal arrangement had provisions offering side-payments to states to encourage them to adopt behaviours they would not otherwise have adopted. Besides sanctions and rewards, IEIs can seek to increase the capacity of member states to fulfill their commitments or reduce their opportunities to violate their commitments. Capacity-building measures have become an increasingly common element in IEIs that include developing states who may lack the financial or technical ability to comply with their provisions (Haas/Keohane/Levy 1993). Although not frequently observed, as environmental concern increases one might expect provisions imposing controls on the export of certain pollutants to states that lack the indigenous capacity to produce them as a way of reducing the ability of those states to pollute. Several recent IEIs have adopted strategies based on simply increasing the flow of information through prior informed consent procedures that assume that states are engaging in behaviours they themselves would not engage in if they were fully aware of the consequences of those behaviours (O'Neill 2000).

5.2 Constructivist Mechanisms

Another strain of thinking is that IEIs influence state behaviour through a "logic of appropriateness" in which state behaviour is explained as a function of the identities states adopt and the behaviours considered appropriate to those identities. In this model, the behaviours of states results not from decisions about what is in the state's interest but rather from assessments of what identity the state seeks to promote or project and what is the behaviour appropriate to that identity. After initial assessments such as that, state behaviour also is likely to reflect the influence of the habit of compliance or conformance with treaty norms.

According to this view, IEIs can induce behaviour change by promoting improvements in and diffusion of scientific and technical knowledge. Through the process of scientific investigation and assessment, not only do states identify and improve their understanding of their material interests but they also develop new identities and roles over time. The process by which scientists working on behalf of a government to understand the environmental impacts of human behaviour is likely not only to increase their understanding of those impacts but is also likely to influence their commitment to both environmental goals and international pursuit of those goals. These processes have been identified in both the scientific developments surrounding the Mediterranean Action Plan and LRTAP (Haas 1990; Levy 1993). IEIs also can promote new norms and alter the discourse and rhetoric that surround an environmental issue making it more difficult (though surely not impossible) to sustain arguments that economic or security interests should take precedence over environmental ones (Litfin 1998; cf. Engels in this volume). At an even broader level, IEIs may facilitate behavioural change and environmental problem through a diffuse but nonetheless important process of dynamic social learning in which the ability to manage environmental problems collectively improves over time (The Social Learning Group 2001).

6 How Much Do IEIs Matter?

Arguing that IEIs matter does not imply anything about how much they matter relative to alternative ways of inducing behavioural change and environmental improvement. Comparisons across different approaches to inducing such changes have not yet been seriously engaged by the research community investigating international environmental politics. However, that community as a whole has identified an interesting array of efforts to induce such changes.

Certainly, state policies and behaviours that do not include IEIs have a broad range of influences on environmental behaviour. Potentially one of the biggest influences of states on the environment lies in the unintended, but nonetheless large, effects of the processes of technological development and economic globalisation. These processes often do not involve intergovernmental coordination and their environmental impacts are often not considered but they still have major environmental impacts. Although these are often assumed to be negative, increasing evidence shows that dynamics can produce a race to the top as well as a race to the bottom. Of course, explicit coordination of economic policies is increasingly common at both the global level within the World Trade Organization and at the regional level within the European Union, the North American Free Trade area, and other regional trade arrangements. Increasingly, these intergovernmental economic efforts are choosing or being forced to include environmental considerations in their policies. Important environmental impacts also result from the often organic process of policy diffusion by which the national environmental policies of one country are imitated by other countries that view those policies as effective ways to deal with environmental problems that have large negative domestic influences.

Non-corporate actors in civil society have been playing active roles in influencing environmental behaviour globally. NGOs have devised a wide range of programmes designed to reduce human impacts on the environment. From shaming corporations engaged in environmentally harmful behaviour to promoting eco-tourism to devising a variety of eco-labels to facilitating debt-for-nature swaps, environmental NGOs have adopted numerous strategies the effectiveness of which have yet to be evaluated relative to IEIs. Alongside these specific efforts are the broader and more diffuse influence of transnational environmental movements that shape the identities, interests, and behaviour of citizens throughout the world (Princen/Finger 1994; Wapner 1996). Scientists engaged in global environmental assessments and in epistemic communities also wield significant influence over the behaviour of states and the private and public citizens that compose states in ways that may be much more far-reaching and fundamental than IEIs (Haas 1992; Clark/Mitchell/Cash/Alcock 2002).

Private actors operating at both the domestic and international level also appear to be having important influences on the type and extent of environmentally harmful behaviours. Economic and political forces are increasingly leading many multinational corporations to view it as in their best interests to alter their business practices in ways that have environmental benefits, regardless of what competing corporations are doing. In other cases, they are coordinating their behaviour through private regimes such as the International Standards Organization (ISO) in ways that may well alter corporate behaviours far more than do corresponding intergovernmental efforts. Multinationals also have begun coordinating such efforts with nongovernmental organisations, as evident in the efforts of the Forestry Stewardship Council to serve as an independent auditor of logging industry practices (Dudley/Elliott/Stolton 1997). In all these cases, whether involving state, nongovernmental, or private actors, important questions remain about both how effective these various efforts are individually, how effective they are in the aggregate, and how they compare to IEIs both in their effectiveness and in the conditions that influence such effectiveness.

7 Other Considerations

This discussion has focused on the effectiveness of IEIs defined in terms of their influence on behaviour and environmental quality. Before concluding, it deserves mention that several aspects of IEI effectiveness have not been discussed here and several effects of IEIs are not captured in the relatively limited sense of effectiveness that has been used here.

The preceding discussion has conceptualised effectiveness in a relatively static sense of comparing each IEI relative to some counterfactual state of affairs. Yet, the effectiveness of an IEI can be as readily, and perhaps more appropriately, judged in a more dynamic as well as relative sense. The effectiveness of an IEI is likely to depend in no small measure on where it stands in its "lifecycle" (Gehring 1994). Although work has only just begun in this arena, we might well expect IEIs to exhibit a particular temporal profile in which IEIs have low levels of effectiveness initially, become increasingly effective over time as both the IEIs themselves and their member states learn necessary skills, and decrease in effectiveness after passing some point of maturity. Whether following this or some other trajectory, it seems unlikely that we can make an assessment of an IEI at one point in its lifecycle that is equally valid for all other points in that lifecycle. We might also be interested in the effectiveness of a regime conceptualised in terms of its ability to respond to exogenous changes in the problem being addressed, or what has been called regime "robustness" and flexibility (Young 1999a). This might include the ability of the IEI itself to engage in both simple forms of learning (finding new ways to achieve existing ends) and complex learning (pursuing new ends) (The Social Learning Group 2001).

Another important aspect of effectiveness that is only now beginning to engage significant scholarly attention is the relative effectiveness of different IEIs (Mitchell 2002). Assessing relative effectiveness involves attempting to compare whether one IEI is more effective than another in similar circumstances. This raises not insignificant problems of identifying metrics that allow meaningful comparison of IEIs that address different environmental problems which are not readily or even obviously comparable. Scholars are, however, increasingly recognising that for research on effectiveness to be policy relevant it must provide guidance to negotiators regarding which of the available design options is likely to be most effective in addressing a given problem in particular circumstances (Helm/Sprinz 1999; Sprinz/Helm 1999; Miles et al. 2002).

It is also worth noting that IEIs have a wide range of effects that go well beyond the central and intended effects on regulated behaviours and environmental quality (Young 1999a). Scholarship has yet to engage questions of how the efforts of IEIs measure up in terms of their efficiency in the use of resources to induce such behavioural changes. The costs incurred in developing and implementing an IEI are rarely discussed let alone carefully evaluated. Even more rare are efforts to identify and quantify economically the benefits that derive from an IEI. Obviously both these tasks are difficult both theoretically and empirically. Yet they would be necessary elements to any effort to determine whether IEIs are efficient or cost-effective. Nor have scholars begun to seriously examine how the efforts of IEIs to improve environmental quality influence levels of economic equity around the world or have other secondary (i.e., non-intended), but nonetheless important, effects in the world of international politics.

8 Conclusion

International environmental institutions can influence the behaviour of states and the quality of the environment that their behaviours, in turn, influence. Of course, not surprisingly, not all IEIs realize their potential to wield influence. At times this reflects poor institutional design, while at other times it reflects the influence of a range of factors that would make it difficult for an IEI of any design to alter existing behavioural patterns. In short, IEIs matter sometimes. The foregoing has not delineated a fully integrated model of factors that determine IEI effectiveness, but has provided a list of the factors that previous scholarship has delineated as important to research on these and related issues. Much research remains to be done before we will have a full understanding of why some IEIs work so well and others work so poorly. Making progress in that effort will require theoretical efforts to devise compelling, comprehensive, and integrative models of how IEIs influence behaviour; methodological efforts to complement the large set of qualitative case studies that have already been conducted with quantitative methods that engage questions of relative effectiveness and look for patterns that can only be perceived by looking across IEIs; and substantive efforts to examine the large share of hundreds of multilateral environmental agreements that have not yet received any scholarly attention. Pursuing those efforts in the years ahead may allow scholars interested in international environmental politics to provide the policy relevant research necessary to guide negotiators in improving existing international environmental policy and devising new international environmental policies to address the range of environmental problems we are likely to encounter in the decades ahead.

References

Andresen, Steinar (1997): The International Whaling Commission: The Failure to Manage Whales Effectively. Paper Presented to the International Studies Association. 18-22 March; Toronto

Bernauer, Thomas/Peter Moser (1996): Reducing Pollution of the Rhine River: The Influence of International Cooperation. In: Journal of Environment and Development; Vol. 5; No. 4; pp. 391-417

Biersteker, Thomas (1993): Constructing Historical Counterfactuals to Assess the Consequences of International Regimes: The Global Debt Regime and the Course of the Debt Crisis of the 1980s. In: Rittberger (ed.): Regime Theory and International Relations. New York; Oxford University Press; pp. 315-338

Brown Weiss, Edith/Harold K. Jacobson (eds.) (1998): Engaging Countries: Strengthening Compliance with International Environmental Accords. Cambridge (MA); MIT Press

Chayes, Abram/Antonia Handler Chayes (1995): The New Sovereignty: Compliance with International Regulatory Agreements. Cambridge (MA); Harvard University Press

Chayes, Antonia Handler/Abram Chayes/Ronald B. Mitchell (1995): Active Compliance Management in Environmental Treaties. In: Lang (ed.): Sustainable Development and International Law. London; Graham and Trotman; pp. 75-89

Clapp, Jennifer (1994): Africa, NGOs, and the International Toxic Waste Trade. In: Journal of Environment & Development; Vol. 3; No. 2; pp. 17-45

Clark, William C./Ronald B. Mitchell/David W. Cash/Frank Alcock (2002): Information as Influence: How Institutions Mediate the Impact of Scientific Assessments on Global Environmental Affairs. Faculty Research Working Paper RWP02-044 of the Kennedy School of Government. Cambridge (MA); Harvard University

Downs, George W./David M. Rocke/Peter N. Barsoom (1996): Is the Good News About Compliance Good News About Cooperation? In: International Organization; Vol. 50; No. 3; pp. 379-406

Dudley, Nigel/Chris Elliott/Sue Stolton (1997): A Framework for Environmental Labeling. In: Environment; Vol. 39; No. 6; pp. 16

Fearon, James D. (1991): Counterfactuals and Hypothesis Testing in Political Science. In: World Politics; Vol. 43; No. 2; pp. 169-195

Franck, Thomas M. (1990): The Power of Legitimacy Among Nations. New York; Oxford University Press

Gehring, Thomas (1994): Dynamic International Regimes: Institutions for International Environmental Governance. Frankfurt (Main); Peter Lang

Haas, Peter M. (1989): Do Regimes Matter? Epistemic Communities and Mediterranean Pollution Control. In: International Organization; Vol. 43; No. 3; pp. 377-403

Haas, Peter M. (1990): Saving the Mediterranean: The Politics of International Environmental Cooperation. New York; Columbia University Press

Haas, Peter M. (1992): Banning Chlorofluorocarbons. In: International Organization; Vol. 46; No. 1; pp. 187-224

Haas, Peter M./Robert O. Keohane/Marc A. Levy (eds.) (1993): Institutions for the Earth: Sources of Effective International Environmental Protection. Cambridge (MA); MIT Press

Hasenclever, Andreas/Peter Mayer/Volker Rittberger (1997): Theories of International Regimes. Cambridge (UK); Cambridge University Press

Helm, Carsten/Detlef Sprinz (1999): Measuring the Effectiveness of International Environmental Regimes. Report 52 of the Potsdam Institute for Climate Impact Research. Potsdam

Keohane, Robert O./Marc A. Levy (eds.) (1996): Institutions for Environmental Aid: Pitfalls and Promise. Cambridge (MA); MIT Press

King, Gary/Robert O. Keohane/Sidney Verba (1994): Designing Social Inquiry: Scientific Inference in Qualitative Research. Princeton (NJ); Princeton University Press

Koremenos, Barbara/Charles Lipson/Duncan Snidal (2001): Rational Designs: Explaining the Form of International Institutions. In: International Organization; Vol. 55; No. 4; pp. 1-32

Krasner, Stephen D. (1983): International Regimes. Ithaca (NY); Cornell University Press

Levy, Marc (1993): European Acid Rain: The Power of Tote-Board Diplomacy. In: Haas/Keohane/Levy (eds.): Institutions for the Earth: Sources of Effective International Environmental Protection. Cambridge (MA); MIT Press; pp. 75-132

Litfin, Karen T. (ed.) (1998): The Greening of Sovereignty in World Politics. Cambridge (MA); MIT Press

March, James/Johan Olsen (1998): The Institutional Dynamics of International Political Orders. In: International Organization; Vol. 52; No. 4; pp. 943-970

Matthews, G. V. T. (1993): The Ramsar Convention on Wetlands: Its History and Development. Gland, Switzerland; Ramsar Convention Bureau

Miles, Edward L./Arild Underdal/Steinar Andresen/Jorgen Wettestad/ Jon Birger Skjaerseth/Elaine M. Carlin (eds.) (2002): Environmental Regime Effectiveness: Confronting Theory with Evidence. Cambridge (MA); MIT Press

Mitchell, Ronald B. (1994a): Intentional Oil Pollution at Sea: Environmental Policy and Treaty Compliance. Cambridge (MA); MIT Press

Mitchell, Ronald. B. (1994b): Regime Design Matters: Intentional Oil Pollution and Treaty Compliance. In: International Organization, Vol. 48; No. 3; pp. 425-458

Mitchell, Ronald B. (1996): Compliance Theory: An Overview. In: Cameron/Werksman/Roderick (eds): Improving Compliance with International Environmental Law. London; Earthscan; pp. 3-28

Mitchell, Ronald B. (1998): Sources of Transparency: Information Systems in International Regimes. In: International Studies Quarterly; Vol. 42; No. 1; pp. 109-130

Mitchell, Ronald B. (2002): A Quantitative Approach to Evaluating International Environmental Regimes. In: Global Environmental Politics; Vol. 2; No. 4; pp. 58-83

Mitchell, Ronald B./Patricia Keilbach (2001): Reciprocity, Coercion, or Exchange: Symmetry, Asymmetry and Power in Institutional Design. In: International Organization; Vol. 55; No. 4; pp. 893-919

Mofson, Phyllis (1996): Zimbabwe and CITES: The Reciprocal Relationship Between State and International Regime. Paper Presented to the International Studies Association Conference, 16-20 April. San Diego

O'Neill, Kate (2000): Waste Trading Among Rich Nations. Cambridge (MA); MIT Press

Parker, Richard W. (1997): Choosing Norms to Promote Compliance and Effectiveness: The Case for International Environmental Benchmark Standards. In: Brown Weiss (ed.): International Compliance with Nonbinding Accords. Washington (D.C.); American Society of International Law; pp. 145-203

Parson, Edward A. (1993): Protecting the Ozone Layer. In: Haas/Keohane/Levy (eds.): Institutions for the Earth: Sources of Effective International Environmental Protection. Cambridge (MA); MIT Press; pp. 27-74

Parson, Edward A./Owen Greene (1995): The Complex Chemistry of the International Ozone Agreements. In: Environment; Vol. 37; No. 2; pp. 16-22

Peterson, M. J. (1992): Whalers, Cetologists, Environmentalists and the International Management of Whaling. In: International Organization; Vol. 46; No. 1; pp. 147-186

Peterson, M. J.(1993): International Fisheries Management. In: Haas/Keohane/Levy (eds.): Institutions for the Earth: Sources of Effective International Environmental Protection. Cambridge (MA); MIT Press; pp. 249-308

Princen, Thomas (1996): The Zero Option and Ecological Rationality in International Environmental Politics. In: International Environmental Affairs; Vol. 8; No. 2; pp. 147-176

Princen, Thomas/Matthias Finger (1994): Environmental NGOs in World Politics: Linking the Local and the Global. New York; Routledge

Rittberger, Volker/Michael Zürn (1991): Regime Theory: Findings from the Study of East-West Regimes. In: Cooperation and Conflict; No. 26; p. 171

Sprinz, Detlef/Carsten Helm (1999): The Effect of Global Environmental Regimes: A Measurement Concept. In: International Political Science Review; Vol. 20; No. 4; pp. 359-369

Stein, Arthur A. (1983): Coordination and Collaboration: Regimes in an Anarchic World. In: Krasner (ed): International Regimes. Ithaca (NY); Cornell University Press; pp. 115-140

Sylvan, David/Stephen Majeski (1998): A Methodology for the Study of Historical Counterfactuals. In: International Studies Quarterly; Vol. 42; No. 1; pp. 79-108

Tetlock, P. E./A. Belkin (eds.) (1996): Counterfactual Thought Experiments in World Politics: Logical, Methodological, and Psychological Perspectives. Princeton; Princeton University Press

The Social Learning Group (ed.) (2001): Learning to Manage Global Environmental Risks: A Comparative History of Social Responses to Climate Change, Ozone Depletion, and Acid Rain. Cambridge (MA); MIT Press

Victor, David G./Kal Raustiala/Eugene B. Skolnikoff (eds.) (1998): The Implementation and Effectiveness of International Environmental Commitments. Cambridge (MA); MIT Press

Wapner, Paul (1996): Environmental Activism and World Civic Politics. Albany (NY); State University of New York Press

Wilder, Martijn (1995): Quota Systems in International Wildlife and Fisheries Regimes. In: Journal of Environment and Development; Vol. 4; No. 2; pp. 55-104

Young, Oran R. (1991): Political Leadership and Regime Formation: on the Development of Institutions in International Society. In: International Organization; Vol. 45; No. 3; pp. 281-308

Young, Oran R. (1998a): Creating Regimes: Arctic Accords and International Governance. Ithaca (NY); Cornell University Press

Young, Oran R. (1998b): The Effectiveness of International Environmental Regimes: A Mid-Term Report. In: International Environmental Affairs; Vol. 10; No. 4; pp. 267-289

Young, Oran R. (1999a): Effectiveness of International Environmental Regimes: Causal Connections and Behavioral Mechanisms. Cambridge (MA); MIT Press

Young, Oran R. (1999b): Governance in World Affairs. Ithaca (NY); Cornell University Press

Andreas Obser

Learning in International Public Policy Networks. Managing Institutional Interplay between National and International Forest Programmes[1]

1 Introduction

The article takes up individual lines of reasoning articulated in the contribution of Ron Mitchell in this book on 'when and how international institutions matter'. International institutions do matter and they ought to. The emphasis here will be on Mitchell's 'how' questions, such as how the management of international institutions influences social learning in a given field like international forest policy. Furthermore, it is argued that the form matters. The form international institutions assume affects vitally their role in and effectiveness for social learning. A core and concrete feature of contemporary international institutional arrangements is their multilateral form. Multilateralism is described (Ruggie 1993: 7f) as generic institutional form of international partnerships and must not be confused with formal multilateral organisations or secretariats, a relatively recent form and still of only relatively modest importance. Multilateralism refers to coordinating relations among three or more states in accordance with certain organising principles.

The complex interplay between public, private, local and global arenas has influenced outcomes of forest policies for several decades. The surrounding circumstances characterise less a radical shift in paradigms than a gradual evolution of policy and management approaches (Reidar 1998; World Bank 1998). They include a shift in emphasis from plantation forestry to social forestry, which is from the timber supply issues that concern foresters to the fuelwood, employment and income-generation concerns of developmentalists. The shift to community participation reflected the emerging role of the social activists. They focused on a more equitable distribution of timber and non-timber forest products, particularly to the stewards of those products. Treatment of forests as ecosystems with functions ranging from watersheds and

---

[1] This chapter summarises and integrates the findings of the projects "International Forest Policies" (Hartmut Elsenhans and Andreas Obser, University of Leipzig) and "Multilevel Governance" (Andreas Obser, University of Potsdam). The author gratefully acknowledges the financial support and intellectual stimulation by DFG's Global Environmental Change Programme and its interdisciplinary Working Groups.

habitats for biodiversity to carbon sequestration reflected the increasing voice of the international environmental NGOs. The most recent development appears to be the increasing role of policy analysts in international, forest-related debates (World Bank 1998).

Agenda 21 and the Forest Principles reflect the gradual change in paradigm. Both no longer focus on tropical forests alone but address all types of forests worldwide and call for holistic instead of sector-bound approaches as well as for a shift from state forest monopolies to pluralistic structures. This is reflected in the term forest governance, which emphasizes that there is a role for civil society, forest users, the private sector and government agencies outside of the forest administration in determining how forests are used. Forest governance focuses on clarifying the relationships, rights and responsibilities of stakeholders and on providing a framework to design the structures, mechanisms and linkages to tackle existing and future challenges (Facharbeitskreis Waldwirtschaft 2002).

Multi-level governance has emerged as an important analytical framework and linking strategy in the International Arrangement on Forests (IAF). Focusing on National Forest Plans (nfp), the paper will analyse the current allocation of forest policy functions across multiple levels of governance, including an increasing number of international arrangements such as the United Nations Forum on Forests (UNFF), the Collaborative Partnership on Forests (CPF) and various global environmental conventions. The growing popularity of decentralisation and multi-stakeholder dialogues in many countries has further accentuated the shift to a more multi-levelled governance logic of nfps. Thus far, the often ad hoc and incremental process through which forest policy tasks disperse across different levels of governance has created a confusing pattern of overlapping responsibilities. It is argued, however, that nfps could and should serve as learning-oriented transmission belts in multi-level arrangements.

2 Analysing Forest-Related International Public Policies

2.1 Evolution of International Public Policies

Many crises reflecting the international forest policy agenda today are attributed to an under-provision of 'global public goods' (Kaul, Grunberg et al. 1999) and 'international public goods' (Ferroni/Mody 2002) also called global policy outcomes (compare (A) in Figure 1). They are considered as a new emerging class of such goods (Kanbur, Sandler et al. 1999). A major reason why public policymaking has not adjusted to global, present-day challenges is explained by three major gaps: first, a jurisdictional gap, i.e., the discrepancy between the global boundaries of today's major policy concerns and the essentially national boundaries of policymaking; second, a participation gap, which results from the fact that we live in a multi-actor world but international cooperation is still primarily intergovernmental; third, an incentive gap, because moral suasion is not enough for countries to correct their international spillovers or to cooperate for the global public good. To make international public policymaking work, the research group at UNDP asks for policy reforms to create a clear jurisdictional loop, reaching from the national to the international (regional and global) level and back to the national. Further, a participation loop is requested, in order to bring all actors into the process – governments, civil society and business, all population groups, including all generations, and all groups of countries. Finally, there is a quest for an incentive loop, for ensuring that cooperation yields fair and clear results for all (Kaul, Grunberg et al. 1999).

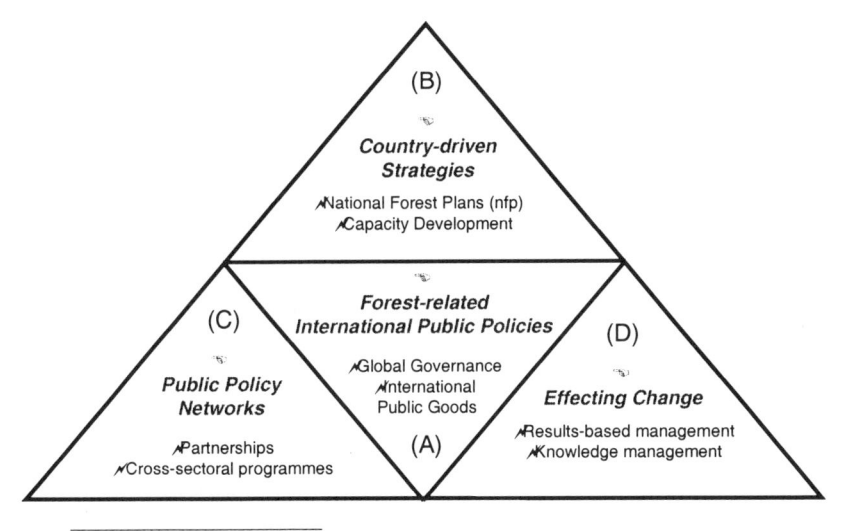

(B) Country-driven Strategies
⤳National Forest Plans (nfp)
⤳Capacity Development

(A) Forest-related International Public Policies
⤳Global Governance
⤳International Public Goods

(C) Public Policy Networks
⤳Partnerships
⤳Cross-sectoral programmes

(D) Effecting Change
⤳Results-based management
⤳Knowledge management

⤳ = contemporary agendas of forest policy change and
⤳ = selected issues relevant to international public policymaking

Figure 1: Contemporary agendas of policy change and selected issues relevant to forest-related international public policies

The last decade has seen the emergence of international public policy networks (Reinicke 1998; Benner, Obser et al. 2001; Benner, Reinicke et al. 2002), involving international organisations, governments, businesses as well as not-for-profit organisations that have joined forces around particular issues (compare (C) in Figure 1).

They have become an important feature in the decentralised system of global governance, indicating the shift from vertical integration and purely state-driven cooperation in multilateral regimes and international organisations towards a system of networked governance that cuts across sectors (public, private, voluntary) as well as levels (local, regional, national, international). International public policy networks seek to remedy collective action inertia by creating issue-focused partnerships and processes for reaching agreement on priorities, procedures and reciprocal obligations toward specified outcomes (Ferroni 2000: 8). International organisations often play central roles in these networks, stimulating various institutional changes that indicate a fundamental change in the roles and responsibilities international organisations perform in the international political system.

2.2 Analytical Framework

What analytic tools are available and which have to be developed in order to explore the complex and contingent interdependencies in international public policymaking? An analytical framework is meant to be a platform for investigating the predictive power of complementary or competing theories and models used in other (sub-)disciplines that surround regime effectiveness analyses in theories of international relations. The framework does not constitute any proper theory in itself. A major objective is to pursue a governance-oriented style of explanatory research on international public policy that creates openings for an integration of analytical methods that are standardly employed in international relations, comparative politics, network analysis and public administration. One objective is to explain the phenomenon of international public policy networks as a new mode of governance in world affairs. The framework should be used as a foundation for investing the predictive power of complementary or competing theories, rather than be limited to the use of only one theory (Ostrom, Gardner et al. 1994: 26).

Major benchmarks for the development of an international public policy framework are approaches like the Institutional Analysis and Development Framework (IAD) suggested by Elinor Ostrom and Larry Kiser (Kiser/Ostrom 1982) and further developed at the Workshop of Policy Analysis and Political Theory (Oakerson/Walker 1997) or 'Actor-Centered Institutionalism' mainly developed by Renate Mayntz and Fritz Scharpf at the Max-Planck-Institute in Cologne (Mayntz/Scharpf 1995; Scharpf 2000). Elinor Ostrom is particularly concerned with maintaining a clear distinction between the terms 'framework', 'theory', and 'model', which represent different levels of conceptualisation. The 'framework' is defined as an organising schema that categorises concepts that can be used to build different theories of any given empirical phenomenon. The term 'model' is reserved for more detailed representations of specific situations (Ostrom, Gardner et al. 1994). Correspondingly, the framework should be considered as a meta-theoretical framework or a generalised way to organise different institutional approaches in order to conduct global public policy analyses. With regard to the theory-practice gap, the framework aims at overcoming the factors that hinder the potential of scientific inquiry into the management of international public policies and programs to evolve into a transdisciplinary discussion about what-to-do and how-to-do questions in public policymaking.

An application of the institutional analysis and development framework (Oakerson 1994) to the implementation of international environmental programs re-poses the informational assumptions (e.g. selfishness, complete information, consistent alternative ranking and maximisation of expected utility) in favour of addressing the micro-meso link such as the relationship between individual behaviour and organisational action (Young 1991). The relevance of institutional frameworks in administrative and organisational analysis, like the advocacy coalition approach or the IAD framework, for international regime analysis (Keohane/Ostrom 1995) cannot be addressed in more detail here. However, the role of ideas as independent variables is acknowledged. Drawing on a more contractual view in the analysis provides a conceptual framework for linking institutional schools of thought both in public administration (Majone 1996) and in international politics (Goldstein/Keohane 1994) that focus on the role of ideas, interests and institutions in policy-making.

3 The Demand for Synthetic Frameworks in International Public Policy Analysis

Research in international and comparative politics (compare (A) and (B) in Figure 2) often deals with the same question; in the case of forestry, for example, the nature of deforestation, the conduct of non-tariff barriers like certification on international timber trade and the consequences of different political institutions. Yet, several scholars see a pronounced gap between these two subfields of political science. Mainstream neorealist research in international politics has difficulties in considering governance effects of sub national actors, while most of comparative research rarely scales up national and sub national governance effects beyond the territorial border of nation states. The theoretical reductionism provides the motivation to bring theories of domestic and international politics closer together (Caporaso 1997).

Of most interest is research that is both explanatory and comparative, and which focuses on techniques and functional aspects associated with global governance. Those studies help us to identify theoretically significant variation in the overall importance and causal forms of global governance effects across issues, countries and institutions. 'Good international governance' in modern times requires attention not only to shifting relations between international institutions, governments, citizens and the private sector (compare (C) in Figure 2), but also to the effective functioning of governments (Collingwood 2003; compare (D) in Figure 2) and international institutions themselves.

```
                        (B)
               Public Policy and
             Distributed Governance
           How can we reinforce national
       capacities and implement nfp processes?

                The effectiveness of
                international regimes
   (C)                                        (D)
                 International institutions,
 Interorganisational  like the IAF/UNFF/CPF     New
     Networks        matter but how?      Public Management
                         (A)
 How can we support and implement      How can we strengthen
 forest partnerships and cross-sectoral  accountability and learning in forest
         programmes?                          policies?
```

(A) = Theories of International Relations (B) = Theories of Comparative Politics
(C) = Policy Network Theories   (D) = Public Administration Theory
📖 = contemporary sub-disciplinary concepts of social science, and
🔑 = key questions for explaining and implementing forest-related international public policies

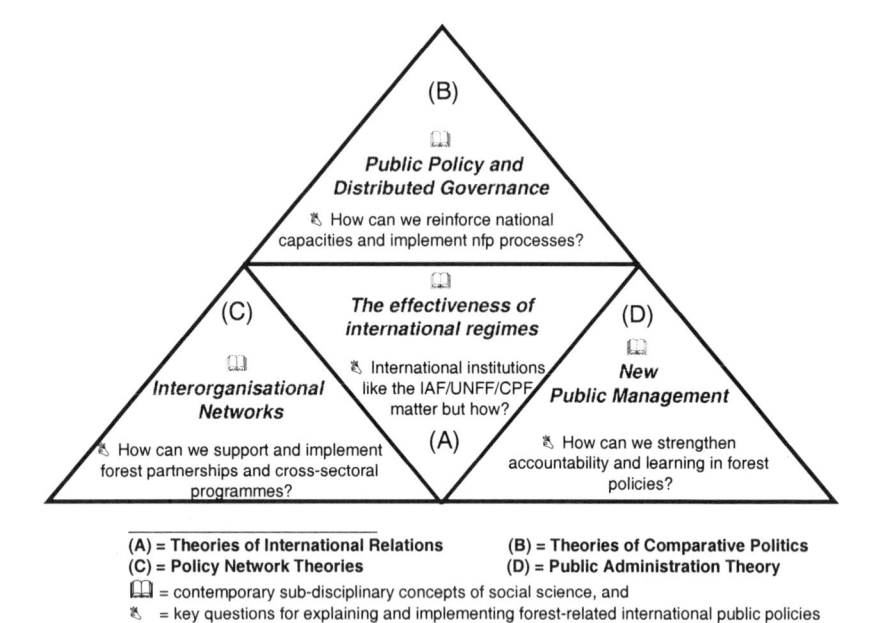

Figure 2: Contemporary social science debates and key questions for analysing forest-related international public policies

'Distributed governance' – a term coined in a recent publication of OECD – is concerned with the protection of the public interest in the increasingly wide variety of government organisational forms (Organisation for Economic Co-operation and Development (OECD) 2002). The term captures the notion of proliferating public organisations operating with some degree of separateness from core government agencies. Governance variation can not only illuminate comparative research but also better inform international public policymaking. Beside the reduction to either internal variables or external variables, other political science theories reduce their analyses to either state-centric or society-centric variables (see Figure 3).

	society-centered approaches	state-centered approaches
national and subnational variables	reductionist ← integrative →	reductionist
	↘ synthetic ↙	
international and regional variables	reductionist ← integrative →	reductionist

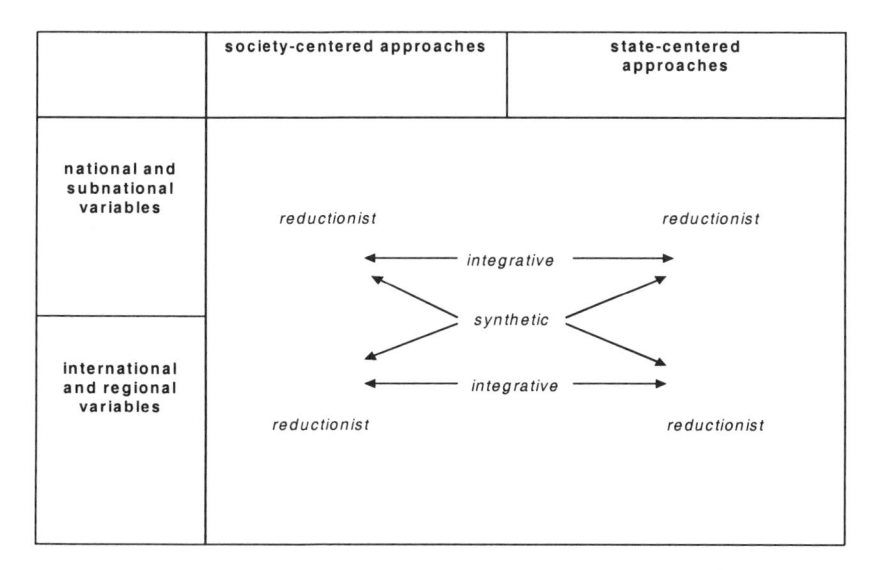

Figure 3: Conceptual requirements to analyse complex models of global governance that incorporate public and private actors (Source: Grande/Risse 2000: 247)

Regulation theories focus on states' or governments' public policy techniques that are intended to promote the social and economic well being of the public. These theories were long based on a tenet of the state as the central and hierarchical control authority. On the other side, political pluralism is originally based on the idea that within a political system or institution power is or should be shared between varieties of groups. Grande and Risse (2000) developed a conceptual framework in order to classify individual political science approaches and to be able to combine them better for addressing complex issues of governance capacity in times of globalisation. Basically three different approaches have been identified: (i) reductionist approaches, that focus on either internal, external, society- or state-centric variables exclusively; (ii) integrative approaches, that still separate internal and external perspectives but which attempt to integrate society- and state-centric research strategies, and (iii) synthetic approaches, which endeavour to unravel the divide between internal and external factors as well as the reduction to either public or private actors (see Figure 3).

In the past decade, there has been a major growth of interest in political economy and institutions. Special attention is given to the outputs and outcomes of political processes and institutions. Politics is conceptualised as an independent rather than a dependent variable in order to ask whether politics matters (Benz 1997; Mair 2002). In an effort to define and measure regime performance Arild Underdal introduces a typology of public policy research into regimes analysis (Underdal/Young 2003). He differentiates outputs, outcomes and impacts of global institutions. Accordingly, outputs are defined as procedures and arrangements that are needed to transform an international policy idea on paper into practice or to make it operational. Outcomes are defined as behavioural changes such as compliance of individual actors that are traced back to the implementation of international public policy. The ultimate measure however, are impacts which refer to problem-solving capacity in the sense of attributable changes in the status of the problem a regime is designed to address (Hanf/Underdal 1995; Hanf/Underdal 1997).

There has been a major growth of interest in institutional change and institutional analysis in political science. In the literature at least three different kinds of institutionalisms are differentiated in political science, e.g. historical, rational choice and sociological institutionalism (Hall/Taylor 1996). Despite differentiation between the institutionalist approaches, many scholars agree that the various approaches should be seen as complementary, rather than separate (Ostrom 1990). Neo-institutionalism is less constitutional than the old institutionalism. Economic analysis plays a more central role in exploring the role of markets and globalisation. Furthermore, neo-institutionalism is more connected to social and political theory, and less to political philosophy, than its predecessor and more engaged in political economy (Apter 1987). Hence the state as an instrumentality in its own right, its steering trends and traditions and how it determines the nature of the private sector, is at stake (Peters 1999).

4 Across the Great Divide: Integrating International and National Forest Policies

The concept of international regime (Krasner 1983) helps to describe multilateral arrangements through which states cooperate to regulate transborder activity. International regimes are sets of implicit or explicit principles, norms, rules and decision-making procedures applicable to a specific area of international politics (Keohane 1984). In the case of the forest there is – at least in strict terms and definitions (Levy, Young et al. 1995) – no international regime. During the United Nations Conference on Environment and Development in Rio de Janeiro (UNCED 1992), the international community could not agree on a legally binding instrument on forests. Instead, governments adopted Chapter 11 "Combating Deforestation" of Agenda 21 and the "Forest Principles" (compare Figure 4 and 5).

Chapter 11 and the Forest Principles are both not legally binding. Although they represent a significant step in that direction, a shared operational international vision still needs to be developed. However, many international agreements reached in recent years have profound implications for forest policies and programs in developing countries. There is active and increasing international cooperation on forest issues, but no legal instrument deals specifically with the protection and management of forests.

In February 2000, at the conclusion of its mandate, the Intergovernmental Forum on Forests (IFF) recommended the establishment of a new international arrangement on forests, composed of a policy forum and a collaborative partnership on forests. In October 2000, acting on the recommendations of the IFF and the decision of the Commission on Sustainable Development (CSD), ECOSOC established the UNFF, with universal membership. The UNFF succeeds the five-year process (1995-2000) of the *ad hoc* Intergovernmental Panel on Forests (IPF) and Intergovernmental Forum on Forests (IFF). As part of the new international arrangement on forests, ECOSOC also invited the heads of relevant international organisations to form a collaborative partnership on forests to support the work of the UNFF and to enhance cooperation and coordination among its participants (Collaborative Partnership on Forests (CPF) 2002).

No one can deny the immense importance placed by numerous actors on issues of sustainable forest management. Yet, despite all the international activity, little progress has been made (Poore, Blaser et al. 1998). Forests continue to be degraded and lost, and the international community could not agree upon creating an effective forest regime such as a global forest convention. The UNFF, like its forerunners IPF and IFF, is still criticised by many observers for endless discussions, controversies, a targetless Agenda 21 and Forest Principles and a plethora of recommendations emerging from the various international institutional settings.

The list of international organisations as well as the multiplicity of international instruments and initiatives indicate that almost all issues of international forest politics have already been addressed at the international level. Some analysts consider the existing instruments that are clearly binding under international law as inadequate with regard to either the level of detail they go into or their practical feasibility. They therefore contain regulatory gaps with regard to specific issues at the implementation level. Furthermore, instruments that deal with specific issues in sufficient depth and detail are not legally binding and are therefore formally inadequate. Different options for future regulation of forest issues at the international level are proposed: (i) forest protocols in existing conventions; (ii) establishment of a global forest convention; (iii) country-specific implementation of the Forest Principles and Chapter 11 of Agenda 21; (iv) integration and harmonisation of existing instruments; (v) continuation and institutionalisation of the current international process (Skala-Kuhmann 1996).

IAF	= International Arrangement on Forests *(since 2002)*
CPF	= Collaborative Partnership on Forests *(since 2001)*
UNFF	= United Nations Forum on Forests *(since 2001)*

Eight-Country Initiative (2000)
Six-Country Initiative (1998)

IFAG	= International Forestry Advisers Group *(since 1989)*

IFF	= Intergovernmental Forum on Forests *(1997-2000)*
IPF	= Intergovernmental Panel on Forests *(1995-1997)*
ITFF	= Interagency Task Force on Forests *(1995-2000)*

CSD	= Conference on Sustainable Development *(since 1992)*
CBD	= Convention on Biodiversity *(since 1992)*
CCD	= Convention on Combating Desertification *(since 1994)*
FCCC	= Framework Convention on Climate Change *(since 1994)*
UNCED	= United Nations Conference *(1992)* → Agenda 21 → **Forest Principles**
GEF	= Global Environment Facility

TFAP	= Tropical Forest Action Programme *(1985-1992)*

Figure 4: Chronology of international forest policy

Critics of the international forest processes are pessimistic about prospects for major changes in international collaboration on forests and do not attribute any significant influence to the UNFF Secretariat. International forest policy is said to remain a self-help system, organised through interstate arrangements rather than through the quite restricted powers of the Secretariat. Politics is here often conceived as zero-sum game where only the interests and bargaining power of states count. A number of states still reason that the case has not been made for a convention yet, that the time is not yet ripe for a convention and that concentrating all efforts on negotiating a convention might result in a loss of momentum, so consensus-building on forest issues should continue simultaneously.

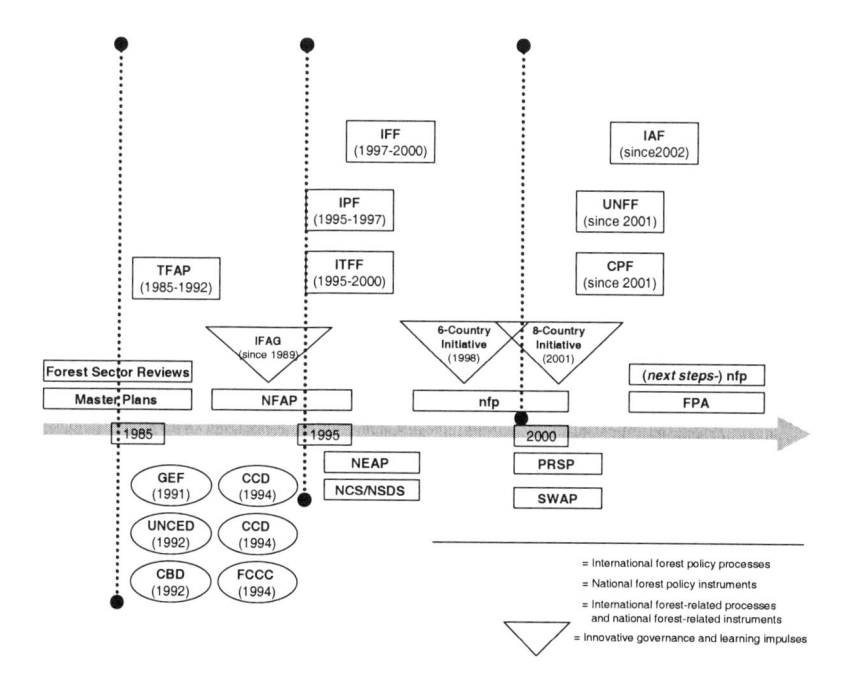

Figure 5: Governance phases, layers and initiatives in international forest policy

In its struggle against vested interests and policy inertia the new UNFF Secretariat will increasingly rely on policy analyses and problem-solving capacities of vertically integrated institutions in resolving problems that are too complex or controversial to be dealt with in a simply sequential, pluralist or horizontally integrated approach of collective international organisations. The UNFF Secretariat is the administrative body where the coordination and harmonisation of an efficient and effective forest regime – in the absence of a legally binding convention – is pursued. It is argued that only further institutionalisation, in particular novel features of vertical interplay, support synergistic effects of existing instruments and ensure the necessary production of coordination and orientation services for forest-related international public policies.

In the following paragraphs, individual novel features of (inter)national institutional interplay and learning will be illustrated. They represent common policy processes and new implementation strategies that transcend the national/international divide in forest policies.

4.1 Provision of Policy Services through Networked International Organisations

Most international regimes include at least one formal international organisation as service provider for the collaborating states in a regime (compare (A) and the reasonable links to (C) in Figures 1 and 2). Four key functions are frequently referred to international organisations in the development of international regimes: (a) the facilitation of agreements, (b) the altering of states' and NGOs' influence in the formation of and implementation of regimes, (c) the promotion of compliance with regime rules and (d) the legitimisation of particular ideas or international practices. In the case of the forest there is a network of international organisations, i.e. the Collaborative Partnership on Forests (CPF), jointly providing international policy services on behalf and in support of the UNFF Secretariat.

CPF's forerunner, the ITFF, was established in 1995 to support the IPF (1995-97) and, subsequently, the IFF (1997-2000). The provision of services had been based on a notion of division of labour or, so to speak, a horizontal form of institutional interplay at the level of international organisations. The ITFF consisted of eight international forest or forest-related organisations (Figure 6) and it was chaired by the FAO, as Task Manager of Chapter 11 of Agenda 21.

The ITFF members supported the IPF/IFF process by assisting in the preparation of the reports of the UN Secretary-General on various IPF/IFF programme elements, contributing to the implementation of IPF/IFF proposal for action and by enhancing coordination on forest-related matters among its members. Furthermore, CIFOR, DESA, FAO, ITTO, UNDP and UNEP supported the IPF/IFF Secretariat through secondments of staff. The ITFF was considered one of the main institutional legacies of the IPF/IFF process. Both the IPF and IFF recognised the valuable contributions made by the ITFF and commended the ITFF as an example of an effective mechanism for inter-agency collaboration.

In response to ECOSOC's recommendation, the CPF was established at its inaugural meeting on 4-5 April 2001 in Rome. The initial membership of the CPF consists of eight founders, the members of the ITFF. The CPF membership will, however, be strengthened to include about a dozen members in total. Invitations are being issued to the Secretariat of the United Nations Framework Convention on Climate Change (FCCC), the Secretariat of the Convention to Combat Desertification (CCD) and the Secretariat of the Global Environment Facility (GEF) to join the CPF. A few other organisations may also be approached to explore their interest in joining the CPF and their potential contribution to CPF objectives.

Current and former founding Members of ITFF (1995-2000) and CPF (2001)

- CBD   = Secretariat of the Convention on Biological Diversity
- CIFOR   = Center for International Forestry Research
- DESA   = Department of Economic and Social Affairs of the United Nations Secretariat
- FAO   = United Nations Food and Agriculture Organization
- ITTO   = International Tropical Timber Organization
- UNDP   = United Nations Development Programme
- UNEP   = United Nations Environment Programme
- World Bank

Future Prospects for extended Network-Membership at CPF

- Other UN agencies
- Regional processes
- International and regional development banks
- EC   = European Commission
- WTO   = World Trade Organization
- IFAG   = International Forestry Advisors Group
- PROFOR   = Programme on Forests

Figure 6: Membership of the CPF

The CPF consists of international organisations, institutions and instruments that have the capacity, programmes and substantive resources to facilitate the UNFF process, in particular the implementation of the IPF/IFF proposals for action and other relevant internationally agreed actions on forests. The CPF members have stressed, however, the importance of strengthening the work of the CPF by inviting other partners to join in its specific activities, as well as the importance of sharing information on the CPF work with a wide audience. A CPF Network is being established to facilitate cooperation and interface between the CPF and other partners (Collaborative Partnership on Forests (CPF) 2002).

The CPF Network will be open for the participation of interested international and regional organisations, institutions and instruments, including NGOs, private sector entities and other major groups. The Directory of Forest-related Institutions, maintained by FAO, serves as a starting point for developing the CPF Network. The CPF Network participants could include, for example: United Nations agencies; regional processes (such as the Pan-European Forest Process, Amazon Cooperation Treaty, Central American

Forest Commission, etc.); European Commission (EC); World Trade Organisation (WTO); International Forestry Advisors Group (IFAG); Programme on Forests (PROFOR); international and regional development banks; International Union of Forest Research Organisations (IUFRO) and other international or regional forest research and information institutions; international environmental and development NGOs and organisations or associations representing indigenous peoples, the forestry industry, forest owners and other private sector entities as well as other major groups.

```
                International Arrangement on Forests (IAF)


                    UNFF    <------>    CPF


       Intergovernmental Process          Inter-agency Partnership

              ↕                                   ↕

       Multistakeholder Dialogue  <------>   CPF Network
```

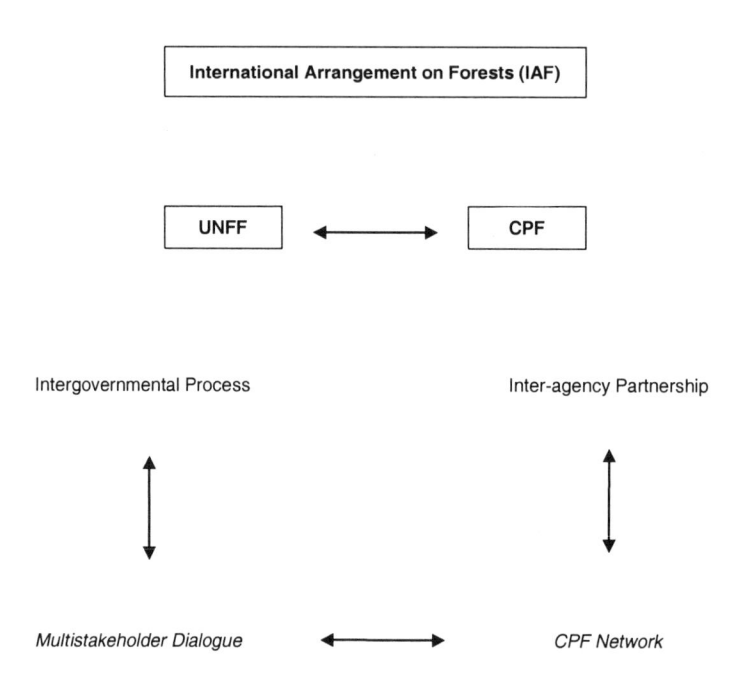

Figure 7: The relationship between the multi-stakeholder dialogue in UNFF and the CPF Network (Source: Collaborative Partnership on Forests (CPF) (2001)

It has been emphasised that the CPF Network and the UNFF multi-stakeholder dialogue are two distinct processes (see Figure 7). Multi-stakeholder dialogues are a provision of ECOSOC resolution E/2000/35 and are designed to provide an opportunity for the UNFF to receive and consider input from representatives of major groups. The UNFF is the intergovernmental forum for policy development and multi-stakeholder dialogues will be held at each meeting of the UNFF to provide an opportunity for major groups to contribute their expertise, concerns and views to policy deliberations. The CPF is an inter-agency partnership whose role is to promote coordinated and cooperative action in support of the UNFF, and the CPF Network is envisioned as a mechanism to enable meaningful involvement of other relevant organisations, institutions and instruments in the work of the CPF. Therefore, it is important to clarify that the CPF Network will not offer the opportunity for a dialogue with governments in addressing matters relating to forest policy, but will help channel inputs from various organisations, institutions and instruments, which support the implementation of IPF/IFF proposals for action. This distinction in the roles of the CPF Network and multi-stakeholder dialogue must be borne in mind as the CPF Network is formed and its working modalities are elaborated (Collaborative Partnership on Forests (CPF) 2001).

The CPF meeting in August 2001 also addressed the issue of a lead-agency system, similar to the practice during the ITFF. It was decided that the term 'focal agency' be used instead to reflect equal partnership and shared responsibility in facilitating and coordinating the work of CPF on a particular issue.

4.2 Provision of Policy Services through Independent Expert Bodies and Country-Led Initiatives

Efficiency is generally expressed as the ratio of output to input in any comparable unit of measure. It is difficult to have a precise measure of efficiency in international policy-making, but it has become a stronger tool for evaluation of regime effects (compare (B) and the reasonable links to (C) and (D) in Figures 1 and 2). In times of scarce financial resources and UN reform, an important function of international secretariats is the production of coordination and orientation services, and their efficiency in promoting them. Efficiency in international service production implies improving productivity (i.e. increasing output per unit of input) as well as reducing waste and indirect costs (i.e. negative side effects such as overlaps, duplication, conflicts and competition).

International organisations are institutions of collective choice for the most part corresponding to the unanimity rule or special forms of qualified majority in international decision-making. These forms of collective decision-making entail excessive transaction costs for international secretariats in discovering opportunities for policy innovation. Independent expert bodies are not caught in two-level games (Evans, Jacobson et al. 1993). They are insulated from the electoral cycle in domestic politics and zero-sum games in international bargaining. Such institutions sometimes succeed in issue areas that are too controversial to be dealt with by a secretariat of an ad-hoc intergovernmental forum. "The politics of efficiency is the process by which diffuse, ill-organised, broadly encompassing interests sometimes succeed in overcoming particularistic and well-organised interests. [...This] process cannot be understood without acknowledging the role of ideas as independent variables. The significance of non-majoritarian institutions in this context is due to their ability to focus public attention on a particular issue, to diffuse policy ideas, and to translate such ideas into concrete decisions." (Majone 1996)

There had been a practice by the IFF Secretariat of employing independent expert bodies to perform some specific task rather than to perform it themselves, that is to say to delegate rather than to make. This change reflects a special form of contracting out by international secretariats. The conventional concept of contracting out refers to the process of governments to buy particular services for reasons of more efficient production processes from outside rather than promote them in-house. Firms move towards vertical integration in order to eliminate the profit margins of intermediaries or to secure sources of supply or markets. A similar practice by international secretariats is defended on the grounds that the delegation of secretariat services stimulates more efficiency in international policy processes.

As in the case of politics of efficiency, politics of credibility becomes an increasingly important topic for the UNFF Secretariat. It faces a situation of 'governance without government' or – to put it in the terminology of new institutional economics – a situation of 'incomplete contracting' (Milgrom/Roberts 1992). The use of the term contract designates not only a legally binding forest convention, but also informal and tacit agreements among actors engaged in international forest politics. Majone (1996: 825) states that "...[o]ne response to contractual incompleteness is an arrangement, known as 'relational contracting' (Williamson 1985), where the parties do not agree on detailed plans of action, but on goals and objectives, on the criteria to be used in deciding what to do when unforeseen contingencies arise, and dispute resolution mechanisms to resolve disagreements."

In the absence of coercion in policy-making of international forest politics, the UNFF Secretariat will be willing to delegate such discretionary authority. The novel features of the UNFF Secretariat to delegate important policy-making powers to independent expert bodies might explain a strategy for achieving credible commitments in situations of incomplete contracting. There have been a number of expert-based and country-led initiatives directly linked to the policy processes of the UNFF and its forerunner IFF (International Institute for Sustainable Development (IISD) 1996). Three of them addressed the interdependence between international and national forest policies in particular: (i) the long-term scheme of the International Forestry

Advisers Group (IFAG) and the action schemes of (ii) the Six-Country-Initiative and (iii) the Eight-Country-Initiative (compare Figure 5).

The IFAG is an informal forum of advisers from the major international organisations and donor countries. The group has identified its most important task as advising on how donors can support sustainable forest management in developing countries (Savenije 2000: 37). In the past the FAG, and before that Tropical Forestry Advisers Group was very much involved in the TFAP/NFAP process (Oksanen, Heering et al. 1993; Oksanen, Salmi et al. 1994). The IFAG and its forerunners have always had an important function in international forest policies as a think-tank, in monitoring and as an important institutional memory. During the first phase of its existence (up to the early nineties), the FAG was largely concerned with the practical co-ordination and monitoring of the implementation of the TFAP process, which included mobilising and coordinating donor support. Besides this, the FAG also put a great deal of energy into promoting the exchange of experience and advancing the conceptual development of TFAP. Later, especially after the UNCED, attention became increasingly focused on international policy development.

The implementation and monitoring of the IPF Proposals for Action, the IFF recommendations, and now the multi-year programme of work of UNFF currently make up the framework of IFAG activities. The most important guiding principle in getting this across is how to enhance and support nfp processes. The FAG now sees its most important function as actively thinking along with the IAF process of implementing the IPF Proposals; it therefore has close contacts with the UNFF and the CPF. In this role, the IFAG has already proved capable of providing valuable services to international forest policies. Criticism has frequently been raised as the IFAG is still largely made up of donor advisers, whereas its mandate is global. There is an increasing need for regionally organised advisory groups made up of forest advisers from the developing countries themselves. This could guarantee a process of information exchange between countries about their individual processes that better matches their own needs and possibilities. The importance of this has now been more or less recognised and is being actively propagated by the IFAG (Savenije 2000: 38). Regional expert and coordination schemes, such as at the ASEAN Secretariat, are currently being developed.

In 1998, the so-called government-led Six-Country-Initiative "Putting the IPF Proposals for Action into Practice" was launched, in which three developed countries together with three developing countries agreed to undertake a joint effort to support the implementation of the international proposals for action that were formulated by the IPF prior to the creation of the IFF and the UNFF (Six-Country Initiative 1998). The initiative focused on the fact that no actual ways and means have been indicated for implementing the IPF proposals at national level. Hence, the objective was to enhance the implementation of the Proposals at national level and to develop guidance for consideration by the IFF (and the countries involved) based on the experience gained in their respective "translation" processes. The six countries criticised the formulations in the IPF Proposals for Action for not always being entirely clear and a significant number of proposals for being either fragmented or overlapping with others. It is therefore not always possible to implement them directly at national level. On the basis of country case studies, each of the six countries has studied how the IPF Proposals relate to its specific national context and planning process and vice versa (Savenije 2000: 33). The six case studies were conducted with the participation of relevant stakeholders and their institutions, from both the public and private sector. Another interesting part of the initiative has been the implicit equity and reciprocity between the three donor countries and the three developing countries that have decided to study their individual forest policies in a similar and mutually agreed manner. The approach and the results of the Initiative were positively received at IFF. The countries involved in the Six-Country Initiative decided to continue the process, albeit largely on an individual basis. In Indonesia, Uganda, Germany and also Australia, processes are underway for assessment of the IPF proposals and their integration into national policies by developing nfps. Some countries are embarking on similar processes using the revised Practitioner's Guide presented to the IPF (FAO/UNDP 1999). Other countries have been invited to do the same. The Netherlands has been considering joining the ongoing initiative. Additional expert meetings are scheduled to examine the progress of this innovative partnership approach.

In 2000, the Eight-Country-Initiative "Shaping the Programme of Work for the UNFF" capitalised on the Six-Country-Initiative. It had been organised and steered by Australia, Brazil, Canada, France, Iran, Malaysia, Nigeria and Germany. The Initiative has worked in close collaboration with the then extant IFF Secretariat and the international organisations and secretariats of international conventions, which formed the ITFF, and now the CPF. Furthermore, the initiative has a transparent organisation and is open to all interested countries, as well as to the NGO community and representatives of the private sector and other major groups. It has aimed to assist the international community in developing the programme of work for the UNFF and its concept and basic elements. Accordingly, the initiative has been focused on implementation of forest-related measures, bearing in mind that the UNFF aims to launch a 'plan for action' for the implementation of the IPF/IFF Proposals for Action. Special emphasis has been placed on capacity building, exchange of experiences on the nfp framework and the implementation of the "international forest regime". Emphasis was placed on issues of coordination of instruments, programmes and initiatives of international institutions relevant to the UNFF, including relevant aspects of the structure and work of the then still to be created CPF. In the last analysis, the initiative provided important organisational and content-related contributions to the extant IFF Secretariat in preparing a Secretary General's Report for consideration at the UNFF's first session.

Summarising the effects of the IFAG and the two country- or government-led initiatives, an important characteristic of vertical institutional interplay in international secretariats is that their success depends on affecting the attitudes and habits of involved states besides the more technical matter of managing complex interdependencies. The aim of modifying state's expectations reflects the special context by which credibility of a secretariat's policy-making becomes an essential condition of policy innovation. This is because the UNFF Secretariat – in the absence of a legally-binding forest convention – cannot bind states' legislature and a majority coalition of member states in the UNFF International forest policies are always vulnerable to reneging and hence lack credibility. Delegation to independent expert bodies and country-led initiatives appears to be a novel and efficient feature of achieving innovative and credible policy commitments by intertwining expert communities of international and national administrations.

4.3 Reinforcing National Capacities and Implementing National Forest Programmes (nfps)

To some experts it still appears that the greater the degree of international political consensus reached, the less explicit, specific and implemental the subsequent recommendations appear to be on the ground (World Bank 1999: 1). It is legitimate therefore to ask: is it really worth the effort to seek more specific commitment at the international level? Alternatively, should we seek a specific strategy and commitment to change at an individual country level (compare (B), (C), and (D) in Figures 1 and 2)? Two major currents are made responsible for this: (a) the lack of hierarchy and (b) the political economy in international forest politics. In international relations research, both framework conditions are not new phenomena, on the contrary. Neoinstitutional international relations research and knowledge, however, is clear on this: international forest policies like at the UNFF and policies at the national and sub--national level like in National Forest Programmes (nfp) are and ought to be complementary and not separate.

In 1997, the Intergovernmental Panel on Forests (IPF) endorsed, among others, the concept of nfp that are understood as comprehensive cross-sectoral forest policy processes with flexible entry points. The concept of nfps has been widely discussed during the past decades, especially in the context of the formulation and implementation of National Forest Plans (NFP), National Forestry Action Programmes (NFAP), Forestry Master Plans and Forest Sector Reviews (compare Figure 5). Various international institutions and cooperation agencies have promoted these frameworks as a means of achieving sustainable forest development, especially in developing countries. The nature, scope, context and impact of these frameworks often differ very considerably and usually need to be adjusted in order to form an effective conceptual and operational framework for implementing the IPF's Proposals for Action and for promoting sustainable forest management. Hence, there have been intensive discussions within the IPF on what form such policies, plans and processes should take. Experience of past and current processes has played an important role in these discussions. During all the discussions, however, it was also apparent that many countries are in fact strongly opposed to any outside body prescribing the form their forest planning should take (Savenije 2000: 11ff).

The World Bank's (2000) evaluation on its own and other actors' forest strategies summarises former inter-agency coordination and nfp-forerunners as follows: FAO-supported NFPs and World Bank-encouraged NEAPs have often not worked. The NFPs, which succeeded the Tropical Forest Action Plans in 1985, were supported by the FAO, the World Resource Institute (WRI) and the World Bank. In due course, however, the World Bank and the WRI dropped their support for these programs because they were 'top-down' and narrow in scope. The NFPs continued as FAO initiatives carried out by developing country governments with the support of several bilateral donors and the European Union. The World Bank, meanwhile, encouraged countries to develop NEAPs, which in many ways resemble NFPs, but with a broader scope and often variable treatment of issues in the forest sector. The report argues further that the World Bank, FAO and the donor community have not streamlined or coordinated their activities to bring about essential policy and institutional reforms that reflect the concerns of all stakeholders. What is needed is a better-coordinated, country-driven approach (cf. ibid., 33).

To enhance the implementation of the IPF Proposals for Action and the agreed forest-related action incorporated in other international agreements and conventions at country level, the IPF introduced the concept of national forest programmes (nfp's). From the outset, the IPF has always stressed that responsibility for designing and implementing these national processes primarily lies with countries themselves. At the same time, it has been argued that national forest plans should not be established in isolation but should have a certain degree of international coherence and co-ordination in view of the global dimensions and inter-relationships of sustainable forest management.

Nfp Principles

- National sovereignity and country leadership
- Consistency with the constitutional and legal framework of the respective country
- Consistency with international agreements and national commitments
- Partnership and participation of all interested parties in the nfp process
- Holistic, cross-sectoral approach to forest development and conservation
- Long-term and iterative process of planning, implementation and monitoring

Figure 8: Principles of a National Forest Programme (nfp)

The Facharbeitskreis Waldwirtschaft (2002: 6f) characterises a nfp as follows: it (i) is not a programme in the sense of a master plan, but a participatory dialogue process with defined outputs; (ii) deals with policy processes not only at the national, but also at sub-national and local levels; (iii) takes global and regional aspects into account; (iv) deals not only with forests but with all forest related sectors; and (v) covers not only forest policy development but also its implementation on the ground. Nfps aim at building transparency, promoting consensus between stakeholders and clarifying their mandates, tasks, rights and obligations. They result in agreed objectives, policies and strategies on sustainable forest management and in specific action for implementation. Decentralised consultation and decision-making is an integral part of the nfp process.

4.4 Forestry as a Governance Issue: Partnership-Building and Cross-Sectoral Approaches

An international public policy framework further relies on concepts used in the analysis of interorganisational networks (compare (C) linked to (A) and (B) in Figures 1 and 2). Network analysis of interactions between official and unofficial actors in the forest governance process implies a significant degree of structuring to interactions and can be extended to cover relationships within international institutions and within governments as well as between private and public actors (Peters 1999: 20). Interorganisational network concepts contribute to the development of models that capture the complexities and dependencies that determine the courses of action that are possible among and between governmental jurisdictions and multiple carriers of forest governance.

The term forest governance reflects a change in paradigm that calls for (i) networked instead of centralised structures and (ii) holistic instead of sector-bound approaches. In the last few years this new thinking in forestry has led to two complementary processes of change (compare Figure 5):

— the emergence of nfps, and related Forest Partnership Arrangements (FPA), as the leading framework for forest-sector reform; and
— a shift from project-based aid delivery to sector-wide approaches (SWAPs), strengthening donor co-ordination and support for a single, nationally-led sector policy and expenditure programme, that is adjusted to broader planning frameworks, such as developing countries' Poverty Reduction Strategy Papers (PRSP).

These processes are considered complementary, as a nfp is a comprehensive policy framework within which to co-ordinate sector development and a SWAP is a delivery mechanism to channel aid in support of that framework (Wells, Schreckenberg et al. 2002: 1).

Up to the 1960s and 1970s, the forestry planning concepts were primarily "top-down" and from a macro-economic perspective directed towards the profitability of productive activities that were often conceived in large-scale projects (Savenije 2000: 21). The importance of forests for the population and other not directly productive functions gradually received more attention and concepts such as "sustainability", "bottom-up planning", "participation" and "multifunctional forest management" gradually emerged. Since the 1980s, this has led to the introduction of several more highly integrated policy and planning frameworks and concepts to enhance forest management in developing countries. These conceptual trends in the past, together with ongoing processes, have actually been consolidated in the formulation of the framework of the nfp principles and in the 1990s extended by the FPA. FPA should be understood as instruments designed to coordinate and guide the activities of international and national actors within the context of national forest policy frameworks for the achievement of sustainable forest management (Liss 1999). Concerning the institutional and legal options for FPAs a distinction has to be drawn between national and international FPAs, since both instruments have different parties and participants and vary in their objectives (Skala-Kuhmann 1997). FPAs may be established at the national level, for example, between government institutions and donors as well as at sub national or local level, such as between forest administration, local communities, NGOs and the private sector.

At national level, nfps are said to have potential for integrating all the 'magic bullets' such as certification and forest fora into a system for continuous improvement (Bass 2002). Since the 'magic bullets' have tended to make the good forest players better, and left the bad alone, a focus on stopping illegal activities may be desirable. But the principal need is to improve local governance for 'forest goods and services' – which itself is often the best tactic to forge demand for effective forest governance and for integration 'at the top'. Limitations relate to continued (inter)governmental action without local involvement. It is not only the path from UNCED to UNFF that affected forest policy and management. It is also the spread of democracy, the increasing importance of civil society and noticeable activities of local and indigenous NGOs at the local level. The critical question is how best to balance 'top-down' and 'bottom-up' governance modes.

Isolated solutions to forest governance often fail as they deal with only the proximate cause of the problem and not the underlying cause, which may be extra- or cross-sectoral policies, such as for trade, finance and land use. The institutional and policy conditions for a SWAP are rarely ideal. It takes time to secure donor co-ordination, partner country ownership and changes in planning, budgeting and management processes. Nfps face similar obstacles. In a sector characterised by competing and vested interests, an nfp is likely to be highly political. Consensus may be difficult to obtain. Nfps also vary greatly. Some are genuinely inclusive with strong linkages to extra-sectoral processes. Others are narrow technocratic exercises with limited cross-sectoral impact. So, rather than impose a blueprint for sector-wide support to nfps, the Code encourages movement along a continuum, from project-level interventions through jointly financed programme packages to full integration into national budgetary procedures. This may help to institutionalise the iterative cycles of policy formulation, implementation, lesson learning and adjustment that are central to the nfp concept (Wells, Schreckenberg et al. 2002). The authors further recommend an initial focus on project-level interventions that may be most appropriate where donors focus their efforts on civil society.

The borderline between national FPA and the 'Code of Conduct' as recently proposed by a research group at the Overseas Development Institute (odi) is fluent (Wells, Schreckenberg et al. 2002). Both include a statement of principles and guidelines governing the behaviour of partners. As the role of the state is increasingly seen as setting the regulatory framework in which the private sector and civil society can function, codes of conduct provide a means to set standards and to manage the public/private interface. They also help to define mutual expectations in other forms of public partnership, including those between donors and recipients of international aid. The Code, however, is more process-oriented in its treatment of cross-sectoral challenges of forest governance. It provides a framework by which sector-based support might secure broader governance reform and achieve cross-sectoral benefits.

Development policy experts are increasingly concerned with questions of governance, i.e. with the rules under which power is exercised in the management of a country's resources and the relationships between the state and its citizens, civil society and the private sector (Brown, Schreckenberg et al. 2002). Brown and his colleagues continue to reason that, although there have been failures as well as successes, the sector has considerably more experience with governance issues than do most others, and this experience has been garnered at all levels – local, national and international. With regard to the interface between forestry and poverty alleviation, it is argued that forestry brings to life key governance concerns. Thus, progress in the forest sector can potentially lever wider gains in good governance. With donors increasingly preoccupied with good governance as a precondition for poverty reduction, the authors make the case for forestry as an entry point for governance reform.

4.5 Mainstreaming and Learning through Results-Based Management (RbM)

What is public management research good for in forest governance (compare (D) as fundamental management principle of (A), (B) and (C) in Figures 1 and 2)? First, public management concepts are expected to help us to better bridge the gap between practice and theory of forest governance. Second, results-based management is considered a major challenge for effective forest governance.

The gradual expansion of the international forest policy agenda must be seen in connection with the expansion and mainstreaming of the international development agenda, i.e. the introduction of the logic of the Comprehensive Development Framework (CDF) at the end of the 1990s. This framework is a set of principles proposed by the World Bank to improve the quality of aid to developing countries (World Bank 1999). The core principles of CDF also affected the international policy dialogue on forests in terms of: (i) a holistic, long-term perspective; (ii) partnership between government, the private sector and civil society; (iii) government commitment to policy reform and (iv) results orientation. The first three principles have been referred to in more detail in the former chapters. The fourth principle and its impact on the change of paradigm in international forest policy will be addressed in the following paragraphs. Results-based management is about making management a priority, alongside forest policy priorities. Public management research informs us about the strengths and weaknesses of results-based management in forest policies.

The last two decades were determined by two parallel developments in the theory of government, governance and public administration: besides (neo)institutionalism (neo)managerialism has also resurged, often attended by network analyses. The launch of a project of analytical reconstruction in public administration contributed to movements of 'reinventing government' (Osborne/Gaebler 1993), 'new steering model' (KGSt 1993), 'new public management' (Schedler/Proeller 2000; Barzelay 2001), 'good governance' (Collingwood 2003) and the like. Some scholars are uncertain about the potential of theory development, for example for forest governance, as well as the degree of practical utility, as scholarship on public management took off in many directions and at the same time consolidated existing 'knowledge enclaves'. It is not only the divide between policy and implementation in forest governance, it is also a gap between political science and public management research that needs to be bridged. An increasing number of scholars aims at demonstrating that political science can make larger contributions to contemporary public management research and *vice versa* (Barzelay 1997).

In an applied research approach that follows the rationale to 'design complexity to govern complexity' Ostrom (1995) comes to the conclusion that small-scale forest institutions at the community and local level and large-scale forest institutions at national or international level alike are not a sufficient solution by themselves, but that all of them are necessary parts of the multilevel governance systems needed for the future of forests (Keohane, McGinnis et al. 1992). Although there is no blueprint for international forest policy that can be used to create effective institutions, design principles can be derived from respective studies, which can be taught in research and training activities. George (1993:18) has substituted the theory-practice agenda with three different questions, which are slightly modified in order speak to the rationale and terminology of the challenges addressed in this paragraph: What is the relationship between forest-related public policy research and practice? What kind of knowledge is most relevant for assisting international public policymaking on forestry? How can this type of knowledge be developed by scholars and how can it be employed effectively by decision-makers, as in nfps?

In development cooperation, mainstreaming means the widespread adoption of a new policy, a new approach to the delivery of public services or a new method of program management, taking full account of the country context (Picciotto 2002). While there have been variations in the nfps launched and implemented, there have been many common aspects. For example: the focus on performance issues and on achieving results; the devolution of management authority and responsibility; an orientation to stakeholder needs and preferences; an emphasis on participation and teamwork; the reform of budget processes and financial management systems; and the application of modern management practices (Organisation for Economic Co-operation and Development (OECD) 2001). A central feature of contemporary nfps is the emphasis on improving performance; that is, on ensuring that governments' and international institutions' activities achieve the desired results. RbM can be defined as a broad management strategy aimed at achieving important changes in the way government agencies operate, with performance improvement (achieving better results) as the central orientation.

Focusing on individual forest projects as the unit of analysis for RbM has increasingly come under criticism. Limitations of the project logframe include its lack of strategic and long-term focus, and its inappropriateness for dealing with newly emerging SWAP modes that are jointly supported by numerous development partners (ibid, 9). There are currently joint efforts to develop performance measurement systems for broader country programs, such as for nfps – usually defined as sets of related projects or non-project activities sharing the same development objective within a partner country and across different sectors related to forestry. The nfp approach is a much more comprehensive and strategic approach to RbM than the project approach. The unit of analysis is not a single project but a whole nfp that typically includes many activities implemented by different donor agencies and partner organisations over a relatively long period.

5 Conclusions

One of the important challenges for sustainable forest policy is to manage programs that are delivered by more than one organisation or individual. International regimes and global policy networks are increasing forms of contemporary forest policy learning and management at the international, political, regional and ecological levels alike. Both, international (e.g. UNFF) and national (e.g. nfp) forest policies increasingly have to be managed outside a vertical hierarchy and must include some strategies for fostering cooperation and negotiation in multi-stakeholder situations. There are specific institutional and organisational arrangements for collaborative forest management. It is necessary to characterise different network situations and subsequent implications in order to develop design principles for effective global forest governance.

Forest management has become a pioneer field for the creation of such policy networks. The problems of structuring forest networks addresses problems which also emerge elsewhere because of the necessity to define the structures which constitute an otherwise rather amorphous issue area and on which actors involved have to agree, and this, in such a manner that the network is reinforced through this agreement. Forest management has been addressed by various networks, which have developed over time. These gained in cohesion when the structure of the network was changed. Hence, forest management can give insights into the requirements, which have to be fulfilled in order for a network to increase its cohesion and learning effects.

The significance of vertical interplay in the context of independent expert bodies in the policy-making process of international regimes is due to their ability to focus public attention on a particular issue, to disseminate international policy knowledge, and to translate such knowledge into concrete international but also country-specific decisions. Hence, forms of vertical interplay on the basis of delegating policy-making powers to independent expert bodies are important features with regard to efficient and credible policy-making in international regimes. The comparative advantage and the added value of independent expert bodies is referred to their expertise and commitment that contributes to a problem-solving, rather than to a bargaining, style of policy-making.

Forest governance is about guiding. It is characterised as a learning process whereby an organisation, a country or the international community reinforces modes of self-governance. This process is complex and changing. It depends on the dynamics of communication and control. In the dynamic environment of IAF and nfp new modes of partnership and new modes of production of knowledge and sharing of knowledge have evolved. The path-dependent and complex development of international forest policy illustrates that a massive stock of know-what and know-why information on forests is available, although doubts increase about the validity of causal conclusions drawn (Angelsen/Kaimowitz 1999). Know-how and know-who in forest governance yet have remained tacit and underdeveloped. The FPA and Codes of Conduct, in particular, pick up this thread.

References

Angelsen, A./D. Kaimowitz (1999): Rethinking the Causes of Deforestation: Lessons from Economic Models. In: The World Bank Research Observer; Vol. 14; No. 1; pp. 73-99

Barzelay, M. (1997): Researching the Politics of New Public Management: Changing the Question, not the Subject. Summer Workshop of the International Public Management Network, Potsdam

Barzelay, M. (2001): The New Public Management. Improving Research and Policy Dialogue. Berkeley C.A. et al.; University of California Press

Bass, S. (2002): Forests in Sustainable Development. A Quick Report Card on Progress Since Rio. London; International Institute for Environment and Development (IIED)

Benner, T., A. Obser, et al. (2001): Global Public Policy: Chancen und Herausforderungen vernetzten Regierens. In: Zeitschrift für Politik; Vol. 4; pp 27-54

Benner, T., W. H. Reinicke, et al. (2002): Global Governance: Globalisierung gestalten – Regieren in Netzwerken. In: Die Mitbestimmung; Vol. 1

Benz, A. (1997): Policies als erklärende Variable in der politischen Theorie. Theoreentwicklung in der Politikwissenschaft – eine Zwischenbilanz. In: A. Benz/W. Seibel (eds.): Baden-Baden; Nomos Verlagsgesellschaft; pp. 303-323

Brown, D., K. Schreckenberg, et al. (2002): Forestry as an Entry Point for Governmance Reform. London; ODI

Caporaso, J. A. (1997): Across the Great Divide: Integrating Comparative and International Politics. In: International Studies Quarterly; Vol. 41; No. 4; pp. 563-592

Collaborative Partnership on Forests (CPF) (2001): Draft CPF Network Concept Paper. New York, N.Y.; UNFF

Collaborative Partnership on Forests (CPF) (2002): CPF Network Concept Paper. New York; CPF

Collingwood, V., Ed. (2003): Good Governance and the World Bank. Washington; World Bank

Facharbeitskreis Waldwirtschaft (2002): People and Forests. Opportunities for Improving Livelihoods, Alleviating Poverty, and Saveguarding the Environment through Sustainable Forest Management. Eschborn; GTZ

Ferroni, M. (2000): Reforming Foreign Aid. The Role of International Public Goods. Washington, D.C.; World Bank Operations Evaluation Development

Ferroni, M./A. Mody, Eds. (2002): International Public Goods: Incentives, Measurement, and Financing. Boston and Washington, D.C.; Kluwer Academic Publishers and the World Bank

Food and Agriculture Organization of the United Nations (FAO)/United Nations Development Programme (UNDP) (1999): Practitioner's Guide to the Implementation of the IPF Proposals for Action. Rome and New York; FAO and UNDP

Goldstein, J. and R. O. Keohane, Eds. (1994). Ideas and Foreign Policy. Ithaca, N.Y.; Cornell University Press

Grande, E./T. Risse (2000): Bridging the Gap. Konzeptionelle Anforderungen an die politikwissenschaftliche Analyse von Globalisierungsprozessen. In: Zeitschrift für Internationale Beziehungen; Vol. 2 (Oktober); pp. 235-266

Hall, P. A./R. C. Taylor (1996): Political Science and the Three New Institutionalisms. Political Sciences; Vol. 44; No. 5; pp. 936-957

Hanf, K./A. Underdal (1995): Domesticating International Commitments. The International Politics of Environmental Management. In: Underdal, A. (ed.): The International Politics of Environmental Management. Kluwer Academic Publishers, for the European Science Foundation

Hanf, K./A. Underdal (1997): The Domestic Bases of International Environmental Agreements. Final report of a project funded by the European Commission

International Institute for Sustainable Development (IISD) (1996): Report of the Second Meeting of the CSD Intergovernmental Panel on Forests 11-22 March 1996. In: Earth Negotiation Bulletin; Vol. 13; No. 14; pp. 1-13

Kanbur, R., T. Sandler, et al. (1999): The Future of Development Assistance: Common Pools and International Public Goods. Washington, DC; Overseas Development Council

Kaul, I., I. Grunberg, et al. (1999): Defining Global Public Goods. Global Public Goods. International Cooperation in the 21st Century. In: I. Kaul, I. Grunberg and M. A. Stern (eds.): Global Public Goods. International Cooperation in the 21st Century. New York; Oxford University Press; pp. 2-19

Kaul, I., I. Grunberg, et al., Eds. (1999): Global Public Goods. International Cooperation in the 21st Century. New York; Oxford University Press

Keohane, R., M. McGinnis, et al., Eds. (1992): Proceedings of a Conference on Linking Local and Global Commons. Conference held at Harvard University, April 23-25, Harvard University, Center for International Affairs and Indiana University, Workshop in Political theory and Policy Analysis

Keohane, R. O. (1984): After Hegemony: Cooperation and Discord in the World Political Economy. Princeton, N.J.; Princeton University Press

Keohane, R. O./E. Ostrom, Eds. (1995): Local Commons and Global Interdependence: Heterogeneity and Cooperation in Two Domains. London; Sage

KGSt (1993): Das neue Steuerungsmodell. Begründung, Konturen, Umsetzung. Köln; KGSt

Kiser, L. L./E. Ostrom (1982): The Three Worlds of Action: A Metatheoretical Synthesis of Institutional Approaches. In: E. Ostrom (ed.): Strategies of Political Inquiry. Beverly Hills, CA; Sage: pp. 179-222

Krasner, S. D., Ed. (1983): International Regimes. Ithaca, N.Y.; Cornell University Press

Levy, M. A., O. R. Young, et al. (1995): The Study of International Regimes. In: European Journal of International Relations; Vol. 1; No. 3; pp. 267-330

Liss, B.-M. (1999): Nationale Waldprogramme. Konzept für einen Politik- und Planungsrahmen zur nachhaltigen Bewirtschaftung der Wälder. Eschborn; GTZ

Mair, S. (2002): Die Globalisierung privater Gewalt. Kriegsherren, Rebellen, Terroristen und organisierte Kriminalität. Berlin; SWP

Majone, G. (1996): Public Policy and Administration: Ideas, Interests and Institutions. In: R. E. Goodin/H.-D. Klingemann (eds.): A New Handbook of Political Science. New York, Oxford University

Mayntz, R./F. Scharpf (1995): Der Ansatz des akteurszentrierten Institutionalismus. In: R. Mayntz/F. Scharpf (eds.): Gesellschaftliche Selbstregelung und politische Steuerung. Frankfurt a.M.; Campus Verlag; pp. 39-72

Oakerson, R./S. T. Walker (1997): Analyzing Policy Reform and Reforming Policy Analysis: An Institutionalist Approach. In: D. W. Brinkerhoff (ed.). Policy Studies and Developing Nations: An Institutional and Implementation Focus. Greenwich, C.T.; JAI Press; pp. 21-51

Oakerson, R. J. (1994): Institutional Analysis and the Conduct of Policy Reform: Seeking New Rules of Economic Organization in Cameroon. Study prepared for the U.S. Agency for International Development, Decentralization: Finance and Management Project

Oksanen, T., M. Heering, et al. (1993): A Study on Coordination in Sustainable Forestry Development, Report prepared for the TFAP Forestry Advisers' Group (Draft 5/6/93)

Oksanen, T., J. Salmi, et al. (1994): Options for Improving the Effectiveness and Efficiency of National Forestry Programmes. Helsinki, Finland; INDUFOR OY

Organisation for Economic Co-operation and Development (OECD) (2001): Results Based Management in the Development Co-operation Agencies: A Review of Experience. Background Report. Paris; OECD

Organisation for Economic Co-operation and Development (OECD) (2002): Distributed Governance. Agencies, Authorities, and other Government Bodies. Paris; OECD

Osborne, D./T. Gaebler (1993): Reinventing Government. How Entrepreneurial Spirit is Transforming the Public Sector. New York, N.Y.; Plume

Ostrom, E. (1990): Governing the Commons. The Evolution of Institutions for Collective Action. Cambridge, UK; Cambridge University Press

Ostrom, E. (1995): Designing Complexity to Govern Complexity. In: S. Hanna/M. Munasinghe (eds.): Property Rights and the Environment. Social and Ecological Issues. Washington D.C.; The Beijer International Institute of Ecological Economics and the World Bank; pp. 33-46

Ostrom, E., E. Gardner, et al. (1994): Rules, Games and Common Pool Resources. Ann Arbor; University of Michigan Press

Peters, B. G. (1999): Institutional Theory in Political Science. The 'New Institutionalism'. London; Continuum

Picciotto, R. (2002): The Logic of Mainstreaming: A Development Evaluation Perspective. In: Evaluation; Vol. 8; No. 3; pp. 322-339

Poore, D., J. Blaser, et al. (1998): No Forest without Management. Sustaining forest ecosystems under conditions of uncertainty. In: Tropical Forest Update; No. 8; Vol. 4; pp. 10-13

Reidar, P. (1998): From Industrial Forestry to Natural Resources Management. Lessons Learnt in Forestry Assistance. Stockholm; Swedish International Development Cooperation Agency (SIDA)

Reinicke, W. H. (1998): Global Public Policy. Governing without Government. Washington, D.C.; Brookings Institution Press

Ruggie, J. G., Ed. (1993): Multilateralism Matters. The Theory and Praxis of an Institutional Reform. New York, N.Y.; Columbia University Press

Savenije, H. (2000): National Forest Programmes. From Political Concept to Practical Instrument in Developing Countries. Wageningen; International Agricultural Centre (IAC)

Scharpf, F. W. (2000): Interaktionsformen. Akteurzentrierter Institutionalismus in der Politikforschung. Opladen; Leske + Budrich

Schedler, K. and I. Proeller (2000): New Public Management. Bern; Verlag Paul Haupt

Six-Country Initiative (1998): Putting the IPF Proposals for Action into Practice. Proceedings of the International Expert Consultations. Baden-Baden; DSE (German Foundation for International Development)

Skala-Kuhmann, A. (1997): The Forest Partnership Agreement. Outline of the Concept and Considerations from a Legal Point of View. Eschborn, Germany; Support to International Programmes in Tropical Forestry (TWRP), Sectoral Project of the GTZ

Underdal, A./O. Young, Eds. (2003): Regime Consequences: Methodological Challenges and Research Strategies. Dordrecht; Kluwer Academic Publisher

Wells, A., K. Schreckenberg, et al. (2002): Negotiating Partnerships for Governance Reform: the Draft Code of Conduct for Forest Sector Development Cooperation. London; ODI

World Bank (1998): Forests and the World Bank: An OED Review of the 1991 Forest Policy and its Implementation. A Design Paper (draft). Washington, D.C.; World Bank

World Bank (1999): Discussion Paper. Coordinating Forest Sector Approaches and Policies Internationally: Some ideas for joint policy work within the Interagency Task Force on Forests (ITFF). Wasington, D.C.; World Bank (mimeo)

World Bank (1999): A Proposal for Comprehensive Development Framework (A Discussion Draft). Washington, D.C.; World Bank

Young, O. R. (1991). Political Leadership and Regime Formation. In: International Organization; Vol. 45; No. 3; pp. 281-308

Timothy Moss

Solving Problems of 'Fit' at the Expense of Problems of 'Interplay'? The Spatial Reorganisation of Water Management Following the EU Water Framework Directive[1]

> "The realization that institutional problems in water resources development and management are more prominent, persistent, and perplexing than technical, physical, or even economic problems has fostered as much frustration as insight among analysts and planners in water resource agencies" (Ingram et al. 1984, p. 323).

1 Introduction

This paper deals with a particular type of institutional change: the policy-driven reform of supranational environmental legislation and its anticipated impact on existing national, regional and local institutions of resource management. It takes as an example the EU Water Framework Directive (WFD), which came into force in December 2000, and investigates how the future introduction of river basin management across the EU is likely to affect the spatial organisation of water management within Member States. For students of institutional and environmental change the WFD is intriguing and illuminating for two reasons. Firstly, by institutionalising at a supranational level the concept of river basin management the Directive raises important issues of compatibility with well-established national and sub-national institutions of water management, particularly those not organised around river basins. Secondly, by establishing the river basin as the spatial unit for future water management the Directive follows a powerful ecosystem logic of managing water according to biophysical, rather than political-administrative, boundaries.

---

[1] This paper presents results from a project funded by the German Research Council (DFG) within the Priority Programme "Global Environmental Change – Social and Behavioural Dimensions". The author would like to thank the DFG for its generous support. Thanks are due also to Vera Tekken, Jochen Monstadt and Thomas Weith, who helped research part of this paper.

This paper investigates these two key issues by applying and testing an analytical framework provided by the Science Plan of the international project "Institutional Dimensions of Global Environmental Change" (IDGEC) of the Human Dimensions Programme (Young 1999). It examines how the institutionalisation of river basin management by the WFD represents a classic case of trying to solve problems of spatial 'fit' arising from managing a biophysical system along political-administrative territories. It then queries whether, in overcoming this dilemma, problems of 'interplay' between water and other relevant institutions – such as for spatial planning, agriculture or nature conservation – may be exacerbated by creating a different territorial unit for water management.

On the surface it is a study of the quest for the right scale at which to manage a natural resource: water. This may appear a straightforward and, indeed, superfluous task given the wealth of literature from environmental sciences advocating the river basin or catchment as the natural territorial unit for water management. Our objective, however, is not to question the validity of the river basin management concept but to investigate the implications of introducing or strengthening river basin management for existing institutional configurations (Göhler 1997). For despite unequivocal calls for river basin management from environmental policy-makers and researchers, the practice of reforming institutions of water management towards a more catchment-based approach has – as examples from around the globe illustrate – proved very difficult. The statement in the introductory quotation still holds true today.

This paper goes beyond the immediate issue of the functional suitability of organising water management around river basins, therefore, to explore a set of challenges relevant to research on environmental institutions which emanate from the implementation of the WFD. These challenges all relate to spatial dimensions of institutional change. The first is the need to reorder responsibilities and distribute new tasks among water management bodies at national, regional and local levels. Here we examine what experiences with river basin management and the plans for implementing the WFD can tell us about multi-level governance of an environmental resource in the EU. The second challenge addressed is the effectiveness of institutional reform 'from above'. The issue at stake here is whether the WFD can stimulate institutional innovation within the Member States whilst being sensitive to existing national styles of water management. The third challenge relates to the adaptability of existing institutions to pressures for change: in our case the ability of institutions of water management at regional and local levels to meet the WFD's requirements for river basin management. Finally, we aim to draw lessons from the changes envisaged by the WFD on the nature and value of interplay between distinct but functionally related institutions at local and regional levels. Given the importance of integrating land use and water resource management to river basin management in general, and the WFD in particular, we focus on the interrelationship between institutions of land-use and water management planning. By addressing these issues we hope, in sum, to create greater sensitivity among researchers of institutional change for its spatial dimensions at sub-national levels.

The paper begins with a review of the international literature on river basin management in order to establish whether and how problems of institutional 'fit' and 'interplay' are addressed in the scientific community of water specialists. The following section explores how far the WFD and recent EU water policy reflect and build on this knowledge, in terms of recognising the advantages of an ecosystem approach to water management and showing sensitivity towards the potential negative effects of the institutional changes demanded. The potential impact of the Directive on the spatial organisation of water management is explored in a case study of Germany, selected as a Member State where water has traditionally been managed around political-administrative units rather than river basins. The adaptability of existing institutions to the required changes is assessed with a comparison between past and future institutional arrangements in Germany and an analysis of the views and implementation plans of relevant organised actors at different spatial levels. The paper concludes with lessons drawn from the case study, relating in particular to the need for an integrated approach to solving problems of spatial fit and institutional interplay.

2 River Basin Management as an Instrument for Overcoming Problems of Fit

Boundary Problems and Environmental Governance

The problem of fit has been identified by the IDGEC project as one of three clusters of factors which strongly shape the performance of institutions that govern human/environment relations (Young 1999, p. 45; Young 2002). The basic idea is that the effectiveness of an institution is diminished where its characteristics do not match the characteristics of the biophysical systems it addresses. One obvious dimension concerns spatial fit; that is, the degree to which a resource regime covers the same geographical area as the natural resource it is designed to influence. Examples are fishery conservation regimes which cover the entire migratory range of fish and the need for global institutions to deal with emissions of climate gases. There are though many other dimensions, besides the spatial, at which fit can be sought. Identifying and responding to problems of fit requires a systems approach, looking beyond the immediate problem of resource over-use or point-source pollution to the wider causal effects and seeking linkages between these and characteristics of human systems. Systems linkages of this kind can extend in many directions – i.e. not just spatially – making it difficult to determine appropriate system boundaries for institutions. Bearing this in mind, creating better fit involves "structuring institutions in ways that maximise compatibility between institutional attributes and biogeophysical properties" (Young 1999, p. 48).

Problems of spatial fit are familiar to political scientists, economists and geographers interested in determining optimal units of governance for various policy fields, in particular relating to the distribution of public goods. Mancur Olsen's principle of fiscal equivalence has long held that the responsible level of government should coincide with the range and scope of the public good's effects on welfare (Olsen 1969). The related theory of fiscal federalism also argues for a link between the spatial extent of a problem and the spatial remit of political decision-making bodies and jurisdictions (Kirsch 1984). The central argument is that lack of fit causes spatial externalities, benefiting free-riders and harming others beyond the spatial reach of the responsible institution. Recent research on regionalisation and decentralisation processes within the EU takes a similar line in identifying growing incongruence between the spaces of problems and political boundaries as a major source of institutional ineffectiveness (Holzinger 2000). In such cases

"disparities between functional space and political territory can arise which can only be removed by the reorganisation of political territories or by functional cooperation between the responsible jurisdictions" (Holzinger 2000, p. 12, translation).

Environmental problems present a particular challenge since the spatial context of natural resources cannot, in most cases, be altered. The onus of problem-solving lies, therefore, on changes to institutional arrangements. This is reflected in the rich literature on the management of common pool resources, where boundary problems between biophysical and human systems play an important role (Ostrom 1990; Ostrom/Gardner/Walker 1994). The issue of spatial fit has, indeed, been central to attempts to redesign institutions to follow the characteristics of specific ecosystems. Here, the spatial mismatch between institution and ecosystem – at local, regional and national as well as international levels – is not just an obstacle but the heart of the problem. As Lipschutz argues:

"We take it for granted that ecosystemic boundaries have little correspondence to political, economic and social institutions at the international level [...]. But the same poor fit is true at the national and even the local levels: For historical and economic reasons, the jurisdiction of virtually all governments matches poorly to nature. This suggests environmental governance is problematic where one looks." (Lipschutz 1999, pp. 102-3).

Perhaps the most radical expression of this spatial approach to environmental governance is the bioregionalism movement. Conceived in the United States in the 1970s, bioregionalism seeks to use the "distinctive boundaries" of natural systems as a reference for human agency and – on a philosophical plane – as a means of rediscovering connections between the natural world and the human mind (Sale, cited in Pepper 1996; cf. Dodge, cited in Aberley 1999). Strongly rooted in notions of communal self-reliance, the bioregionalist movement spawned bioregionalist groups around the country, often around river basins or "watersheds"[2]. The river basin, with its clearly delineated boundaries of a river system, offered bioregionalist groups an ideal spatial framework for organising and managing relations between humans and the environment. "Watershed consciousness" became a catchphrase to express cultural identity with a natural place (Parsons 1985). Since the 1990s the language of bioregionalism has, interestingly, been appropriated by environmental policy makers and resource managers "to assist in conceptualising experiments in institutional and organisational form" (Aberley 1999, p. 34). The most common examples relate to the restructuring of regional governance units to match river basin boundaries.

River Basin Management: a Classic Case of Responding to Problems of Spatial Fit

If the river basin is one of the most clearly defined territorial units of an ecosystem, how far does the literature on river basin management reflect the above debates on the need to overcome problems of spatial fit? The attraction to water managers of using the river basin as the territorial unit for managing water resources has, indeed, always been to address what Mitchell and Pigram have called "the political boundary problems that plague integrated resource management" (cited in Downs et al. 1991, p. 300). Effective protection of water resources, in terms of both quality and quantity, depends on a management concept which reflects the complexity of water-based ecosystems, the multiple anthropogenic uses of water and the interaction between biophysical and human systems (Voigt 1997). Policies or strategies which address only a part of the water system, such as a stretch of a river or a point source of pollution, without considering the broader context run the serious risk of ignoring, or even creating, negative external effects. By managing water resources for a whole river basin – i.e. from the source to the mouth of a river as well as laterally from the river bed to the watershed – it is hoped to address the interdependencies between, in particular, upstream and down-

---

2   It should be noted that the term "watershed" is used in American English to mean the whole river basin or catchment, whereas in British English it refers to the dividing line between two adjacent river systems. In this paper where the term is used without inverted commas it is in the British English sense.

stream effects, water quality and water quantity, and water and adjacent land-use resources (OECD 1989).

Although there are various interpretations of what comprises integrated river basin management (see below), it is generally held to include elements of the following list from Downs et al. (1991, p. 304): water management (quality, hydrological regulation); river channel management (channel control); land management (land degradation control, land-use regulation); ecological management (preservation, diversity); management of human activities (socio-economic benefits). A more detailed explanation of the concept of river basin management is given by Marchand and Toornstra (1986).

The argument that river basin management is the best way of protecting water resources in an integrated way is reflected in virtually all the major international policy documents on water management, from Agenda 21 of the Rio Conference on Environment and Development to statements from the World Bank (Quarrie 1992; World Bank 1993). For example, Chapter 18.9 of the Agenda 21 document states that "integrated water resources management, including the integration of land- and water-related aspects, should be carried out at the level of the catchment basin or sub-basin". The European Water Charter calls for "the management of water resources [...] based on their natural basins rather than on political and administrative boundaries" (cited in Newson 1997, p. 283). The UN's Economic Commission on Europe recommends: "The whole catchment should be considered as the natural unit for integrated, ecosystems-based water management" (UN-ECE 1995, p. 13). Interest in an integrated, ecosystem approach to water management – and thus in river basin management – has recently been strengthened by debates on sustainable development following the 1992 Rio Conference.

Support for river basin management is, moreover, not restricted to policy-making communities. As Newson points out: "It is axiomatic to almost all water managers that the river basin is the appropriate scale" (1996, p. 12). The ecosystem logic underpinning river basin management is today accepted by most hydrologists, water biologists and ecologists, as well as by an increasing number of water engineers. In the language of institution theory the growing international support for river basin management amongst water managers represents the institutionalisation of a scientific concept (Lepsius 1997). The river basin approach to water management has in recent years matured into an informal or fundamental institution, in the sense of becoming a guiding principle for the water management community in many countries.

The institutionalisation of river basin management has not, of course, been restricted to the informal sphere. For decades river basin management has been applied across the globe as a formal institution, i.e. as an operational regime. In 1935 the Tennessee Valley Authority became the first major organisation to coordinate the management of water resources within a single drainage basin and became an model imitated worldwide (Downs et al. 1991;

Mitchell 1990). Today, applications of river basin management can be found in many – particularly industrialised – countries, such as the watershed conservancy districts in the USA, the basin agencies in France and river catchment planning in England and Wales (Newson 1997).

Problematising the Quest for Perfect Fit

Experiences with the many practical applications of river basin management demonstrate, however, serious limitations to the logic of overcoming problems of spatial fit by reorganising water management around natural boundaries. The Tennessee Valley Authority, in the past a model for water managers in industrialised and developing countries, is today more commonly held up as a lesson on the negative effects of knowledge transfer insensitive to national or local contexts (Downs et al. 1991; Newson 1996, 1997). Since the late 1980s the literature on river basin management has, on the basis of extensive empirical evidence, begun to challenge the notion of creating perfect spatial fit which underlies a purist interpretation of river basin management. The principal criticisms broadly relate to physical, political-administrative and socio-economic problems.

Even in hydrological terms, river basin management does not solve all boundary problems. The river catchment or basin follows surface water, not groundwater, boundaries. Its geographical range may well not correspond at all to that of groundwater acquifers, resulting in spatial misfit which can negatively affect the integrated management of surface water and groundwater resources (OECD 1989). Physical boundary problems can also occur where water supply networks or artificial waterways, such as canals, cross from one river basin to another.

The most intractable problems emanate from creating a spatial unit for water management at odds with existing political-administrative territories. In overcoming problems of spatial fit within the water sector, river basin management creates new spatial misfits with other institutions. This can limit the effectiveness of institutions of river basin management in several ways. Firstly, it challenges their political legitimisation and accountability. River basin authorities are territorially distinct from democratically elected bodies of local and regional government and are, therefore, not accountable to them. In some countries, such as France, steps have been taken to compensate for this "democracy deficit" with elected representatives on river basin committees, but the essential problem of political independence from local and regional government remains. What is advantageous for the spatially integrated management of water resources can prove damaging when, in a crisis such as a major flooding incident, the accountability of river basin authorities becomes a political issue. Secondly, solving boundary problems within the immediate institutions of water management creates new boundary problems with other policy fields which have a major impact on water use, such as urban development, agriculture, forestry, transportation and energy. This spatial mismatch with other institutions – discussed in more detail below under problems of institutional interplay – can act as a barrier to effective cooperation between different institutions. In England and Wales, for instance, the different spatial remits of water management and land-use planning are held partially responsible for the low level of policy linkage on water issues (Slater/Marvin/Newson 1994; Slater 1997).

On a more fundamental level, structuring water management along an eco-system boundary has often encouraged water managers to focus on biophysical, rather than socio-economic, problems of water management. As Pepper has observed, regions defined by natural features alone have only limited social and economic meaning (1996). The quest for perfect biophysical fit can result in important social and economic factors, such as water consumption patterns, pricing disincentives to save water or the supply logic of water provision, to be overlooked. A lack of sensitivity towards these forces has contributed to the criticism that river basin management in practice is often too techno-centric and heavily reliant on regulatory tools, allowing little scope for market based incentives or instruments of persuasion (Downs at al. 1991; Pepper 1996; Newson 1997).

The perfect spatial fit, to conclude, does not exist. The replacement of existing institutional units by institutions oriented around biophysical systems will inevitably create new boundary problems and fresh mismatches. Rather than try to identify the ideal river basin management institution we need to consider the territorial unit of the river basin in a broader context of overlapping social, economic, political and physical spaces (Lipschutz 1999). Reflecting on spatial misfits produced by river basin management, a comparative study of ca. 100 cases of river basin management worldwide cautioned: "The key is to determine the rationale for the choice of spatial management unit, and to consider the relative merits of adopting the catchment area as the management unit" (OECD 1989, p. 15).

3 The Impact of River Basin Management on Institutional Interplay

Problems of Interplay as a Factor of Institutional Effectiveness

A second cluster of factors identified by the IDGEC Science Plan as central to the performance of institutions has been termed the problem of interplay

(Young 1999, 2002). The basic idea is that "the effectiveness of specific institutions often depends not only on their own features but also on their interactions with other institutions" (Young 1999, p. 49). Interest in interplay has arisen in response to cases where institutional reform has failed to produce the expected results owing to incompatibility with existing institutional arrangements. The history of environmental policy is rich in examples of deliberate institutional change where inadequate consideration has been given either to how the intervention affects other institutions or to how its own effectiveness is influenced by the wider institutional framework. Recent efforts to introduce carbon emission taxes, for instance, reveal strong institutional dependence on transport policy and rural development strategies. Young identifies two dimensions to the problem of interplay (1999, p. 50): functional linkages involving the unavoidable interdependencies of two or more institutions (e.g. between agricultural production and land-use regimes) and political linkages where actors seek better integration between two or more institutional arrangements (e.g. those for public health and organic farming in the wake of the recent BSE crisis in Europe). A further distinction is drawn between vertical linkages cutting across different levels of social organisation (e.g. local, regional, national) and horizontal linkages of a cross-sectoral nature on the same level of social organisation.

These are boundary problems of a different kind. The boundaries at stake here relate not to physical territories, but to political responsibilities and social spheres of influence. It is along these boundaries, where the jurisdictions and interests of organised actors overlap, that conflict between formal institutions most commonly arise (Mitchell 1990). It is important to appreciate that problems of interplay are, of course, not restricted to formal institutions. Social activities are shaped by different – sometimes even competing – institutional logics, just as organisations can be infused with values from various informal institutions (Friedland/Alford 1991, cited in Hanf/Jansen 1998). This paper, however, is concerned primarily with interplay between political or formal institutions, referring to informal institutions only where they help explain incompatibilities between formal institutions.

Fit Versus Interplay? The Dilemma of River Basin Management

How suitable is river basin management for solving problems of institutional interplay arising from the protection of water resources? Is there not a real danger that, in the pursuit of better spatial fit, river basin management may exacerbate existing problems of interplay with other water-relevant institutions? As we have already noted, reorganising water management around the river catchment or basin gives rise to spatial mismatches between the new river basin bodies and other organisations which are structured around political-administrative territories. The literature on organisational aspects of river basin management has identified such differences in spatial remit as a significant hindrance to trans-sectoral cooperation over water-related issues. For Newson, one of the principal problems of river basin management is the "policy gap" between land-use planning and water management planning resulting from the different spatial scopes of the two planning regimes (1997, p. 343). The underlying argument in this literature is that the effective protection of water resources cannot be achieved by institutions of water management alone. The quality and quantity of water resources are affected by a wide range of human activities – from agriculture to electricity generation, from recreation to industrial production – each framed by its own institutional arrangements. For this reason good institutional interplay is essential for effective water protection.

Intriguingly, an integrated approach to water resource issues is a key feature of river basin management. Besides its geographically comprehensive perspective of managing water within a whole basin, the concept of river basin management is holistic in its approach to interactions between human and natural systems. It draws on a rich body of knowledge loosely termed integrated water management developed in response to the ineffectiveness of one-dimensional and isolated solutions to water resource problems. Mitchell identifies three possible interpretations of integrated water management, based on a review of the literature (1990). The most straightforward form involves the systematic consideration of the various dimensions of water and their interdependence (e.g. quality and quantity; surface water and groundwater). The task here is to ensure adequate linkage between various water management functions, such as water supply, wastewater disposal or flood protection. A second, more comprehensive interpretation of integrated water management addresses the interactions between water, land and the environment. In this case the management tasks cross sectoral boundaries between land and water use, for example with floodplain management, the reduction of diffuse-source pollution or the preservation of water-dependent habitats. The third, most far-reaching form of integration looks beyond physical impacts to the interaction between water and economic and social development. This approach is rooted in the debate on sustainable development and addresses, in addition to the above, the role of water in, for instance, electricity generation, transportation or recreation.

The concept of river basin management is open to all three approaches; in practice there exist examples of each and of combinations of them. What is significant in terms of our interest in spatial organisation is that the management of water resources around the biophysical territory of a river basin is founded on the first approach with its emphasis on integration within the water sector. Broader interpretations of integrated water management which include interactions between water and other sectors and their institutional arrangements are therefore likely to encounter difficulties as a result of the kinds of spatial misfits described earlier.

Coping with the Dilemma: Lessons from Past Experience

How, then, are water managers to overcome the dilemma of pursuing more advanced forms of integrated water management in cooperation with other water-relevant institutions in a spatial framework which – by creating new spatial misfits – may well make institutional interplay more difficult? Empirical studies of experiences with river basin management indicate that a flexible and contextually sensitive approach can help to overcome this dilemma. Many of the difficulties experienced in the past emanated from the attempt to introduce a blueprint of river basin management – based for instance on the Tennessee Valley Authority – in a very different context. They revealed how important it is for institutions of river basin management to respect the political traditions and culture of the host country or region (OECD 1989; Newson 1996, p. 15). Furthermore, river basin management can be suggestive of a organisational 'fix' which – it has been claimed – appeals to water managers who are keen to avoid more fundamental changes in attitudes, work patterns or lifestyles (Kinnersley 1988, p. 93-94).

Past experience argues that the processes and mechanisms involved in implementing river basin management are of greater importance than the availability of an ideal organisational model. This is the conclusion drawn by Mitchell:

"... there is never a perfect 'fit' among legitimisation instruments, functions and structures. As a result, use is made of various processes and mechanisms to overcome the problems which occur because of imperfect matches. It is often these processes and mechanisms, informal and formal, which facilitate co-ordination and integration" (Mitchell 1990, p. 214).

River basin management, to be effective, depends on coordinating mechanisms capable of bridging the gaps between the relevant institutions and organisations (OECD 1989). The task of winning broad support for a more integrated, holistic approach to water management demands extensive consultation with a wide range of parties. For most water managers consultation exercises with professional groups beyond the immediate water sectors is unfamiliar territory. River basin management demands more than merely disseminating information and collecting opinions in the context of a formal planning procedure. It requires complex negotiation and bargaining processes with other parties relevant to water resource management and the creation of new partnerships to solve basin-specific problems (Newson 1997). Beyond professional groups it is important to engage the wider public in debates on the future of the river basin, not only to ease acceptance of river basin strategies but also to tap relevant local knowledge. The central message is that river basin management, to be effective, requires a more open and interactive form of regional environmental governance, involving a wider range of stakeholders.

A second point raised in the literature is the need to consider the appropriate scale for particular institutional arrangements (OECD 1989). Many cases of river basin management have encountered serious problems when taking either too detailed an approach at the level of the whole river basin or too broad an approach at the local level. Mitchell recommends, for instance, distinguishing between the strategic level of a whole basin, where the need is for a comprehensive perspective covering all water-relevant issues and institutions in general terms, and the operational level, where tasks should focus on those water functions (including human impacts) of particular relevance to that locality (1990, p. 4).

Finally, the dominance of the ecosystem logic underpinning the river basin management concept should not blind us to a wide range of other motives influencing the way river basin management is applied in practice. River basin management is not only a biophysical construct, it is also a social construct in the sense that it is seen by its proponents as an optimal way of achieving specific policy objectives or of promoting certain power interests. The policy objectives underpinning river basin management have varied widely over time and space. In the USA river basin management was originally a response to drought and limitations to urban development (Mitchell 1990), in Spain it was in the 1920s and 1930s an important tool for modernising agriculture (Swyngedouw 1999), whilst in England the central motives shifted from land drainage via flood protection to securing adequate water supply (Newson 1997). The introduction of river basin management had the – often deliberate – effect of strengthening the hand of certain political, economic or professional groups at the expense of others. In Spain, for example, it was used by a new generation of wealthy farmers as a tool to undermine the traditional water regimes of the landed aristocracy (Swyngedouw 1999). When implementing river basin management it is, therefore, essential to be aware of the hidden agendas behind the rhetoric and the potential winners and losers of institutional change.

4 The Water Framework Directive and the Institutionalisation of River Basin Management Across the EU

Institutional Change from Above: Introducing the Water Framework Directive

How far is existing knowledge on the difficulties of institutionalising river basin management, as outlined above, reflected in the WFD? In the following section we are particularly interested to discover whether the lessons on how to solve problems of fit and interplay with river basin management have influenced both content and style of the WFD. The WFD (2000/60/EC) came into force on 22 December 2000 (EC 2000). This Directive is designed to provide "a transparent, effective and coherent legislative framework" for Community water policy (Preamble, para. 18). The overall aim is to establish a legal framework within which to protect surface waters and groundwater in the EU using a common management approach and following common objectives, principles and basic measures (EC 2000; cf. Blöch 1997). The core environmental objective is to prevent the deterioration of aquatic ecosystems and to restore polluted surface waters and groundwater to a "good" status in terms of ecological and chemical, as well as water quantity, parameters within a specified time frame (Art. 1). Additional objectives are to promote the sustainable use of water resources and to alleviate the effects of floods and droughts.

The WFD marks a departure from past EU water policy in a number of ways. On the one hand it harmonises existing EU legislation on water management, removing many of the inconsistencies and gaps which had emerged over the years between the ca. 30 directives relating to water protection. It provides for the first time a coherent framework for EU water policy. On the other hand the WFD sets EU water policy on a new footing, in terms of the environmental objectives, regulatory style and spatial organisation of water management in the EU. The WFD establishes the river basin as the unit for water management planning across the EU, strengthens the combined approach to pollution prevention, introduces economic analyses of water use, provides the general public with rights of participation in planning processes and establishes a detailed system of monitoring and reporting. These innovative elements relate, therefore, not simply to standards of water protection but above all to organisational aspects of water management.

In the language of institution theory the WFD represents a deliberate reform to a formal institution (the EU's water policy regime) designed to induce change to formal institutions of water management at lower levels of spatial hierarchy (i.e. within the Member States). The implementation of top-down changes from a "peak regime" onto multiple smaller regimes is fraught with difficulties, as is documented in the literature (Ostrom 1990; Lipschutz 1999). Referring to resource regimes in general Lipschutz delivers a warning which could well be levelled at the WFD:

"Legislation originating 'from above' is rarely able to take into account the valid concerns of all stakeholders in a resource because of a lack of information about the institutional history and path dependency of a resource management system, which are of critical importance to its revision" (Lipschutz 1999, p. 106).

Our interest lies in explaining how the WFD is likely to affect institutions of water management at national and sub-national levels in terms of the changes that will be required and the ability of existing institutions to adapt to these changes. This relates to a number of distinct but interrelated strands of research into institutional change. The WFD presents, firstly, an interesting case of multi-level governance involving institutions at supranational, national and sub-national levels (Mayntz/Scharpf 1995, pp. 44, 50). It is illuminating, for example, to explore how far Elinor Ostrom's critique of centralised institutional solutions to environmental problems can be applied to the WFD (Ostrom 1990), or whether it leaves scope for distinctive sub-national styles of integrated water management. More specifically, the WFD contributes to the ongoing debates on whether processes of European harmonisation are eroding national policy styles and how far national forms of environmental governance compete for influence over EU legislation (Jordan/O'Riordan 1995; Héritier 1996; Héritier/Knill/Mingers 1996; Börzel 1999). Finally, the WFD offers insight into the relationship between formal and informal institutions (on the distinction between the two, see Göhler 1997; Dietl 1993; Jordan/O'Riordan 1997). Being itself an expression of a recent shift in perceptions and assumptions within the EU over how water should be managed, the WFD is an example of change to a formal institution precipitated by change to an informal institution. This development reflects a deeper understanding of institutional change as a reconfiguration of formal and informal institutions over time (Häder/Niebaum 1997; Göhler 1997; Eisen 1996).

Resolving Problems of Spatial Fit with the Water Framework Directive

One of the principal changes initiated by the WFD is the establishment of the river basin as the territorial unit for managing water resources across the EU. The main tool of the WFD is, indeed, the river basin management plan (Art. 13). The EU's new water policy, substantiated in the WFD, builds unequivocally on the ecosystem rationale underpinning the concept of river basin management. As early as 1996 a key Communication on EU water policy by the European Commission stated that new demands on water management "would require integrated water management planning on a river basin basis" (CEC 1996, p. 18). The Commission's Directorate General for the Environment is today even more explicit on the need to overcome problems of spatial fit: "The best model for a single system of water management is management by river basin – the natural geographical and hydrological unit – instead of according to administrative or political boundaries" (Homepage DG Environment).

The concept of river basin management is institutionalised principally in Article 3 of the WFD. This requires Member States to identify river basins within their territory and assign them to River Basin Districts. These River Basin Districts form the spatial unit for all environmental objectives and specified measures under the WFD, comprising primarily obligatory river basin management plans, programmes of measures, river basin and economic analyses, public information, monitoring programmes and reports. River basins covering more than one Member State are to be assigned to an international River Basin District. All these requirements must be implemented at the same time in all River Basin Districts according to a strict and detailed timetable. For the first time river basin management will be institutionalised throughout the EU. Yet the WFD deliberately falls short of specifying how each Member State should organise this complex process internally. Member States are not obliged to set up new river basin authorities but only to ensure "appropriate administrative arrangements, including the identification of the appropriate competent authority" for each River Basin District (Art. 3). Following heated opposition – in particular from Germany – to an earlier draft which made river basin authorities obligatory, the current formulation was chosen out of respect for national (and sub-national) styles of water policy and management (for the criticisms, see Breuer 1997). In this way, it is hoped that the WFD will stimulate institutional and organisational change within Member States by providing a common framework for action and detailed specifications for individual measures (e.g. river basin management plans) without actually prescribing to Member States how these measures should be put into practice.

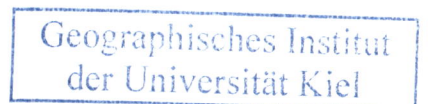

The introduction of River Basin Districts and river basin management plans is, interestingly, not the only way in which the WFD will affect the spatial organisation of water management in the Member States. A second institutional innovation concerns greater sensitivity to regional circumstances. In response to past criticism that EU-wide emission limit values or environmental quality standards made no allowance for the very different conditions and needs of water management across the Member States, the WFD calls for programmes of measures to respect this diversity and for "decisions to be taken as close as possible to the locations where water is affected or used" (Preamble, para. 13). This appeal is substantiated by allowing the reference parameter for the "very good status" of surface water bodies to vary according to different river types. It is expected that there will be ca. 20 reference types for Germany alone, permitting a degree of regional differentiation and context sensitivity new to EU water policy.

The WFD can, indeed, be said to herald the regionalisation of water management in the EU. Besides river basin management and regionally differentiated reference standards, a stronger emphasis on environmental quality standards within the combined approach to pollution prevention will have a far-reaching impact on land-use patterns (Art. 10). By setting objectives for the ecological and chemical quality of surface water bodies and the chemical quality and availability of groundwater resources the WFD directs interest at the multiple sources of pollution and over-exploitation within a whole river basin and its sub-basins. Point sources of pollution, such as sewage treatment plants or industrial emitters, will remain important in future but attention will need to focus more on diffuse sources, emanating primarily from agriculture, urban development and other forms of land use. The combined approach for point and diffuse sources introduces, in other words, a new, spatial dimension to pollution prevention which covers all water-relevant activities within a river basin. This raises the issue of institutional interplay and the degree to which it is addressed in the WFD.

Considering Problems of Interplay and Implementation

Institutional interplay is not referred to explicitly in the WFD, being a matter of operational responsibility for the individual Member States. It is, though, strongly implicit in the combined approach to pollution prevention and in the stipulations on river basin management planning. If water managers are to adopt a more integrated approach to water protection, taking a wide range of human impacts into account, they will need to cooperate to a far greater extent than in the past with organisations outside the sphere of water management, in particular in the fields of land-use planning, nature conservation and agriculture.

Indicative of the recognition of the need for greater interaction between stakeholder groups is the emergence of new instruments of water management within the WFD. Past EU legislation sought to protect water resources in the main by establishing uniform technical standards for emission levels or environmental quality across the EU. The WFD retains this focus in part – for example, emission and quality standards relating to specified priority substances in Article 16 and Annex X – but draws on a wider range of instruments to pursue its objectives. Supplementing the more conventional regulatory instruments are several novel market-oriented and participatory tools.

The economic analysis of water use, for instance, forms a part of the ex-ante evaluation of the characteristics of a River Basin District (Art. 5 and

Annex III). On the basis of this knowledge Member States are to apply the principle of full cost recovery for water services, including "environmental and resource costs", at the same time ensuring "adequate incentives" for efficient water use and the "adequate contribution" to water costs by each category of water user – generally households, industry and agriculture (Art. 9 and Annex III). How these requirements are to be interpreted is a question currently being addressed at the European level by a Working Group of Water Directors within the Common Implementation Strategy (CEC 2001) and at the national level with a pilot project on the Main river (Kessler 2001). Depending on which costs are included and how they are calculated and allocated, the principle of full-cost recovery and the new transparency over cost calculations could seriously reshape the economic relationships between different stakeholder groups.

To take a second example, the WFD institutionalises forms of public consultation and information in water management in the EU (Jekel 2002). Article 14 establishes public information and consultation as a component of future river basin management planning. Member States are to "encourage the active involvement of all interested parties" in implementing the WFD. Specifically, they will have to publish a timetable and work programme for the production of river basin management plans, an interim overview of significant water management issues identified in the River Basin District and draft copies of the plan. In addition the public is to be granted access to relevant background documents and information. Here, again, the specifications in the WFD are vague, reflecting the differences of opinion between Member States over what public participation should involve. There is no definition of who the "public" of a River Basin District are; for instance, whether it refers to any interested party or just to those resident in the District. It is also unclear whether participation is limited to providing information to the public and considering their comments or should be more inter-active, involving consultation meetings and even a stake in the decision-making process. There is a strong argument for saying that, regardless of the text of Article 14, the need to gain support for water protection measures required by the WFD will make some form of active consultation unavoidable (Hagenguth 2001, p. 19; LAWA 2002 Teil 3, pp. 48-49, 72, 75).

Conclusion: The New Style of Governance Underpinning the Water Framework Directive

The WFD is often criticised – in particular by environmental groups – for possessing inadequate powers of enforcement. There are indeed many loopholes in the WFD, notably the options for exemptions and/or delays in achieving "good" status for water bodies. The danger of inadequate and ineffective implementation needs to be taken seriously. Ultimately, much will depend now on how the WFD is implemented and interpreted in each of the Member States.

What is often overlooked, though, is that the WFD does not rely wholly on the EU's (limited) powers of regulation over water management but on other kinds of sanctions and incentives which have the potential to stimulate institutional change within and between individual Member States. The WFD encourages a new style of decision making in and beyond the water community which is more open, more consultative and more participatory. Within River Basin Districts we can expect the emergence of complex – and often controversial – negotiations over future river basin management plans and programmes of measures conducted by a wide range of policy-makers and planners and drawing on the inputs from interest groups and individual citizens. Moreover, the EU will in future possess the power to sanction Member States not only for non-enforcement of technical standards or non-fulfilment of environmental objectives, but also for failing to meet organisational requirements, such as the production of river basin management plans, programmes of measures or reports to the European Commission. The power of the Commission to monitor progress has been strengthened by the use of uniform and detailed reporting procedures for all Member States under Article 15.

This style of governance envisaged by the WFD, it should be noted, mirrors a wider shift in EU environmental policy since the early 1990s away from a command and control approach towards the use of more market-based instruments backed up by incentives for greater self-regulation and public involvement (Héritier 1996; Héritier/Knill/Mingers 1996; Philip 1998). This trend is in part a pragmatic response to low implementation levels using regulatory instruments and in part a consequence of the dominant logic of liberalising or privatising public services (Héritier 1996). Against this background the Commission is keen to consolidate existing legislation while attempting to raise environmental standards as economic development and new technologies permit (Philip 1998). Pressure in this direction is also coming from individual Member States, notably the UK, which are themselves less reliant on regulatory instruments. Indeed, the history of the WFD is an interesting case of conflict between two national logics of environmental policy-making in the UK and Germany. While the UK prefers the use of environmental quality standards and 'least-cost' technologies, Germany traditionally relies more on emission controls using Best Available Techniques. These differences were further accentuated over the WFD because river basin management is standard practice in the UK, but not in Germany. The final version of the WFD can therefore be classified, to use Héritier's terminology, as a "British home-run with concessions" in the sense that key features of the British model of water management, such as river basin management, environmental quality standards and cost-efficient water use, were adopted but are complemented by elements characteristic of the German approach, notably emission values for priority substances (Héritier 1996, pp. 479-483). It is the purpose of the following case study to ascertain how the German model of water management will need to adapt to accommodate the changes required by the WFD.

5 Reshaping Existing Institutions: A Case Study of Implementation Plans in Germany

The Spatial Organisation of Water Management Prior to the Water Framework Directive

The changes to the spatial organisation of water management resulting from the WFD will be greatest in those Member States where river basin management is least developed. Germany is a prime example of a country where water management is traditionally organised around political-administrative units, making it well suited to a case study of institutional change towards better spatial fit.

Responsibility for water management in Germany is divided between public authorities at different spatial levels in accordance with the federal structure of government (on the following Kraemer/Jäger 1998). There are essentially three tiers to the German institutional model of water management: federal, state and municipal. Legislative authority over water issues rests primarily with the 16 states (*Länder*). The federal Water Management Act provides merely a legal framework which allows considerable scope for substantiation in the water legislation of each state. Federal legislative functions have, though, increased in recent years to meet the need for uniform emission standards and compliance with EU directives (Kahlenborn/Kraemer 1999). Executive authority is similarly concentrated on the state, rather than the federal, level. The state water authorities, with up to three territorial sub-units, possess the principal policy-making, planning and regulatory powers. Several federal ministries exercise advisory or supervisory functions in ensuring standards are met on individual aspects of water management. The Federal Waterways Directorate is unusual in possessing substantial executive powers over navigable waterways which it exercises via its regional offices (Kahlenborn/Kraemer 1999). Operational functions – in particular, the provision of water supply and sewage disposal services, but also the maintenance of smaller watercourses and flood protection measures – are primarily the responsibility of local authorities, many of which operate their own water utilities.

The principal advantage of this multi-level system of governance is that it ensures a high degree of formal political legitimacy to institutions of water management in Germany. Each water authority – whether at federal, state or municipal level – is politically accountable to a democratically elected parliament or council. The main drawbacks – besides the lack of spatial fit with river basins – lie in institutional diversity between the 16 states and problems of vertical institutional interplay, in particular between federal and state levels. Indicative of the need for improved coordination and harmonisation of German water policy is the growing importance of the Working Group of the Federal States on Water Problems (LAWA), an inter-state consultative body with close links to the relevant federal ministries and to the European Commission (Kraemer/Jäger 1998, pp. 208-9, 271).

Elements of river basin management do exist in Germany but they are supplementary, not central, to the above water management institutions and their impact is often limited by spatial misfit to political-administrative territories (Interview 6). The principal instruments of water management planning are at least partially oriented around river catchments or reaches (Betlem 1998; Umweltbundesamt 1998). Water management framework plans, required by §36 of the Water Management Act, cover river basins, urban areas or parts of these whilst water management plans are for short reaches of heavily polluted watercourses. However, these plans stop at state borders, the only exception being the framework plan for the Berlin metropolitan area produced jointly by the states of Berlin and Brandenburg. Furthermore, the framework plans – although required by law – are not legally binding for either authorities or users, whilst the management plans, which are legally binding, are voluntary. As a result the framework plans have generally proved fairly ineffective and only a very limited number of management plans have been produced, mostly for the heavily polluted watercourses in Northrhine-Westphalia (Hoffmeister 1994; Umweltbundesamt 1998). Being highly detailed, these plans have taken as many as 13 years to be introduced, rendering many out of date before they are even complete (Umweltbundesamt 1998).

Several organisations of water management have been created to improve management coordination across the administrative boundaries of a watercourse or river basin. At the international level, river commissions for the protection of the Rhine, Elbe, Danube and Oder rivers represent voluntary, contractual forms of cooperation between national or sub-national authorities. These international river commissions vary greatly in their technical and spatial responsibilities (there exist 4 distinct commissions for different reaches of the Rhine and its tributaries) and are concerned primarily with the river itself, rather than the whole basin. Their principal influence is via action programmes focused on improving water quality and flood protection (Umweltbundesamt 1998).

Within Germany inter-state cooperation is partially institutionalised in the form of working groups of state water authorities for each of the major river systems, such as the Elbe, the Rhine and the Weser. As with the international river commissions, these working groups produce action plans and programmes which are not legally binding but are designed to give guidance to water authorities. The Action Programme for the Rhine, for instance, sets emission limit values for pollutants. The Integrated Ecological Plan for the Weser is distinctive for addressing the impact of a wide range of human activities along the whole river system and its floodplains (Henneberg/Schilling 1998). On a smaller spatial scale there exist various forms of inter-ministerial cooperation between states, often to tackle a localised water management problem. These can be relatively formalised, as is the case with the Inter-ministerial Working Group for the Lausitz (LIWAG) to manage water resource problems resulting from long-term lignite mining on the Saxony-Brandenburg border, or regular meetings of departmental heads, as between the water authorities of Berlin and Brandenburg (Interviews 2, 4 and 5).

Inter-municipal cooperation along river reaches or catchments is institutionalised in several forms, albeit limited to specific territories or tasks. The nine statutory river associations (*sondergesetzliche Wasserverbände*) of the state of Northrhine-Westphalia are the closest Germany has to operational organisations of river basin management. Created in the early twentieth century to cope with extreme demands on water resources in the Ruhr industrial region these associations operate facilities of wastewater treatment, water supply and reservoirs and maintain watercourses for a whole catchment of a tributary of the Rhine. Membership is compulsory for local authorities, municipal water utilities and private companies that abstract or discharge significant amounts of water in the catchment. Recently, these associations have shown a growing interest in a more integrated approach to water quality and quantity issues as well as in better consultation with local stakeholders (Interview 8; Kolisch/Londong/Renner 2000). The inter-municipal water management associations (*Wasser- und Bodenverbände*) also have a long historical pedigree, developing unevenly across the country and differing greatly in their operational priorities. Funded by landowners with property adjacent to watercourses, their principal task is to maintain ditches and smaller watercourses in the interest of flood protection and drainage. Although required by law to respect natural and landscape functions, water management associations are often criticised for serving the water needs of the farming community at the expense of ecological quality (v. Alvensleben 2000; Interview 11). A more integrated approach to the management of small watercourses has recently been promoted by the principal professional association of water specialists, the ATV-DVWK, which has set up voluntary working groups, called *Gewässernachbarschaften*, in several states to raise awareness of ecological management practices by means of educational courses, meetings and field trips (Interview 8).

Finally, it is worth noting that up until 1990 a form of river basin management was standard practice in East Germany. From the 1950s onwards both the organisational structure and the instruments of water management planning of the GDR were designed around 7 (later 5) river basins rather than political-administrative boundaries. This early orientation towards river basin management was only partly driven by concern for integrated water management. More important was the state planning logic of centralising control of water resources at the expense of municipal influence in order to secure strategically important water supplies for industrial and household use (van der Wal/Kraemer 1991; Umweltbundesamt 1998). Nevertheless, several features of river basin management under the GDR – notably the spatial organisation and uniform methods of reporting – can be regarded as valuable contributions to implementing the WFD (Umweltbundesamt 1998, p. 36). Some river basin structures indeed survived the territorial reorganisation of water management following unification in 1990: the regional water authorities of Brandenburg's state environment agency, for instance, follow river basin boundaries largely (Interview 5). The irony of having to reinstate river basin management little more than 10 years after it was dismantled in the interest of strengthening renascent municipal and state authorities is not lost on those who witnessed this earlier phase of institutional change.

Given the generally limited and isolated forms of river basin management in Germany it is not surprising that spatial misfit between river basins and the territories of water management institutions has given rise to the kind of boundary problems described earlier. On the other hand, one might expect that the spatial fit between water and land-use planning authorities has aided institutional interplay in a given territory. On paper the relationship between the two planning regimes has a sound legal basis, with clauses on spatial planning in the Water Management Act, a requirement for water management planning to respect spatial planning objectives and detailed procedures for consulting water authorities over spatial planning set down in federal and state legislation (Jacobitz 1994). In practice, however, it is commonplace for local authorities to build roads, houses or commercial estates on floodplains, along river banks or in water protection areas contrary to water protection policies (Kahlenborn/Kraemer 1999).

Several factors have in the past contributed to ineffective institutional interplay between water management and land-use planning. The inadequacies of water management planning instruments – outlined above – have limited the forcefulness of water protection policies. Local authorities, equipped with considerable (spatial) planning authority, often resent and resist what they regard as an intrusion by state water planning authorities. The objectives of spatial planning at the state and regional level are often too unspecific to lend weight to state water policy. Furthermore, interaction between water management and land-use planners is typically limited to formal consultation procedures during planning processes (Interview 8). The norm is for planning authorities, as representatives of the public interest, to submit written comments to a draft plan by another body rather than engage in discussion. It is quite common for the wording and zoning of a regional plan relating to water protection, for instance, to be suspiciously similar to those of an existing water management plan, indicating that no real weighing up of the different planning perspectives has taken place at all (Jacobitz 1994; Hoffmeister 1994; Interview 11). More generally, institutional interplay is hampered by strong functional division of responsibility in German administration. From the federal to the municipal level issues of water management, spatial planning, nature conservation and agriculture are commonly the responsibility of separate organisational units (Kahlenborn/Kraemer 1999). Even where these fields are under one administrative roof, as is the case in the state environment ministries of Brandenburg or Northrhine-Westphalia, sectoral thinking remains entrenched (Interview 3). To summarise, spatial fit between different institutions at any one level of the administrative hierarchy is clearly in itself no guarantee of effective cooperation between them.

Institutionalising River Basin Management: Initial Steps Towards Better Spatial Fit

Given the importance of political-administrative territories to water management in Germany and its limited, if varied, experience with river basin management, the WFD will necessitate major changes to the way water protection is spatially organised in the future (Stratenwerth 2002, p. 324; Holzwarth/Bosenius 2002). The challenge currently facing water managers in Germany is to reform existing institutions in such a way that they are compatible with both the WFD and the country's federal system of government. Having successfully opposed an early draft which would have required the creation of new river basin authorities, Germany's water authorities now need to demonstrate how they can improve spatial fit with the river systems they manage within a federally structured framework.

The debate on implementing the WFD is being conducted primarily by the state water authorities in conjunction with the Federal Environment Ministry under the auspices of the inter-state working group LAWA (Irmer 2000). The LAWA has produced guidelines for water authorities covering technical, legal and organisational issues as a way of ensuring the speedy and – if possible – uniform implementation of the WFD in all 16 states. The main focus of the discussion currently is on legal implementation – i.e. changes to existing legislation explicitly required by the WFD – which must be completed by

December 2003. In terms of spatial organisation, the principal changes to the federal Water Management Act, amended in 2002, identify River Basin Districts on German territory, make obligatory the coordination of water management planning across state boundaries, establish the river basin management plan and programme of measures as the principal instruments of water management planning, set quality standards for surface and ground water and to establish a framework for public participation in the planning process (Deutscher Bundestag 2002). On the basis of these changes, state water laws and ordnances are currently being reformed, specifying in detail how the WFD is to be implemented organisationally. This applies in particular to allocating the river catchments within a state to a River Basin District, determining the procedure for drawing up river basin management plans, including public participation, and institutionalising forms of cooperation and exchange with states of the same River Basin Districts. One of the main changes will be to instruments of water management planning. Although some methods and data from existing water framework and management plans will prove useful in future (Umweltbundesamt 1998, pp. 67-9), experts are in no doubt that the new river basin management plan and the programme of measures drawn from it will need to cover a much wider range of issues (Leymann 2000). In particular, they will need to address the interrelationship of upstream and downstream water use, the reduction of diffuse sources of pollution within the whole river basin, the efficient use of resources and public participation (Umweltbundesamt 1998, pp. 68-72).

One of the toughest challenges, central to resolving the dilemma of following two different spatial logics of governance, is how to adapt existing organisational structures, responsibilities and procedures to satisfy both. The problem for Germany is exacerbated by its geographical characteristics. Germany's natural river basins vary enormously in size, from the Rhine basin with an area of 100,000 km² and a population of 34 million in Germany alone to the German part of the Oder basin of just 5,600 km² and 0.4 million inhabitants. All but one of its major river basins are trans-national, covering 9 neighbouring countries in- and outside the EU. The Elbe basin covers 10 of Germany's 16 states, the Rhine basin 8 states. The future task of cross-border and inter-state coordination is, therefore, huge.

In accordance with the WFD 10 River Basin Districts have been identified in Germany. It is now necessary to identify a "competent authority" for each full or partial River Basin District on German territory. The key question is which existing body is to be entrusted with responsibility for each River Basin District and what coordinating and planning authority it will be allowed to exercise (Hagenguth 2000). From the outset it was clear that there should be no new river basin authority created for the parts of a River Basin District in Germany (see the reservations above). The issue at stake was whether state water authorities should transfer some planning sovereignty by inter-state contract to a new coordinating body for a River Basin District or whether they should retain their full powers and rely on looser coordination in the form of a river basin secretariat for day-to-day management and regular meetings of representatives of the state water authorities (Hagenguth 2000). At a meeting of the Environment Ministers' Conference (UMK) in 2001 it was resolved to avoid any transfer of sovereignty and pursue the latter model. The activities of the coordinating bodies for German River Basin Districts are to be limited to collecting data, drafting the river basin management plan and communicating, where necessary, with the international coordinating body. Enforcement will be the responsibility of the individual state water authorities. With this decision the state water authorities circumvented jurisdictional problems of spatial fit between River Basin Districts and the federal structure of administration and ensured no loss of formal power to an independent body. The model of loose coordination has the additional advantage of being able to build on existing organisations of trans-boundary cooperation, the inter-state working groups for the major rivers (e.g. ARGE Rhein, ARGE Weser). However, it has the considerable drawback of relying heavily on the ability of participating state water authorities to reach unanimous agreement on most issues and to sell the agreements made to their respective governments. Given the potential conflicts of interest with ministers responsible for finances, agriculture and spatial planning the loose model of coordination may yet prove a major weakness when it comes to drawing up the river basin management plans and implementing the programmes of measures.

A second organisational dilemma is whether to sub-divide the larger River Basin Districts into smaller sub-basins, each with its own management plan and even organisational structure. Article 3 of the WFD allows for this, leaving the decision to individual Member States. In Germany it is widely felt that a single plan for, say, the whole Rhine or Elbe basin cannot adequately reflect the diverse characteristics and needs of their main tributaries (Umweltbundesamt 1998; Irmer 1999; Interview 6). In these cases it makes sense, for hydro-morphological as well as institutional reasons, to introduce river basin management at the sub-basin level and aggregate these plans into a common plan for the whole basin. This allows for more context-sensitive planning, facilitates public participation, eases the task of coordination within the whole basin and permits the use of existing forms of cooperation. Agreements have been reached, for instance, to sub-divide the Rhine basin into 11 and the Elbe basin into 5 sub-units according to river catchment boundaries. Within the largest River Basin Districts a further sub-division into smaller catchments has been made. Interestingly, these smallest planning units don not follow the catchment boundaries precisely but are adapted to accommodate political-administrative jurisdictions. This is justified by proponents as a way of avoiding the impracticalities of water planning boundaries running through the middle of towns and cities, minimising administrative upheaval and bridging the gap between the two systems of spatial organisation (Interviews 5 and 6). Critics warn that by focusing activities on the sub-basin level within each state, the state water authorities may be less interested in a coordinated approach across the whole basin.

Actor Viewpoints on the Institutional Changes

So far we have analysed institutional change in Germany in terms of reforming laws, instruments and organisational structures – i.e. the formal institutions of water management. What the analysis is revealing is how far the alternatives under discussion are being shaped by what the leading actors regard as the right way of doing things – i.e. by informal institutions. It is worthwhile at this point, therefore, to reflect on the degree to which the spatial reorganisation of water management initiated by the WFD meets with the approval of the main actor groups. It might be assumed, given Germany's tradition of managing water along political-administrative boundaries, that water managers there would resist the imposition of river basin management from Brussels. In fact, rather surprisingly, all the principal water policy-making, regulatory, planning and service bodies in Germany welcome the strengthening of river basin management by the WFD. Whether the Federal Environment Ministry, the LAWA, state water authorities, the Association of Water Engineers (BGW) or the German Association of Water Management, Wastewater and Solid Waste (ATV-DVWK), all agree with the principle of managing water resources across political boundaries for a whole river basin (Fuhrmann 2000; Schmitz 1998; Interviews 2, 5, 6, 7 and 8). More than this, they generally welcome the form of river basin management established by the WFD, with its emphasis on monitoring water quality standards, uniform planning methods and sensitivity towards regional differences (Interview 6). While acknowledging a number of potential problems of adapting existing institutions and emphasising the premature status of debate on implementation, water managers in Germany – as elsewhere – largely follow the ecosystem logic underlying the WFD. They approve of its holistic approach, the greater attention to diffuse sources of pollution, the pressure for improved trans-boundary cooperation and the requirement for better data. Interestingly, the spatial planners interviewed also welcome the strengthening of river basin management. For them the WFD represents an important step towards a more integrated approach to water management which relates to their own professional task of considering competing claims on land use.

A further reason for water managers in Germany to welcome the WFD is essentially political. Recently, water protection has lost some of its political urgency as the quality of many rivers and lakes has improved markedly. Water protection strategies and economic restructuring have succeeded in raising water quality and reducing demand but, in doing so, have weakened the willingness of politicians to fund additional protection measures. "And it is at this point", the LAWA chairman points out, "that the WFD with its ecological, holistic approach was sent to us as a gift. Whoever takes water protection seriously must be delighted. The WFD has come right on cue" (Leymann 2000, p. 8, translation). In addition, water managers widely anticipate that a more integrated approach to water management, which considers the wide range of human impacts, will strengthen their hand in policy-making and planning processes vis-à-vis other policy fields. In particular, they hope to gain greater influence via the WFD over forms of land use damaging to water resources (e.g. Interview 2). While some water managers view this in terms of a power shift at the expense of other policy fields, others prefer the notion of sharing responsibility for water management across a wide institutional spectrum.

The broad welcome from water managers to river basin management should not blind us, however, to some important differences of opinion over implementing the WFD. The state water authorities are fearful of losing influence to the federal level in the course of harmonising water policy and to any coordinating body for a River Basin District which seeks to assert its independence from state authorities. They are similarly wary of delegating any planning authority to the statutory river associations or enforcement tasks to municipal water management associations. The influential ATV-DVWK, by contrast, has long criticised state particularism over water management, calling for a stronger role for the federal government. It favours coordinating bodies with real powers and the active involvement of existing river basin organisations, such as the river associations in Northrhine-Westphalia and its own *Gewässernachbarschaften* in an implementation strategy (Interviews 7 and 8). The Association of Water Engineers (BGW), representing water and sewage utilities, is similarly critical of past state influence and had hoped the WFD might simplify water management structures in Germany but is now sceptical, fearing additional bureaucracy and costs resulting from the co-existence of state and river basin structures (Interview 9; Schmitz 1998). Water utilities are particularly attracted by the prospects of using the polluter-pays principle to improve water quality before it reaches water treatment plant, thus saving them considerable investment costs.

Institutional Interplay: The Open Questions

The optimistic attitude of most water managers in Germany towards the institutionalisation of river basin management in principle is tempered by a fair degree of uncertainty – even among the well-informed and influential – over how the WFD is likely to alter existing processes and structures of water management in Germany in practice. The impact on the water authorities at federal and state level, if still not finalised, is at least the subject of intensive debate among those responsible. Far less consideration has been given as yet to the wider implications of the WFD to institutional arrangements beyond the legislative framework. Largely uncharted are, for instance, the potential impact on local authorities and their water/sewage utilities, modes of allocating costs of implementation across state boundaries, forms of engaging the public, the future role of existing forms of river basin management (such as the municipal water associations) and the willingness of actors from other policy fields to cooperate in pursuing the objectives of the WFD. These unresolved issues all relate to institutional interplay, whether between different water organisations, with other water-relevant institutions or between water managers and the general public. As we have noted earlier, river basin management, to be effective, needs to ensure good interplay as well as fit.

Leading water managers in Germany do recognise that there is much more to implementing the WFD than adjusting the legal and organisational framework: "The WFD will demand considerable changes to our past ways of thinking and working in the water sector if we are to take a spatial and context-sensitive approach to water protection" (Leymann 2000, p. 25, translation). Water management under the WFD will require greater cooperation and coordination within and beyond the water sector. There is talk of the emergence of new environmental partnerships as more effective means of water protection than traditional regulatory instruments (Fuhrmann 1999, p. 122, Interview 13). However, if those responsible for implementation focus their efforts on following the letter, rather than the spirit, of the WFD the danger is that the resolution of important issues of interplay not specified in the text of the Directive will be sidelined or seriously delayed: "The prospect of water authorities spending the next nine years exclusively on developing water management plans and ignoring their wider impact is very real indeed" (Leymann 2000, p. 7, translation).

Looking at vertical institutional interplay within the water sector, we can observe how the solutions currently under discussion are focused on the future tasks of the state water authorities. The coordinating bodies to be established for each of the 10 River Basin Districts in Germany will be composed solely of state officers, with no representatives from federal or municipal authorities, let alone from other relevant stakeholder groups. This raises questions as to the effectiveness of such bodies if, for instance, they do not include a representative from the influential Federal Waterways Directorate. Local authorities and their water/sewage utilities have criticised state and federal bodies for not engaging them in discussions on the WFD in the past on the grounds that their involvement is only necessary when legal implementation is complete (Lattmann 2000; Interview 8). By then, they argue, it will be too late to affect real change: "We have always said this is a great opportunity to reshape water management together. Truly together and not with the authorities on one side handing out instructions and the addressees on the other having to pay up" (Interview 8, translation).

A further example of unresolved interplay is over the river associations in Northrhine-Westphalia. Although these organisations have long been responsible for collecting data, compiling water management plans and negotiating with stakeholders for whole river catchments, the state water authorities are keen to ensure they control river basin management functions, taking on some tasks previously performed by the inter-municipal river associations (Knitsch 2000; Interview 8).

While it is quite likely that water managers from different organisations, with their common interest in water protection, may be able to reach agreement on a plan or programme of measures, enforcement will require the support of others outside the water sector. The effectiveness of the WFD will depend much on horizontal institutional interplay, in particular with land-use planning, agriculture and nature conservation. It is recognised amongst state water authorities that the WFD's goal of "good status" for water bodies cannot be achieved by water managers alone (Leymann 2000; Interviews 1 and 2). Interestingly, most water managers do not see any major problems of communication emerging from having different territorial units for water management planning and land-use planning (Interviews 3, 5 and 6). This view reflects partly their confidence in the continued influence of state authorities over water management but partly also the expectation that river basin management will create greater pressure for cross-sectoral cooperation in practice. A more integrated approach to water management will, it is felt, require others to cooperate over water protection issues. Some state water authorities, as in Bavaria, Hesse and Saxony, are actively engaging with government agencies, local authorities, interest groups, NGOs and business organisations directly affected by the WFD. In the state of Baden-Württemberg an advisory group on the WFD has been established, including representatives from municipal associations, state ministries for rural development and economics and local business. In addition the water authorities there are conducting an intensive publicity campaign on the WFD. In many other states, however, water managers appear reluctant to consult other interest groups over their implementation procedure or to inform them of the WFD's implications.

The need to cultivate better relations within and beyond the water sector will be particularly apparent when it comes to allocating the costs of implementing the WFD within a River Basin District. As yet, very little consideration has been given to suitable mechanisms for funding the WFD. It is widely expected that the WFD will give rise to substantial additional costs necessary to cover both new administrative tasks (e.g. monitoring) and the water protection measures themselves (Interview 6). If water managers are to acquire these additional funds they will need to persuade politicians and water users of the benefits of improved water protection. They will also need to co-opt funds earmarked for nature conservation, river management and sustainable agriculture if they are to meet some of the new environmental objectives in target areas.

Equally problematic will be establishing a modus for distributing costs between different localities and states of a single River Basin District. If, to take one topical example, it is ascertained that the most cost-effective way of improving the water quality of the rivers and lakes of the Berlin metropolitan region is to reduce the use of nutrients in agriculture upstream rather than upgrade the city's sewage treatment plants, who will have to pay (Interviews 1, 2, 3 and 5)? According to the territorial principle currently practiced, each state is responsible for arranging the funding of measures on its own territory. In our example, the cost burden currently falls on the water utility of Berlin rather than the farmers of Brandenburg. Clearly, new mechanisms for allocating costs across state boundaries will need to be found which offer adequate incentives for the most cost-effective measures for the whole river basin. The redistribution of costs affects not just state authorities. If, in our example, the decision was made to limit nutrient inputs upstream the costs would fall initially on farmers in Brandenburg and the savings would benefit primarily the Berlin water utility. Finding an acceptable mechanism for cost allocation is likely to take considerable time and effort, particularly in view of the difficulties of identifying the cause of diffuse source pollution. If the timetable for implementation is not to be endangered, this issue must be addressed soon.

Finally, consulting and informing the public is a further dimension of interplay where discussions on implementation are as yet only partially developed. Water managers in Germany have little experience of engaging with the general public: past water management plans have not required public involvement (Umweltbundesamt 1998). Moreover, limited experiences with formal public participation procedures, as in the context of environmental impact assessments, often discourage further contact. Article 14 of the WFD, requiring consultation of the public in drawing up river basin management plans, poses a major challenge to German water managers. In its implementation guidelines the LAWA distinguishes between measures to engage the general public and those directed at organised groups affected by the WFD (LAWA 2002, Part 3, pp. 48-49, 72, 75). It also points to the need for different forms of engagement at different spatial levels and at different stages of the implementation process. The Federal Environment Ministry has also produced ideas on how to meet the requirements of Article 14 (Jekel 2002).

At the level of the states, however, there are substantial differences in the degree of importance attached to engaging the public and the activities conducted or planned. Some state water authorities prefer a minimalist interpretation of the legal requirements and are not intending to engage with the public until the first drafts of the river basin management plans are complete. Then they only plan to make information on the relevant issues and the draft plan publicly available by means of official journals, newspapers and the internet. Public participation is regarded there as a legal obligation rather than a means of developing a wider understanding of the issues and gaining support for the plans and measures. Other states, by contrast, are contemplating or already enacting more pro-active forms of public participation. Public opinion there is actively sought in preliminary consultation processes as a way of creating awareness of the WFD's objectives and minimising the risk of conflict over the selection and enforcement of particular measures. It is these same states which also look beyond Article 14 to engage voluntarily with those interest groups directly implicated in the WFD, either as polluters or as organisations responsible for enhancing the environment. They see important advantages in informal, flexible approaches to cooperation with bodies outside the water management sector on whose support they will have to rely in order to deliver many of the environmental objectives set out in the WFD.

6 Conclusion

The process of implementing the WFD has only recently begun but already the contours of the future organisation of river basin management in Germany are becoming apparent. From this it has been possible to identify the extent to which the lessons from past experiences of river basin management have been learnt and to highlight areas where further reflection is needed.

This paper has used a conceptual framework for analysing the effectiveness of institutions in terms of their ability to solve problems of fit and interplay in order to identify some of the chief strengths and weaknesses associated with reorganising water management around river basins rather than political-administrative territories. The principal message emerging from past empirical analyses of river basin management is that the quest for the perfect spatial fit is fundamentally flawed. Addressing problems of spatial fit via river basin management is an important way of conceptualising and managing the complex interactions between human and water systems. However, creating new water management institutions around biophysical systems inevitably creates new boundary problems and fresh mismatches with existing water regimes and other institutions. Rather than try to identify the universal river basin management institution we need a more flexible approach, adapting the model to the physical, socio-economic and institutional characteristics of a specific river basin. This means addressing problems of interplay between institutions, both within and beyond the water sector, alongside problems of fit. The objectives of integrated river basin management cannot be achieved by water managers alone.

Our analysis of the WFD and early plans to implement it in Germany show that whilst the problem of spatial fit is widely recognised by water managers, even where river basin management is not standard practice, the importance of institutional interplay to the success of river basin management is not yet fully reflected in the debate. The WFD is not explicit on mechanisms of interplay, although it does create some openings relating to public participation, diffuse sources of pollution and cost recovery. Much will depend on how each Member State interprets the Directive and recognises the need for cooperation with other stakeholder groups in practice. Initial steps towards implementing the WFD in Germany suggest that issues of institutional interplay may well get sidelined, or at least postponed, as a result of the water authorities' prime concern with meeting their most immediate obligations and protecting their own position in the new structures and procedures of river basin management. This tendency, if not corrected, could exacerbate conflicts of interest with other stakeholder groups at a later date when it comes to defining policy objectives, prioritising water protection measures and allocating costs within a River Basin District. The WFD presents an opportunity for a more transparent, consultative and participatory form of regional governance for water protection. Whether this opportunity will be seized is, as yet, unclear.

References

Aberley, Doug (1999): Interpreting Bioregionalism: A story from Many Voices. In: McGinnis (ed.): Bioregionalism. London/New York; Routledge; pp. 13-42

Betlem, Ilja (1998): River Basin Planning and Management. In: Nunes Correia (ed.): Selected Issues in Water Resources Management in Europe. Vol. 2. Rotterdam/Brookfield; Balkema; pp. 73-104

Bley, Joachim (2000): Die Umsetzung der EU-Wasserrahmenrichtlinie am Rhein. In: Länderarbeitsgemeinschaft Wasser (LAWA): EU-Wasserrahmenrichtlinie – Programm für die Zukunft im Gewässerschutz. Symposium zur Einführung der EU-Wasserrahmenrichtlinie am 13./14. Dezember 2000. Schwerin; LAWA; pp. 115-120

Börzel, Tanja (1999): Europäisierung und innerstaatlicher Wandel. Institutionelle Anpassungsprozesse untersucht am Beispiel Deutschlands und Spaniens. Unpublished Paper Presented to the Research Colloquium European Integration; 4 May

Breuer, Rüdiger (1997): Die Fortentwicklung des Wasserrechts auf europäischer und deutscher Ebene. In: Deutsches Verwaltungsblatt; 15 October; pp. 1217-1223

Commission of the European Communities (CEC) (1996): European Community Water Policy. Communication from the Commission to the Council and the European Parliament of 21 February 1996. Brussels; CEC

Commission of the European Communities (CEC) (2001): Common Strategy on the Implementation of the Water Framework Directive; 2 May; Unpublished manuscript

Deutscher Bundestag (2002): Siebtes Gesetz zur Änderung des Wasserhaushaltsgesetz. Drucksache 14/7755

Dietl, Helmut (1993): Institutionen und Zeit. Tübingen; Mohr

Downs, Peter W./Kenneth J. Gregory/Andrew Brookes (1991): How Integrated is River Basin Management? In: Environmental Management; Vol. 15; No. 3; pp. 299-309

Eisen, Andreas (1996): Institutionenbildung im Transformationsprozeß: Der Aufbau der Umweltverwaltung in Sachsen und Brandenburg 1990-1994. Baden-Baden; Nomos

European Community (EC) (2000): Directive 2000/60/EC of the European Parliament and of the Council of 23 October 2000 Establishing a Framework for Community Action in the Field of Water Policy. In: Official Journal of the European Communities; 22 December; L 327/1-72

Fuhrmann, Peter (1999): Institutionelle und organisatorische Auswirkungen der Wasser-Rahmenrichtlinie in Deutschland. In: Hessisches Ministerium für Umwelt, Landwirtschaft und Forsten: Europas Wasser. Die Wasser-Rahmenrichtlinie der Europäischen Union. 3. Wiesbadener Wassersymposium. Wiesbaden; Hessisches Ministerium für Umwelt, Landwirtschaft und Forsten; pp. 113-122

Fuhrmann, Peter (2000): Perspektiven aus der Sicht der LAWA. In: Länderarbeitsgemeinschaft Wasser (LAWA): EU-Wasserrahmenrichtlinie – Programm für die Zukunft im Gewässerschutz. Symposium zur Einführung der EU-Wasserrahmenrichtlinie am 13./14. Dezember 2000. Schwerin; LAWA; pp. 21-26

Göhler, Gerhard (1997): Wie verändern sich Institutionen? Revolutionärer und schleichender Institutionenwandel. In: Göhler (ed.): Institutionenwandel. Opladen; Westdeutscher Verlag

Häder, Michael/Hendrik Niebaum (1997): Pfadabhängigkeit in der Umweltpolitik. In: Metz/Weidner (eds.): Umweltpolitik und Staatsversagen. Perspektiven und Grenzen der Umweltpolitikanalyse. Festschrift für Martin Jänicke zum 60. Geburtstag. Berlin; Edition sigma; pp. 463-472

Hagenguth, Rolf (2000): Organisatorische Gestaltungsmöglichkeiten in Deutschland. In: Länderarbeitsgemeinschaft Wasser (LAWA): EU-Wasserrahmenrichtlinie – Programm für die Zukunft im Gewässerschutz. Symposium zur Einführung der EU-Wasserrahmenrichtlinie am 13./14. Dezember 2000. Schwerin; LAWA; pp. 109-114

Hagenguth, Rolf (2001): Organisatorische Umsetzung der EU-Wasserrahmenrichtlinie in Deutschland. In: Wasser und Abfall; No. 6; pp. 18-21

Hanf, Kenneth/ Alf-Inge Jansen, (1998): Environmental Policy – the Outcome of Strategic Action and Institutional Characteristics. In: Hanf/Jansen (eds.): Governance and Environment in Western Europe. Harlow; Longman; pp. 1-16

Henneberg, Simon Christian/Jan Schilling (1998): Ökologische Gesamtplanung Weser – Ziele und Umsetzung. In: Wasser & Boden; Vol. 50; No. 9; pp. 3-14

Héritier, Adrienne (1996): Muster europäischer Umweltpolitik. In: Diekmann/Jaeger (eds.): Umweltsoziologie. Kölner Zeitschrift für Soziologie und Sozialpsychologie; Sonderheft 36; pp. 472-486

Héritier, Adrienne/C. Knill/S. Mingers (1996): Ringing the Changes in Europe. Regulatory Competition and Redefinition of the State. Britain, France, Germany. Berlin; Walter de Gruyter

Hoffmeister, Jochen (1994): Die Bedeutung großräumiger wasserwirtschaftlicher Pläne im Verhältnis von Raumplanung und wasserwirtschaftlicher Fachplanung. In: Akademie für Raumforschung und Landesplanung (ARL): Wassergütewirtschaft und Raumplanung. Probleme der Zusammenarbeit und Lösungsansätze. Hannover; ARL; pp. 135-156

Holzinger, Katharina (2000): Optimale Regulierungseinheiten für Europa. Flexible Kooperation territorialer und funktionaler Jurisdiktionen. Unpublished Paper Presented to 21st Scientific Congress of the DVPW, 1-5 October in Halle

Holzwarth, Fritz/Udo Bosenius (2002): Die Wasserrahmenrichtlinie im System des europäischen und deutschen Gewässerschutzes. In: von Keitz/Schmalholz (eds.): Handbuch der EU-Wasserrahmenrichtlinie. Inhalte, Neuerungen und Anregungen für die nationale Umsetzung. Berlin; Erich Schmidt; pp. 27-46

Ingram, Helen M./Dean E. Mann/Gary D. Weatherford/Hanna J. Cortner (1984): Guidelines for Improved Institutional Analysis in Water Resources Planning. In: Water Resources Research; Vol. 20; No. 3; pp. 323-334

Irmer, Harald (1999): Die Umsetzungsplanung nach den Vorstellungen der Länderarbeitsgemeinschaft Wasser. In: Hessisches Ministerium für Umwelt, Landwirtschaft und Forsten: Europas Wasser. Die Wasser-Rahmenrichtlinie der Europäischen Union. 3. Wiesbadener Wassersymposium. Wiesbaden; Hessisches Ministerium für Umwelt, Landwirtschaft und Forsten; pp. 11-18

Irmer, Harald (2000): Die LAWA-Arbeitshilfe: Ein pragmatisches Instrument zur fachlichen Umsetzung. In: Länderarbeitsgemeinschaft Wasser (LAWA): EU-Wasserrahmenrichtlinie – Programm für die Zukunft im Gewässerschutz. Symposium zur Einführung der EU-Wasserrahmenrichtlinie am 13./14. Dezember 2000. Schwerin; LAWA; pp. 49-54

Jacobitz, Karlheinz (1994): Sicherung der Gewässergüte als gemeinsame Aufgabe der Raumplanung und der Wasserwirtschaft. In: Akademie für Raumforschung und Landesplanung (ARL): Wassergütewirtschaft und Raumplanung. Probleme der Zusammenarbeit und Lösungsansätze. Hannover; ARL; pp. 1-20

Jedlitschka; J. (1998): Die Wasserrahmenrichtlinie der Europäischen Union und der Gewässerschutz. In: Korrespondenz Abwasser; Vol. 45; Nr. 9; pp. 1670-1678

Jekel, Heide (2002): Die Information und Anhörung der Öffentlichkeit nach der EU-Wasserrahmenrichtlinie. In: von Keitz/Schmalholz (eds.): Handbuch der EU-Wasserrahmenrichtlinie. Inhalte, Neuerungen und Anregungen für die nationale Umsetzung. Berlin; Erich Schmidt; pp. 345-364

Jordan, Andrew/Timothy O'Riordan (1995): Institutional Adaptation to Global Environmental Change (I): Social Institutions, Policy Change and Social Learning. Norwich; CSERGE Working Paper GEC 95-20

Jordan, Andrew/Timothy O'Riordan (1997): Social Institutions and Climate Change: Applying Cultural Theory to Practice. Norwich; CSERGE Working Paper GEC 97-15

Kahlenborn, Walte/R. Andreas Kraemer (1999): Nachhaltige Wasserwirtschaft in Deutschland. Berlin/Heidelberg; Springer-Verlag

Kessler, Peter (2001): Die ökonomische Seite der Wasserrahmenrichtlinie. In: Wasser und Abfall; No. 11; pp. 16-18

Kinnersley, David (1988): Troubled Water. Rivers, Politics and Pollution. London; Shipman

Kirsch, G. (1984): Federal Fiscalism. In: Wirtschaftswissenschaftliches Studium; No. 3; pp. 118-119

Knitsch, Peter (2000): EU-Wasserrahmenrichtlinie – Stand der Umsetzung. In: Wupperverband (ed.): Flussgebietsmanagement beim Wupperverband. 3. Symposium am 30.05.2000; pp. 8-11

Kolisch, Gerd/Jörg Londong/Joachim Renner (2000): Integrated and Sustainable River Basin Management by German River Associations. In: Water21; October; pp. 38-41

Kraemer, R. Andreas/Frank Jäger (1998): Germany. In: Nunes Correia (ed.): Institutions for Water Resources Management in Europe. Vol. 1. Rotterdam/Brookfield; Balkema; pp. 183-325

Länderarbeitsgemeinschaft Wasser (LAWA) (2002): Arbeitshilfe zur Umsetzung der EG-Wasserrahmenrichtlinie. Version dated 27 February; Unpublished working paper on www.lawa.de/

Lattmann (2000): Perspektiven aus der Sicht der kommunalen Spitzenverbände. In: Länderarbeitsgemeinschaft Wasser (LAWA): EU-Wasserrahmenrichtlinie – Programm für die Zukunft im Gewässerschutz. Symposium zur Einführung der EU-Wasserrahmenrichtlinie am 13./14. Dezember 2000. Schwerin; LAWA; pp. 33-36

Lepsius, M. Rainer (1997): Institutionalisierung und Deinstitutionalisierung von Rationalitätskriterien. In: Göhler (ed.): Institutionenwandel. Opladen; Westdeutscher Verlag; pp. 57-69

Leymann, Günther (2000): Bedeutung der Wasserrahmenrichtlinie für die Bundesländer und Konsequenzen. In: Länderarbeitsgemeinschaft Wasser (LAWA): EU-Wasserrahmenrichtlinie – Programm für die Zukunft im Gewässerschutz. Symposium zur Einführung der EU-Wasserrahmenrichtlinie am 13./14. Dezember 2000. Schwerin; LAWA; pp. 7-11

Lipschutz, Ronnie D. (1999): Bioregionalism, Civil Society and Global Environmental Governance. In: McGinnis (ed.): Bioregionalism. London/New York; Routledge; pp. 101-120

Marchand, M./F. H. Toornstra (1986): Ecological Guidelines for River Basin Development. Leiden; Centrum voor Milienkunde, Rijksuniversiteit

Mayntz, Renate/ Fritz W. Scharpf (1995): Der Ansatz des akteursorientierten Institutionalismus. In: Mayntz/Scharpf (eds.): Gesellschaftliche Selbstregelung und politische Steuerung. Frankfurt am Main; Campus Verlag; pp. 39-70

Mitchell, Bruce (1990): Integrated Water Management. In: Mitchell (ed.): Integrated Water Management: International Experiences and Perspectives. London/New York; Belhaven Press; pp. 1-21

Newson, Malcolm (1996): Land, Water and Development: Key themes driving international policy on catchment management. In: Cresser/Pugh (eds.): Multiple Land Use and Catchment Management. International Conference, 11-13 September; Aberdeen; The Macauley Land Use Research Institute; pp. 11-21

Newson, Malcolm (1997): Land, Water and Development. Sustainable management of river basin systems. 2nd ed. London/New York; Routledge

Olson, Mancur (1969): The Principle of "Fiscal Equivalence": The Division of Responsibilities among Different Levels of Government. In: The American Economic Review; No. 59; pp. 479-487

Organisation for Economic Co-operation and Development (OECD) (1989): Water Resource Management. Integrated Policies. Paris; OECD

Ostrom, Elinor (1990): Governing the Commons. The Evolution of Institutions for Collective Action. Cambridge; Cambridge University Press

Ostrom, Elinor/Roy Gardner/James Walker (1994): Rules, Games, and Common-Pool Resources. Ann Arbor; University of Michigan Press

Parsons, James J. (1985): On "Bioregionalism" and "Watershed Consciousness". In: The Professional Geographer; Vol. 37; No. 1; pp. 1-6

Pepper, David (1996): Modern Environmentalism. An Introduction. London/New York; Routledge

Philip, Alan Butt (1998): The European Union: Environmental Policy and the Prospects for Sustainable Development. In: Hanf/Jansen (eds.): Governance and Environment in Western Europe. Harlow; Longman; pp. 253-276

Quarrie, J. (ed.) (1992): Earth Summit '92: The United Nations Conference on Environment and Development. London; Regency Press

Schmitz, Manuela (1998): Bürokratie- und Kostenschub durch die neue EU-Wasserrahmenrichtlinie? In: Wasser Abwasser; Vol. 139; No. 5; pp. 264-274

Slater, Simon (1997): River Basin Management: Development Responses within the Context of Catchment Management Planning in England and Wales 1990-1996. Ph.D. dissertation; University of Newcastle upon Tyne

Slater, Simon/Simon Marvin/Malcolm Newson (1994): Land Use Planning and the Water Sector. In: Town Planning Review; Vol. 64, No. 4; pp. 375-397

Stratenwerth, Thomas (2002): Die Bewirtschaftung nationaler und internationaler Flussgebiete. In: von Keitz/Schmalholz (eds.): Handbuch der EU-Wasserrahmenrichtlinie. Inhalte, Neuerungen und Anregungen für die nationale Umsetzung. Berlin; Erich Schmidt; pp. 323-342

Swyngedouw, Erik (1999): Modernity and Hybridity. Nature, "Regeneracionismo" and the Production of the Spanish Waterscape, 1890-1930. In: Annals of the Association of American Geographers, September

Umweltbundesamt (1998): Studie zu den Möglichkeiten und Problemen der praktischen Umsetzung der vorgeschlagenen EG-Wasserrahmenrichtlinie, insbesondere der dort vorgesehenen River Basin Management Plans, auf der Grundlage ausgewählter Planungsinstrumente in Deutschland. Berlin; Umweltbundesamt

United Nations Economic Commission for Europe (UN-ECE) (1995): Protection and Sustainable Use of Waters. Recommendations to ECE Governments. Water Series No. 2. New York/Geneva; United Nations

van der Wal, Henriette/ R. Andreas Kraemer (1991): Die Wasserwirtschaft in der DDR. Forschungsstelle für Umweltpolitik der Freien Universität Berlin. Unpublished manuscript

Voigt, Manfred (1997): Die Nutzung des Wassers. Naturhaushaltliche Produktion und Versorgung der Gesellschaft. Berlin/Heidelberg; Springer

von Alvensleben, Reimar (2000): Gewässerunterhaltung in Brandenburg aus umweltökonomischer Sicht. In: NABU Landesverband Brandenburg: Wasser in der Landschaft. Jubiläumsband zum 5. Naturschutztag des NABU Brandenburg. Potsdam; NABU; pp. 19-28

Watson, R. Drennan (1996): Integrating Catchment Management: The Human Dimension. In: Cresser/Pugh (eds.): Multiple Land Use and Catchment Management. International Conference, 11-13 September; Aberdeen; The Macauley Land Use Research Institute; pp. 125-137

World Bank (1993): Water Resources Management. A World Bank Policy Paper. Washington (D.C.); The World Bank

Young, Oran (1999): Institutional Dimensions of Global Environmental Change. Science Plan. IHDP Report No. 9; Bonn; IHDP

Young, Oran (2002): The Institutional Dimensions of Environmental Change. Fit, Interplay, and Scale. Cambridge (MA); MIT Press

Interviews with representatives from:

1. The Senate Department for Urban Development of the State of Berlin, 13 July 2000
2. The Senate Department for Urban Development of the State of Berlin, 17 July 2000
3. The Ministry of Agriculture, the Environment and Spatial Planning of the State of Brandenburg, 18 July 2000
4. The Joint Planning Department of Berlin and Brandenburg, 31 August 2000
5. The State Environment Agency of Brandenburg, 7 September 2000
6. The Federal Ministry for the Environment, Nature Protection and Nuclear Safety, 13 September 2000
7. The German Association of Water Management, Wastewater and Solid Waste (ATV-DVWK), 13 September 2000
8. The River Association of the Wupper (Wupperverband), 14 September 2000
9. The Association of Gas and Water Engineers (BGW), 24 October 2000
10. The environmental group Grüne Liga, 30 January 2001
11. The Regional Planning Office for Uckermark-Barnim, 7 February 2001
12. The Regional Planning Office for Lausitz-Spreewald, 9 February 2001
13. The Ministry of Environment and Transport of the State of Baden-Württemberg, 24 April 2000

Florian Dünckmann and Claudia Mayer

Using Market Institutions for Sustainability: Environmental Production Standards in the Coffee Trade

Institutions do not only exist in political arenas but also in "free markets" which are always controlled by a large number of different regulations, rules and standards[1]. In the following paper we will take a closer look at the design, performance and effects of a particular type of market internal institutions that is becoming increasingly important on the world market: environmental production standards.

Since the 1980s an increased awareness of global ecological and social problems and contamination of food can be observed among consumers in industrialised countries. Accordingly the demand on the world market for 'responsible products' – i.e. products that possess specific attributes – is increasing. These attributes are physical (e.g. pesticides-free), social ("fair trade") and/or environmental (e.g. nature conservation during the production process), and are promoted in advertising campaigns. Frequently a certificate on the package attests to the special attributes of the product. Certification is linked to specific, voluntary product standards (i.e. standards concerning properties of the final product) and production standards (i.e. standards concerning properties of the production process). Significantly, due to the demand for environmentally friendly products, market production standards are offering new possibilities to enhance sustainable environmentally friendly production patterns in producing countries in the developing world.

The crucial step for the implementation of production standards is the certification of products or companies. Certification is understood as a "...system by which the conformity of products, services etc. to an applicable standard is determined and confirmed" (Rundgren 1997, p. 14).

The trade in environmentally friendly products is creating new tasks and new actors in the field of certification. In the first instance there are the organisations that are formulating new standards and seek to establish them on the market. They are often to be found outside the free market, i.e. these are either non-governmental organisations, scientific institutions or international organisations. Although they are not an integral part of the market, they can only achieve their aims if they can ensure that producers participate and that consumers accept the label. Closely linked to these organisations (and in

---

[1] This paper presents results from a research project funded by the German Research Council (DFG) within the Programme "Global Environmental Change – Social and Behavioural Dimensions". The authors would like to thank the DFG for its generous support.

some cases even identical) are organisations that monitor the implementation of the standards during production and trade, and certify their conformity. Unlike the organisations that formulate the standards, the controlling organisations are often private companies that are in immediate competition for clients – in this case, producers.

1 Standards as Internal Market Institutions

Environmental standard labels, as well as trade marks, can be understood as market internal institutions as they ensure that a certain quality gets passed on from the ecological producer to the ecologically conscious consumer. These institutions not only provide the consumer with information, they also fulfil the role of "reference point" in terms of reputation and customer loyalty to the marketer, in this case the coffee roaster. Certified and conventional food can hardly be differentiated by taste. The consumer is prepared to pay a higher price for certified products for an indirect product quality that is not otherwise discernible to him or her. This increases the danger of confusing or misleading the consumer (Dörtelmann 1997). The trust and confidence of the consumer are of fundamental importance for the entire trade with certified products. As these can be easily undermined, it is important to embed the trade in a system of reliable controlling institutions.

Trustworthiness, predictability and voluntary production standards are significant not only from a consumer perspective. For farmers and processing concerns the application of standards of organic production are generally expensive and require a re-organisation of production procedures at high cost. On the one hand the producers need the guarantee that they will be compensated by higher prices for certified produce, for their investment in building up a new network of trading partners, and the risk of crop losses due to limited means of control of pests and diseases in ecological production. This is especially crucial during the phase of conversion from conventional to organic agriculture. On the other hand it is vital to ensure that farmers not producing according to the standards do not benefit from higher market prices associated with the application of the standards. This would remove the incentive for farmers to convert their production systems (usually at high cost). Institutional control of environmental production standards is thus vital to ensure fair play and provide the right incentives.

1.1 Institutions: Costs and Benefits

According to the new institutional economy (North 1998), institutions fulfil a vital role in the economy. The social sciences perceive institutions on the one hand as a limiting factor for human action. On the other hand they also open new avenues for action, as institutions make the actions of others (and therefore the consequences of their own action) more predictable. If we translate these two characteristics into economic figures, we can compare "costs" (e.g. opportunity costs) and "benefits" (e.g. reduced transaction costs) of formal institutions. Successful institutional constellations are a reliable frame for economic activity that is flexible, whilst not blocking innovations.

How can institutions bring economic benefit? For the development of a market for products that are produced without damaging the environment, it is crucial that the trading partners are accountable within an explicit framework and that the product information as well as the price guarantee to the producers are credible. What is the basis for the necessary trust between producers, trade and consumers, if there are no formal production standards? One alternative is an integrated production chain: one company that covers all steps from production to sale on the retail market. In this case all the potential markets that exist along the production chain are excluded. This alternative causes high internal production costs. Another possibility is building trust through personal contacts. Ideally the consumer knows the farm and has first hand knowledge of the environmentally friendly production. However, such personal contact is connected with high transaction costs and can only exist in small niche markets.

Environmental production standards can be seen as a substitute for either personal contact or the merging of all production stages within one company. In reality hybrid forms exist that combine different elements of the three principles (markets with formalised standards / hierarchically regulated producer-consumer relations within one enterprise / direct interaction between consumer and producer on the basis of trust).

1.2 The Contribution of Market Internal Institutions to Solving Environmental Problems

How can production standards contribute to the improvement of the environmental situation in producing countries? Even rigorous policy can only solve environmental problems that occur in the same country. Ecological damage through export oriented agriculture is clearly a global problem. Although the consequences of environmental destruction are most severe on local and regional level, its roots can be traced back to existing world market structures and to demand from industrialised countries. In these cases political measures and agreements are necessary on a global level. But such international regimes have frequently proved to be complicated, ineffective and "tooth-less" (Ruloff 1999, Keohane et al. 1993, Paarlberg 1993). Voluntary production standards now have the of making possible the monetary quantification of the environmental dimension possible. This offers a way of internalising the externalised costs for ecological responsibility into the price of the product. As "money talks more clearly than the reprimanding silence of nature" to the producers, voluntary production standards are often seen as a promising tool to address global change (Gawel 1994).

The formulation of successful production standards steered by the market has proved to be a difficult challenge: producers and consumers represent the outer ends of a complex production chain that includes a number of actors with various interests. The standard has to provide a stable "bridge" between production and consumption and this is only possible if there are enough incentives for companies along the production chain. If a standard is formulated in such a way that it will hinder the production or the marketing of certified products, then it will not persist in the market. Contrary to legal obligations, the survival of market-internal voluntary production standards is dependent on their acceptance by all actors involved. This is largely achieved though a comparative market advantage in new niches in an otherwise saturated market.

Environmental standards therefore have to fulfil requirements that reach far beyond the simple function as a communication instrument in international trade. In order to promote environmental conservation, the production standard should be in a position to enhance or even induce a fundamental change in agrarian production. To achieve this the standards have to be ecologically sound and have to be adopted by many producers. From a social point of view it is important to work towards a fundamental redistribution of the resources and value-adding processes along the production chain. Social activists argue that ways have to be found that will favour the disadvantaged on the world market: the small scale farmers. Especially for these groups, environmental production standards must provide market advantages and stability. It is difficult to achieve these far-reaching ecological and social aims as voluntary production standards operate within the logic of the market and can only be successfully implemented through positive incentives.

In this article we will raise some problems that arise in the formulation, supervision and implementation of environmental production standards in the coffee sector. There are two frameworks for the analysis presented in the scientific framework of the IHDP (International Human Dinemsions Programme on Global Environmental Change) (Young et al. 1998) for the examination of institutional dimensions of global change: Problems of Fit and Problems of Interplay.

Problem of fit: Do the characteristics of the institutions match the characteristics of the system that it should be applied to? Is the functional logic of the environmental production standards appropriate to environmental, farming and processing conditions in the market sector? As pointed out earlier, modernised production is linked to a number of different ecological and social problems. Which of these problems (e.g. soil erosion, water pollution, species extinction) should be addressed with a specific production standard? Is this problem relevant for the ecological situation at the local, regional and global level? How effective is the standard for improving the environmental situation?

Problem of internal interplay between different standards: Market based production standards as well as trade marks have to survive the "hostile environment" of a free market. In which ways are standards competing with each other? What are the critical, key resources provoking competition and how scarce are these? What are the consequences of this competition? Will the "best standard" survive, or are there other factors that determine the survival of a standard? On the other hand, is harmonious co-existence of standards or even co-operation possible?

Problem of external interplay between standards and legislation: The effectiveness of production standards is not only determined by their internal modus operandi and market conditions. National legislation and international frameworks represent important institutional systems that define and limit the arena of free market forces. Pioneering legislating organisations such as the EU have recognised that environmental production standards can make a contribution towards guiding global change. Consequently, since the early 1990s legislation has been in place to enhance and regulate the organic market in Europe. Are these rules appropriate? Alternatively is it only the rules of the free market that are able to create the right conditions for an effective standard? And what effect does other legislation (e.g. environmental, tax and trade legislation) have on producer and consumer countries?

2 The Problem of Fit: How Do Production Standards in Coffee Trade Affect the Environment?

2.1 The Socio-ecological Dilemma of Coffee Production

Coffee is a typical colonial product – its production areas are nearly exclusively in the countries of the South, while the consuming markets are mainly in the industrialised countries. In its production chain coffee thus crosses the gap that separates the first world from the third world.

This has significant consequences for the pricing structure: if one excludes short term price fluctuations due to shortages resulting from adverse weather conditions, the coffee market is to a high degree determined by consumer preferences. Since the International Coffee Agreement expired in 1989, a strong demand for cheap coffee led to a decreasing price trend on the world market. Due to the strong dependence of single producers, entire production regions and countries on coffee, the decreasing price on the world market triggered increased production. This was exacerbated by mechanisation in the production process. Overproduction resulted in further deterioration of prices on the world market (Masserat 1993). This 'vicious circle' formed by falling prices and overproduction has a negative social impact on the countries in the South. Small scale producers face poverty due to a weak market, and seasonal labourers on coffee plantations often suffer under bad working conditions.

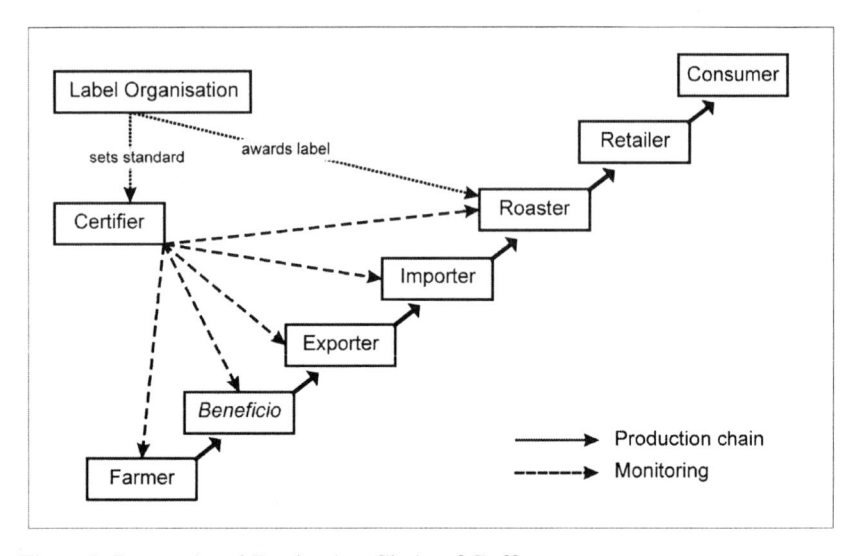

Figure1: International Production Chain of Coffee

Besides this social dimension, the structure of the world market also has negative consequences for the environment of the producing regions. The intensification and mechanisation of production systems, requiring a high input of pesticides and insecticides, has resulted in higher levels of erosion and increasing contamination of the soil, groundwater and surface water. During the first step of processing coffee (washing, peeling and drying of the coffee beans) in the so-called beneficios considerable air and water contamination take place (UNCTAD 1993).

Coffee production also has a negative effect upon nature conservation: On the one hand the expansion of coffee plantations into forest areas has destroyed the natural habitat of several species. On the other hand there is high pressure on the forest ecosystems of coffee producing countries due to the high demand for fuel wood for processing coffee. An even bigger threat is posed by the conversion of traditional shade tree coffee cultivation to mechanised open cultivation. Shade tree cultivation not only reduces the susceptibility of coffee to pests; it also prevents erosion and provides natural nutrients. The diversity of indigenous tree species in the traditional coffee production system provides an important habitat, especially for insects and birds. Traditional coffee production areas in Central- and South America are important winter feeding grounds for North American migrating birds. Intensified methods of coffee production have resulted in the ecological impoverishment of the areas. This development is of special concern where the last 'forests' in the region are the traditional shade tree cultivation areas, as in parts of Guatemala and El Salvador (Rice/Ward 1996, CEC 1999).

2.2 The Impact of Environmental Production Standards

The ecological effectiveness of production standards depends to a high degree on their adaptability to characteristics of environmental systems with which they interact. In the case of coffee, environmental systems include more than just the bio-physical context. The technical specifications of the production and processing of coffee, as well as the economic frame of production and trade have to be taken into account. In general, the effectiveness of environmental standards depends upon two factors: on the one hand their strictness and the range of influence of their obligations and on the other hand consumer preferences, i.e. the market shares of the product (UNCTAD 1993, pp. 8f).

2.2.1 Organic Production: Focused in Uncontaminated Food

The standards for organic agriculture do not represent a uniform set of rules but rather an international network of generally compatible standards. All rules are focused on the prohibition of synthetic pesticides and fertilisers as a common key element. In most cases the control of production and trade is exercised by private certification companies (e.g. OCIA, BCS, Eco-Cert, Ecologica) or para-statal organisations (e.g. Skal, Krav).

Large parts of the population in Europe, the USA and Japan are aware of organic agriculture. Due to repeated food scandals the market share of organically produced food is increasing steadily (Willer/Yusefi 2000). Due to this increasing market share controlled organic production has the best chance of all environmental standards to influence the agricultural sector sustainably. High acceptance with the consumer is mainly based on two factors: Firstly the key message "this product was produced without the use of any artificial substances" has recruited new consumers to the market. On the other hand these products serve an existing interest in healthy, uncontaminated food. Market analysis suggests that increased health awareness in the middle classes is the primary cause of increased demand, especially in the USA.

Coffee is the most significant product of the South in this context. The main area of coffee production is clearly Latin America (ITC 1999, p. 134). In any event, in the case of coffee the use of fertilisers and pesticides in production has little impact on the final product. This is because the roasting process of even conventionally produced coffee burns away nearly all chemical traces. The fact that organic coffee is still benefiting from the health trend is based on the misunderstanding that this product is healthier than coffee produced conventionally.

For the environmental situation of the producing areas, abstaining from using artificial substances naturally results in a lower contamination of soil and water, and a reduction of health risks for workers due to toxic fertilisers or pesticides. However, habitat and species protection should not be overlooked, especially considering the fact that production areas for coffee are often identical with centres of the highest global biodiversity (McLean 1998, p. 4). The conservation of biodiversity in natural ecosystems is not an obligation in organic production. Although there are recommendations by IFOAM regarding organic production of coffee that promote, for example, the establishment of buffer strips or the protection of indigenous primary forest, these are not legally binding. There is thus no mechanism to prevent the establishment of an organic coffee plantation on cleared primary forest land.

The conservation of tree species diversity in the coffee plantations is also of great significance. In this respect the system of shade tree cultivation is important. Ecological surveys have concluded that shade tree cultivation is not only a good habitat for migrating birds, but also for up to 74% of the species diversity of a natural forest (Saxenian 1996, p. 226). The technical characteristics of this means of production offer both advantages and disadvantages: the improvement of the microclimate and many soil-chemical and physical indicators are very positive (Muscheler 1998). On the other hand, humidity levels are higher and this can trigger fungus infections of the coffee plants. Plantations should thus be established in such a way that they emulate natural conditions in the area (see Figure 2).

Ecological frame conditions

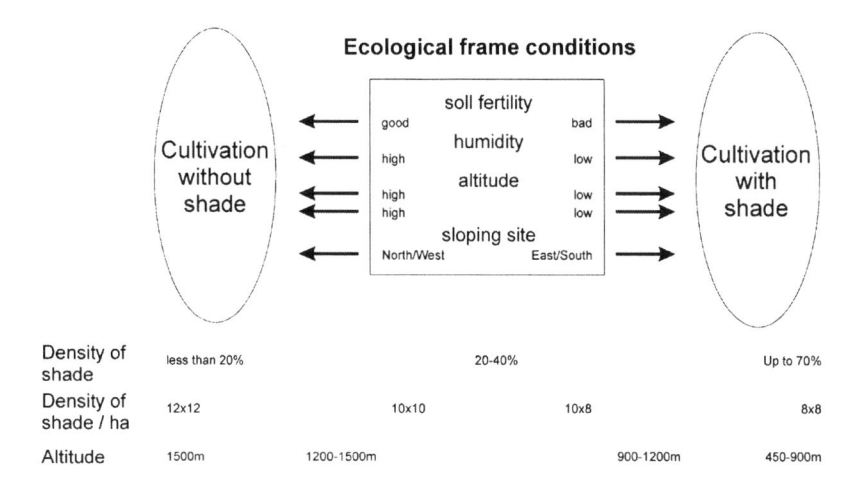

	Cultivation without shade				Cultivation with shade
		good	soil fertility	bad	
	←	high	humidity	low	→
	←	high	altitude	low	→
	←	high		low	→
		North/West	sloping site	East/South	

Density of shade	less than 20%		20-40%		Up to 70%
Density of shade / ha	12x12	10x10		10x8	8x8
Altitude	1500m	1200-1500m		900-1200m	450-900m

Source: Muschler 1999

Figure 2: Factors for Shade Trees

The controlled organic production of coffee occurs mainly in a shade tree system, as it improves the natural supply with nutrients dramatically. To which degree the shade tree culture contributes to species and habitat protection is highly depended on the varieties of tree species used. Specialised shade tree cultivation that uses exclusively one species of shade trees (mostly Inga-Species) like mono cultures is home to only a small number of plant and animal species (Rice/Ward 1996, p. 10). This important context is not reflected in the standards for organic production.

2.2.2 Bird-friendly-Coffee: a "Scientific" Standard

As a consequence of this concern the Bird-friendly-Coffee concept was created with the explicit aim of conserving the biodiversity in coffee producing areas. In 1997 the Smithsonian Migratory Bird Centre (SMBC) developed this standard for coffee that was focused on the conservation of traditional shade tree cultivation of coffee. The label was to ensure that ecologically valuable and diverse production systems would be rewarded, as they play a significant role in the protection of species and their habitat. Virtually only ecological criteria were considered for registration. For example, the species composition and density of trees in a plantation is regulated. It is also not acceptable to have plantations within nature conservation areas.

The narrow aim of maintaining a habitat for migratory birds is reflected in the name, and the entire PR campaign is essentially of a pragmatic nature, informed by the belief that this message reaches consumers in the USA most effectively. However, the focus is clearly on land stewardship and environmental conservation. As this label is currently only obtained in combination with organic production, it guarantees an optimal combination of environmental and species conservation in the production cycle of coffee.

However, even with this standard problems of fit can be seen, although at a different stage. The label was conceptualised on the basis on scientific knowledge without concrete, existing demand in the North American market. For this reason the interest of the consumer had to be raised actively through PR activities. The demand for Bird-friendly Coffee and the label is often perceived as a negligible addition to the existing demand for organic coffee. Consequently, the prices paid for this coffee are relatively low. Furthermore, the roaster has to pay 25 cents per pound to SMBC so little of the additional price reaches the actual producer. Therefore the Bird-friendly-Coffee can only contribute to the maintainance of ecologically significant traditional production systems that are already using the traditional tree shade culture due to lack of capital.

2.2.3   EcoOK: "Sustainability" as the Goal

Similar problems are found with the EcoOK label. This label is awarded by the Rainforest Alliance, a network of Latin-American NGOs engaged in environmental protection. The vary aim of the organisation has been to achieve the conservation of tropical forest on as large a scale as possible. Accordingly the EcoOK standard is geared towards large production units.

Contrary to organic agriculture and Bird-friendly-Coffee standards, EcoOK tries to address a variety of problem areas and thus enhance sustainable production by including aspects that are not covered by any other certificate, e.g. explicit regulations regarding environmental conservation and working conditions.

In environmental respects the standard is more flexible than the organic certificate. The use of synthetic substances is accepted to a certain degree and the transformation phase is regulated by a dynamic and hierarchic point system that allows a step-by-step improvement of production systems. This leaves enough leeway for the producers to adapt over time.

As the criteria focus on the requirements of the producer, marketing aspects have been largely neglected. Until recently there were hardly any structures in place to control the integrity of the coffee along the production chain (the so-called "audit trail"). Furthermore, the wide spectrum and flexibility of criteria proved to be problematic for marketing. The principle of "minimizing and strictly managing the use of agrochemicals" is very diffuse and not easily understood. Sustainability is a very abstract product characteristic and thus difficult to convey to the customer. Consequently the demand for this label is limited and its real potential to influence land use sustainably is very low.

These examples demonstrate clearly that marketing and trade have to be considered in the formulation of production standards. The problem of fit is not only limited to production but can occur at any stage of the production chain. As a means of mediating supply and demand, voluntary instruments that show a strong bias towards the requirements of production or marketing will make a limited contribution towards sustainable land use. Therefore, when looking at problems of fit one has bear in mind that successful institutions have to match with the physical as well the socio-economic environment.

2.3 Eco-Farms as Islands in the Conventional Coffee Environment: the Example Costa Rica

A general problem concerning all environmental production standards is the question of the spatial approach. As the standards have an impact on the market, every producer (company or co-operative) represents the spatial unit where the ecological improvements are realised. Where strict standards are applied, there is a great danger that they are adopted only by few ecological producers. These small islands of ecological practice are unlikely to have much impact on the regional environmental situation.

An example illustrating this problem is Costa Rica, with a highly modernised process of coffee production. More than 70% of the coffee lands are under open, unshaded cultivation, and only 30% are under shade tree cultivation. Research shows that very few farmers have decided to enter the organic market. Bird-friendly-Coffee™ and EcoOK coffee are not produced in Costa Rica and only 500ha are farmed organically – this is only 0.5% of the coffee production area. Environmental production standards have hardly contributed to significant ecological improvements. Why is the outcome so negative?

Apart from two exceptions, all 200 organic producers are small scale producers with a production area of 2ha on average. For these fincas a conversion to organic agriculture does not imply a radical change of the production process as the capital for artificial fertiliser and pesticides is extremely limited. For capital intensive large scale producers working with high yield varieties on unshaded plantations, cutting out fertilisers and pesticides would result in changing the entire production system, at a high risk. As Costa Rican coffee is highly valued on the international coffee market due to its good quality, the incentive of an expected additional financial benefit through organic production does not outweigh the risks attached. Furthermore, organic production limits potential buyers to a few certified beneficios.

For the small scale farmers the smaller harvest and therefore lower income during the conversion to organic agriculture pose a challenge as the coffee can not yet be marketed as "organically produced". Furthermore, the certification of the production is an expense that is especially difficult for small-scale farmers to bear. The smaller the producer (or co-operative, as group certification is permitted), the higher the relative costs of the official control of production according to the standards of private certifiers. The costs can be up to 9 US$/qq (equivalent to 46.6kg green coffee). To bear these costs, the producers have to take out loans or are strongly dependent on their buyers. Buyers frequently cover the costs for the certification but in turn retain the exclusive right to buy the harvest in the coming years. Large scale producers have higher personnel costs and therefore higher production costs, as additional work cannot be done by family members as is often the case with small scale producers. Another factor is the scarcity of organic fertiliser, which leads to a tendency towards higher prices. The majority of the large scale producers perceive the organic market as a fashion.

The beneficios rely rather on industrial standards like the ISO14.001 standard. In this case the demand for certification does not arise from individual consumers, but from European retail chains. Due to their internal purchasing policies these retail chains are passing the impulse for ISO certification along the supply chain.

2.4 No Standard Can Solve all the Problems on Its Own

Although organic farming is more widely spread in other producing countries (esp. Mexico, Peru and Guatemala), the results from Costa Rica show that environmental production standards have to meet favourable socio-economic conditions (capital extensive agricultural systems, low cost production, external support during conversion, etc.) to be successful.

In the light of these problems of fit of the various production standards we may observe that each standard is addressing a certain area of the multi-dimensional environmental problems and is following a certain strategy. A standard that can enhance a comprehensive sustainability while not overstretching the producers and at the same time can address the consumers does not exist. It is conceivable that this objective could be achieved through the combination of various standards. The next chapter will explore what the relations between the various standards are.

The example of Costa Rica also demonstrates that environmental production standards on their own are not able to induce a fundamental change in export-oriented agricultural production, as the focus on individual producers limits the improvements to small, geographically isolated areas. Besides, the capital intensive producers that are responsible for many environmental problems prove to be especially resistant to the economic advantages of the ecological niche market. Environmental production standards cannot replace national environmental legislation. The ways in which the two institutional systems (market internal institutions and legislature) can complement or hinder each other will be discussed in a further chapter.

3 Problem of Internal Interplay: What Are the Consequences of Competition between Environmental Standards?

Coffee is a global product, produced in diverse natural and agricultural settings for a variety of consumer groups with specific preferences. No standard could ever be attractive to large scale producers in Brazil and small scale farmers in Mexico at the same time. A price-conscious and health-conscious consumer is not attracted to the same label as an environmentalist concerned about development in the South. Considering this multi-facetted market pattern, it is not surprising that a variety of environmental standards for coffee exists.

Do these standards exist independently from each other? Can one simply add up the market shares? Is every new standard to be welcomed as it is an expression of increasing responsibility of the coffee sector? Will additional standards win over new producer and consumer groups? Or are the labels always in competition with each other and harmful to the basic principle of sustainable production because they are confusing to the consumer?

All these initiatives call on the solidarity of the coffee drinker with the people and the ecology of the producing countries. If one understands this solidarity as a limited resource, mainly used by standards and labels to demand a higher price compared to conventional coffee, it becomes clear that various production standards cannot be seen in isolation as they are either in direct competition or at least impacting on each other. A producer or a label owner (e.g. a roaster) that wants to start producing "ethical coffee" will have to decide on one or a combination of standards considering the price range of the buyers. The consumer will have to assess the different benefit and costs of the various labels in comparison with one another. In a situation of strong competition the attention span of the consumer can be seen as the critical resource. The problem of "using" this resource effectively is compounded by the lack of information about the different motives and aims of the various standards. Consequently it does matter if the certified coffee is the only one on the supermarket shelf, or if similar labels are offered. If a label is successful "in the store", then all parts of the production chain will adapt quickly.

However, environmental production standards, although they are in competition with each other, are not perceived in a differentiated way by the consumer and therefore stay linked to one another in the mind of the consumer. The revelation of inappropriate methods to control the implementation of a standard does not lead to a strengthening of its competitors, but rather severely weakens the trust of the consumer in production standards in general, and can thus lead to difficulties for other initiatives as well. Production standards are therefore in a situation of "dependent competition".

How strongly the labels are competing with each other depends naturally on the similarity of the aims and the spatial overlap of the production and consumer regions. In the following section we shall explore the situation of competition between different standards.

3.1 Voluntary Commitment

Some companies are generally critical towards control of their production through an independent institution. As an alternative to third party certification, some large coffee roasters and retail chains that are potentially under pressure from consumers have formulated their own standard for a voluntary commitment. These relate to an environmentally friendly purchasing policy, i.e. the companies commit themselves to buy exclusively coffee that is produced according to a certain standard. The principles for purchasing practised the large North American retail chain Starbucks and the "From farm to fork" programme by the international retail chain Ahold are examples of experiments to promote a "greening" of supply chains (see also Wycherley 1999). Some sectors of the coffee industry are also formulating its own catalogue of criteria. The Speciality Coffee Association of the USA has a mission statement that includes a comprehensive catalogue of guidelines, from quality control to sustainability. The European coffee industry is currently developing a statement for "responsible business".

In a survey regarding the voluntary commitment of companies, Utting (2000) concludes that commitment on its own does not induce a fundamental change in the methods of production. Although some initiatives are serious about the approach, it remains often contradictory, fragmented and minimalist. The constraints of the market are too strong to enable a company to fundamentally change its way of production voluntarily without any direct incentives.

Environmental activists, in particular, view these "codes of conducts" with distrust. In the past they have too often been purely PR measures, used to protect the company against public defamation or, in extreme cases, boycott. In these cases voluntary standards were used to distract attention from the absence of real change. In this way the voluntary commitment acts in competition to company based standards such as ISO 14.001, as they are undermining the certification through an independent third party. An example for this is the food company Procter & Gamble, which stated in 1997 that its own environmental management system complied to the intentions of ISO 14.001. Due to costs and bureaucracy a certification was not envisaged (ISO 14.001 update 1997).

3.2 Organic and Integrated Agricultural Production in Competition

Such voluntary obligations are competing for public acceptance with other standards that advertise products, and not companies. But there are other areas of competition. Willer and Yusefi (2000, p. 70) see initiatives for integrated agriculture as the biggest threat to organic agriculture. In the case of EcoOK the integrated agriculture approach is also linked to a label. It is therefore not surprising that the introduction of the EcoOK label was heavily criticised by representatives of the organic agricultural movement. They perceived the label as being in competition for market share, and were concerned about the soft standards that would erode the level of regulation that had been achieved within organic agriculture. Representatives of the fair trade movement critiqued the lack of consideration for the right of labourers to join trade unions in the standard, which nevertheless claimed to address social aspects. Especially harsh criticism was expressed when the Rainforest Alliance cooperated with the fruit company Chiquita in the banana production. It was felt that if NGOs with their labels were to be taken over by multinational companies, the integrity of all environmental production standards would be endangered.

Representatives of Rainforest Alliance on the other hand perceive the market as large enough to allow co-existence of "high bar standards" like the organic production and labels with less demanding guidelines like EcoOK. An insistence on strict guidelines would cement the niche existence of environmental standards and would exclude the spatially more relevant group of large scale producers. Furthermore, the Rainforest Alliance argues that in the face of urgent ecological improvements, organic agriculture has failed to have a broad impact.

3.3 Harmonising the Standards of Organic Agriculture

In the case of organic agriculture, the various existing standards tend to co-exist rather than compete. They are generally similar guidelines, but are not always well co-ordinated. Although well harmonised internationally, the free trade of organic products is sometimes hampered as governmental and private standards differ minimally from each other. An example of this is Sweden whose own national standard for organic agriculture, formulated by the semi-state foundation KRAV, sets slightly higher standards than those laid down by the EU guidelines. The consequence is that coffee that has been already imported into Europe as organic has to be re-certified for the Swedish market.

Such incompatibility not only costs money and administrative effort, but can also lead to insecurity on the part of producers and prevent them from taking part in a supposedly obscure and excessively regulated economic sector. This problem has been recognised and the Codex Alimentarus of the FAO will henceforth play the role of the "standard of standards". IFOAM is also trying to standardise guidelines as well as the qualifications of inspectors so as to ensure continuous quality control.

3.4 Co-operation between Standards

Not in all cases are labels in competition with each other. Some labels with different foci can supplement each other well. Such double or triple certification could improve the one-sidedness of existing labels and could be a step towards sustainability. Furthermore, the linking of Bird-friendly-Coffee to the existing control procedures of organic agriculture demonstrates that co-operation between labels often leads to a reduction in costs for monitoring and certifying production processes. On the consumer side, the established standard of organic agriculture could make new customer groups accessible for the Smithsonian Institute.

Most common in the coffee market in Northern Europe is the combination of organic production and "fair trade" labels that guarantees a minimum price enabling the producers and small-scale farmers to lead a dignified life. The link between these two labels is so strong that many consumers perceive organic coffee as equivalent to fair trade coffee. This situation can largely be explained by looking at the history of both standards: both expanded in the 1980s and were addressing rather similar consumer groups. Especially in the coffee trade, the fair trade label was offering organic coffee from an early stage. As the contacts to the producers are now well established and direct trade relations exist it would be difficult to separate both standards today.

3.5 Diverging Pathways

In the light of this successful co-operation, a possible integration of several labels into one standard has been discussed for some time. The primary aim is to reduce the number and diversity of labels and to address consumers more effectively. Nevertheless, most actors are critical of this approach. On the one hand they argue that too many producers could not fulfil all requirements and would therefore be excluded. However, this problem could be addressed through a flexible "umbrella" label that includes all sub-labels. But none of the initiators is willing to give up their own label for the sake of a "super-seal".

An example of expressed strong self-confidence was the proposal of the US Organic Coffee Association (ORCA) that its standard for organic production be accepted as a "super-seal". They argued that most of the organic coffee plantations were using shade tree cultivation anyway, and that the existing market price for organic coffee was higher than the minimum prices of fair trade coffee. This proposal by the representative body of importers, roasters and large-scale producers of the organic sector indicates that they perceive labels such as the Bird-friendly-Coffee™ and fair trade as superfluous.

Rice and McLean (1999) conclude from their survey of the possibilities of a joint labelling initiative of shade tree culture, fair trade and organic production that it is not so much the contents, but rather fear of survival on the part of the various label operators that prevents the implementation of a joint label. The study reveals that behind each standard are not only concepts but also actors such as companies or NGOs that have already invested in "their" standard. They are pursuing their own interests with their own strategies. The development of a standard never happens on a level playing field, where an "ideal" standard is designed according to ecological and social criteria. Institutional change is always "path-dependent", i.e. it is influenced by the chronology of historical events, the formation of strategic alliances and competition (North 1998, pp. 109ff.; see also the contribution of Troja in this book). The aspiration that environmental standards would be more efficient in steering global trade than environmental policy appears unrealistic. We cannot assume that under these circumstances the best standard will persist on the market. Is the solution intervention by government to level the playing field, in order to ensure that the best possible standard can be achieved?

4 Problem of External Interplay between Standards and Legislation

Environmental institutions embrace a wide spectrum of functions between the poles of the "free" market and state intervention. With increased state intervention the market incentives for environmental production diminish. On the other hand a market orientation implies less influence of the state on implementation of environmental conservation and more emphasis on economic incentives.

```
┌─────────────────────────────────────────────────────────────────┐
│          International and national institutional area          │
│   ┌─────────────────────────────────────────────────────────┐   │
│   │ state production   contributions/   private label   voluntary │
│   │                    certificates                      commitment│
│   │                                                         │   │
│   │           environmental   organic agriculture  ISO 14001│   │
│   │           legislation     certification                 │   │
│   └─────────────────────────────────────────────────────────┘   │
│      state intervention  ◄──────────────►  market logic         │
└─────────────────────────────────────────────────────────────────┘
```

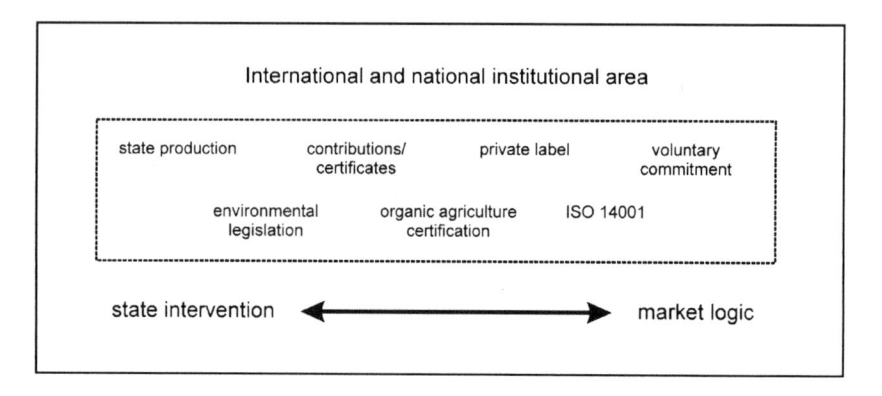

Figure 3: Environmental Institutions in the Market-State Intervention Continuum

In the case of state production, services are not provided by the market, as semi-public companies cover the entire process (see also the contribution of Moss in this book). At the other end of the continuum are voluntary commitments. In this case innovations are implemented according to the standards of the trading concern. As explained previously, the functionality of an environmental production standard depends on its flexibility and on acceptance by the other actors in the production chain. Furthermore, the efficiency of a production standard does not exclusively depend on the internal system and market conditions. Legislation and international frameworks are important institutional systems as they limit and define the arena of the free market. Coffee as a product of the world market falls under legislative conditions at various administrative levels, primarily global and national. In the following section the national and international framework conditions will be explored in terms of their enabling or hindering effect.

4.1 Legislation of Organic Production in Consumer Countries

Private standards for organic agriculture have existed since the 1970s. At the beginning of the 1980s, as market shares for organic products increased, stricter regulation of the sector was demanded. This was intended primarily to protect the consumer. As there was no legal mechanism to protect customers from false or misleading product information the confidence of the customers in organic labels was undermined. The term "natural" had been abused to such an extent that consumer confidence was lost. It was vital to prevent a erosion of the term "organic". The European Union Directive (EU) No

2092/91 "regarding organic agriculture and the adequate labelling of agricultural products and food" has been legally binding since 1993. It defines the obligatory requirements for marketing a product as organic in all member countries of the European Union.

The decree also regulates the import of organic products from "third countries" to the EU (see EU 2092/90 and Schmidt/Haccius 1996). Protection of the customer is clearly the focus. However, producers are also protected from unfair competition and abuse of certification. Although the health aspect is dominant the entire production chain is controlled. This is intended to prevent mixing of organic and conventional products. Regulations regarding the use of resources and possible negative environmental effects of processing are becoming more and more significant.

How can one assess the influence of governments on environmental standards which are steered by market forces? Apart from a higher degree of bureaucratic effort required for the import of coffee, the consequences are almost entirely positive. The legal foundation of the standard contributed to increased confidence on the part of consumers for a product quality that is difficult to assess directly. Furthermore it was now possible to limit the "flood" of labels. The uniform standard also enhanced inter-European trade. This background helps to explain the continuous growth in market share of organic products in Europe in the last decade.

In the light of this positive experience, an act was formulated to regulate organic agriculture in the USA, the heartland of deregulation. In its essence it emulates the European example. This was a rare case in that an industry requested federal government regulations for its own sector. Protection of consumers and the exclusion of dishonest competitors were the priorities.

4.2 Global Environmental Governance

As much as legal regulations of environmental production standards are supposed to enhance fair internal competition, they are debated in the frame of international law governing competition. In the debate on the integration of environmental standards into the World Trade Organisation (WTO) system, the member states have not reached agreement. In the debate about ecological minimum standards the differentiation between product and production standards is fundamental. All member states of the WTO have the right to demand the application of national standards regarding safety in the workplace, health regulations and environmental protection. However, imports cannot be rejected due to health or environmental problems occurring during production or processing in the producing country (see Windfuhr 1999, pp. 15f).

The reason lies in the principle of non-discrimination and equality of member countries which the WTO has had to ensure since its foundation in

1995. Article III of the GATT agreement prohibits discrimination against countries exporting products of the same quality, as well as discrimination against its producers. This regulation concerns national tax rates and duties, but also applies to all acts and regulations, including those relating to organic labelling (see Landmann 1997, p. 7). The question remains whether products with an environmental label can be considered equal to an equivalent product that lacks this label, or if sufficient product differentiation is achieved through the labelling process. Furthermore it is arguable whether or not Article III also affects regulations that do not determine production, but the methods of production. As environmental labels also include criteria regarding the production process, it could be possible that in their present format they are not consistent with GATT Article III. The consequence would be that the standards have to be conceptualised in such a manner that they respect the national legislation regarding resource conservation.

A possible consequence could be that the WTO establishes conditions which lead to the abolition of labels that regulate minimal standards (as in the organic production by the state) or specify the type of production without impact on the nature of the product. So far no legal judgements have determined that a state-regulated government programme is not consistent with the anti-discrimination principle. To avoid law suits such as the tuna-dolphin case[2], the existing state regulated certification programmes have no regulations for resource use in the processing phase.

Private standard programmes are not obliged to honour this principle. They are thus at liberty to regulate the production process, as is the case with EcoOK. The EcoOK norms go further, as they also demand measures to protect the environment without direct influence on production. Segments of the production chain are controlled to prevent contamination with other substances. Resource use and its possible negative environmental impact is monitored. The same applies to the standard of Bird-friendly-Coffee: production is regulated without a direct impact on the nature of the product. This would infringe the anti-discrimination regulation of the WTO.

If international regulations prohibit importing countries from governing the production process, the governments of the producing countries must take action to promote resource management and environmental conservation in the production process.

4.3 Environmental Legislation in Costa Rica

This realisation is not new and has been implemented by the Costa Rican government: the national environmental policy is one of the most progressive

---

[2] The techniques being used to catch tuna were resulting in the death of dolphins, and this was seen as just cause for imposing a ban on the import of tuna into the USA.

in Latin America. Nevertheless the different interests of the various actors are reflected in the regulations. This results in different approaches manifested in the regulations for each of the segments of the production chain.

In Costa Rica organic production is regulated by the ley de la agricultura orgánica. The aims of this act were to protect consumers and prevent abuse of organic labels whilst also enabling Costa Rica to be part of the EU third-country list, which eases the importing procedures. It is a requirement of the EU for this listing that the country has a national policy regarding organic agriculture equivalent to that of the EU. The differences between these regulations are slight: all actors that want to adopt the standard have to be registered by the Ministry of Agriculture and have to cover all additional costs incurred in certification. However, a governmental programme to support organic agriculture does not exist.

The Costa Rican policy is still strongly focused on conventional agriculture. The Coffee Institute that provides extension services to producers has virtually no extension staff that could advise about organic production. As always, the conventional technology is supported by the national Coffee Institute. Since 1988 some acts have aimed at regulating the use of agro-chemicals. Some chemicals ("the dirty dozen") were prohibited, and for other highly toxic chemicals a maximum allowable application was defined. But implementation has proven difficult. Enforcement of the legislation, requiring expensive soil samples, is very costly. The highly toxic chemicals are often cheap and are used by producers for economic reasons. The trade in agro-chemicals is lucrative for a number of actors. Furthermore, anxieties about potential loss of foreign currency earnings due to loss of production keep the national government committed to the conventional technology approach.

Apart from the coffee policy, other legislation supports the producer indirectly in the conversion process towards standard programmes. The Costa Rican soil conservation act is an example of this. It follows an advisory approach instead of sanctions. Alternative measures for soil conservation are illustrated, as are ways of maintaining soil fertility. Furthermore it offers incentive systems such as further education, tax reductions and access to loans. Unfortunately these are little known to producers and therefore not often used.

In the recent past the coffee policy has focused more on the expansion of organic agriculture. With falling prices for coffee on the world market, the growing organic niche market is increasingly seen as a solution. Divergent pathways are present in the acceptance or rejection of institutions. Once a technological path is taken it is difficult to abandon it, especially if powerful interest groups do not see an advantage in institutional change. But if changes promise an advantage for influential interest groups they are pursued. Co-operation amongst interest groups is a basic requirement for a multi-sectoral environmental policy. Over-utilisation of resources, as for example the enormous water pollution and fuel wood consumption in the roasting process, could have a negative impact on other activities that are bringing foreign currency into the country (e.g. eco-tourism). In the legal regulation of the drying of coffee fruit formulated in 1992 it is possible to identify the interests of the various sector policies. The "Convenio de Cooperación Interinstitutional", an agreement between the National Coffee Institute, the Ministry of Agriculture and the Ministry of Environmental Affairs, prescribes a four-phase, 80% reduction of water use contamination by peel debris for all processors (see ICAFE 1998). The first phase aims at a reduction of water used in the process of peeling the coffee fruit. The used water is supposed to be recycled with adequate technology or must be disposed of in a purified state in phase 2. Phases 3 and 4 comprise dry peeling, as well as aerobic and anaerobic water treatment.

According to official statistics more than 80% of the beneficios adopted the new technology (see ICAFE 1999). Impressive figures demonstrate the positive effect on the environment. Whereas in 1992 4m3 water was used per Quintal (qq) coffee, today the consumption is reduced to 0.15-1.2 m3 water per Quintal (qq) (own data 2000). The water volume is reduced due to the non-hydraulic transport of the coffee fruit, the recycling of the water in various stages of the process and the purification of the water after peeling and washing.

Initially all processors experienced difficulties in achieving adequate product quality. The recycled water reduced the fermentation time in the water. Experience was needed to identify the optimal fermentation time required. Along with these "costs of learning" the processors also had to invest in technical equipment.

There were and are no state financed support programmes for the implementation of the necessary new technology[3]. More then 50% of the processors had to take up a loan (own data 2000). Contrary to market internal instruments, the national environmental regulations do not offer compensation through a higher price. Consequently the smaller beneficios had a higher cost per unit coffee than the larger companies. To close this financial gap, the processors in Costa Rica certify with ISO 14.001 to achieve a competitive advantage. They thus created a combination of state and market institutions to resolve tensions between ecology and economy.

For the benificios the main advantages of national environmental regulations is the extension service. The National Coffee Research Institute has undertaken a number of surveys to optimise technology, and offer seminars and support. NGOs, supported by international donor funds, also undertake research. The first private-public-partnerships have also been established.

---

3 The costs varied between US$ 150.000 and US$ 600.000 depending on the size of the processing unit and the necessary improvements. Some companies had to buy new land to build sediment tanks.

Reduced fuel wood consumption during the drying process is not yet regulated by legislation. The reason is the absence of technological alternatives: the drying of the coffee must take place in the rainy season. In most regions this renders the use of solar energy useless. More efficient methods of using fuel wood are being explored in the context of certification with ISO 14.001.

4.4 Tax Policy in Costa Rica

While organic agriculture and natural resource management is supported by environmental regulations, trade policy has a hampering effect. In particular, the calculation of export tax must be examined in this context. The tax is charged according to the export price and not according to the volume exported. In times of falling world market prices, exporters pay less tax. At first glance this regulation makes sense. But exporters of organic coffee are disadvantaged as they have to pay more tax due to the higher price of certified coffee.

The import of organic products to the EU requires higher bureaucratic effort than the import of conventional products. Companies that would like to import products from non-EU countries have to comply with the EU regulations. Furthermore the countries have to be generally certified. This means that organic coffee can be imported from countries that are on the EU list of "third countries" or certified countries. It is important that the organisations specified in the regulations have indeed been monitoring production, processing and export. Organic coffee from non-EU countries that are not part of the third country list can only be imported once the importer gets special permission to import the product.

Many importers feel that the requirement to disclose their trade contacts and the increased bureaucracy hinder their entry into this market segment. Imports became even more difficult as a result of the 2000 regulation by which every certified product has to be physically accompanied by a certificate. In the context of necessary control, these restrictive barriers can only be eased to a limited extent.

4.5 Using Synergies

International and national environmental regulations in combination with market internal instruments can have an enhancing or hampering effect. While the international guidelines aim at harmonising standards and try to prevent discrimination ("protectionism in a green coat"), the advantages of national government action should be seen in two ways:

Firstly, if the organic market was not regulated by the state, a number private programmes would exist. These would not be able to fulfil the functions of a label as demonstrated by the numerous "bio-scandals" in Europe during the 1980s. Government regulations are thus necessary to prevent confusing the consumer with a multiplicity of labels, and to protect the consumer from dishonest suppliers.

Secondly, it is important that problems are addressed in a certain time frame: if grave and irreversible damage occurs (as in the case of water being polluted by processing facilities), rapid action is required. This cannot be addressed by international regulations without compromising the sovereignty of states. Instruments that achieve their influence through changes in the relative prices of commodities and thus influence the adaptation of practices operate over long periods of time and are too slow if rapid action is demanded (see Troja 1998, pp. 49f).

Looking at the degree of adaptability of the Costa Rican processors to existing environmental standards it should be noted that only 1% of coffee is produced organically. The impact of state regulations is much more effective and could additionally lead to the adoption of a market internal environmental label. But political and administrative support are preconditions for environmental regulations, and may not be forthcoming if they are seen to have a negative influence on economic interests.

In future possible synergy effects between environmental improvement through state legislation and economic incentives through market internal instruments should be used. Neither market instruments nor state regulations alone can solve the social dilemma. New creative forms have to be found to combine an ecological impact with an increased competitive advantage.

5 Conclusions

The requirements of environmental production standards are high: they should support environmentally friendly production systems and at the same time open up new economic avenues for the people involved. How can they fulfil these expectations? A general answer cannot be given. The environmental problems of coffee production are complex and multidimensional and the different standards only address a relatively small part of them, in accordance with the focus area chosen in each case (e.g. use of chemical inputs, soil erosion, loss of habitats). Each standard has its own problem of fit: either to match with the physical properties of the environment or with the requirements of the market.

However, it is not useful to try to understand each of the standards in isolation, as the interplay between them is a complex one ranging from competition to co-operation. The crucial competitive capacity of a standard that gives it a "cutting edge" is determined by its position in the market, i.e. when it comes to addressing and convincing the consumer. Similar to the conventional sector, the attention of the customer is the key resource that determines market competition in the market for certified coffee.

However, state and multilateral environmental and trade legislation also have both supporting and limiting impacts. Problems with adaptation are not necessarily due to the internal functions of a standard, but have to be understood in the context of the legislative environment, especially in the area of trade and environmental policy. The effect of a standard programme can therefore not be seen in isolation but always has to be seen in relation to the impact of other formal institutions.

If environmental standards are to do justice to the complexity of the socio-ecological dilemma, they have to fulfil a number of diverse criteria that are difficult to combine with each other. On the one hand economic efficiency is highly significant and is reached through reduced transaction costs or higher profits. The former can only be realised if the various legislation is harmonised. The alternative is that the organic sector remains a niche market where personal contact replaces costly transaction costs. However, this will not achieve the ecological aims of the standards as impact will remain very limited. In the recent past the transaction costs of all certification programmes have risen due to new or increased monitoring and control mechanisms. Clearly higher profits are only achieved in organic agriculture due to higher price levels. There is increased inter-dependence amongst actors along the production chain and insecurity as to whether the benefits of the higher prices achieved from the consumer do indeed reach the producers to cover the higher costs. These problems have not yet been addressed adequately.

The second important criterion is ecological effectiveness. This depends on broad acceptance amongst producers, traders and consumers of the strictness of the application of regulations and the existence of appropriate agricultural and processing techniques adapted to the regional and local framework conditions.

Increased demand in the coffee trade can thus induce new, more environmentally adapted processes and practices. These can have a broad impact as the multiplicity of standards creates a situation in which "everyone finds something". Nevertheless, a significant improvement of the environment in producer countries cannot yet be observed, as currently too few producers participate in organic, sustainable production. To achieve far greater environmental impact, state measures are more effective. Non-implementation of conservation measures can be sanctioned. The actors can respond individually to new state regulations, contrary to market internal institutions where the entire production chain has to be included.

Environmental production standards are clearly not the magic tool to solve all the problems of global change overnight. Thus far they have not even triggered noticeable change in the coffee industry as a whole. The "discovery of the market" does not replace the responsibilities of national and international environmental policy. In the contrary: with the introduction of environmental market internal institutions a new and complex field for political measures (e.g. market regulation, support programmes, agricultural extension) has been created. First attempts to link the guiding mechanisms of market and state regulations can already be identified.

References

CEC (Commission for Environmental Cooperation)(1999): Measuring Consumer Interest in Mexican Shade-Grown Coffee: An Assessment of the Canadian, Mexican and US markets. Montreal

CEC (2000): Experts Workshop on Shade-Grown Coffee, Oaxaca, Mexico, 29-30 March 2000, Backround Note for Participating Experts. Oaxaca

Gawel, Erik (1994): Ökonomie der Umwelt – ein Überblick über neuere Entwicklungen. In: Zeitschrift für angewandte Umweltforschung; Vol. 7; pp. 37-84

ICAFE (Instiuto del Café de Costa Rica)(1998): Leyes y Decretos Relativos al Café. San José

ICAFE (1999): Liquidación Final de la Cosecha 1998-1999. San José

ITC (International Trade Centre)(1999): Organic Food and Beverages: World Supply and Major European Markets. Geneva

Keohane, Robert/Peter Haas/Marc Levy (1993): The Effectiveness of International Environmental Institutions. In: Haas/Keohane/Levy (eds.): Institutions for the earth. Sources of effective international environmental protection. Cambridge; pp. 3-24

Landmann, Ute (1999): Umweltzeichen und ethische Warenzeichen: Werden sie im Rahmen des internationalen Handelsabkommen GATT/WTO anerkannt?. In: GTZ (ed.): Reader zu Umwelt- und Sozialstandards. Eschborn

Massarat, Mohssen (1993): Endlichkeit der Natur und Überfluß in der Marktökonomie – Schritte zum Gleichgewicht. Marburg

McLean, Jennifer (1998): Merging Ecological and Social Criteria for Agriculture: the Case of Coffee. Washington D.C.

Muscheler, Roland (1999): Arboles en Cafetales, Modulo de Enseñanza Agroforestal 5 CATIE/GTZ. Turialba

North, Douglas (1998): Institutions, Institutional Change and Economic Performance. Reprint; Cambridge

Paarlberg, Robert (1993): Managing Pesticide Use in Developing Countries. In: Haas/Keohane/Levy (eds.): Institutions for the Earth, Sources of Effective International Environmental Protection. Cambridge; pp. 309-350

Rice, Paul/ Jennifer McLean (1999): Sustainable Coffee at the Crossroads, a Report to the Consumer´s Choice Council. Washington D.C.

Rice, Robert/Justin Ward (1996): Coffee, Conservation, and Commerce in the Western Hemisphere. How Individuals and Institutions Can Promote Ecologically Sound Farming and Forest Management in Nothern Latin America. Washington D.C.

Ruloff, Dieter (1999): Kompatibilitätsprobleme internationaler Regime: Theoretischer Hintergrund und Forschungsfragen. In: Bernauer/Ruloff (eds.): Handel und Umwelt. Zur Frage der Kompatibilität internationaler Regime. Opladen; pp. 13-40

Rundgren, Gunnar (1997): Building Trust in Organics – A Guide to Setting up Organic Certification Programmes. Jamestown, Tholey-Theley

Saxenian, Michael (1996): Conservation through Sustainable Enterprise. In: Proceedings of the 1st Sustainable Coffee Conference, Sept. 1996. Washington D.C.; pp. 263-267

Schmidt, Hans-Peter/Manon Haccius (1996): EU-Regulation 'Organic-Farming': A Legal and Agro-Ecological Commentary. Eschborn

Troja, Markus (1998): Umweltpolitik und moderne Ökonomik; der Beitrag der neuen politischen Ökonomie und der Institutionenökonomik zur Erklärung umweltpolitischer Entscheidungsprozesse. Studien zur internationalen Umweltpolitik No. 9. Münster

UNCTAD (United Nations Conference on Trade and Development)(1993): Fostering Sustainable Development in the Commodity Field. Experiences Concerning Environmental Effects of Commodity Production and Processing: Synthesis of Case Studies on Cocoa, Coffee and Rice. Washington D.C.

Utting, Peter (2000): Business Responsibility for Sustainable Development. UNRISD Occasional Paper 2. Geneva

Willer, Helga/M. Yuseffi (2000): Organic Agriculture World-Wide. Stiftung Ökologie und Landbau – Special Edition No. 74. Bad Dürkheim

Windfuhr, Michael (1999): Durchsetzung sozialer und ökologischer Standards im Welthandel – ökologisches und soziales Labelling. In: GTZ (ed.): Reader zu Umwelt- und Sozialstandards. Eschborn

Wycherley, Ian (1999): Greening Supply Chains: The Case of the Body Shop International. In: Business Strategy and the Environment; Vol. 8; No. 2; pp. 120-127

Young, Oran (1999): Institutional Dimensions of Global Environmental Change: Science Plan. International Human Dimensions Programme on Global Environmental Change Report No. 9. Bonn

Part II: Linking Institutions to Social Practice

Heiko Breit

Introduction

Whereas Part I of this book shed light on the effectiveness of institutional arrangements in providing or securing public goods by policy makers, the contributions of Part II demonstrate that institutional change cannot be reduced to a "top-down process". Formal institutions only change by the social practice of social actors which is always embedded in cultural worldviews and social rule systems. Moreover, formal institutions themselves and their functions are interpreted within the framework of cultural norms, values and understandings. This wider conceptual approach and understanding of institutional change is presented in the second part of the book. Here, the relationship between formal institutions and *informal* institutions is analysed. Worldviews, shared beliefs, knowledge dispositions, norms, non-codified regulations, values, expectations and social relations play a central role for social learning processes.

Several questions will be addressed in the contributions to Part II. To what extent do highly complex institutional arrangements depend on worldviews, intersubjectively shared norms and values, social relations and individual responsibility? How do informal institutions interact with each other and how do they interact with formal institutions? What types of dynamics do we find at different levels of society: individual and collective action; values, norms and social relations; interacting societal subsystems? What kinds of changes do they undergo, how do these changes occur and what do they imply for institutional change in general?

Informal institutions can be seen as a direct link to social practice and interaction processes of social actors. They integrate objective and subjective action frames and bridge the gap between individual thinking and social functioning. Knowledge about informal institutions helps to understand the reasons why changes which are conceived as necessary sometimes succeed and sometimes fail. However, it would be shortsighted to understand them only as "constraints" or independent variables of institutional change. New or more environmentally sound institutions such as policy regimes, environmental legislation or sets of organisational units established to manage an environmental problem can also be the outcome of changing risk perceptions, values and social relations based on notions of responsibility or justice. Informal institutions can also, therefore, initiate processes of change and provide the grounds for legitimacy of formal institutional arrangements by increasing awareness and concern for environmental problems.

This perspective on informal institutions and social action includes a broad variety of ways of seeing, ways of doing and ways of speaking. Different worldviews and risk perceptions are part of and contribute to different forms of social practice including different forms of communication. The contributions of Part II therefore call for a multi-dimensional approach and an interdisciplinary perspective. Often, this includes the notion of participation which involves not only a variety of social actors but also social actors at different levels of social organisation, both system- and action-oriented, private and public, local, national and international and individual and collective.

The three papers of this section make use of the disciplinary perspectives of sociology (Engels), cultural psychology (Breit/Döring/Eckensberger) and cultural anthropology (Widlok). They seek answers to the questions outlined above. The first analyses discourses on climate change in the realms of science, politics and the mass media in two different national contexts (Germany, USA). The second contribution focusses on social actors' individual responsibility for remedial action which is understood as depending on their perspective of the scope for within formal institutions such as law and politics. The third paper analyses a number of interacting layers of a complex property regime, exploring both culturalist and individualist approaches to institutional change in one setting in Namibia.

These different disciplinary approaches represent different societal levels: national and international discourses of societal subsystems, ideal types of individual arguments in civil society and clusters of social relationships in a specific local arena. Each paper analyses informal institutions as *differences* in the "ways of seeing" (perceptions of environmental risk), "ways of doing" (modes of behaviour or social practice) and "ways of speaking" (discourses about environmental problem-solving).

Engels demonstrates that no global consensus exists on how to deal with the problem of global climate change. She discusses the question of how risk discourses help to institutionalise a specific risk perception by de-institutionalising others. However, these processes of institutionalisation may be valid in one national setting but confront conflicting perceptions and institutionalised solutions in other national settings. Breit, Döring and Eckensberger show how different understandings of individual responsibility can be interpreted as a result of justice judgements rather than the result of objective (and more or less external) conditions. These justice judgements can themselves be subject to change as they become more complex and represent more advanced levels of moral orientation. Widlok describes the differentiated dynamics of analytical layers such as cultural values, cultural regulations, social relations and social actions, and analyses how changes which take place at one layer trigger off changes at another layer or sometimes clash with changes (or the lack thereof) at any of the other layers.

In this way the contributions help elucidate interactions between informal and formal institutions and between local contexts of social practice and global processes of change. Differences in risk discourses between science, politics and the media, differences in the complexity of justice judgements and related concepts of individual responsibility and differences in institutional layers with changing cultural values, regulations, relations and social actions do not only emphasise the importance of informal institutions for social learning, but also demonstrate that institutional change does not occur in a one-dimensional and monolithic way. Institutions do not change as complete entities or as tightly knotted packages, but rather in a discontinuous way with varying speeds and dynamics at different levels. Worldviews collide and either permeate one another or remain mutually exclusive; different justice judgements coexist or compete in public discourses; and innovations only touch upon certain layers whereas others remain untouched by them. The findings in these contributions furthermore show an overlap between environmental institutions and other institutions which may, at first sight, have nothing to do with human-environment interactions. Pathways of social learning for environmentally sustainable institutions, therefore, are deeply rooted in day-to-day social practice, depending on the interaction between different formal institutions (economics, law, politics, administration), between different informal institutions (informal norms, values, interests) and, lastly, between informal and formal institutions.

Anita Engels

Institutionalisation of Ecological Risk Perceptions: The Role of Climate Change Discourses in Germany[1]

1 Introduction: Perceptions of Global Climate Change

Public perceptions of climatic events have changed dramatically over the past two decades. Once, climate change (or weather) was widely thought of as a natural source of calamities to which humans can only try to adapt. Moreover, the climate in one world region appeared more or less unconnected to other regions' climates. However, in the 1990s a new perception emerged and became dominant. Now, the world climate is perceived as one interconnected global system. And, most importantly, it appears to be a system with which humans have interfered dangerously, which humans have actively put at risk and the evolution of which is dependent on human activity. What once was perceived as a natural source of good and bad has now changed into a manmade ecological risk. Accordingly, global environmental management is a new guiding principle for international politics. It was the institutionalisation of the new risk perception that enabled societies to react to this ecological risk. This chapter analyses the process through which this new perception was institutionalised in Germany between 1975 and 1995. It discusses this process as an example of social learning. The main finding is that this institutionalisation made possible the adoption of strict targets for a national climate protection policy. However, this refers to the national context only. It will also be argued that this risk perception may not be appropriate anymore for the rapidly changing world of international environmental politics. Negotiations between many different nation-states often require social learning at a higher, transnational level. In cases like these, the de-institutionalisation of old and the re-institutionalisation of new risk perceptions may also be a necessary step of social learning.

---

1   This chapter summarises the results of a project by Peter Weingart, Petra Pansegrau and Anita Engels at the Institute for Science and Technology Studies (IWT), University of Bielefeld, Germany. The project on "Climate communications between science, politics and the mass media" was funded by the German Research Council (DFG) as part of the German section of the International Human Dimensions Programme (IHDP) (see Weingart et al. 2000; 2002).

2 Worldviews, Risk Perceptions and Social Action

Risk perceptions are embedded in broader and more general worldviews. The neo-institutionalist approach in sociology allows the understanding of institutional change in terms of the emergence and stabilisation of worldviews (for an overview, see Hasse/Krücken 1999; Jepperson 2001). Worldviews include assumptions about what the world is like, which problems we have to deal with and which solutions are appropriate to tackle these problems (Thompson/Rayner 1998). In other words, our worldviews tell us who we are and how we are supposed to act.[2] These worldviews do not simply exist, but they evolve over time and become stabilised. With regard to environmental problems a worldwide reconceptualisation of nature itself occured within the last 100 to 150 years. Whereas at the end of the 19th century nature was often depicted in spiritual terms, by the end of the 20th century a nature-as-ecosystem concept has gained worldwide prominence (Frank 1997). In this concept "each component of nature is dependent on the larger natural system for exchanges of energy and matter. *Homo sapiens* is but one species in the larger biosphere, which itself is subsumed within a larger physical universe (...). The basic notion in the ecosystem model is that nature, including a naturalized human society, constitutes an integrated physical system" (Frank 1997, p. 418). The rise of a science-based worldview of nature as the ecosystem on which society depends in an encompassing sense helped establish a worldwide environmental regime. Environmental concern is now a global concern shared by individual actors, organisations and even nation-states on a worldwide scale and embodied in a multitude of international environmental treaties (Meyer et al. 1997; Frank et al. 1999; Frank et al. 2000).

In contrast to these broad and sweeping changes that occured over relatively long time periods this chapter is confined to a more concrete example of risk perception – that of global climate change – and to a more short-term perspective that takes into account two recent decades only. However, it can be demonstrated that even in this "short" period fundamental changes in the perception and the definition of the problem have occured.

Climate change is not directly perceivable, and science has identified huge uncertainties. There is no worldwide consensus on what the problem is and how it should be treated. With regard to climate change several distinct risk perceptions exist, incompatible with one another (Thompson/Rayner 1998, p. 294). They exist in parallel, and groups that adhere to these incompatible views are struggling for dominance at every level of decision making, from local municipalities to the international sphere of treaty negotiations. The identification and definition of the problem, therefore, is a non-trivial and

---

2 For a discussion of a typology of worldviews and their implications for morality, see Breit/Döring/Eckensberger in this volume.

conflictuous process. However, it is not totally undetermined or arbitrary either. Stabilisations (often in the form of consensus) have emerged over time, a process which will be termed in the following the institutionalisation of ecological risk perceptions. Institutionalisation means stabilisation and the development of some degree of persistence. Once institutionalised, risk perceptions get accepted as normal, obvious and natural; they are not questioned anymore and do not require further sanctioning (Zucker 1977). This taken-for-grantedness is a powerful source of the effectiveness of institutions (Berger/Luckmann 1967).

Ecological risk perceptions as understood in this chapter are examples of *informal* institutions. They are non-codified and they are the outcome of an unplanned and unintended process rather than that of willful action. In his chapter on the spatial reorganisation of water management in the European Union, Moss mentions paranthetically the institutionalisation of a scientific understanding of a resource management problem, namely the ecocentric view which helped generate new management forms (this volume). Here, the institutionalisation of a specific understanding of the climate change problem is placed centre stage. Risk perceptions provide an orientation for actors and they separate legitimate and appropriate forms of action and actorhood from the illegitimate and the inappropriate. Social practice is thus embedded in informal institutions. Social learning, in this sense, refers to the stabilisation and normalisation of a respective risk perception. Often this process involves the creation of new *formal* institutions such as new policy regimes, environmental legislation or a new set of organisational units to manage the environmental problem, so it also says something about the interplay between formal and informal institutions (Young 2002).[3] However, the process of institutionalisation also bears the danger of losing too much flexibility. Particularly in the case of formal institutions institutional path dependency precludes many alternative options, and institutional capture renders innovations difficult or even impossible (Dobbin 1994; Walker 2000). Thus, sometimes phases of destabilisation and de-institutionalisation are needed to allow for new forms of social practice to emerge (Jepperson 1991).

3 Discourses and the Institutionalisation of Risk Perceptions

Debates about climate change are not new, they date back to the classical age and have resurfaced in different forms and guises ever since (von Storch/Stehr 2000). However, the question is why it was in the 1980s and

---

3 On the importance of formal institutions for climate change, see O'Riordan/Jordan (1996).

1990s that this issue gained such a prominence in public debate and was placed on the political agenda then. Discourse analysis can provide useful answers to this question, and this section will briefly elaborate the theoretical approach that was adopted in the project.

Discourses abound. They stabilise and legitimise risk perceptions, they generate problem definitions and general frames in which issues can be understood, and they constitute actors and actorhood in a given field and provide scripts for legitimate action (Meyer/Jepperson 2000). If discourses gain prominence they tend to have effects of control, discipline and normalisation in many aspects of social life (Foucault 1990). Discourses emerge around specific issues and evolve over time. They structure areas of knowledge and social practice (Fairclough 1992). Stabilisations can be observed as well as discursive shifts. Where do these discourses come from? In this project it is assumed that there is not one overarching societal discourse but that a multitude of discourses exist, sometimes as if in parallel universes, sometimes interfering with each other rather directly (Weingart/Engels/Pansegrau 2000). Several societal fields can be identified that produce discourses of a specific kind. Science, politics and the mass media have been in the centre of this analysis, as three important locations where discourses often emerge.[4]

"Science" here means the set of institutes, universities and expert bodies that engage in research and use scientific theories and methodologies to generate new and generalisable understandings of the world or, in more applied fields, to provide knowledge and technologies with which all kinds of problems can be addressed. The search for new questions is the driving force that produces discourses in this field. "Politics" here means those formal institutions that generate decisions which are binding for a certain electorate, with the national electorate at the centre of the analysis. The need to win elections and to create an identity which is different from that of the political opponent is the driving force for discourses in politics. The "mass media", finally, are the ensemble of printed or broadcasted publications that appear in great number and address in a very general sense the broader public. The newsworthiness and the attraction of issues for the imaginary reader is the main driving force of media discourses. Interactions between these societal fields and the different discourses they generate is an important source for the institutionalisation of world views and ecological risk perceptions.[5]

---

4   For a more complete account of theories and methodologies applied in this project, see Weingart et al. (2002).

5   It should be mentioned that this type of discourse analysis privileges the view on the unplanned and unintended outcomes of social processes over the analysis of willful acts of individual actors. Even though interventions by actors of course take place it is assumed here that discourses constitute actors and actorhood. However, this is obviously a theoretical choice rather than an ontological statement.

4 Analysing Discourses: The Data Used

Discourses on climate change can be analysed in the form of texts of written or spoken language that are the typical forms of expression in the fields of science, politics and the mass media: scientific publications, political debates and press articles. The analysis is based on a huge body of texts that cover the period from 1975-1995.

The scientific discourse manifests itself in scientific publications, i.e. peer-reviewed articles, monographs and edited volumes, and contributions to periodicals of scientific associations. However, the production of scientific literature on climate change and related issues is so overwhelming that it was necessary to select a smaller sample of central articles that have influenced the scientific discourse.[6] Bibliometric analysis (citation rates) was used to determine the centrality and importance of authors and publications, and 23 articles were selected covering the full period of 1975-1995.

The political discourse is documented in the proceedings of debates in the German Bundestag (national parliament) and in related commissions. The analysis is based on verbatim minutes of every plenary session of parliament dealing with climate change (115 sessions) and minutes of working sessions of the parliamentary commission on "Environment, Nature Conservation and Nuclear Safety", established in 1987, in which climate change figured as a topic (45 sessions).

The climate change discourse in the mass media, finally, also required a careful selection of sources. The sample consists of 478 news texts from the weekly news magazine, *Der Spiegel*, and the daily newspapers the *Frankfurter Allgemeine Zeitung* and the *Süddeutsche Zeitung*. News coverage on climate change in *Der Spiegel* is completely covered in this sample; coverage in the *Frankfurter Allgemeine Zeitung* is added for six selected years, and a special series of the *Süddeutsche Zeitung* is included.[7]

Discursive events were identified that resulted in the stabilisation of specific meanings and definitions (taken-for-grantedness), or in discursive shifts. For each of the three discourses, a discourse profile was identified, comprising the chronological order of distinct phases, central definitions and metaphors, and basically the discursive means by which climate change is established as an arena of political decision making in each of these spheres. The main results will be summarised in the sections below.

---

6   Between 1990 and 1995 scientific publications on climate change per year nearly quintupled in Germany (Schwechheimer 1997).
7   For a full account of methodological choices and the sources that have been analysed, see Weingart et al. (2000), and Weingart et al. (2002), Pansegrau (2000); for an early account of the results, see also Engels and Weingart (1997).

5 The Perception of Global Climate Change in Germany

Broader attention for global climate change in Germany originated in the field of science. At the beginning of the 20th century it was difficult to imagine that the global climate would ever become an important field of research. Even though some basic theories about the world climate, its most important driving forces and the possibility of a manmade global climate change were already known by then (Arrhenius 1896, Fourier 1827), important technologies to observe the earth and generate a reliable overall picture were lacking. Satellites and computers, the key technologies in this field, only became broadly available in the 1970s and 1980s, and for German scientists later than for leading American scientists.[8] However, through a series of international conferences scientific attention for the issue began to rise, so that in the first decade of the analysis (1975 – 1985) a scientific discourse on global climate change slowly emerged.

Driven by a general concern for potentially negative impacts of global climate change on human life on earth, the scientific discourse focused on several aspects that helped link the physical and bio-chemical properties of the earth's atmosphere to human action. Trace gases were identified as driving forces for major climatic dynamics. These trace gases were then separated by source as either natural or anthropogenic, and while natural sources were considered important, attention shifted more and more to anthropogenic sources. They were linked to human activities such as industrial production, energy consumption, agricultural practices, etc. Early on, the scientific discourse identified two different groups of ‚culprits': industrial nations emitting trace gases because of their high levels of fossil fuel consumption and developing countries causing atmospheric problems through deforestation and rapid population growth. Industrial countries' emissions had greatly accumulated in the past and were continuing to do so in the present, whereas developing countries' influence on the climate was predicted to grow more important in the future. By identifying human causes for future climate change and potential impacts of this change on human life, the scientific discourse created a view on climate and climate change that was centred around human activities. Climate appeared as a global system with which humans inadvertantly interfered. The "interferability" of such a large-scale system was an important change of perception, implying for the first time that this global system could be the object of wilful human manipulation in the form of global environmental management[9] to stop the impending man-made climate change through some kind of technical or political measures (Engels/Weingart 1997).

---

[8] The German meteorologist Hermann Flohn, personal communication, September 8, 1995.
[9] See also some results of the social learning project on global environmental management (The Social Learning Group 2001a, b) in Huber's contribution to this volume.

In this same period the German Parliament only rarely dealt with climate change as an issue (Graph 1). If at all, politicians emphasised scientific uncertainties that did not seem to imply a need for new policies. In parliament climate change was mostly seen as a potential issue for research, but not as a legitimate issue for political decision-making.

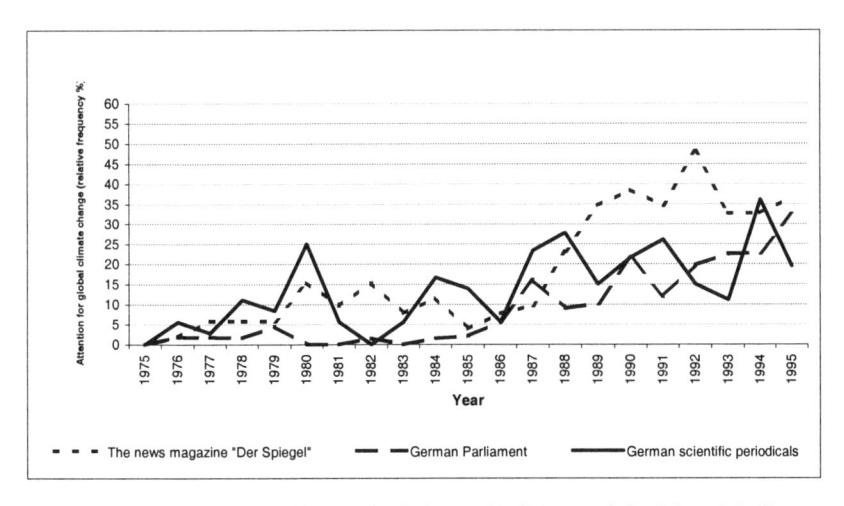

Graph 1: Global Climate Change in Science, Politics and the Mass Media

The mass media in Germany reacted slightly differently. Early article headlines show that the media, and in particular the news magazine *Der Spiegel*, sensationalised scientific scenarios and depicted global climate change as a deadly threat. Articles were titled "Death in the greenhouse" (*Der Spiegel* 9/1979), "All over in 50 years" (*Der Spiegel* 11/1980), and "Heading for the catastrophe" (*Der Spiegel* 21/1981). However, even though climate change appeared in the print media more often than it appeared on the agenda of the German Parliament, it did not become a dominant theme before the late 1980s (Graph 1). So both the amount of attention for climate change and the way in which it was perceived as a problem varied substantially accross the three fields of science, politics and the mass media.

Some important events provided the background for the developments in the second decade of the analysis (1986-1995). The nuclear accident of the Tschernobyl plant in 1986 provoked a rapid and longlasting politicisation of the German public over environmental concerns and the question of how to secure Germany's future energy consumption (Hatch 1995). In the aftermath of the accident a new Ministry for Environment, Nature Protection and Nuclear Safety (BMU) was created, and for the first time environmental policy was institutionalised as an independent policy domain. As polls indicate, environmental concern was one of the public's most important concerns at that time; it even became the most important concern in 1989 before it fell back behind the more immediate concern for the process of the German reunification (IPOS 1991).

These events helped discourses on climate change to gain momentum. In 1986 a group of energy experts (the Working Group Energy of the German Physical Association) published a memorandum warning politicians and the public of an impending climate catastrophe with impacts that would be felt rather directly, such as the flooding of the German plains caused by the melting of the arctic iceshields. Among other possible ways to prevent this horror scenario, the memorandum suggested the extended use of nuclear energy to curb down energy related CO_2 emissions. This warning triggered attention both in the mass media and in the German Parliament. Some members of parliament used the warning to exert pressure on the government. The language of urgency used in the warning helped to do that. At first, the government reacted in the same manner it had done before – emphasise the uncertainties and define it as a research problem. However, pressure grew stronger and after only a few months the scientists' warning had attracted so much attention that it could not be ignored or dismissed anymore. Soon after, the warning (in a slightly modified form) was backed up by the German Physical Association and the German Meteorological Association, a move that strengthened the warning's credibility and institutional leverage (DPG/DMG 1987).

Parliament appointed an Enquête Commission to assemble scientific facts, define the problem and suggest ways to deal with it. The scientific discourse grew more important in these years. General attention to climate change rose in all three fields. In contrast to the different discursive developments in the first decade, the second decade under study reveals more congruent dynamics. The discourses on climate change in science, politics and the mass media reinforced and amplified one another. The scientific discourse provided more elaborate knowledge on the amount to which each country contributed to the global problem through its country specific emissions (Subak 1996), on the potential impacts of climate change on human societies and on available policy options to either prevent climate change or adapt to its negative consequences. Even though in later publications scientific warnings were less dramatic and did not use the term climate *catastrophe* anymore the initial warning attracted broad media attention. The mass media adopted the term climate catastrophe and used it as an organising metaphor, i.e. a metaphor that structures the perception of the problem. In the political discourse the term climate catastrophe gained prominence as well. To the end of the period under study this metaphor was used in parliamentary debates to evoke the urgency and the seriousness of the problem. Through the rising media attention for climate change political pressure grew stronger. The media also transformed the inherent uncertainty of a scientific hypothesis into the certainty of the future catastrophe and thus created the political need to act (Pansegrau 2000). The Enquête Commission played an important role especially in its first working period from 1987 to 1990, when it served to consolidate the scientific facts around climate change and provided the necessary credibility of this scientific assessment through consensual reports (Enquête Commission 1990a, 1990b, 1990c, 1991).

By the early 1990s perceptions of climate change in Germany had changed considerably. The scientific discourse had communicated the warning and in the following years consolidated the knowledge base that served as a scientific assessment of the risk. The media discourse made climate change a public issue, treated the scientific warning as the certainty of the coming catastrophe and called for urgent and drastic political action. The political discourse switched from a mode of passive observation to a mode of promoting political action at all levels of society and, in particular, through international negotiations. This resulted in the 1990 commitment of the German government to a 25 percent reduction of domestic CO_2 emissions. The perception of the risk of man-made climate change had been institutionalised by then, and it was institutionalised as the coming catastrophe that called for urgent action and wide-ranging political regulation. The following section will discuss the implications of this new risk perception for the development of a climate protection policy in Germany.

6 The Power of Discourse: From the Natural to the Political Arena

Several elements of the new risk perception need mentioning here, as they have important implications for the range of potential solutions that appear as possible and legitimate:

- the interferability of the earth's climate,
- the global dimension of the problem,
- the self-identification as the culprit and therefore responsibility for averting the catastrophe and
- the perceived need for changes in lifestyles and very general features of current society.

The scientific discourse generated a view on climate that was centered around human action. The interferability of the world climate was an important precondition for the development of political programmes to prevent climate change. It means shifting the boundaries between the natural and the artificial toward a new area for legitimate political intervention. Only if the global climate of today was 'artificial' or man-made in character, could governments hope to have a stance for environmental regulation. If, on the other hand, the climate's evolution was driven by purely natural factors, humans could not possibly hope to change its future course. The repercussions of this discursive shift were felt in the political discourse from the late 1980s on, but it took a few more years before it became institutionalised as a general frame of reference for political action. The perception and evaluation of extreme weather events like heavy rainfall and storms demonstrate this dynamic clearly. When the Minister of the Environment reported in the parliamentary commission on "Environment, Nature Conservation and Nuclear Safety" on possible causes of severe floods that occurred in Germany in early 1988, he took unusually heavy rainfalls as proof of the *natural* character of the event.

In the Rhine area, the precipitation of March 1988 was the highest in the last 100 years, *a fact proving the natural cause of this dramatic flood development.* (...) One cannot direct one's attention to one spectacular flooding only, *as no one can do anything about precipitation* (...). (Report of Töpfer in the committee on causes of the flood catastrophe in the areas of Rhine, Main and Danube; 4.5.1988, protocol: 25/8; 25/14; 11th legislative period; emphasis added).

Just a few years later, this pattern of reasoning was questioned and no longer considered legitimate. A series of storms in spring 1990 was used to criticise the slow progress of a climate protection policy:

(Member of Parliament): Hurricanes, storm tides and the climate protection policy of the government – this is on the agenda. The storms of the past weeks have with incredible force cut aisles through our forests, removed roofs and let storm tides roll against the coast. Sylt reports a 10 meter landloss, insurance companies report damages in the billions and many people were directly affected. (...) Do you really want to wait until even stronger storms destroy our parliament? (...) Shall hail from tropical thunderstorms destroy the harvest? Are 30, 40 million metres of destroyed wood in our forests in 4 weeks not enough? Do you want to wait until millions of refugees flee the consequences of climate change and knock on our doors? (11th legislative period, 200th session, 8.3.1990, pp. 15477-78).

The debate about possible causes of the extraordinary floods in 1995 show even more clearly that, compared to 1988, a new risk perception was institutionalised:

(Member of Parliament): We discussed the effects of the flood catastrophe here in the Bundestag just a few weeks ago. We reached a relative consensus that climatic changes were playing a considerable role in it. (13th legislative period, 30th session, 29.3.1995, p. 2257)

Quotes like these indicate that by 1995 the perception of the interferability of the world climate was institutionalised to the point that human action was directly responsible for extreme weather events, and in return also for preventing these events in the future.

The global dimension of the problem of climate change is another important element of the new risk perception. In connection with the term climate catastrophe the all-embracing framework of the global catastrophe implied that climate change emerged as a meta-problem that included all other environmental crises on earth. In parliament, this was reflected in many of the debates, growing stronger in the wake of the UN Conference on Environment and Development in Rio de Janeiro in 1992, with quotes stemming both from members of the government and the opposition.

(Undersecretary of Parliament): The changes of the world climate due to the slow accumulation of the earth's atmosphere with carbon dioxide and other trace gases reveal a completely new dimension of environmental policy. (11th legislative period, 194th session, 8.2.1990, p. 14880)

(Member of Parliament): Because we still waste so much energy, we are already responsible for current climate changes, for growing environmental damages and for radioactive dangers. Without a drastic reform of our energy supply we will directly give rise to the impending climate catastrophe. (11th legislative period, 215th session, 20.6.1990, p. 17094)

(Member of Parliament): The health and the lives of all people and the balance of the whole biosphere on earth is at stake. We are at risk in a global sense, and only globally are we capable of taking up this challenge and succeeding. I think only together can we survive. (11th legislative period, 232nd session, 26.10.1990, p. 18458)

(Member of Parliament): To prevent the climate catastrophe is not a question of the environment but a question of the organisation of societies and therefore of politics. ... This is about the question of the sustainability of human society. (12th legislative period, 23rd session, 25.4.1991, p. 1558)

(Member of Parliament): I want to remind you of this: Climate protection is ultimately about the preservation of civil society. We only have this one planet. (13th legislative period, 6th session, 20.1.1995, p. 794)

The institutionalisation of a perception of climate change as a truly global problem that potentially endangers human life on earth helped to create political commitment and made possible the declaration of the stringent CO_2 reduction target of 25 percent.

This target was also an expression of another element of the new risk perception: the self-identification as culprit and therefore acceptance of responsibility for averting the catastrophe. The political discourse was centred around domestic action, albeit in an internationally co-ordinated way. The perception that was generated was strongly influenced by notions of justice and fairness. It was perceived as the only right way that those responsible are liable for damages and should seek to prevent damages in the first place. This view more or less excluded developing countries from being responsible and accepted their needs for further economic development. It was further supported by a whole range of scientific attempts to identify policy options that would allow Germany to substantially reduce its country specific emissions even in the absence of international co-operation. The Enquête Commission discussed the viability of different energy production and consumption paths (Enquête Commission 1990a, 1990b). Some years later the Wuppertal Institute for Climate, Environment, Energy published a study on options for a sustainable Germany which had been commissioned by two NGOs (BUND/Misereor 1996). In later years it proved problematic to implement the deep cuts in Germany's emission levels (Bach 1995), but the voluntary reduction target of 25 percent from 1990 symbolised the specificity of this risk perception.

In line with this, another aspect of the risk perception needs to be emphasised. The global dimension of the problem, its urgency and the self-identification as a culprit opened the way for some radical concepts of change. Not only technical options were discussed but also more radical notions of a new type of society, one that was not oriented towards more and faster production, mobility and consumption, but on the contrary a more post-materialist society in which slowness, solidarity and less consumption were valued. This is not to say that this was a majority perception but concepts like this gained broad public attention through media coverage and through publications like those of the Wuppertal Institute. Even though this was not seriously discussed in parliament, current lifestyles were part of the problem definition that was generated by the political discourse, and changing them appeared an important element of the solution. Other solutions were less acceptable because they were perceived as the direct continuation and even intensification of lifestyles that had been identified as unsustainable and unfair. Two policy options which later gained prominence in the international negotiations fall into this category. The first was all kinds of flexible mechanisms that would allow developed countries to avoid domestic emission reductions by funding reductions abroad, or allow companies to sell and buy emission reduction units as it suited them best.[10] The second was the option to increase a country's capacity to absorb greenhouse gases from the atmosphere rather than decrease the amounts of emissions to the atmosphere. This was discussed in connection with the role of forests and other forms of biomass as a sink for CO_2. The political discourse in Germany centred around the question whether these options should be allowed for others; it never became really acceptable as an option for Germany itself.[11]

This enumeration of elements is only a selection but represents the most important dimensions to the new perception of global climate change, of Germany's role in it, and of the role of individual action. The most important argument here is that this discursive development produces a selective risk

---

10   See Articles 4, 6 and 17 of the Kyoto Protocol.
11   This is in sharp contrast with some other European countries, such as Norway and the Netherlands.

perception which includes some aspects of a problem (and a selection of options for a solution) while excluding others. It is the power of the discourses that leads to the impression that this specific worldview is the only appropriate one, the only legitimate one. The risk perception generated through these discourses appears to be self-evident after some time – it becomes institutionalised. The following section will discuss problems of institutionalisation and de- or re-institutionalisation.

7 Institutionalisation and Discursive Stability

One important indicator for the institutionalisation of the perception of anthropogenic climate change as a risk is its diffusion from the field of environmental policy to other policy domains. This can be shown in the parliamentary debates that address climate change. In the first decade under study, climate change figured almost exclusively as an item in its own right on the parliamentary agenda, i.e. it was dealt with in a direct way. This happened, for instance, when a member of parliament addressed the ruling government to inquire if a particular scientific study indicated direct implications for future climate change for Germany. In contrast, in the second decade, it has been more often dealt with indirectly. Items on the agenda are energy policy, transportation policy, the federal budget or the public funding of R&D, but climate change is linked to them, for instance, the impact of a specific transportation policy on global climate change (Graph 2). The only exception to this pattern occured at the time of the earth summit in Rio de Janeiro, but after that the relative frequency of issue linkages on the agenda has increased substantially. This indicates that climate change was firmly institutionalised on the political agenda as it appeared in so many other political debates that were not linked to climate change before.

The institutionalisation of a particular risk perception is discussed here as a form of stabilisation at the level of national decision-making in a world of potentially unlimited different perceptions. On the international scene, the science on climate change was often attacked by sceptics as too uncertain, too precocious and too dramatising (Lindzen 1990). In Germany, a consensus on the underlying science base emerged relatively early. It was through the mutual support of science, politics and the media that doubts about the reality of climate change did not become a dominant aspect of the risk perception, but were more or less excluded as non-legitimate. The mass media had early on transformed the uncertainties of the scientific hypotheses into the certainty of the impending catastrophe.

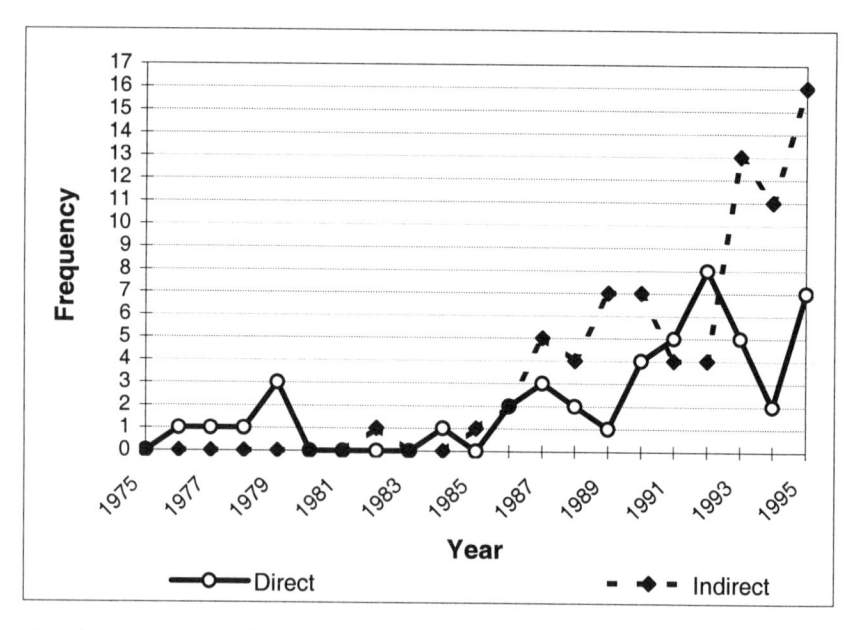

Graph 2: Direct / Indirect References to Climate Change in the German Parliament

Science and politics joined forces in the form of the first Enquête Commission to bring together a reliable knowledge base from which political options could be discussed and assessed. The Enquête Commission, which had both scientists and members of parliament in its ranks, went through a painstaking process of public hearings, a broad-ranging study programme and numerous internal meetings to bring about a consensual assessment of climate change (Kords 1996). The main report of the Enquête Commission (1990a) was not just another scientific report; it was perceived as a credible and trustworthy document that was approved by both scientists and politicians. Internationally, the Intergovernmental Panel on Climate Change (IPCC) provided at the same time a similar assessment aimed at solidifying scientific claims on climatic developments, the scope of the problem and necessary steps to prevent the change (see also Siebenhüner in this volume). The IPCC report (Houghton et al. 1990) was also generated in a difficult process with the broad inclusion of several hundred scientists, and was meant to provide the scientific background for the international climate negotiations. Although the IPCC reports were regarded internationally as very influential for the course of the negotiations, they did not play an important role in the parliamentary debates in Germany. Whereas in the political discourse in Germany in the first decade under study many international – in particular American – scientific sources were quoted and used to support this or that position in the debate, a kind of nationalisation of perceived scientific policy advice took place within the course of the second decade under study. First, climate research was institutionalised in a number of institutes and research programmes, so that German expertise was available to the political discourse. Second, in parliamentary debates, reference to German research institutes and German scientists largely replaced reference to international sources. And third, the first report of the Enquête Commission that was widely perceived as most influential in Germany is better known and was cited more often in the political discourse than the first report of the IPCC which has hardly been mentioned at all (Cavender/Jaeger 1993; Krück/Bray 1999). This does not imply ignorance of international sources, but rather that the credibility of the scientific expertise is possibly connected to its cultural and spatial proximity. The development of a consensual scientific knowledge base that is backed by the German research community was thus the central mechanism through which a specific perception of climate change was institutionalised. Sceptics with strong influence on the international scene could not break this consensus once it was institutionalised in Germany, even though they had some news coverage (Hornschuh 1999).

This example also shows that the emergence of informal institutions, such as new risk perceptions, often implies changes in formal institutions or even the creation of new formal institutions. In the case discussed in this paper, it led to changes in the German research landscape and the creation of diversified national climate change expertise. The German climate protection policy manifested itself in numerous policy documents, budgetary programmes and new legislation, and can therefore also claim the status of a formal institution. But the interactions of formal and informal institutions should not be seen in a uni-directional way. The formal institution of the Enquête Commission as a high-ranking advisory body to the federal parliament provided a form in which a politically supported scientific consensus could develop on which the new risk perception was founded.

As already mentioned, the metaphor of the climate catastrophe became the dominant framework for thinking about climate change both in the media and the political discourse. Together with the global dimension of the problem, it called for urgent and wide-ranging political regulation. For a while, global climate change appeared as the all-embracing problem of mankind, under which all other environmental problems could be subsumed. However, as the implementation of the 25 percent reduction target proved difficult, this global framework became a legitimatory problem in the political discourse. The action plans of the government did not seem far-reaching enough to cope with such a problem.

In the aftermath of the UN conference in Rio, the government's statements thus began to show signs of a re-interpretation of climate change. Now it was increasingly described in less dramatic terms, namely as part of a broader problem called sustainable development.

(Dr. Töpfer, Federal Minister for the Environment): Both the Law of Cyclical Economy and Waste currently under discussion and its effects on responsibility for new products in the entire waste sector, from packaging to cars, are the direct consequence of a conference that made sustainable development ... its central focus. I just want to make this clear, *so as not to narrow everything down to the climate situation, as important as its consideration may be.* (12th legislative period, 147th session, 12.3.1993, pp. 12648/49; emphasis added).

(Dr. Töpfer, Federal Minister for the Environment): Let me say something concerning the motion of the SPD. *It is somewhat disappointing that it deals almost exclusively with the climate question. Our follow-up is considerably more comprehensive.* Our follow-up ... has something to do with development and environmental issues and thus with Agenda 21, dealing with the question of how we can overcome poverty without putting a strain on the environment. Hence we should be aware of the fact that *we have to do more than to consider the climate,* ... as important as this undoubtedly is. (12th legislative period, 152nd session, 22.4.1993, p. 13014; emphasis added)

It became obvious that the expectation of a coherent global environmental management approach was an excessive expectation for the government, and that it had to rely on the usual forms of incremental policy-making instead.

Institutionalisation means stabilisation and normalisation. Changing a once institutionalised solution often proves difficult (Oliver 1992). So far, the stabilisation of risk perceptions has been emphasised as a necessary step to focus on some solutions, i.e. to gain capacity for acting. But what if problems of implementation become overwhelming and demand a new way of seeing the respective risk, as well as new ways of acting and finding solutions? What if new aspects of a problem appear which cannot easily be integrated into a specific risk perception? The danger of institutional capture or lock-in in the sense of too much stability is the flipside of the coin. Social learning thus requires an appropriate balance of stability and change in order to improve institutional capacities to deal with long-term environmental problems. This will be discussed in the following section which gives an example of difficult adjustments to rapidly changing political conditions. The basic ecological risk perception on climate change in Germany stabilised in the first half of the 1990s. However, international negotiations on a binding climate treaty only started in 1995, and developed their most important dynamics from 1997 onwards, beginning with the Kyoto Protocol. The next section will therefore deal with the question of how this specific risk perception helped Germany to negotiate internationally.

8 Differences in Risk Perceptions – Worlds Apart in the International Negotiations?

The overall question of this section of the book is how institutions and social practice interact. This chapter focusses on a perspective that looks at ways in which institutions generate and guide social practice. For an approach which is more centred around actorhood and the question of how social practice can form institutions, or be a precondition for their efficacy, see Breit et al. in this volume. Here, the institutionalisation of a particular risk perception is seen as a way of linking institutions and social practice. Risk perceptions define a problem, identify and legitimise appropriate ways of reacting and de-legitimise other options. Individual action happens on the grounds of these perceptions, but also action of corporate actors such as governments or political administrations. A risk perception is often implicit and does not undergo a formal process of recognition. However, once it is institutionalised it shapes the outcomes of political decisions (Goldstein/Keohane 1993). It is assumed here that risk perceptions like the one described above helped generate the German position in the course of the negotiations. Moreover, their institutionalisation occurred of course not only in Germany, but in many other places elsewhere. It is easy to see that from differences in risk perceptions differences in national positions emerge that make international negotiations a very difficult process. A comparison of the position of the United States and Germany illustrates this clearly.

From a certain perspective one would expect Germany and the U.S. to have similar positions with regard to climate change, the definition of the problem and the identification of appropriate solutions. They are both industrialised countries with large populations and high rates of greenhouse gas emissions. However, early on in the negotiations it became obvious that the two countries are almost diametrically opposed in their assessments. In the U.S., the science on climate change was met with much more scepticism than in Germany. No strong consensus emerged, either on the scientific base of the risk perception or on the acceptability of different solutions. In contrast to Germany, where a dominant risk perception was institutionalised in the early 1990s, in the U.S. the issue of climate change and the respective policy options were deeply controversial (White 1998). The view that became most important, though not generally accepted, was very economically oriented and defined the climate change problem in terms of costs and benefits. The resulting positions of the national delegations in the course of the negotiations differed in fundamental ways (Table 1).

Dominant Perception of Climate Change in Germany	Dominant Perception of Climate Change in the U.S.
Optimism about capacities for short-term emission reductions and win-win-options	Pessimism about high costs of short-term reductions
Pessimism about the dangers of the global climate catastrophe	Optimism about human capacities for adaptation
Dominance of notions of fairness and justice	Dominance of notions of costs and benefits
Excluding developing countries from direct responsibility	Insistence on responsibility of developing countries
Rejection of sinks	Reliance on sinks
Rejection of flexible mechanisms	Reliance on flexible mechanisms
Acceptance of changes of lifestyles	Rejection of change of lifestyles

Table 1: Comparison of the perception of climate change in Germany and the U.S. [12]

Driven by the perception of the impending catastrophe, the German position was based on general pessimism about the negative impacts of climate change. It was also based on an optimism towards human capacities to curb emissions quickly and thus prevent climate change in the first place. The position of Germany was dominated by notions of fairness and justice; the earth needed special protection and industrialised countries were identified as culprits. Conversely it was accepted that developing countries, for reasons of fairness, have the right to develop without immediately curbing their emissions. In the course of the negotiations, several options for how to reduce emissions were discussed. The use of sinks, i.e. the capacity of forests and biomass to absorb CO_2 from the atmosphere, rather than emission reductions was one of these options, as was the use of flexible mechanisms, such as Joint Implementation and Emissions Trading. Germany rejected both these options for a long time. It was perceived as inappropriate and illegitimate to concentrate on sinks instead of reducing sources, and on reducing emissions abroad rather than domestically.

The U.S. position was the opposite in all these respects (Victor/Salt 1995; White 1998; Coppock 1998; von Moltke/Rahman 1996). For a long time, climate change was not perceived as a very important problem as humans have huge capacities to adapt to adverse changes. However, pessimism over the human capacities for short-term emission reductions dominated. As the

---

[12] The table is based on our own analysis on Germany, and on interviews and literature on the U.S. (among others Victor/Salt 1995; Krücken 1997; White 1998; Coppock 1998; von Moltke/Rahman 1996).

framework of costs and benefits gained some prominence it was calculated that it might be economically more rational to seek to reduce emissions in the very long term and to begin strengthening adaptation capacities. All possible options that avoided early domestic emission reductions seemed appropriate from this perspective. The U.S. therefore strongly advocated options such as sinks and flexible mechanisms (Ehrmann/Oberthür 1997). The two positions of Germany and the U.S. seemed to be incompatible with one other. Indeed they were, as they originated from two different risk perceptions. These differences between the U.S.' understanding and that of many other countries culminated in the total rejection of the Kyoto Protocol by the U.S. Government in 2001, which was agreed upon by the majority of others. This is not to claim that risk perceptions were the only explanatory factor for the differences in the negotiations; several possible explanations such as the political system, basic features of the economy, including the supply and consumption of energy, of course also apply to some of these variations (see also Rowlands 1995). However, in a world in which national interests are often hard to define even by the respective governments the role of worldviews, perceptions, or more generally "ideas" in international negotiations and regime formation is increasingly recognised (Finnemore 1996; Goldstein/Keohane 1993; see also Mitchell in this volume).

From this rather sketchy comparison of two national risk perceptions we can only speculate on more fundamental questions about the origin of the differences. It would be worthwhile to analyse the role of more general worldviews and of deeper cultural differences in which the formation of national policies is embedded. However, these questions are beyond the scope of this paper.

The institutionalisation of a specific risk perception and a respective problem definition on climate change clearly helped to put the issue on the political agenda in Germany. The image of impending climate catastrophe, backed up by a credible and trustworthy science base, also helped to induce political action, a stringent national reduction target and domestic climate protection programmes. However, it only identified certain options as legitimate and appropriate and excluded others. This became a problem in the negotiations where a clash of problem definitions seriously hampered agreement over an international climate treaty.

9 Conclusions and Outlook

In this chapter, the institutionalisation of a risk perception was analysed. This was manifest in a picture of the atmosphere which is centred around human activity and intervention. It thus enabled governments to anticipate man-made climate change and develop a range of policy responses. However, no global consensus exists on how to deal with the problem of global climate change. The chapter described the stabilisation in the form of a national consensus that helped to institutionalise a specific risk perception in the German context.

This risk perception helped to identify legitimate and appropriate policy options and dismiss others. A risk perception in this sense is an informal institution, as it is non-codified and the outcome of an unintentional process. In this specific case, it was mainly shaped by the interaction of science, politics and the mass media – societal fields which in themselves reflect and bundle the cacophony of social voices.

The examples also showed related changes in the arrangement of formal institutions and demonstrated the interactions between formal and informal institutions.

The institutionalisation of climate change as a global impending catastrophe helped to establish this problem on the political agenda. It can therefore be interpreted as an example of social learning. However, problems emerged both domestically and internationally with this particular problem perception. Domestically, it created the call for more far-reaching and more fundamental institutional changes than the political process was capable of realising. Internationally, huge differences became apparent between the specific risk perception that had been stabilised in Germany and those of other countries, among them the United States. Thus, in the international negotiations a clash of risk perceptions occurred that led to serious deadlock.

Social learning can thus mean both stabilisation and change of specific risk perceptions. Moreover, reacting to global environmental changes is a multi-layer phenomenon which refers to the problem of interplay between these different layers of policy formulation and implementation. This process is difficult but not impossible to shape and control intentionally. Recognition of these problems would be a first step to avoid deadlock situations. Internationally, it would be necessary to refrain from making absolute one's own risk perception and develop a will to compromise. However, this is difficult as discursive developments lead to a naturalisation and normalisation of the risk perception, resulting in each of the negotiating parties thinking that they act on the basis of the same truth and the same world. This problem refers to the need for procedures and capacities for conflict management, a perspective that is pursued in the contribution by Troja in this volume. The main argument of this chapter is, however, that a specific risk perception (consensus, catastrophe, urgency, etc.) was necessary to establish a national policy, but that it might not be appropriate for future international negotiations. Reflexive mechanisms are needed which help overcome blind spots and find an appropriate balance between stability and change.

References

Arrhenius, Svante (1896): On the Influence of Carbonic Acid in the Air upon the Temperature of the Ground. In: Philosophical Magazine; Vol. 41; No. 251; pp. 237-277

Berger, Peter L./Thomas Luckmann (1967): The Social Construction of Reality. New York; Doubleday

Cavender, Jeannine/Jill Jäger (1993): The History of Germany's Response to Climate Change. In: International Environmental Affairs; Vol. 5, pp. 3-18

Coppock, Rob (1998): Implementing the Kyoto Protocol. The Kyoto Protocol Will Be a Worthwhile Agreement Only if it Adopts a Long-Term Strategy in its Implementation Plan. In: Issues in Science and Technology; Spring; pp. 66-74

Dobbin, Frank (1994): Forging Industrial Policy. The United States, Britain, and France in the Railway Age. Cambridge; Cambridge University Press

DPG/DMG (1987): Warnung vor drohenden weltweiten Klimaänderungen durch den Menschen. In: Physikalische Blätter; Vol. 43; pp. 347-349

Ehrmann, Markus/Sebastian Oberthür (1997): Spring in Climate Negotiations? In: Environmental Policy and Law; Vol. 27; No. 3; pp. 192-196

Engels, Anita/Peter Weingart (1997): Die Politisierung des Klimas. Zur Entstehung von anthropogenem Klimawandel als politischem Handlungsfeld. In: Hiller/Krücken (eds.): Risiko und Regulierung. Soziologische Beiträge zu Technikkontrolle und präventiver Umweltpolitik. Frankfurt a.M.; Suhrkamp, pp. 90-115

Enquête Commission ("Vorsorge zum Schutz der Erdatmosphäre") (1990a): Schutz der Erde: Eine Bestandsaufnahme mit Vorschlägen zu einer neuen Energiepolitik, Band 1. Bonn; Economica/Karlsruhe; C.F. Müller

Enquête Commission ("Vorsorge zum Schutz der Erdatmosphäre") (1990b): Schutz der Erde: Eine Bestandsaufnahme mit Vorschlägen zu einer neuen Energiepolitik, Band 2. Bonn; Economica/Karlsruhe; C.F. Müller

Enquête Commission ("Vorsorge zum Schutz der Erdatmosphäre") (1990c): Energie und Klima, 10 Bände. Bonn; Economica/Karlsruhe; C.F. Müller

Enquête Commission ("Vorsorge zum Schutz der Erdatmosphäre") (1991): Schutz der Erde. Bericht der Enquête-Kommission "Vorsorge zum Schutz der Erdatmosphäre" des 11. Deutschen Bundestages, Band 1. Bonn; Economica

Fairclough, Norman (1992): Discourse and Social Change. Cambridge (UK); Polity Press

Finnemore, Martha (1996): Norms, Culture, and World Politics: Insights from Sociology's Institutionalism. In: International Organization; Vol. 50; No. 2; pp. 325-347

Foucault, Michel (1997): Politics, Philosophy, Culture: Interviews and Other Writings 1977-1984, ed. with an introduction by Lawrence D. Kritzman. New York et al.; Routledge

Fourier, Jean-Baptiste (1827): Mem. Acad. Sci. Inst. Fr. 7, 569

Frank, David (1997), Science, Nature, and the Globalization of the Environment, 1870-1990. In: Social Forces; Vol. 76; No. 2; pp. 409-437

Frank, David/Ann Hironaka/John Meyer/Evan Schofer/Nancy Tuma (1999): The Rationalization and Organization of Nature in the World Culture. In: Boli/Thomas (eds.): Constructing World Culture: International Nongovernmental Organizations Since 1875. Stanford; Stanford University Press; pp. 81-99

Frank, David/Ann Hironaka/Evan Schofer (2000). The Nation-State and the Natural Environment Over the Twentieth Century. In: American Sociological Review; Vol. 65; pp. 96-116

Goldstein, Judith/Robert O. Keohane (1993): Ideas and Foreign Policy: An Analytical Framework. In: Goldstein/Keohane (eds.): Ideas and Foreign Policy: Beliefs, Institutions, and Political Change. Ithaca (NY); Cornell University Press; pp. 3-30

Hasse, Raimund/Georg Krücken (1999): Neo-Institutionalismus. Bielefeld; transcript-Verlag

Hatch, Michael T. (1995): The Politics of Global Warming in Germany. In: Environmental Politics; Vol. 4; No. 3; pp. 415-440

Hornschuh, Tillmann (1999): Skepsis als Schema? Zur Bedeutung des "Backlash". In: Der Berichterstattung über anthropogenen Klimawandel in den deutschen Printmedien. Unpublished Paper; University of Bielefeld

Houghton, John T./G.J. Jenkins/J.J. Ephraums (eds.) (1990): Scientific Assessment of Climate Change – Report of Working Group I. Cambridge, (UK); Cambridge University Press

IPOS (1991): Einstellungen zu Fragen des Umweltschutzes 1991. Ergebnisse jeweils einer repräsentativen Bevölkerungsumfrage, im Auftrag des Bundesministeriums für Umwelt, Naturschutz und Reaktorsicherheit, Förderkennzeichen 101 07 112

Jepperson, Ronald L. (1991): Institutions, Institutional Effects, and Institutionalism. In: Powell/DiMaggio (eds.): The New Institutionalism in Organisational Analysis. Chicago; University of Chicago Press; pp. 143-163

Jepperson, Ronald L. (2001): The Development and Application of Sociological Neoinstitutionalism. Robert Schuman Centre for Advanced Studies; EUI Working Papers RSC 2001/5

Kords, Udo (1996): Tätigkeit und Handlungsempfehlungen der beiden Klima-Enquete-Kommissionen des Deutschen Bundestages (1987-1994). In: Brauch (ed.): Klimapolitik. Berlin et al.; Springer; pp. 203-214

Krück, Carsten P./Jutta Borchers (1999): Science in Politics. A Comparison of Climate Modelling Centres. In: Minerva; Vol. 37; No. 2; pp. 105-123

Krück, Carsten P./Dennis Bray (1999): Wie schätzt die deutsche Exekutive die Gefahr eines globalen Klimawandels ein? Eine Meinungsumfrage zum Risikomanagement in der Umweltpolitik. Hamburg; Unpublished Research Paper

Krücken, Georg (1997): Risikotransformation. Die politische Regulierung technisch-ökologischer Gefahren in der Risikogesellschaft. Opladen; Westdeutscher Verlag

Meyer, John/David Frank/Ann Hironaka/Evan Schofer/Nancy Tuma (1997): The Structuring of a World Environmental Regime, 1870-1990. In: International Organization; Vol. 51; pp. 623-651

Meyer, John/Ronald L. Jepperson (2000): The 'Actors' of Modern Society: The Cultural Construction of Social Agency. In: Sociological Theory; Vol. 18; pp. 100-120

Oliver, Christine (1992): The Antecendents of Deinstitutionalization. In: Organization Studies; Vol. 13; pp. 563-588

O'Riordan, Tim/ Andrew Jordan (1996): Social Institutions and Climate Change: In: O'Riordan/Jäger (eds.): Politics of Climate Change: A European Perspective. London, New York; Routledge; pp. 65-105

Pansegrau, Petra (2000): "Klimaszenarien, die einem apokalyptischen Bilderbogen gleichen" oder "Leck im Raumschiff Erde". Eine Untersuchung der kommunikativen und kognitiven Funktionen von Metaphorik im Wissenschaftsjournalismus anhand der Spiegelberichterstattung zum anthropogenen Klimawandel. Unpublished Dissertation; Bielefeld University

Rowlands, Ian H. (1995): Explaining National Climate Change Policies. In: Global Environmental Change; Vol. 5; No. 3; pp. 235-249

Subak, Susan (1996): The Science and Politics of National Greenhouse Gas Inventories. In: O'Riordan/Jäger (eds.): Politics of Climate Change: A European Perspective. London, New York; Routledge; pp. 51-64

The Social Learning Group (2001a): Learning to Manage Global Environmental Risks. Volume 1: A Comparative History of Social Responses to Climate Change, Ozone Depletion, and Acid Rain. Cambridge (MA); MIT Press

The Social Learning Group (2001b): Learning to Manage Global Environmental Risks. Volume 2: A Functional Analysis of Social Responses to Climate Change, Ozone Depletion, and Acid Rain. Cambridge (MA); MIT Press

Thompson, Michael/Steve Rayner (1998): Cultural Discourses. In: Rayer/Malone (eds.): Human Choice and Climate Change. Volume 1: The Societal Framework. Columbus (OH); Battelle Press

Victor, David/Julien E. Salt (1995): Keeping the Climate Treaty Relevant. In: Nature; No. 373; 26 January; pp. 280-282

von Moltke, Konrad/Atiq Rahman (1996): External Perspectives on Climate Change. A View from the United States and the Third World. In: O'Riordan/Jäger (eds.): Politics of Climate Change: A European Perspective. London, New York; Routledge; pp. 330-345

von Storch, Hans/Nico Stehr (2000): Climate Change in Perspective. Our Concerns about Global Warming Have an Age-Old Resonance. In: Nature; No. 405; 8 June; pp. 615

Weingart, Peter/Anita Engels/Petra Pansegrau (2000): Risks of Communication: Discourses on Climate Change in Science, Politics, and the Mass Media. In: Public Understanding of Science; Vol. 9; pp. 261-283

Weingart, Peter/Anita Engels/Petra Pansegrau (2002): Von der Hypothese zur Katastrophe. Der anthropogene Klimawandel im Diskurs zwischen Wissenschaft, Politik und Massenmedien. Opladen; Leske+Budrich

White, Robert M. (1998): Kyoto and Beyond. Future Actions in Response to the Threat of Climate Change Should Emphasize Adaptation and New Energy Technology. In: Issues in Science and Technology; Spring; pp. 59-65

Young, Oran (2002): The Institutional Dimension of Global Environmental Change. Fit, Interplay, and Scale. Cambridge (MA); MIT Press

Zucker, Lynne G. (1977): The Role of Institutionalization in Cultural Persistence. In: American Sociological Review; Vol. 42; No. 5; pp. 726-743

Heiko Breit, Thomas Döring and Lutz H. Eckensberger

Politics, Law and Citizens' Responsibility. Justice Judgements in the Everyday Reconstruction of Environmental Conflicts[1]

1 Introduction

Our contribution deals with citizens' understanding of formal institutions such as law and politics. With regard to responsibility for environmental damages in the past and risk management in the future this understanding entails a variety of different concepts about individual, collective and institutional commitment and their interrelationship. It is maintained that the range of these ideas depends on the complexity of justice judgements.

Justice judgements entail the ability to co-ordinate divergent perspectives and actions in conflicts. They can be defined at different levels of abstraction. Our investigation demonstrates how different justice judgements on environmental risk affect the degree to which individuals feel that they themselves or others are responsible for ecological remedial action. This question is linked to how citizens judge themselves and others with respect to civil participation in the institutional framework of law and politics.

The analysis is based on 180 semi-structured interviews on conflicts about a coal-fuelled power plant, water use and agricultural production. We could identify four different perspectives or ideal types on the basis of the interrelationship between risk interpretations, responsibility and solidarity formulated in answer to the question: "Who can do what and who has the obligation to do something?"

The fruitfulness of this typology for explaining civil engagement is demonstrated for the case of a civic action group. Its purpose, its goals, successes as well as its ultimate failure are judged and valued differently in accordance with the four types presented.

Before presenting these results the relation of justice judgements and institutions as well as their function in civil society has to be clarified. Subsequently a short introduction will be given to the theoretical and methodical framework applied.

---

[1] This paper is based on data from different projects funded by the German Research Council (DFG), conducted at the University of Saarland, Saarbrücken and the German Institute of International Educational Research (DIPF), Frankfurt/Main. The authors would like to thank Ingrid Plath for her critical remarks.

2 Civil Society, Citizens' Responsibility and Environmental Protection

According to Castoriadis (1987) institutions encompass *functional* and *imaginary* components that are closely interrelated. The formal organisation of economic and juridical systems, institutionalised power or religion are only effective because they are respected as shared societal systems of symbols and meanings which are the basis of worldviews. We attempt to analyse this symbolic or imaginary component of institutions and reconstruct the different ways in which people perceive formal institutions in conflicts between economy and ecology. In doing so, we consider their understanding of formal institutions as expressed in constitutions, laws, regulations and statutes from the *interaction perspective* of social practice. This perspective is constituted by cultural and individual rule systems and non-codified norms such as morality and conventions.

Taking informal institutions into account is crucial for understanding social learning and institutional change. Formal institutions are, to a great extent, embedded in a web of shared beliefs and culturally transmitted meanings as they are represented in informal institutions. The political acceptability of legal control, technological innovation and price control largely depends on whether they are agreed upon or acknowledged by citizens. If the acceptance of formal institutions (economy, law, politics, administration) requires informal institutions (morality, conventions, values), then informal institutions are a necessary condition for the *effectiveness* of institutional changes. The functionality of formal institutions must be broadly accepted in everyday life in order to maintain political control and to motivate social agents to develop individual responsibility for ecological remedial action.

It is the interaction of formal rules, informal norms and enforcement characteristics that shapes institutional change. Usually social sciences propagate that formal institutions can be changed intentionally, whereas informal norms often only appear to constrain institutional change (North 1990). However, informal institutions also provide indispensable *input* into initiating institutional change. For instance the now widely accepted criticism of the dangers of nuclear technology was initially not articulated within expert systems but by environmental groups. Moreover changes in formal, structured expert systems also depend on informal institutions because expert cultures are also rooted in the common sense opinions of their members (Beck 1992).

Consequently coping with environmental risks requires new institutions on the basis of *social learning* (The Social Learning Group 2001). Social learning is a field of enormous breadth in social sciences that we cannot discuss here. In the present context we understand social learning as occurring at the interface between different informal institutions (informal norms, values, interests), between formal institutions (economics, law, politics, administration) as well as between informal and formal institutions.

The significance of informal institutions for social learning in environmental contexts is based on the fact that ecological risk management depends broadly on interpretations and worldviews (see Engels in this volume). However, interpretations and worldviews vary across individuals, cultures and contexts. This leads to conflicts in risk evaluations. Such conflicts, like any other type of conflict, must be restrained and resolved by institutions as well. According to Offe (1999) the most esteemed types of institutions are those which are seen and justified as "morally plausible". They are morally plausible when and if there are reasons which prevent them from being deemed unjust or hypocritical.

The moral plausibility of institutions is an essential background for legitimate politics and institutional change in democratic societies. However, the functioning of a democratic civil society is not solely guaranteed by formal institutions and political representation. In addition to formal institutions powerful organisations, interest groups and established political parties constitute the framework of a democratic social constitutional state (Habermas 1996). These organisations can only act successfully if members of civil society are prepared to take on responsibility within the framework of their duties, interests and ability to act.

Since the eighties the role of an active public in "civil society" has increasingly attracted the attention of social scientists (Cohen/Arato 1992; Rödel/Frankenberg/Dubiel 1989). This interest arose as a result of the changes in political landscapes brought about by social movements, civic action groups and non-governmental organisations.

The importance of active citizens' engagement for institutional change is particularly evident in ecological risk management. The framework of problem solving provided by market forces, law and science (new sources of energy, catalytic converters etc.) has to be complemented by the *personal responsibility of citizens to act*. The protection of the environment and nature cannot be achieved by sanctions and coercive measures alone. It is inconceivable without aesthetic experiences, individual commitment to action and recognition of the necessity of institutional changes. For instance, attempts to bring about changes directly by way of price regulation are soon met with limited acceptance, as is clearly shown in the recent example of an energy tax in Germany.

Through the political commitment of citizens the general public can be made aware of the dangers of technology and the consequences of unlimited consumption with respect to the environment and nature. Involvement in environmental organisations, civic groups, "green" parties and NGOs with a global reach, such as Greenpeace and the Rainforest Alliance, could help sensitise the public to official politics and the established "expert culture"

(Beck 1992). In Germany the awareness of ecological risks occupies a high priority in public consciousness.

But what motivates people to become politically active, to get involved in environmental organisations or civic action groups, or at least, as consumers, to be willing to buy expensive environmentally sustainable products? From Hobbes and Adam Smith to Karl Marx the familiar old answer is: they safeguard their *own interests*.

However, it is not clear what the concept of *interests* actually entails. In philosophy and the social sciences the topic is generally treated rather vaguely and encompasses a wide spectrum of meanings ranging from the particularity of self-assertion under economic pressure to the universality of interests in a "good life" which includes a reasonable coexistence of all people in an invaluable environment where nature is cherished. By contrast, the concept of economic interests is more definite but also more narrowly formulated. It refers to the realisation of subjective preferences. According to the liberal model the "invisible hand" of the market, maximising individual benefits, should lead to the optimisation of societal conditions for everyone, or at least for the majority of members of society.

However, this model of the so-called "homo-oeconomicus" loses its theoretical validity when its consequences for environmentally sustainable action are scrutinized. The maximisation of individual benefits has been showed to endanger the preservation of the commons (Ostrom 1990). Consequently, in economics games theory has begun to play an increasingly important role. Insight into environmental dilemmas should lead to a shift from the rationale of expecting short term (immediate) profits towards institutionally secured co-operation in the future (Frey 1992). Such a rational calculation is endangered however by "free riders" who profit from what individual benefits provide, even if they themselves have not contributed to it. Conversely, the commitment of activists does not always pay off. On the contrary: environmentally sustainable action is, for the most part, still saddled with financial burdens. Free riders may perhaps be clever enough to recognise the long-term benefits of environmentally sustainable action, but ultimately they hope that others will care for the preservation of nature and that they themselves can profit from this. This leads to the expectation that if the individual benefits perspective is projected so far into the future that it is necessary to take following generations and people in faraway regions, such as the third world, into consideration, then self-interest should lose its appeal. This kind of reasoning also applies to respect for animals and nature.

In cases of environmentally sustainable action, when the power of formal institutionalised measures alone do not bring about success, laws and politics as well as technical innovation and the incentive of price regulation must be supplemented by the commitment of people. They share culturally embedded values and uncodified norms in informal institutions which reach beyond the short and long term *interest of maximising individual benefits*. Environment and nature are also important objects of cultural values and symbols. This is especially evident with regard to publicity. Nature and environment represent more than just economic resources and mere general conditions of individuals or collective actions. They are grounded in aesthetic concepts of a successful lifestyle and the "good life". Their protection, therefore, triggers political commitment.

However, it is extremely controversial where the line should be drawn between material standards of living and possible renunciation of these for sustainable development. In view of the global dimension of ecological contexts, the support for sustainable development cannot be separated from issues of solidarity and justice which always concern questions of economic wealth.

At this point civil social action appears on the scene (see also Dünckman/Mayer in this volume). Democratic, social and ecological questions remain inseparable (Breit 2002). Civic action, according to the political theories of Locke, Rousseau and Kant, implies that citizens have the capacity to solve conflicts despite by immediate contradictory interests and diverging private worldviews (see Troja in this volume).

On the other hand simply trusting that individuals will feel responsibility and make commitments that go beyond the perspective of maximising individual benefits proves to be a weak argument and does not generate confidence in achieving a solution to existing environmental problems. The well-established fact that environmental awareness does not go hand in hand with environmental action gives cause for scepticism (De Haan 1995). Is the notion of civil society therefore, in a negative sense, utopian? Or is it possible to establish institutions through citizens' willingness to act and to co-operate? Where are the obstacles? Our research reveals to what extent mutual commitment is found in the context of economic-ecological conflicts by demonstrating qualitative differences in the patterns of discourse as manifested in private as well as public argumentation.

3   Citizens' Responsibility and Moral Judgements

To analyse such patterns of discourse *moral consciousness* is central. It has a structuring influence on meaning systems and worldviews, i.e. in the imaginary component of institutions. Morality is salient for the attribution of individual, collective and institutional responsibility and is therefore a necessary condition for a functioning civil society.

But what does *morality and moral consciousness* mean? Those who remain committed to morals today expose themselves to uncomfortable questioning. Can one really rely on morals to initiate or to anchor institutional change? Is this desirable, considering that moral concepts differ across cultures and between people? Is a liberal societal constitution based on moral burdens or rather on freedom of thought and a rational legal system?

These questions are all justified, implying that morality is an ambiguous notion. It also seems to be reserved for private interactions and therefore is regarded as inadequate for societal functionality (Luhmann 1995). But we agree with Durkheim (1991) that moral perspectives are unavoidable in everyday interaction and informal institutions. Morality plays an important role in the negotiation of differing interests and therefore has societal functions. Moral concepts also are the social basis of obedience and revolt as Moore (1978) describes them. They therefore are the essence of the *legitimisation processes of decision-making in formal institutions such as law and politics.*

When outlining the *societal* functions of morality, the concept of morality should not be confounded with altruism or care, as used in various psychological approaches. In the context of our research, morality is understood as the core of mutually accepted notions of *justice,* as typically formulated in cognitive theories of morality in philosophy, from Kant to Habermas (1993).

To be more exact, by defining morality as justice, we are talking about moral judgement *structures* and not about the concrete contents of moral norms. *Contents* of moral norms have different cultural meanings and vary in different contexts. But moral judgements can be interpreted *structurally* as the complexity of social perspectives (Kohlberg 1985) or of different action elements (Eckensberger 1986). This *structure* can be universalised (Kohlberg 1985; Habermas 1990). In the case of *conflicting* norms and values subjects apply different complex justice operations such as equality and equity in order to resolve controversies, e.g. between health and property as well as between ecology and economy.

The theory of moral judgement used has its roots in the research of J. Piaget (1932) and L. Kohlberg (1985). The main result of their investigations is that justice operations come into effect on *different levels of complexity of conflict resolution.* They develop in stages during ontogeny. The levels gradually increase in stages from an egocentric interest perspective to a "moral point of view". The "moral point of view" integrates the interests of all persons involved in conflicting decisions within an idealised, impartial process of communication which also forms the ideal of civil society (Habermas 1996).

Our work differs from recent research on moral judgements in significant points. In contrast to the Kohlbergian tradition we do not use *hypothetical* moral dilemmas, but analyse the significance of moral judgements in everyday conflicts, as in the case of environmental risks. We do not look at the development in ontogeny, instead we study adult persons. Ontogeny of moral judgements does not necessarily reach the final stage. Empirically adults too vary in stage attainment. This is so because development needs stimulating context conditions such as stable emotional care and social recognition, open confrontation with social problems and conflicts, opportunities to participate in the communication process, the possibility to participate in co-operative decision-making processes and responsibility for shaping one's own life as well as that of others (Lempert 1988). These developmental preconditions are not prevalent everywhere or are rare in contemporary societies.

In analysing the structure of moral judgements in interviews which address ecological risks, we are able to determined differences in the complexity of adults' civic responsibility. Our thesis is that different concepts of responsibility for ecological remedial actions are rooted in different justice judgements that in turn are represented by distinct levels of moral judgement. In extending classical research to the investigation of the meaning of moral judgement in real life contexts, we examine the connection of moral judgements with other rule systems.
For this purpose:

— We apply Eckensberger's theory of moral judgement based on action theory (Eckensberger/Burgard 1986; Eckensberger & Reinshagen 1980).
— We connect this approach with Boesch's symbolic action theory (Boesch 1991) which has been further developed by Eckensberger (Eckensberger 1996).

Following Piaget's terminology, we distinguish a *heteronomous* from an *autonomous* moral orientation as external and internal constraints as well as rules aimed at the structure of reasoning. Heteronomy in this context means that actions are interpreted as given and solutions are based to a large extent on intuition. Rules are interpreted as an existing fact. The individual thus takes a rule as being in force and regards it as valid. So reasoning refers to the *factual acceptance* of rules which are also, however, considered *obligatory (and therefore prescriptive)* for everyone.

Autonomy, by contrast, implies mutual respect for intentions and is defined by cultural and everyday needs, norms and values which are intersubjectively taken for granted. The main consequence of an autonomous orientation is the readiness for communicating and co-operating without strategic intentions. This also includes *counterfactual* thinking, this means they refer to what people *should do* rather than to what people *would do* (according to expectations, norms or experiences).

Sphere of Interpretation	Moral Orientation	
	Heteronomous	**Autonomous**
Interpersonal	Conformity to external as well as internal *constraints and rules* in one's own interest	inter-subjective recognition of norms and reciprocal respect, maintaining the community
Transpersonal	functional orientation with the goal of maintaining the system	Orientation towards civil society democracy and human rights

Table 1: Reconstruction of Levels of Moral Judgement

Heteronomous and autonomous moral orientations can occur on two planes of interpreting social reality. First it is specified on the "interpersonal sphere" of concrete relations. It is repeated then on a second, more abstract level, called the "transpersonal sphere". This sphere is constructed or understood in terms of laws, organisations and societal sub-system roles and thus in terms of formal institutions. These two spheres are not identical with informal and formal institutions. We look at formal institutions from the point of view of *informal institutions*, i.e. from the viewpoint of social action and rule systems. However, formal institutions such as law and politics are reconstructed in different ways with consequences for individual responsibility. The complexity of industrial societies and options for institutional action are reconstructed adequately only on the transpersonal sphere. The interpersonal view on power relations, legislation, democratic procedures etc. does not sufficiently reflect functional and non-intended action consequences and reduces functions to social and personal relations (Sennett 1974). Moreover references to individual as well as collective norms and values are merely reflected upon on the transpersonal level, whereas they are accepted without question from an interpersonal perspective. But there is an essential difference between the transpersonal-heteronomous and the transpersonal-autonomous level concerning the interaction between informal and formal institutions. The heteronomous perspective entails regarding nature and society as objective, with a preference for an expert culture aligned to formal institutions such as market rules, nomothetic scientific methods and political decisions. By contrast the transpersonal-autonomous orientation aims at achieving civil society democracy, integrating expert cultures and the perspective and interests of stakeholders (see Troja in this volume).

From the viewpoint of *symbolic action theory* various levels of action such as world-oriented, rule-oriented and self-oriented action can be distinguished. They represent ideas about objective, social and subjective (imaginary) institutions.

On the primary *world-oriented* level actions are oriented towards the perception of facts about the environment and conservation of nature or perceived danger for sustainable development or human health. The means for these ends, with regard to urban and natural aesthetics, are considered here. From the justice perspective these questions lead to the evaluation of *risks*. Risks always entail a close relationship to morality because they involve (a) a reference to the intentionality of the decision to act, (b) a component of uncertainty with respect to the occurrence of consequences and (c) an evaluative dimension concerning the cost/benefit orientation of action (Douglas 1985; Eckensberger/Döring/Breit 2001). If barriers arise on the primary level of action, action regulation is needed. This is understood as an action applied on primary action. The regulation of actions is therefore called secondary action. On this level the concept of "situational control" is a central issue. There are very different notions about what degree of freedom to allocate to members of a society in general as well as to one's self and others. From a moral perspective "control" is closely linked to the question of *responsibility*, i.e. who can and should act. Who is *responsible* for ecological damage, for instance oneself as an unreflective consumer, or politicians and experts? Beyond issues of control, this level concerns different rule systems, i.e. informal institutions in general. These include interests, conventions and moral norms, as well as technical knowledge, aesthetics and religious notions. Finally, the tertiary action level is actor-oriented. It relates to the social positioning of an actor, in other words the orientation of one's identity. Identity regulates the relation of the self to others. Therefore, from the moral perspective, the central notion is "solidarity" and its reach: is it up to us to take future generations into consideration?

To summarise, the real life context of judgement is characterised by (a) the perception of the situational context (*risk*), (b) the possibilities of controlling and changing or influencing the situation (*responsibility*) and (c) reflection on the relationship between the self and others involved in the situation (*solidarity*).

Levels of action	Dimension of analysis	Justice perspective
tertiary level of action actor-oriented	identity	solidarity
secondary level of action action-oriented	control	responsibility
primary level of action world-oriented	perception of facts	risk

Table 2: Conditions of Action Context

Within this framework we carried out qualitative research on environmental risks and action responsibility involved in the building of a coal power plant, the utilisation of freshwater resources and strategies to act in agriculture (Döring/Eckensberger/Huppert/Breit, in press). Altogether, 180 interviews were evaluated. The evaluation aimed at establishing *types of patterns of argumentation*. These types are considered "ideal types" in the sense of Max Weber (1949). The method of formulating ideal types aims at explicating a phenomenon's structure of meaning. Determining the validity of ideal types thus involves two aspects: One deals with the analytical definition of interrelations between the constructs involved – this is precisely what the integration of action levels and moral levels achieves. The second deals with empirically determining the substantive reality of the types themselves. Hence these types are constructions of social scientists derived from a pre-interpreted reality, but they also have empirical status. This evaluation includes alternating empirical (inductive) and analytical (deductive) steps (for more details see Breit 2002, p. 307 f.)

4 Politics, Legal Concepts and Civil Responsibility in the Conflict Between Economics and Ecology

In the following we do not intend to introduce the typology as a whole (see Breit/Eckensberger 1998), but rather to emphasise those aspects which are interesting from the perspective of institutional change and social learning. We will focus on how *responsibility* for ecological remedial action is conceived of and how this interacts with expressing solidarity. The general relation of risk evaluation to responsibility and solidarity has been described elsewhere (Eckensberger/Döring/Breit 2001), but we will consider the issue of risk evaluations in the description of a civic action group. Responsibility for ecological remedial action entails notions of political influence with respect to *changing institutions* and can be reconstructed as varying in complexity on the basis of our typology.

Each of the types is defined according to whether people trust in the power of formal institutions or in the responsibility of the social actors (heteronomy versus autonomy) and whether the preferred mode of exchange is personal interaction at the community level or in terms of functional roles and mechanisms at a societal level (interpersonal versus transpersonal). These variations are rooted in the differing complexities of justice judgements mentioned above.

We will now (1) present the typology and then (2) demonstrate its fruitfulness for explaining civil engagement in the case of a civic action group.

4.1 Justice Based Arguments Regarding the Interaction Between Formal and Informal Institutions

The Interpersonal-Heteronomous Level (Type 1)

Type 1 is driven by notions of law and politics which emphasise the important role of individuals or groups in positions of authority. The difference between informal and formal institutions is not taken into account. The stance taken by the interviewees here is: "It's up to the politicians to change things – the man in the street can't do much at all. If the farmers weren't encouraged to overproduce, they wouldn't need to use such intensive farming techniques."

The IH-types take a self-centred perspective focused on their own interests and even regard this as an ethical obligation for everyone. This ethical obligation is based on the conviction that because of economic and social constraints, there is no scope for action beyond ensuring survival. This "egoism", regarded as necessary in the social world, does not, however, imply "a war, in which everyone fights against everyone else", but rather constitutes the basic ideas shaping the notion of *solidarity*. Social groups and communities are stabilised through the perception of real (and implied) similarities in interests and life-styles. For this type conformity is an essential condition for solidarity, based on a community of people having similar interests. Solidarity is practised predominantly in short-term interest groups.

Questions of *responsibility* are primarily solved by the principle of delegation. Politics, or rather politicians as this concept is intensely personified on this level, are elevated to beings of unlimited power. This hierarchical, sometimes authoritarian, understanding of politics does not necessarily mean that one submits oneself blindly. On the contrary, the hierarchical relationship to politicians makes it possible to hold them responsible for everything and to exonerate oneself. One recognises neither possibilities of influence nor any field of activity for civic action. Therefore, during times of dissatisfaction politicians are made the scapegoat. Politicians are deemed incapable or corrupt. Some of the interviewees are disposed to become active themselves, even in environmental groups or civic action groups (see below), but always only to safeguard their own concrete interests (health, aesthetic and emotional feelings towards nature). There are also obvious contradictions in the world-views of the interviewees. On the one hand they credit politicians with possessing unlimited power, on the other hand politics in general is seen as being powerless in the face of economic interests.

Specifically democratic politics is considered utopian because human anthropology is allegedly oriented towards the pursuit of one's own advantage. Even people who have influence in political institutions or as industrialists refer to their lack of ability to assert themselves against those who really pull the strings of power.

With regard to justice and law, one generally considers these to be uncontrollable and unavoidable sanctioning powers, without which anarchy and disorder would prevail. They convey a feeling of security and serve to protect one's integrity, in that those who break the rules are visibly ostracised as "black sheep" by one's own circle. However, if laws endanger the assertion of one's own interests, then they are interpreted as barriers serving the interests of others or as excessively bureaucratic regulations. In this case laws and rules are regarded as arbitrary and obscure. Under these circumstances it appears legitimate to dodge certain rules which are to one's disadvantage and are therefore considered unjust.

No distinction is made between the constitutional state, law, bureaucratisation, order and politics. All of these either serve to preserve a "natural" order or are seen as interfering with the personal responsibility of the individual. Limits of national politics and legislation are either not considered or are highlighted – often in the same interview – in a fatalistic manner.

The Interpersonal-Autonomous Level (Type 2)

Type 2 is based on trust in the goodwill of socially responsible people and the learning capacity of informal institutions. This type has no real notion of society, its functions and its formal institutions, however. The role of impersonal relations is not seen clearly and not considered in the judgements. Accordingly, it is maintained that the most effective way to encourage environmentally sustainable practices is through informal institutions which allow communication and are based on shared norms. The line of argument taken here is: "All the parties – politicians, farmers and consumers – need to discuss the issues together. The farmers should provide a good product for which the consumers should be prepared to pay more. Politicians should create a favourable context for this to happen and help in raising awareness." Formal institutions are widely distrusted because of their distance from everyday life.

For type 2 interpersonal relations based on shared norms constitute the basis for concepts of *solidarity*. Hence, solidarity is not defined by similarity and conformity as it is in type 1. The type 2 individual trusts that mutual expectations regarding social roles are fulfilled and considers himself/herself a member of the social community. The orientation towards mutual welfare and the cautious trust in the power of inter-subjectively valid norms leave more room for differing interests and pluralistic life-styles within a community.

In contrast to the "principle of delegation" found in the type 1, individuals categorised as type 2 attribute *responsibility* to themselves and rely upon the responsibility of the other members of communities. Politics is no longer exclusively understood as a matter for specific decision-makers in positions of power, but rather as a regulatory means within a community based on rule systems that are taken for granted. This orientation towards inter-subjective standards which are ultimately directed at the preservation of the public weal, corresponds with the trust that people are, in principle, capable of insight and through sincere co-operation can also come to reasonably "good" solutions. This fundamental trust leads to the conviction that people are able to learn and that societal development is headed in the right direction. Nonetheless politicians will always be ascribed a dominant position in the organisation of the community. However, this does not excuse the citizen, as a member of society, from taking personal responsibility for institutional action. After all, politicians are supposed to be dependent on the commitment and the insight of mature and capable citizens to be successful. Politics is therefore perceived from a domestic perspective, thus changing its function. Politicians, as responsible people, do not only have to govern but are also expected to relate to those who are not directly involved in politics. This is necessary for disseminating information and allowing room for social practice because overcoming barriers is defined as a collective effort.

Basic trust is maintained even if disappointment dominates in the actual situation, especially with regard to the honesty and responsibility of politicians and the intransigent egoism of citizens. This type is generally guided by ideas about what people should do. They believe, therefore, that they are resistant to negative experience and remain steadfast even if, in real life, norms are broken.

This *counterfactual* validity of norms gives room for tolerance and restraint. It is important that the barriers confronting the realisation of one's own normative expectations are assessed by super-ordinate goals which include mutual respect. Consequently an effort is made to understand causes and reasons which give rise to deviations from these standards. It becomes increasingly difficult to develop prejudices and to blame scapegoats. Causes and reasons for conflicts are rather attributed to the different interests of actors who are considered part of a community integrated by shared norms. This allows politics, justice (the law) and citizens to be brought together and to be understood as components of shared communitarian interests. Overcoming action barriers is always a matter directly connected with the activities and interactions of the participating protagonists: the industrialist, the politician, the consumer, the scientist etc. In order to resolve these conflicts mutual understanding and learning must be encouraged through institutions by providing space for co-operation.

With respect to law basic agreement exists regarding its role as a controlling and regulatory instrument in the community. This agreement stems from the intrinsic understanding that an *"objective assessment"* of conflicts is necessary. A third person's perspective is needed for a just conflict resolution, a judge. However, one does not want authoritative and hierarchical interference from above either, but rather judgements made with restraint. Such judgements should attend to questions of equality, participation and equity. This is also true for laws. They have to be flexible enough to enable appropriate reactions. They should not exclude different perspectives and encourage co-operation and consensus between politics, science and the public. Correspondingly, the existing legal system is criticised for distancing itself from the public, for over-regulation and for being unjust.

The Transpersonal-Heteronomous Level (Type 3)

In contrast to type 2, type 3 endorses the superiority of formal institutions and organisations, with the consequence of devaluing informal institutions. Objectivity and rationality, backed up by expert systems of science, economics, law and administration, are considered central to political activities and institutional change. Considering stakeholder interests and acceptance of institutional changes by civil society is only a strategic instrument to enable efficient policy. The bottom line on environmental problems would be: "Leave it to the scientists to develop technical solutions so that risks can be controlled; meanwhile politicians should improve conditions for international action and encourage acceptance among the population."

Type 3 does not maintain social coherence by integrating individuals into the community or by following inter-subjectively shared norms. Instead, their concept of *society* is characterised primarily by system-functional entities such as politics, law, technology and science. The main concern is a good (formal) institution, i.e. an efficient organisation as well as the necessary factual and objective knowledge. Persons with a sense of *solidarity* (as called for by type 2) are not needed, but rather persons able to take a professional role within systems of experts or legal communities. However, interpersonal concepts of solidarity are referred to from a functional perspective. Interpersonal social conflict- or problem-solving is considered an "irrational" way of acting.

Type 3 attributes *responsibility* to persons occupying functional roles in a system of formally and institutionally based division of labour. From the perspective of this level, faith and trust in the "good will" of the members of a collective which considers itself a community is seen as simply naive. Politics must be professional, i.e. objective, realistic and therefore aloof from questions of interpersonal interaction at the community level. Committed citizens in consumer organisations, environmental protection movements, civic action groups etc. are seen as irrational, as easily manipulated by the mass media, as too emotional and overly guided by their own interests to be of any use in political processes. Yet it is conceded that "local experts on the scene", social movements and civic action can shed light upon certain topics and make them points of discussion. Therefore, they certainly have a political function.

In principle, formal institutions are considered more rational than the informal. The latter can be seen as an "alarm system", but should generally be considered a barrier to rational decision-making. This happens especially when regulatory policies are implemented which affect the behaviour of citizens and demand their insight and support, for example, regarding the long term benefits of environmental protection.

Politics does not depend on the co-operation with citizens, but rather on interplay with the economy, administration and the system of legal and scientific experts. In this process the responsibility of politics is to reach decisions, even when the facts of the case and the interests have not been clearly sorted out. First and foremost, politicians must take into account the voter's opinion which can be more or less rational. The co-ordination of different system perspectives – legal, economic, political and civil societal – is therefore the most pressing goal of competent political action. In cases of conflict (e.g. between economics and ecology) the only goal is thus to assume a position which promises successful action. The rationality of the system does not guarantee the rationality of action. There are problems of fit as a result of dysfunctional subsystems. However, according to type 3, there seems to be a prevalence of bad decision-making among incompetent politicians who do not fulfil their roles in institutions appropriately.

On this level law is understood as something clearly separate from politics, economics, administration and science. It functions as a sovereign and independent subsystem of society. A logic emerges that differs from that which is scientifically or politically based. It has the authority to make decisions and is heeded, based on procedural rules which can sometimes block reasonable decisions, but are generally necessary for maintaining the system. However the latitude of legal decisions as well as problems of law application and law enforcement turn out to be problematic for the formal law system.

Despite exact procedural stipulations regarding becoming increasingly strict under the domination of global markets, there is always room for individual decision-making within formal institutions. This can be a problem in law application. On the other hand, quite a few of those interviewed considered individual initiative and voluntary action to be fundamental to the functioning of formal institutions. However, such actions are not based on an "autonomous" motive to act, but rather on controlling people through incentives and sanctions.

The Transpersonal-Autonomous Level (Type 4)

Type 4 is the only type that recognizes the importance of the interaction of formal and informal norms. These interviewees underline individual responsibility like the interpersonal-autonomous interviewees but they do not reduce personal responsibility to a social interaction model of society. They consider responsibility as a participatory element of a democratic, civil society which is functionally differentiated. Informal and formal institutions are regarded as being interdependent and are based on a common concept of justice supported by formal institutions such as human rights and democratic constitutions. "Environmental problems require discourse at the level of civil society, in its scientific, political and legal dimensions" is the view taken here.

Forms of universal respect and justice determine the notion of *solidarity* of type 4. The interviewees do not refer to mere self-interest (type 1), to community-relations (type 2), or to the legal or scientific community (type 3), but rather to all persons who could potentially be affected by actions.

To evaluate risks type 4 relies on responsible and competent citizens, rather than on experts as in type 3. Therefore politics is not a separately defined subsystem of societal action, but is understood as something that permeates every aspect of life. Discussion and acceptance of political decision-making through public political discussion is favoured over technocratic solutions. Acceptance is established through competent interaction of manufacturers, consumers, politicians and those who are addressed by politics in communities. Consequently this type endorses processes of negotiation and mediation in cases of environmental conflicts. However, the function of formal institutions is more strongly emphasised than on the interpersonal-autonomous level. In cases of manifest conflicts of interests, informal rule systems are often deemed incapable of achieving solutions. One needs to consider the global connections of economic interests as well as the existing "unreasonableness" of individuals which is rooted in their specific biography.

Therefore political argumentation aims, first and foremost, at co-ordinating informal institutions with public action. Public action should take the form of discourse and argumentation based on adequate knowledge and sufficient information. Then the possibilities of formal institutions can be put to better use and, if necessary, their shortcomings can be surmounted. This is undoubtedly a lengthy and difficult process which requires specific democratic skills of everyone involved.

As far as the law is concerned, it is not only seen as a necessary basis for decision-making but also assessed by the principles of equality and justice. Therefore, it is often viewed directly related to moral principles and ethics (values, conventions). From this perspective it becomes clear that in contrast to the transpersonal heteronomous level informal and formal institutions cannot be seen as separate entities.

As a consequence, individual responsible action reaches above and beyond the framework of formal institutions. However, in contrast to the interpersonal autonomous level, the limits of individual *responsibility* are recognised clearly. These are even considered as a danger to civil society because structural risks, such as unemployment and ecological destruction, cannot be seen as something caused by individuals. Even so, individual responsibility alone would be too weak to induce institutional change and social learning. Society needs a clear formal institutional foundation which interacts with informal institutions. This foundation is the democratic rights of the constitutional welfare state.

In summary, the interpersonal-heteronomous type (1) believes that law and politics should guarantee the conformity and similarity of members of society. In the case of direct contact, formal institutions are experienced as something foreign and interfering. They are an expression of power and authority. The justice perspective, in this case, simply implies "every man for himself". By contrast, the interpersonal-autonomous type (2) attributes the responsibility for achieving a functioning community to the individual self, who is seen as embedded in a community. Politics and law which are represented by role-players, are also assessed by this responsibility. Differing points of view of members of a community present no risk because a belief in people's trustworthiness and honesty exists. Therefore the discussion of norms and values is part of the day-to-day interactions of community members.

	Interpersonal		Transpersonal	
	heteronomous (type 1)	autonomous (type 2)	heteronomous (type 3)	autonomous (type 4)
Politics	Sphere of control of concrete decision-makers	Sphere of mutual responsible action of decision-makers and citizens	System with power of making decisions to control societal development	Actions in public which must be institutionally guaranteed
Law	Restriction of scope for action by the powerful	Authority for normative conflict resolution by personal influence (judge)	Societal sub-system. Positive law as a neutral authority without links to informal institutions	Linked to morality and conventions
Citizens	Oriented towards own interests	Responsible members of the community	Addressees for decisions of politicians and experts	Members of society oriented to enlightenment and emancipation

Table 3: Contextualised Ideal Types of Justice Judgements

The transpersonal-heteronomous type (3) integrates the perspectives of the two previous levels on a higher level. Politics and law can only be approached well detached from everyday interactions, but must integrate functional issues. Formalisation, using criteria such as factuality and objectivity, coupled with proceedings and processes, supports this detachment and leads to a justice perspective based on the objectivity of formal processes such as elections, parliamentary debates, jurisdiction and legislation.

In contrast to this, on the transpersonal-autonomous level (4) there is (again) a turn towards social interactions in everyday practice. However this is no longer a communitarian point of view because functional roles, organisations and societal sub-systems and thus formal institutions as a whole, are still considered as an important part of a just society. The perspectives of level 2 and level 3 are integrated. The interviewees paint the image of civil society which is based on the one hand on formal constitutional proceedings and on the other hand on civil participation from the viewpoint of shareholders. Only the latter makes a genuine civil democracy, based on equality, equity and participation, possible and realistic. This distinction is also important with respect to the institutionalisation of co-operative conflict management procedures, as shown by Troja in this volume.

4.2 Political Action Exemplified by a Civic Action Group

The contextualised types of citizens' responsibility are ideal types of cognitive emotional structures, but how are various goals and motives connected with *concrete political action*? To answer this question a case study of a civic action group will be analysed in terms of the four types. It will be seen that the very same action (participation in a civic action group) has to be interpreted quite differently. The civic action group which was studied a while ago, was formed in reaction to the announcement of plans to build a coal power plant in a mining region. In the long run this plant should secure jobs, but it also presents a considerable risk to the environment (Eckensberger/Sieloff/Kasper/Schirk/Nieder 1992). For this reason some of the residents saw the building plans as a threat to the environment and their health. Consequently a civic action group was created and the members hoped to gain enough political influence to stop the construction plans.

The initial reactions to the building plans and the reasons for becoming committed to the act against these were relatively similar across the members of the civic action group. Some felt individually affected because the consequences of the political-societal decision-making process entailed perceptible negative effects within their "private" sphere. This resembles the attitude expressed by the so called NIMBYS (= Not In My BackYard) (Rayner 1993; Eckensberger/Döring/Breit 2001), people who act only on the basis of their individual interests and anxieties. This is also how the supporters of the power plant saw them. Under the guise of environmental protection, they only seemed to pursue their particular interests. Their accusation was supported to some extent in that those who were affected by the building plans lived in a more affluent residential area. Due to their good work and life situation they seemed to have the security to focus special attention on the questions of health, quality of life, nature and aesthetics. A typical conflict between ecological and economic orientations arose because building the coal power plant was legitimised by the jobs it would create.

In the course of time and as a result of discussions members of the civic action movement developed completely different motivational positions and reasons for their commitment. These positions are based on different notions regarding the possibilities of action in the area of politics, similar to those that we portrayed in the types above.

The "Nimbys" (Type 1, Interpersonal-Heteronomous)

Interviews with the civic action group show that the Nimbys really exist, but they represent only the interpersonal-heteronomous type. The "Nimbys" have similar attitudes to those expressed in the prejudices mentioned about the civic action group. Their risk evaluation is based on self interest and their readiness for action is oriented towards individual success. They felt that the building plans encroached upon their own best interests in health and aesthetics. Therefore they wanted to prevent the construction of the power plant. When it became clear that this goal could not be attained, the entire concept of the civic action group was assessed as a failure. It confirmed their deeply rooted basic assumption that one has little influence over agendas from above. The "Nimbys" interpreted their own commitment in the civic action group as a spontaneous expression of direct personal dismay and against their better judgement. When they realized that there was no stopping the building plans every further activity was seen as a waste of time. They turned their backs on the civic action group, although there was still room for technological improvements. Further civic action group activities were even massively devalued and active members were now regarded as foolish.

The "Communitarians" (Type 2, Interpersonal-Autonomous)

By comparison, the "communitarians", who were just as disappointed that the power plant would be built as planned, were able to adapt their goals to the circumstances and refine them. After the building project could no longer be stopped the goal was shifted to "informing the people" about the environmental damage and presenting themselves as spokespersons for the conservation of nature. Moreover when evaluating risks communitarians also consider social consequences for the community. Therefore they remained active in the civic action group to promote more understanding for its position as the better alternative for everyone even after failing to stop the construction of the plant. These representatives of the civic action group argued that environmental protection and health are communitarian goals. During the course of argumentation stopping the building plans lost its original relevance. Now the mentation stopping the building plans lost its original relevance. Now the "comÌ‹munitarians" asserted that the essential task of the civic action group was to sensitise community members to ecological issues.

The "Negotiators" (Type 3, Transpersonal-Heteronomous)

The most committed representatives of the civic action group are those who can be referred to as "negotiators". During the course of the arguments these persons also changed their conceptions of the political goals of the civic action group. However, they did not advocate achieving a better understanding of the group's intentions. The negotiators adapted their initial positions to propagating the feasibility of at least achieving some of the goals within formal institutions. Risk is understood as loss of control and readiness to act is linked to guaranteeing the successful functioning of a system. Stopping the building plans was no longer discussed. One quickly resorted to reaching compromises and looked for politically feasible positions. In order to act successfully the "negotiator" had to acquire specialised knowledge about power station technology, secondary ecological damage caused by building the power station and national and international environmental law and they had to send for legal expertise and organise public discussions. Civic action was seen as a catalyst with the goal of altering various perspectives of formal institutions, law, politics and technology in the direction of their personal interests. The political public was used as a platform for this purpose. With their arguments the negotiators actually achieved some influence. They demanded legal changes to existing conditions so that technical innovations could be realised which would minimise ecological dangers through a reduction of emissions. Subsequently changes even came about in national legal legislation concerning incineration facilities.

The "Civil Rights Activist" (Type 4, Transersonal-Autonomous)

The "civil rights activists" also aim at changing economic and political decisions within the framework of formal institutions. In contrast to the "negotiator" the feasibility of concrete action plays a role as do fundamental changes in consciousness and in political goals in the direction of sustainable development are achieved. The "civil rights activists", as we have called them, unite the perspectives of the communitarians and the negotiators by way of a broader understanding of civil society commitment within democratic institutions. In their eyes neither enlightenment and comprehension, nor feasibility within the frame of existing institutions alone, are sufficient for initiating institutional change in favour of sustainable development. The "civil rights activist" aims generally at the sustainable development which goes beyond the concrete goal of stopping the building. Their risk evaluation is based on examining structural barriers for social learning and institutional change. Their selective protest is considered a component of a more general social movement. The "civil rights activists" hope to reach into the core of formal institutions (law, politics, economics and science) by enlightening society about the importance of ecology. They also hope to activate long-term potential for being rational in order to promote democratic processes and conflict regulation which they only regard as guaranteed by establishing a just civil society.

Due to this, the civil rights activists' interest in the conflict concerning the power plant was not limited to stopping ist construction. The symbolic and socio-political dimension of the commitment was emphasised. The representatives of this type remained politically active with respect to environmental issues even after discussions about the power plant had ended.

5 Conclusion

The results show that more deeply seated moral standards – justice judgements – play an important role in changing the context of political action, social learning and institutional change. This effect was exemplified by the discussion of a civic action group. Those who merely pursue their own interests when involving themselves in political conflicts (Nimbys, interpersonal-heteronomous) quickly give up when the specific action goal is endangered. Their involvement failed to stimulate any further interest in higher goals. In contrast to this, the second type (the communitarian, interpersonal-autonomous) represents community interests, shows solidarity within a community and feels morally obligated to it. Therefore this type is not as likely to give up when the first dilemma crops up within the public conflict. The third type (the negotiator, transpersonal-heteronomous) diverges strongly from the first two types. The negotiator does not necessarily extract his/her readiness for action from normative feelings of obligation, nor from purely egocentric calculations of how one can reap the benefits of such action oneself. The negotiator is far more interested in the possible realisation of socio-political goals which need management and co-operation with other officials in a *formal* institutional context (science and technique, politics and law). From the perspective of this type, these goals are of central importance for the welfare of the general public. However, one is prepared to compromise and to redefine goals within the bounds of what is feasible in a political system. The readiness for action of this type goes hand in hand with intense activities with regard to searching for information and acquiring competence and this is intensified by the challenge of possible barriers and risks. Such an overaching concept of feasibility is not shared by the representative of the last type (the civil rights activist, transpersonal-autonomous). On the contrary, they harbour doubts regarding the possibility of realising their goals and want first and foremost to prepare the way for fundamental changes in consciousness. Even if their chances for success are minimal their feelings of moral obligation do not allow them to abandon their goals. Hope, despite minimal chances of success, becomes an important regulator for willingness to act.

Social practice, with regard to ecological questions as well as economic conflicts or migration issues, always concerns forms of collective systems of interpretation anchored in real life and based on justice judgements. Contextualised types of justice judgements can lead to varying results in different situations at different times. They realise that under certain circumstances risks also have to be tolerated to avoid social injustice, for instance the construction of a coal fuelled power plant to guarantee employment. What is crucial is the structure or the complexity of justice judgements as an indicator of the quality of democratic conflict-solving processes. Justice judgements represent different ways of integrating various perspectives. In their most complex form they are the foundation of a reasoning civil-society public which also feels responsible for ecological remedial action. The interviewees at this level are aware that democratic conflict-solving processes require formal institutions such as law and politics as well as informal institutions such as public discourse and civic participation. But it is public discourse, with its articulation of different values and interests, that produces the central arena of social learning and, thus, induces institutional change and controls its legitimacy. Therefore participation, negotiation and mediation procedures become a vital issue of civil society. Their success is crucial for sustainable development, all the more so when expert cultures fail to resolve the complex environmental problems facing modern risk societies.

What are the consequences of these findings for the discussion of institutional change and social learning, i. e. the fact that social actors interpret their responsibility to act in institutions so differently? The two interpersonal types reconstruct their action space in institutions at a low level of complexity and thus in a deficient way. This implies that the four described types are not just alternative modes of thinking, but they represent different states of moral complexity. From this point of view they increasingly get closer to the moral point of view. The reconstruction of the institutional frame of modern societies requires the more complex perspective of the transpersonal types. However, the two orientations differ with respect to their trust in social learning. Whereas the transpersonal heteronomous types remain sceptical, the transpersonal autonomous types underline the importance of the interaction between informal and formal institutions. In their opinion formal institutions such as positive law have to be simultaneously independent of and open to informal institutions such as morality and conventions. From a *moral point* of view the transpersonal-autonomous types are more complex than the transpersonal-heteronomous. From the point of view of *efficiency* coping with a specific problem it is an empirical question which way of thinking is more adequate. In the long run, however, the transpersonal-heteronomous type only pursues a system-immanent policy. In this view environmental institutions only react to external problems. Really new structures – institutional change – need the reflective abstraction applied by the transpersonal-autonomous types. They do not seek functional solutions alone but search for new goals. The sphere of this reflective process is public discourse which itself needs an institutional frame. Public discourse requires open institutions which provide room for communication, negotiation and mediation and are prepared to integrate possible results. This occurs if social learning is not only institutionalised in the constitutions and the laws of a democratic state, but also promulgated in the public opinion and mass media. In a pluralistic society value orientations have to be respected, but they also have to be translated into formal procedures guided by a justice perspective. Successful institutional changes for more sustainable relations between humans and their environment, therefore, depend on an environmental policy that enables processes of communication between social actors. Discourse between social actors constitutes the basis for the interplay between formal institutions as well as for the interaction of formal and informal institutions. However the success of discourse and communication depends on established formal institutions – especially those of the education system – which have to impart the competence to co-operate, to communicate and to solve conflicts. Only these skills guarantee an adequate discussion of environmental risks and provide the opportunity for social learning and institutional change.

References

Beck, U. (1992): Risk Society. Towards a New Modernity. London; Sage
Boesch, E. E. (1991): Symbolic Action Theory and Cultural Psychology. Berlin; Springer
Breit, H. (2002): Gerechtigkeit und Natur. Die Reichweite der formalen und universalisierbaren praktischen Vernunft. Saarbrücken; Conte-Verlag
Breit, H./L. H. Eckensberger (1998): Moral, Alltag und Umwelt. In: De Haan/ Kuckartz (eds.): Umweltbildung und Umweltbewußtsein. Forschungsperspektiven im Kontext nachhaltiger Entwicklung. Opladen; Leske + Budrich; pp. 69-89
Castoriadis. C. (1987): The Imaginary Institution of Society. Cambridge; Polity Press
Cohen, J./A. Arato (1992): Civil Society and Political Theory. Cambridge; London
Döring, T./L. H. Eckensberger/A. Huppert/H. Breit (in press): Construction of Risk in Agriculture: Conventional and Ecological Perspectives in a German Region. In: Casimir/Stahl (eds.): Culture and the Changing Environment. Uncertainty, Cognition and Risk Management in Cross-Cultural Perspective. Oxford, New York; Berghahn

Douglas, M. (1985): Risk Acceptability According to Social Sciences. New York; Russell Sage Foundation

Durkheim, E. (1991): Professional Ethics and Civic Morals. With a New Preface by Bryan Turner. London; Routledge

Dworkin, R. (1986): Law's Empire. Cambridge (MA), London; The Belknap Press of Harvard UP

Eckensberger, L. H. (1986): Handlung, Konflikt und Reflexion: Zur Dialektik von Struktur und Inhalt im moralischen Urteil. In: Edelstein/Nunner-Winkler (eds.): Zur Bestimmung der Moral. Philosophische und sozialwissenschaftliche Beiträge zur Moralforschung. Frankfurt; Suhrkamp; pp. 409-442

Eckensberger, L. H. (1996): Agency, Action and Culture: Three Basic Concepts for Cross-Cutural Psychology. In: Pandey/Sinha/Bhawuk (eds.): Asian Contributions to Psychology. New Delhi; Sage; pp. 72-102

Eckensberger, L. H./P. Burgard (1986): Zur Beziehung zwischen Struktur und Inhalt in der Entwicklung des moralischen Urteils aus handlungstheoretischer Sicht. Arbeiten der Fachrichtung Psychologie Nr. 77. Saarbrücken; Universität des Saarlandes

Eckensberger, L. H./H. Reinshagen (1980): Kohlbergs Stufentheorie der Entwicklung des Moralischen Urteils: Ein Versuch ihrer Reinterpretation im Bezugsrahmen handlungstheoretischer Konzepte. In: Eckensberger/Silbereisen (eds.): Entwicklung sozialer Kognitionen: Modelle, Theorien, Methoden, Anwendung. Stuttgart; Klett-Cotta; pp. 65-131

Eckensberger, L. H./T. Döring/ H. Breit (2001): Moral Dimensions in Risk Evaluation. In: Boehm/McDaniels/Nerb/Spada (eds.): Environmental Risks: Perception, Evaluation and Management; Vol. 9; Oxford: Elsevier; pp. 137–163

Eckensberger, L. H./U. Sieloff/E. Kasper/S. Schirk/A. Nieder (1992): Psychologische Analyse eines Ökonomie-Ökologie-Konflikts in einer saarländischen Region: Kohlekraftwerk Bexbach. In: Pawlik/Stapf (eds.): Umwelt und Verhalten. Bern; Huber; pp. 145-168

Frey, B. S. (1992): Economics as a Science of Human Behaviour. Towards a New Social Science Paradigm. Boston, London; Kluwer Academic

Haan, de G. (1995): Umweltbewußtsein. In: Jänicke/Bolle/Carius (eds.): Umwelt Global. Berlin; Springer Verlag

Habermas, J. (1990): Moral Consciousness and Communicative Action. Cambridge; Polity Press

Habermas, J. (1993): Justification and Application. Remarks on Discourse Ethics. Cambridge (MA); MIT Press

Habermas, J. (1996): Between Facts and Norms. Contributions to a Discourse Theory of Law and Democracy. Cambridge (MA); MIT Press

Kohlberg, L. (1985): A Current Statement on Some Theoretical Issues. In: Modgil/Modgil (eds.): Lawrence Kohlberg. Consensus and Controversy. Philadelphia; Farmer Press

Lempert, W. (1988): Soziobiographische Bedingungen der Entwicklung moralischer Urteilsfähigkeit. In: Kölner Zeitschrift für Soziologie und Sozialpsychologie; Vol; 40; pp. 62-92

Loch, D./W. Heitmeyer (eds.) (2001): Schattenseiten der Globalisierung. Frankfurt am Main; Suhrkamp

Luhmann, N. (1995); Social Systems. Foreword by Eva M. Knodt. Stanford (CA); Stanford University Press

Moore, B. (1978): Injustice. The Social Bases Obedience and Revolt. New York; White Plains

North, D. C. (1990): Institutions, Institutional Change and Economic Performance. Cambridge; Cambridge University Press

Offe, C. (1999): Wenn das Vertrauen fehlt. In: Die Zeit; No. 50

Ostrom, E. (1990): Governing the Commons. The Evolution of Institution for Collective Action. Cambridge; Cambridge University Press

Piaget, J. (1932): The Moral Judgement of the Child. London; RKP

Rayner, S. (1991): Cultural Theory and Risk Analysis. In: Golding/Krimsky (eds.): Theories of Risk. New York; Praeger

Rödel, U. /G. Frankenberg/H. Dubiel. (1989): Die demokratische Frage. Frankfurt am Main; Suhrkamp

Sennett, R. (1974): The Fall of Public Man. New York; Alfred A. Knopf

The Social Learning Group (2001): Learning to Manage Global Environmental Risks. Vol. 1: A Comparative History of Social Responses to Climate Change, Ozone Depletion and Acid Rain. Cambridge (MA); MIT Press

Weber, M. (1949): On the Methodology of the Social Sciences. In: Shils/Finch (eds.): Glencoe (IL); Free press

Zürn, M. (2001): Politische Fragmentierung als Folge der gesellschaftlichen Denationalisierung. In: Loch/Heitmeyer (eds.): Schattenseiten der Globalisierung. Frankfurt am Main; Suhrkamp

Thomas Widlok

Institutional Dynamics of Changing Land Care Practices in the Central Namib Desert[1]

1 Introduction

"What are we supposed to learn from a bunch of freaks living on a clearing somewhere in the tropical forest?" Not long ago, this kind of leading question was raised by development policy makers who sought to fend off the claims of anthropologists and other social scientists who claimed that their case studies of small-scale settings in remote parts of the world could contribute to the solution of general issues of development or environmental protection.

The situation has changed insofar as even "exotic bunches" of people tucked away in the forest are considered to be integrated into global processes and insofar as development and conservation experts have discovered the importance of "local culture" and "indigenous knowledge" – and the study of it – for solving global problems such as environmental degradation. However, increasing awareness about the complexity of local social institutions continues to nourish the suspicion that institutional arrangements are not easily transferable from their original setting into any other context. This is true for attempts to import local knowledge and practices into the environmentalist strategies of specialised expert systems (see Widlok in press) but also, conversely, for attempts to understand particular local institutional settings on the basis of general institutional designs (for instance for property regimes, as I will show in this chapter). While the complexity of social institutions in non-Western contexts has been rightly emphasized, partly in an attempt to convince non-social scientists about the importance of recognizing social relations and culture, the main task still lies ahead. This is the task of usefully reducing the complexity of local institutions in order to understand the dynamics of institutional change without uncritically accepting our assumptions of what constitutes different institutional regimes. This contribution tries to

---

1 Field research for this case study was conducted in 1996 as part of a research project funded by the German Research Council (DFG) with supplementary funding by the J. Swan Fund of the Pitt Rivers Museum, Oxford. I am grateful to these institutions for their assistance, to Prof. Michael Casimir who supported my work and to the people of the !Khuiseb valley for their cooperation. I am also indebted to the other members of the working group on institutions in the DFG research programme and to Franz and Keebet von Benda-Beckmann who commented on draft versions of this chapter.

make advances in this direction by critically considering the distinction between "private" and "common" property regimes while continuing our search for comparative analytical tools. My argument proceeds by dissecting a particular social institution, namely the !nara property regime that governs land care practices in the !Khuiseb delta at the central coast of Namibia, into separate layers. This approach allows us to understand social learning in the context of institutional change not in terms of the wholesale import or export of institutional systems. Rather, this case study suggests that in practice institutional change is a product of piecemeal changes taking place on different interconnected institutional layers in a way that generates a particular dynamic. While I maintain that the analysis of layers may be a general tool to understand institutions across diverse cases I expect that every particular setting generates its distinctive dynamic.

The purpose of developing such a layered model is twofold. It should enable us to compare – layer by layer – complex institutions across very different contexts and it should help us to understand the dynamics of institutional change as a consequence of interaction between these layers.

2 The Ethnographic Case Study

The people involved in this case study call themselves =Aoni[2] or Topnaar and they live in the central Namib desert of Namibia. In this desert environment of coastal and inland sand dunes, gravel plains and non-perennial rivers the Khoisan-speaking =Aoni practice a mixed economy consisting of limited lifestock raising, occasional wage labour, foraging on coastal marine resources, and the use of a major endemic food resource, the melon-like !nara (*Acanthosicos horridus*, a cucurbit). Despite their desert environment the =Aoni are not an isolated group. They share a language with other Khoekhoe-speakers in southern Africa, with other Nama groups but also with Damara and even with Hai//om "Bushmen" (see Haacke/Eiseb/Damaseb 1997). They share cultural traits with Nama pastoralists in other parts of Namibia (see Hoernlé 1985) as well as with other people speaking Khoisan languages (Widlok 1993, 1999) and they share a history of colonization and dispossession with other groups of the area, for instance with the Bantu-speaking Herero (see Köhler 1969). One way in which ethnic group boundaries have been drawn in this part of Africa is to identify people according to what they own. The =Aoni or Topnaar have been distinguished from others living in the same

---

2   The Khoekhoe language spoken by the Topnaar includes a number of click sounds which are commonly represented with the help of special symbols, namely =,/,//,! (for details see Haacke/Eiseb/Namaseb 1997).

cultural area or living on the same land on the basis of the main wild resource they own and utilize: the fruit of the *!nara*, an endemic plant of the Namib desert (for botanical details see van den Eynden/Vernemmen/Van Damme 1992, p. 34). This is reflected in the local Nama name "*!naranin*" (*!nara* people) for the =Aoni of the !Khuiseb river valley and in the ethnographic classification of the =Aoni as a "harvesting people". The *!nara* plant, botanically a member of the cucumber family and in appearance similar to a melon, has been used by humans for thousands of years as the archaeological record indicates (Sandelowsky 1977, Kinahan 1991). Ethnographers have linked the archaeological evidence of *!nara* use in the past with the =Aoni of the present. By classifying them as a "harvesting people" (Budack 1983) the =Aoni have been put into a category of their own, set apart from the pastoralists and the hunter-gatherers of central Namibia. There is little information available about the ethnic identity of the *!nara* users who left their mark in the archaeological record but who may not have constituted themselves as a distinct ethnic group at all. However, the =Aoni of today trace their roots as a group to the *!nara* users of earlier times.

The economic importance of the *!nara* has shifted over time. European explorers who landed at the Namib coast already noted that the Khoisan-speaking people of this area ate cooked pulp which in all likelihood was cooked *!nara* (see Moritz 1992, p. 5). As contacts with colonials developed the fatty *!nara* pips gained importance as a trade item. The colonizers became consumers of the *!nara* which they bought from =Aoni and exported to the Cape colony and to Europe. At times colonizers were also disturbed by the *!nara* which provided a food security to =Aoni who used this option to evade being recruited into wage labourhood (Budack 1983, p. 6). *!Nara* are still consumed widely in the area, but today the largest group of consumers may be found in Cape Town which is far away from the =Aoni settlement area. *!Nara* are also harvested and processed by people who may not be identified as =Aoni but as Damara although it has also been observed that newcomers who began harvesting the *!nara* soon identified themselves as =Aoni (Köhler 1969, p. 113).

The Topnaar are not only identified through their association with their major plant resource but also with the specific property regime that regulates the way in which the plant is being used. For Schapera (1930, pp. 290-1) the *!nara* property regime is remarkable because it is a regime of private ownership, a rare instance of private property being institutionalized in this part of Africa. Schapera's notion of "regime" is very fitting here. Private property of *!nara* is not simply an isolated cultural trait but it touches on issues of ethnic identity, it involves individual actions of sanction, social organisation into families and chiefs, and social relationships of inheritance. The notion of an institutionalised practice therefore seems to be appropriate. It contrasts with the communal property regime of land ownership among other Khoisan groups.[3] However, there seem to be some ambivalences when trying to characterize the institutional design of the local property regime as either "communal", "private" or "family-based". To begin with the object of property relations seems uncertain: Is it *land* or its *resources*, *!nara bushes* or their *fruit*? The exact nature of the property relations also remains unclear. "Private property", it seems, is not understood as "individual/personal" nor strictly in opposition to "communal" since a whole family has ownership rights. "Private" appears to be seen in contrast to "public" and "open access" but also in contrast to centrally owned by an individual chief. Both these ambivalences deserve further comment because they remain relevant for the current land care system of the =Aoni and the way it is dealt with by specialists concerned with the !Khuiseb environment.

!Nara grow wild in hammocks on the sand dunes south of the !Khuiseb river valley but in greatest density in the extensive !Khuiseb delta near Walvis Bay. Since the !Khuiseb is a dry river bed except for a few days of a year, and may for many years not reach the Atlantic ocean at all, the delta of the !Khuiseb is a large field of dunes on which the *!nara* plants but very few other edible plants grow. Continual winds and occasional floods reshape this dune field all the time so that *!nara* plants can also be said to move. Moreover, the plant is a creeper with long tendrils so that neighbouring plants easily get entangled. As I will point out in more detail below, in the past the primary object of the property regime of the =Aoni seems to have been the *!nara* plants, and by implication their produce, rather than plots of land. There is evidence that the value of the *!nara* has recently shifted from *!nara* bushes to the land itself, with the *!nara* harvest as a powerful symbol that expresses =Aoni attachment to their land. Today the *!nara* is not only a key element in the definition of =Aoni identity but it also serves as a political tool for defending =Aoni rights to their land that have been under pressure since colonization began. Being officially classified as "Nama" by the apartheid administration, the =Aoni were supposed to be resettled in southern Namibia away from their land and the *!nara* but they have resisted this forced resettlement. It seems that when being asked in the past about the family unit that would legitimately own a field =Aoni refer to the *!hao-!nas* (lit. "in the tribe", often glossed as "clan"), i.e. a division below the level of the ethnic group but above that of a family household. This unit is constituted by a group of genealogically related families that do not all carry the same name but can be

---

3   The =Aoni of today endorse the fact that the *!nara* property regime is outstanding in regional comparison because it provides them with an important ethnic marker. In the words of the present =Aoni Chief: "In contrast to all other Khoi Khoi tribes where the concept of communal ownership prevailed, the *!nara* fields of the Topnaar people are the property of individual lineages. Each and every field is the alienable property of a specific extended family" (Kooitjie 1997). There is no evidence that *!nara* fields have in fact been sold or otherwise alienated but this self-representation also reflects the dominant image of the *!nara* property regime, going back to observations from the 19th century (see Moritz 1992).

identified as unit based on kinship. The =Aoni !hao-!nas encompasses a larger number of individuals and families than those who form the everyday economic unit. At the same time the social system suggests that relatives belonging to one's !hao-!nas are potential partners in the exploitation of a !nara field and that a sufficient basis for trust and common ground exists to pool efforts with them, either in forming a harvesting party or in sharing !nara products and exchanging them for the returns of other economic pursuits such as livestock herding.

3 Environmental Change in the Central Namib Desert

Environmental change in the !Khuiseb valley has been documented in great detail due to the fact that the desert research station Gobabeb, home to the Desert Ecological Research Unit, is located in the !Khuiseb. Here, ecological research over several decades has shown changes in the distribution of density of natural species in the various desert habitats (sand dune desert to the south, gravel plain to the north and a mostly dry river bed rich in animal and plant life at the centre of the !Khuiseb valley). The research has shown that many species useful to the =Aoni are declining, not only the !nara but also for instance game animals. The =Aoni who inhabit the Namib-Naukluft Park but who so far had little say in the way in which it was managed blame this ecological degradation on the various forms of colonial interference, water mining for mines and towns along the lower !Khuiseb, intensive farming by Europeans along the upper !Khuiseb, flood dam construction near the coastal town, but also restrictive nature conservation management in the Namib-Naukluft Park itself.

Primarily due to the presence of the Namib Desert Research Centre at Gobabeb but also because of the incorporation of the area into the Namib-Naukluft Park, the !nara, and the way in which the =Aoni make use of it, has attracted a lot of popular attention. There has been little in-depth field research but many cursory accounts over the decades (Berry 1991; Enviroteach 1995; Grimme 1910; Herre 1975; Pfeiffer 1979; Storad 1991; Visser 1998). These accounts leave no doubt that there have been considerable ecological and social changes over the past decades but the causal links connecting these facts remain unclear. There is agreement on the fact that the distribution of !nara plants and the size and quantity of !nara fruits in the !Khuiseb delta has deteriorated over the last 30 years or so. It is also not disputed that the practices connected with the !nara harvest, in particular the institutionalised property regime, have changed during the same period. However, multiple explanations – some complementary, others mutually conflicting – have been put forward to explain the dynamics that have led to either the ecological change or the social change and to the possible connections between these two processes.

Over the recorded past, ecological changes have affected the distribution and productivity of the *!nara* plants and therefore also the possibilities for its use. Some of these changes, such as the irregular flooding of the !Khuiseb river delta, are "natural" and unpredictable. Others, such as the drop of the groundwater level due to a water extraction scheme and the building of a flood dam, are man-made. *!Nara* subsistence and trade continue up to today but wage labour and other forms of income such as small-livestock holding and a fishing quota produce more income for more =Aoni than *!nara* collecting, processing and trading does today. The *!nara* harvest as an institution is still very relevant for today's =Aoni but complex changes have taken place insofar as the economic dimension of this institution seems to be declining while the political dimension is increasing and insofar as the relation between this institution and other institutionalised forms of economic activity, such as livestock holding and wage labour, are changing. Urbanization, ecological degradation, commercialisation and integration into the world economy have changed the social organisation of the =Aoni and their relations with other groups considerably. A cristallization point for these institutional changes are changing property relations.

The land of the =Aoni is considered state land by the national government and =Aoni were not consulted when state agencies interfered with the ecology of the area by the building of a flood protection wall, the mining of water and the damming of water in the !Khuiseb catchment area. It has been suggested that these measures together with restrictive conservation policies (especially the prohibition for =Aoni to burn unproductive *!nara* plants), changed economic conditions (the increasing number of donkeys grazing on the *!nara*) and changing harvesting practices (for instance the use of iron rods by harvesters) has led to a decline in the size and number of *!nara* (Shilomboleni 1998). All these causes are ultimately man-made but the responsibilities are attributed to different social groups – farmers, miners, town-dwellers, conservationists, planners, harvesters (see Botelle/Kowalski 1996). While some ecologists point out that the availability of water is highly unpredictable in this environment, so that some of the changes observed may be due to irregular natural cycles, the human factor, including institutional change, seems to be crucial in this change.

The decline of the traditional property regime seems to play a major part in the social changes that concern the harvest and use of the *!nara*. Less =Aoni are harvesting *!nara* than in the documented past and less =Aoni families depend on the *!nara*, although the harvesting season has been extended so that it covers almost the whole year. The system of recognized and protected family-fields is largely defunct and the remaining families harvest freely in a number of different fields. At the same time =Aoni complain that the !*nara* is virtually an open-access resource now as town-dwellers, who are not =Aoni, harvest in the !Khuiseb delta. Again the responsibility for these changes has been attributed to various social agents. The decline of the traditional property regime is attributed to weak leadership which failed to protect property rules, to decreasing economic importance of the !*nara* in the =Aoni economy, and to the lack of control granted to the =Aoni by the national administration. Furthermore, =Aoni themselves often draw a direct causal link between the ecological decline of the !*nara* and the practicability of the traditional property regime, putting the blame on external forces for producing ecological change to which they themselves then had to react. Representatives of the Ministry of Environment and Tourism who run the Namib-Naukluft Park have for a long time blamed the =Aoni for detrimentally influencing the local ecology and restricted =Aoni movement in the park and at times threatened to expel them from the !Khuiseb.

I suggest that an analysis of the !*nara* property system in terms of layers, as I will develop below, allows us to account for the diverging assessments of the ongoing environmental change by realizing that individuals within the =Aoni group as well as interested parties from outside this group may be commenting on quite different aspects of what has hitherto been considered to be an undifferentiated institutional package of ownership rights.

4 Towards a Layered Model of Institutions

Comparative anthropological research has shown that forms of private ownership usually coexist with forms of communal ownership basically everywhere, including seemingly simple societies (see Schott 1956). It has become equally important to point out that these property regimes could consist of both formal institutions such as the position of Chief or inheritance rules involving corporate kin-groups and also informal institutions such as habitual practices. In order to avoid any sense of deficiency when discussing the informal "habits" of "simple" societies in contrast with societies that have a tradition of formally codified and written laws, all the above mentioned manifestations can come under the broad category of "institutions" of property.[4]

---

4 It follows that the anthropological study of institutions usually comprises a description of named and formalized arrangements, sometimes reflectively described by actors, as well as of patterns emerging from recurrent behaviour which are only named and identified by the observer.

Institutions in this broad sense may include everything from a formal convention or rule to an informal cognitive foundation of a social grouping or constellation – named or unnamed – that directs practice. It is one of the most fundamental insights of ethnographic case studies that these different forms of institutionalization are seen and understood as conditioning one another. They are either complementary or in conflict with one another in a single complex process of change. Consequently, they require a single analytical framework that distinguishes aspects or layers of institutions rather than types of institutions. The purpose of having such a framework is that it can enable us to do two things. Firstly it helps to split the notion of institutions into components or layers that can be studied ethnographically and comparatively. Secondly it helps us to develop a dynamic model that suggests how these components or levels are related to one another.

In my attempt to develop such a framework I make use of ideas recently developed in the field of legal anthropology. My point of departure is a model which was primarily designed as a descriptive tool and which would allow us to compare diverse property regimes as they are usually encountered by anthropologists working in diverse field situations. Benda-Beckmann and Benda-Beckmann (1999) have proposed a model of institutional layers for dissecting and understanding complex institutionalised property relations. The underlying idea of such a layered model is to overcome the opposition between rules and ideology on the one hand and practice and reality on the other hand (see Benda-Beckmann/Benda-Beckmann 1999, p. 20). Formal and informal aspects of institutions should be re-integrated into a single framework in order to show how they condition one another. The Benda-Beckmanns distinguish four layers: cultural ideals and ideologies, normative and institutional regulation, property relationships, and social practices. This has an important advantage over earlier institutional approaches in that rules, relationships, and practices are no longer "packaged in an institution" (1999, p. 22). Thereby we are equipped to go beyond the investigation of interaction either between (pre-packaged) institutions, each of them an undifferentiated whole, on the one hand or between institutions and apparently institution-free activity on the other. We can improve our understanding of institutional change and the internal dynamics of different layers within an institution. All these layers are connected in social practice but they are independent enough "to warrant an examination of their mutual interrelationships" (1999, p. 22). I subscribe to such a layered model but I propose a graphical representation which contains two important qualifications to the model (see Figure 1).

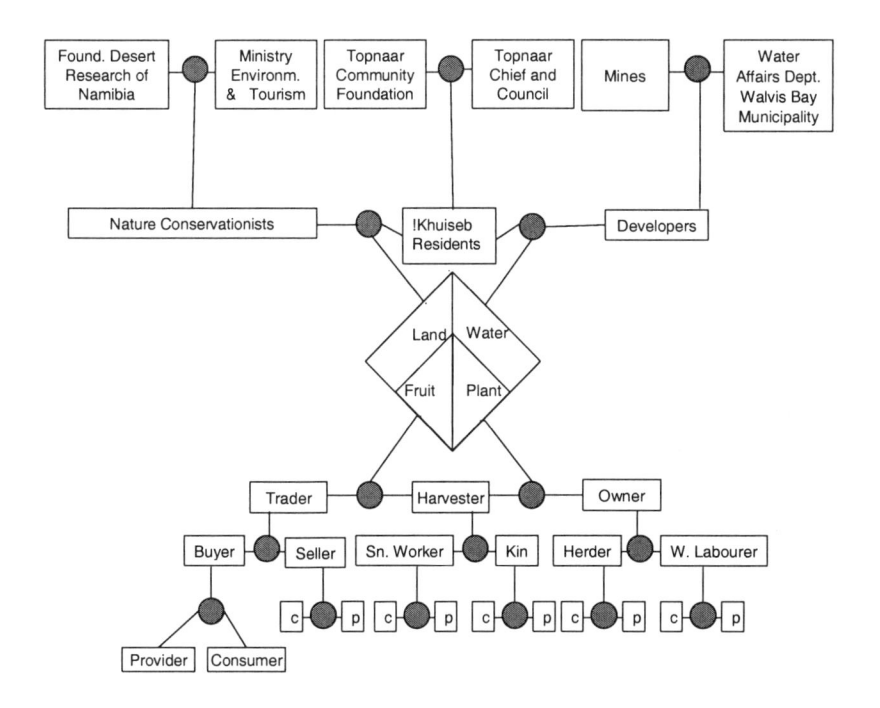

Figure 1: A layered model of the *!nara* property regime

I suggest that it is useful to maintain a sense of that which may be considered the objectification of property relations. With regard to the *!nara* case, but probably this is true more generally, much of the confusion seems to result from the fact that the object of property regulations and relations is not clear. While state environmental agencies underline their sovereign rights over the land on which the *!nara* grows and on which the =Aoni live, other state agencies such as the water affairs administration, the mining companies and the administrators of the urban centre seem to be primarily concerned with the underground water reservoir. The traditional concern of the =Aoni seems to have been the *!nara* bushes more than "plots of land" but this seems to be changing now as the rights in managing the *!nara* come to stand for land rights more generally which offer potential, not just for harvesting *!nara*. Furthermore the social relations that constitute the *!nara* property regime are usefully specified for the *!nara* fruit and the *!nara* plant as will be shown in more detail below. The objectification of *!nara* property regulations is graphically represented with a lozenge, relations are represented with a circle.

213

The second qualification to the model which is contained in the graphical representation concerns the distinction between relations and social actions. Instead of limiting relations to the link between previously identified individual actors, the graphical representation allows to see relations as constituting arenas for action which may then be filled by individual persons (or corporate persons) but which may also be internal to individuals as well as subject to shifts as natural persons take on some fields of action or leave others. The dynamic picture gained through this graphical convention will be described in more detail below. The first necessary step that leads from this discussion is a dissection of the *!nara* property regime into the layers that I have identified above.

5 Dissecting the *!nara* Property Regime

As a first step towards arriving at a more dynamic and realistic picture of the *!nara* property regime I suggest to break up the synthetic statements about "privately owned plots" by investigating separately the different analytical layers of property regimes, namely cultural values, cultural regulations, social relations and social actions.

Cultural Values

The key cultural values in the *!nara* property regime are its exclusiveness with regard to the =Aoni as an ethnic group and its inclusiveness with regard to all =Aoni families. Ethnic exclusiveness is hinted at in descriptions of the *!nara* property regime (see above). Tresspassers of other ethnic groups are severely dealt with since they cannot hold any legitimate ownership rights in the *!nara*, which are – according to the ideal – inherited from one =Aoni generation to the other through the male line. Furthermore "each and every" *!nara* field is claimed by some =Aoni family, leaving no residual area for the use or ownership of others or for open access. But not only are all *!nara* in the area divided into exclusive fields for the =Aoni. Conversely, every =Aoni family has some ownership right in a *!nara* field. Both ideals, that of a comprehensively divided world of *!nara* plants and that of a complete provision for all =Aoni families, are maintained as a value up to this day. The =Aoni chief is often named as the guarantor for these values and his role therefore needs to be discussed in this context.

Since colonization began, chieftainship among the =Aoni has been under pressure, especially during the last century. Colonial interference interrupted the succession of chiefs and there have also been conflicts about succession.

This weakened the =Aoni with regard to the colonial powers and neighbouring groups. Internally the *!nara* property regime did not rely exclusively on the sanctioning power of chiefs being in office but more generally on a shared recognition of the principles of =Aoni social organisation, in particular its identity as an ethnic group and its internal make-up as consisting of family groups. It seems that the property regime was not installed from above but was anchored in the web of =Aoni social organisation which prevented it from collapse in the absence of chiefs. There was no support from external authorities for =Aoni cultural values with regard to ownership since the colonial administration considered =Aoni land to be crown land and their ownership claims and rules therefore as spurious.

The Ministry of Environment and Tourism and the Department of Water Affairs have, if at all, consulted the =Aoni only as one interested party among many others and have carried out their strategies according to their own values, especially the value of "the national good". Despite this general disregard for =Aoni values, the *!nara* fields have been important in the relation between =Aoni and the colonial, now national, administration. The ownership of *!nara* fields is the basis for =Aoni land claims more generally and for their constitution as an ethnic group claiming land ownership in the !Khuiseb valley on the basis of their ethnic identity. The entitlement of all =Aoni families to have access to *!nara* plots has been maintained even under changing ecological conditions. According to the acting chief he initiated a redistribution of family rights to plots when whole stretches of *!nara* fields disappeared due to the building of the Walvis Bay flood dam and due to other measures taken in the interest of a growing urban population and of growth in the livestock and mining industries. Recent urban and industrial developments have exploited the underground water reservoir of the !Khuiseb, threatening the *!nara* fields and consequently threatening to leave some families without access to any *!nara* fields. This development is of great concern to the =Aoni, not only because of its detrimental effects on the *!nara* harvest but more fundamentally because it affects key values of identity and cultural property. The *!nara*, therefore, is best characterized as a =Aoni good, maybe the supreme good of the =Aoni (see Gregory 1997, p. 81). It certainly has value not only as an object of consumption or exchange. The fact that the positive evaluation of the *!nara* is closely connected to a positive self-image of the =Aoni as *!nara* harvesters is also highlighted by the recent re-emergence of *!nara* praise songs in the !Khuiseb which include the following sequences:

"You round food / with many thorns / you many-breasted / foster-mother of the =Aoni children / even if I am far away / I will think of you / you food of my ancestors / I will never forget you" (Kooitjie 1997, p. 2)

There is little doubt that such praise songs did exist in the past but ethnographers who undertook great efforts to record songs in the 1970s were only able to record remnants of these songs. The longest version was obtained from a European farmer who had heard it being sung by an old "Bushman" employee (see Moritz 1992, p. 36). This example of the recreation or revitalization of a cultural tradition shows not only how different cultural values, such as identity and property, are connected but also that they need to be seen in the context of the cultural means of communicating and reaffirming values and of the changing opportunities for institutionalising these values further as cultural conventions and regulations of cultural organisation.

Cultural Regulations

The general cultural values of appropriating the *!nara* for the =Aoni and of guaranteeing access to the *!nara* for all =Aoni families were integrated into a more elaborate cultural system which has been called the *!nara* field or "plot" system. *!Nara* fields were demarcated with "beacons" which served as a cultural sign indicating boundaries and the individual entitlements of families (Budack 1983, p. 4). As I have already pointed out it seems more likely that the property rules in fact applied to *!nara plants* and not to plots of land, taking account of the fact that *!nara* plants "move" as they grow on the shifting sand dunes of the river delta and that the tendrils of individual plants may easily get entangled with one another. There was another cultural tool for detecting trespassing even when it was not observed as a manifest spatial transgression of boundaries. Individual owners claim to recognize the *!nara* pips of their own field by their taste. What may at first to appear to be a mystical skill can still be tested today. I took samples of *!nara* pips from a number of different localities in the !Khuiseb and asked several men and women to taste where a sample came from and to whose harvest they belonged. The results confirmed that there is such a skill of distinguishing *!nara* pips according to taste. The experiment revealed that the size and saltiness of pips varied in relation to the location where the *!nara* plant grew, probably due to the amount and saltiness of water available to the plant. Individuals varied with regard to their skill to match pips with names of places and with individual people harvesting at these places. Such differences in skills were readily acknowledged. But there was no doubt among =Aoni that tasting pips in order to determine their origin is a cultural skill and a legitimate means for the owners to establish the origin of pips. It also suggests that most =Aoni have some sort of socially shared mental map of the *!nara* fields, that is to say some representation about the spatial distribution of *!nara* bushes and people having claims to the fruit gained from these bushes. Furthermore, there are cultural standards of what constitutes a good, tasty *!nara* pip, which largely refer to the colour and taste of pips after they have been cooked. This corresponds to cultural skills involved in cooking the *!nara* properly (such as the selection of suitable ripe !*nara*, the right temperature and duration of cooking the pips). These skills not only help to identify the harvest of an individual but they are also a means of establishing the value of a particular !*nara* as a desirable good in comparison with the !*nara* of other fields and families (see above). Furthermore, the different quality of !*nara* pips is also important for determining the commodity and exchange value of the pips. This is the cultural background for understanding =Aoni complaints about "!*nara* pirates" – that is, mostly non-=Aoni who harvest and trade !*nara* without the culturally recognized skills. These pirates not only upset the established pricing mechanisms between =Aoni harvesters and urban traders, they also more generally threaten the value of !*nara* as a =Aoni good.

=Aoni complaints against "pirates" fall on deaf ears with the administration which appears to follow the policy of various colonial authorities who considered the !*nara* to grow "wild on waste Crown lands and [to be] veld kost, so [that] the law against theft was inoperative" (Rolland quoted in Budack 1983, p. 5). Consequently, all regulations put in place by the colonial administration such as the prohibition to burn old and unproductive !*nara* plants or the prohibition to move freely in the sand dunes are detrimental to the maintenance of the =Aoni property system. The cultural rules governing !*nara* property relations only apply to individuals within the reach of =Aoni cultural organisation. However, within this cultural context the organisation of property claims involves not only relations between owners and (potential) trespassers. Putting up beacons, it seems, was only to underline claims that were already socially recognized. It is therefore unlike the establishment of boundaries with fences in previously communal areas which currently occurs in other parts of Namibia. While owners could not appeal to the administration to safeguard their property rights, they did appeal to the chief and his council who were also known as "parents rich in !*nara*" alluding to their special position with regard to the !*nara* (Budack 1983, p. 5). In other words the cultural organisation of the !*nara* plot system relied on a well-established network and hierarchy of social relations.

Social Property Relations

Property relations are taboo relations because they imply that certain forms of taking and appropriating (and sometimes of giving and alienating) are considered to be forbidden between certain people. However, it is important to note that a taboo relation is still a social relation. It is not the absence of engagement but is characterized by a distinctive restriction of engagement with certain people at certain times for certain purposes. The culturally constructed property taboos that separate the owner of a !*nara* field from others implies that the !*nara* is not freely shared with everybody. However, the owner still engages in social relations with non-owners or other owners. Since these social relations may be eclipsed or "hidden" in taboo relations I will propose (in the following section) a method that elucidates these relations. Products of *!nara* plots do not flow freely among the people related with the =Aoni who harvest *!nara* in the !Khuiseb. Therefore, we need to pay special attention to the engagement not only among owners, but also between owners and non-owners that are involved in the flow of *!nara* products and in establishing the rights in *!nara* plants.

It is important to go beyond the static cultural map of *!nara* "plots" and to consider all relevant social relations involved in the *!nara* property regime. Apart from the relatively instantaneous conflict between owner and trespassers and the relatively fixed genealogical succession of persons leaving an inheritance and those taking it (discussed below), the benefits of *!nara* ownership are distributed in social relations that are formed in the process of *!nara* harvesting. There is no indication that =Aoni sought to sell or buy plots, nor that they received prestige or status owning a particular plot, nor that there was any possibility or interest to accumulate ownership rights in order to make profits, gain interest etc. Inheritance of *!nara* fields seems to have been fairly unproblematic; at least no inheritance conflicts are reported in the records. There are, however, many indications that use rights were complex and subject to manoeuvre and negotiation. The social relations between owner and harvester imply relations between members of the owning family who are active in the *!nara* harvest and those members who are not, as well as relations between harvesters and traders. It is important to note that the composition of harvesting parties seems to always have been flexible. This is certainly the case in the present and for the documented past (Dentlinger 1983). Although harvesters would in most cases be related through ties of kinship or marriage the kinship system does not predetermine who may join a harvesting party this year or next year. Relations between harvesters are informal in the sense of being non-predetermined, as are relations between co-residents who form the main consumption unit and indeed as between co-habitants who form the reproductive unit of the =Aoni. Owners of *!nara* fields can engage with others in a cooperative seasonal harvesting team or they can send out any kinsperson but also a non-=Aoni, usually a Damara, as a worker in the *!nara* fields. The returns would then be shared with these workers. The most common strategy seems to have been to split the household during the *!nara* season so that yields from inland livestock herding and coastal *!nara* harvesting could be pooled or exchanged by members of the household. Sharing the returns means not only receiving some *!nara* as food but also receiving some of the cash or cash economy products gained in the trade of *!nara* pips. For this purpose *!nara* owners also have to engage with urban traders in what for a long time seems to have taken the form of long-term trading partnerships. General traders were, and sometimes still are, providers of all kinds of commodities for the =Aoni who would pay off their debts at harvesting time by trading in their !nara pips.

Social Action

The most influential individual choice in the context of the !nara property regime concerns the intensity of !nara use. The =Aoni never subsisted solely on the !nara but relied on hunting (now no longer possible), livestock raising (now less intensive than in the past) and wage labour (now more intensive than in the past). Harvesting !nara was only one constituent of their mixed economy and it had to be kept flexible in order to account for demographic changes but also for irregular ecological changes that would affect the supply of !nara. At the end of the nineteenth century there were reports that the population had decreased and the !nara increased, leaving tracts of !naras vacant (see Budack 1983, p. 5). Then, after a devastating flood in 1934, harvests were reportedly very low up to the 1950s, leaving some Topnaar without a harvest (Köhler 1969, p. 118). In the 1970s the available !nara were reported to have again exceeded the demand (Budack 1983, p. 5). At the level of individual action this means that every season a person would need to ask him- or herself whether it was worthwhile to move into the !nara fields. Given that most !nara fields are situated in the !Khuiseb delta where there are no permanent =Aoni settlements, moving to the !nara fields often meant abandoning a paid job or leaving livestock in the care of others. Benefitting from this mixed economy implied depending on others as partners in livestock herding or !nara harvesting. With the increase in permanent wage labour opportunities strategies seem to have bifurcated as some =Aoni do not take any active part in the !nara harvest at all while others make much of their living through !nara harvesting. For the latter this means that they have to be more active in trading !nara pips so that they can bridge the times when !naras are lean and so that they can convert some of their harvest into cash income.

Also more recently, some =Aoni convert !nara not only into economic capital through trade but also into symbolic capital in the national politics of community identity and land rights. This is particularly true for =Aoni who are no longer living in the !Khuiseb but who are engaged with administrators and representatives of the media and development NGOs.[5] Although I have

---

5 This is underlined by the results of a workshop in which young people were asked to envisage how they wanted to see the !Khuiseb environment being used in the year 2034 (fourty years ahead). !Nara do not feature in this vision, only in the subsequent discussion it was mentioned that people continue to use the !nara. By contrast a group representation of land use at present (that is in 1994) depicts the !nara prominently in three instances (see Botelle/Kowalski 1995). Note that the !nara also does not feature in the representation

seen many young people among the *!nara* harvesters of the 1996 season, it is certainly true that harvesting in a make-shift shelter in the !Khuiseb delta is an arduous task so that not only young =Aoni but all harvesters try to get regular lifts into the nearby coastal town of Walvis Bay which has all the amenities of modern life including access to a rich spectrum of consumer products.

As a staple food the *!nara* has a rather low reputation among =Aoni, and this has been so at least since the 1970s (see Dentlinger 1977, 1983). Other forms of income are being sought after by =Aoni and those who continue working in the *!nara* fields seek to earn money for more prestigious commodities by selling *!nara* to traders in town. Selling *!nara* helps families pay their children's school fees, as I have been told frequently (see also Botelle/Kowalski 1995, p. 69). This shift of interests is recognized by the =Aoni themselves who often take this as their starting point for explaining the processes of change in which they are involved. In the pursuit of a quick return individuals harvest randomly across the *!nara* fields, disregarding the traditional property regime. In that process they also harvest unripe *!nara*, they do not care or manage *!nara* fields and they use iron rods which can harm the plant. All these developments contribute to the decline of the *!nara* and its fruit.

6 Analysing Institutional Dynamics

Dissecting a property regime into institutional layers allows us to view institutional dynamics in terms of changes that take place at one of the layers and which then trigger off changes at another layer or which indeed may clash with changes (or the lack thereof) at any of the other layers. Disentangling the different layers of an institutionalised property regime may also help to understand why deliberate or involuntary changes to one aspect may only gradually change the property regime and may lead to unintended effects. For instance discontinuing one action, such as burning old *!nara* plants or letting one aspect of the social organisation, such as the *!hao!nati* (clans), fall into disuse may not lead to a demise of the whole institution. A description that accounts for the state of affairs at the various layers promises a more realistic, yet clear, representation of the complexities of an institution such as the property regime under investigation here. The argument which I want to pursue in the remainder of this chapter goes even further than that. The layered model

---

produced by elderly people of !Khuiseb land use in 1944. Again the *!nara* seems to have only been mentioned in passing in the discussion. This may be explained by the fact that the participants in this workshop focused on events surrounding the great flood of 1934 which in fact destroyed many *!nara* plants and the harvest of subsequent years.

not only inventorizes various aspects or suggests that a certain threshold has to be reached for institutional change to take place but can also lead to a dynamic model of institutional change. Moreover, it is possible to characterize different analytic approaches as focusing on opposite ends in terms of this layered model. That is to say, individualistic approaches (e.g. Schweizer 1996) assume that institutional change relies on behaviour change, which then works its way "up" to cultural values. Culturalist approaches (e.g. Douglas 1987) seem to assume that a change of values (in individual cognition or public culture) will eventually trickle down and lead to changes in behaviour. The model suggested here allows for input from either "end" and for indirect influences too, that is for changes in social or cultural organisation triggered by actions and values that are not directly linked to the institution in question. The key assumption is that mutual involvement of people and their social relations are at the centre of institutional dynamics. Relations are the joints that connect values and actions. When social action has a lasting impact on social relations it will change cultural values, too. When value changes have an impact on social relations this will lead to changes in social action. Given the constant flow of individual action on the one hand and cultural invention, forgetting and remembering on the other hand it is likely that most processes of social change take place at both ends, crystallizing at the layer of social relations. With the help of this construction the model allows us to situate activity firmly at the level of the individual actor who changes his or her behaviour or attitude without reducing the process of institutional change to these individual actions because individual acts are amplified and ultimately governed by the layer of social relations. In this model it is possible to see how individual acts gain a momentum that cannot be attributed to individuals alone, but without the need to assume the fictive agency of "a culture" or "a society". A detailed account of the changes affecting the !*nara* property regime should help to illustrate the dynamics outlined here.

The case of the !*nara* harvest lends itself to exemplify the methodological shift from mapping property rights in terms of simply matching people and things towards elucidating complex, layered property relations with the help of a graphic representation. Figure 1 provides an alternative to the way in which =Aoni fields of !*nara* have conventionally been mapped. Instead of mapping the fields topographically it provides a diagram of the analytical layers that make up this particular property regime. It is an attempt to show how the objectification of "!*nara* plants and "!*nara* fruits" is in fact a result of, or "eclipses", the relation between the family owning the field, harvesters possessing the fruit and outsiders trading the !*nara* pips. The use of such a diagram in this context deserves further comment. In the diagram relationships not only connect individual human beings or things but relate terms to one another which can only be reliably identified in and through the relationship itself. For instance, mother and child may be related through physical

221

procreation or legal adoption. One term (that of mother) is logically defined by the existence of another term (that of child). Terms may be filled by different natural persons (men may act as "mothers"), by corporate bodies larger than a single person (a group of classificatory sisters may be "the mother") and natural persons may combine more than one term within them (as in many forms of exchange).

What is true of mothers and children is also true of other relations such as owners and non-owners (see below) or authors and readers. One way of conceptualising and clarifying these relations is through the use of anthropological relationship diagrams, called "Strathernograms" by the late Alfred Gell (1999) who used them to clarify exchange relationships described by M. Strathern. In this graphic convention terms are represented in square boxes, relations are depicted as circles and their objectification in lozenges. The graphic representation is useful because relations between social terms are unlike simple relations between physical entities. Many remain "invisible" unless elicited through analysis. An appearance in the physical world is usually the objectification of more than one social relation (e.g. a book is also an objectification between an author and a publisher and possibly an author and a funding body). Furthermore it is usually made up of terms which are themselves constituted by other relations between other terms or by the same terms (e.g. a book is written by an author who himself has been the reader of other texts and possibly the author of previous texts). This given complexity, a result of the diachronic character of social relations and the embeddedness of human action in a mesh of relationships, is usefully unravelled with the help of diagrams.

We can now start to see the multiple relations that are "hidden" or "eclipsed" in the ownership claims of our case and to introduce differences of hierarchy between them. Distinguishing !nara plants and their produce is not only a matter of material boundary drawing but also a matter of relationships of institutionalized exclusion. This is not only so because ownership rights concern plants rather than land. In their !nara property system =Aoni are not concerned about dividing the !Khuiseb delta geographically or about distributing general land rights. Rather they are concerned about exclusive rights of access to the !nara, that is to say the relations between potential claimants. Figure 1 tries to elucidate all relevant relations on which the harvesting of !nara relies – down to the actions of providing !nara (to dependent family members for instance) and consuming !nara (or its profits).

When analysing the objective returns or benefits of a !nara field it is necessary to begin by distinguishing between !nara harvesters (holding usership rights, possessing harvested !nara pips) and !nara owners (holding ownership rights to a !nara field, being able to exclude non-owners from the plots). Even in the traditional system (as far as we know it) it was possible to be the legitimate user of !nara fruit without ever being the owner of a !nara field. At the same time it was also true that those who procure !*nara* through their harvesting work did rely either on the owners of fields excluding others from harvesting or on traders who help to convert !*nara* into commodities or money. Or to put it more precisely, being the benefactor of a !*nara* field relies on the relation between people with the capacity to work (to harvest), those with the capacity to convert (to exchange !*nara*) and people with the capacity to exclude appropriation (with the necessary kinship links and sanctioning powers). It is through the relation between these capacities that a !*nara* harvest materializes. In the diagram this creates branches representing sub-clusters in the complex relationships governing the !*nara* property regime. Being an owner of the harvested !*nara* fruits also depends on the relation between harvesters and traders. It would be misleading to think of traders as coming in only after the harvest is completed. In fact harvesters enter long-term exchange relations with traders and are continually indebted to them so that traders have legitimate rights to the !*nara* even before the seasonal harvest has started. A harvesting party at any one season would consist of members of the field-owning family plus a flexible number of non-owning harvesters who could gain access to !*nara* through their relationship with the aforementioned members of the owning group. In fact a harvesting group could consist solely of non-=Aoni workers who, however, would still have a relation with the title-holders, either one of cooperation or – more recently – one of competition. In turn their participation in a harvesting party eclipses the relation between providers and consumers. The two terms may be contained within a single person or constituted by a person and his or her dependents. In any case the work of owning and non-owning harvesters is based on the fact that the fruit of this work can be ultimately consumed. Consumption may be indirect insofar as the harvesting party is in relation with trading partners whose presence is based on a relation between more distant parties who demand !*nara* and those who offer something else in return (and again there is a relation of consumers and providers at the end of this line). For the !*nara* harvest to take place successfully and repeatedly in the traditional property regime all these relationships constituting the "!*nara* harvester" seem to be as relevant as the relations which are hidden behind (or underneath) the term of "!*nara* owner". This section of the diagram provides further details on the complex relationships since "the family" which is usually given as the traditional owner of a !*nara* field is based on a web of relations between parties who do not move to the !*nara* fields but who stay behind in the settlements and look after livestock or who have moved into wage labour. !*Nara*, or profits arising from it, are exchanged between harvesting parties and owners who do not contribute directly to the !*nara* harvest. However, they link the harvesters with the owners and thereby with other spheres of the economy, in particular the livestock economy and wage labour. In order to be able to provide outputs from these fields of subsistence the position of non-harvesting owners relies on relations with people (or categories of people) who may ostensibly have nothing to do with *!nara* ownership but who enter the scene insofar as all subsistence activities of non-harvesting owners (with the possible exception of foraging activities) relies on cooperative relations within a household. Raising livestock is based on a relation between those who pool their time and energy with others in order to accomplish the tasks of herding and breeding. This demands some division of labour across age groups (even generations) and across gender (or even spouse exchanging groups). Relations of investing work (i.e. of providing) and of receiving returns (i.e. of consuming) again form the lowest level of the diagram.

There are restrictions to this graphical representation in the form of a single tree diagram. However, with slight alterations to the graphic convention, namely by adding more than one rhizome connected to the objectification (the "resource") in the diagram, the representation becomes more flexible. Thereby the graphical representation shows patterns of relatedness and highlights central positions in the network of relations, in this case the position of the harvesting party and the fact that it links the *!nara* harvest with both the trade of *!nara* and the exchange with other subsistence products.

The diagramatic outline of the *!nara* property regime, as given above, is not only an attempt to visualize the (largely invisible) structure of social relations that are part of this institution but also to unravel the institutional dynamics at work. Changes may originate at either "end" but the diagram allows us to trace them through the complex web of property relations. Following changes from the margins of the diagram we may trace how the values or terms of the property regime have been under pressure, partly because of value shifts in other domains especially that of group sovereignty. The apartheid administration which threatened to resettle =Aoni far away from the !Khuiseb but also the post-independence situation which makes them strive towards establishing a coherent local "community" have pushed the owners of *!nara* fields and fruits to identify strictly in ethnic terms as =Aoni and to delete "non-=Aoni" from the terms of the harvest (even though they cannot get rid of any real person anymore). The reinvention of *!nara* songs and the reiteration of the close symbolic link between *!nara* and =Aoni has led to a situation in which the term "harvesting party" is in effect divided into two terms, namely that of "legitimate =Aoni harvesters" and "illegitimate non-=Aoni harvesters". The diagram illustrates how harvesting was distinguished from owning in the traditional system even though the term "harvester" was linked to that of "owner". Through overemphasizing the identity of harvesters as =Aoni this link is curtailed. Since non-=Aoni owners nevertheless continue to harvest and use the *!nara* this in effect creates a direct relation between traders and the non-=Aoni harvesters, nowadays no longer connected to the owners in the =Aoni property regime. This has triggered off changes in the distribution of shares in the *!nara* harvest in favour of non-=Aoni. The ethnicization of terms has changed social relations in a way that paradoxically gives a larger share of the harvest to non-=Aoni. The interest of many =Aoni owners in turn seems to have shifted from the !nara as a fruit-bearing plant to one that occupies and symbolizes a stretch of land.

At the same time we may follow changes emerging from the centre of the diagram as people living in and around the !Khuiseb have – through their actions – changed the world of this property regime by shifting for instance the *de facto* boundaries in the real world of objects, redistributing the proportions of !nara being harvested, traded, exchanged and so forth shifting the use of !nara land, water, fruit, and plant. In the political debate about land rights, owning !nara plants seems to become more important than possessing fruits. This changes the division with the realm of objectifications (within the lozenge of the diagram) but also the relative weight of the social relations that are hidden behind it. In the !Khuiseb people who were not the direct beneficiaries of the !nara harvest took action that led to a reduction of the harvest available, and that increased the profits from alternative subsistence activities. In terms of the diagram they have altered the division within the lozenges, and possibly its shape and this has repercussions on the relations that constitute this division which in turn effects the terms involved. Graphically speaking changing the central lozenge means that the relations between traders, harvesting parties and non-harvesting owners are no longer as tight as they were before and may be cut off altogether. This means that relations of cooperation and exchange are severed while the subordinate relations of consumption continue so that they now compete directly with one another. Again this leads us to an explanation of another counter-intuitive fact, namely that a reduction of the volume of !nara harvest does not lead to a denser interaction between traders, harvesters and non-harvesters in the fields that remain but rather to greater isolation.

The idealized, balanced graph should not let us forget that the picture at large also changes since the terms that form the building blocks of the diagram are no longer filled by a series of relatively autonomous field owners paired with a group of !nara users but pairs of !nara users in competition with one another. Furthermore, since bounded fields no longer exist it would be more appropriate to talk of nested relations between successive users – varying in number – of the !nara field. In an emerging open access system any new user who enters the scene, or season, forms a relationship with previous users all nested in one another.

7 Conclusion

The =Aoni of the !Khuiseb valley are distinguished from other groups with whom they share linguistic and cultural features with regard to their use of the *!nara*. They are distinguished from others with whom they share the consumption and harvest of the *!nara* by the specific way in which they have institutionalised the property rights in the *!nara*. Early ethnographers with an interest in regional comparison have pointed out that the *!nara* property regime is the only instance of "private ownership" of land among Khoisan groups in southern Africa – without, however, resolving whether the object of these property relations is land, the plants, its fruits or something else, and without resolving what kind of "private" relations are eclipsed in such a property regime. Most recently, policy makers concerned with the mangement of Namibia's biodiversity in protected areas continue to distinguish "private" from "social" benefits in a way that seems to render all communal property to be "private" while "social" is in fact more narrowly defined as "national" (see Barnard 1998, p. 266). These are attempts to apply fixed institutional designs to local property regimes which are, according to the approach developed in this chapter, best understood as specific constellations of institutionalised values, actions and relations. The limits and options for changing local land care systems based on property relations depend on the internal working of these property regimes.

The layered model of institutions and the theoretically informed construction of relationship diagrams proposed here do not preserve all details that may play a role in processes of institutional dynamics. The model reduces the intricacies contained in ethnographic descriptions, in this case or any other case. However, there is reason to believe that the model proposed here can help to overcome some of static dichotomies that continue to haunt not only anthropology but also the social science perspective of environmental change more generally. In the case in question the main dichotomy involved is that between private and communal ownership. The distinction becomes subordinate as we discover clusters of social relationships eclipsed in the property regime governing the *!nara* harvest. The diagram developed above shows that even in a regime that ostensibly involves private ownership relations link trading, ownership of plants and possession of fruits. The terms that are connected by these relations may be covered by individuals or groups or elements of these, since several relations may be incorporated in particular individuals or groups. The *!nara* property regime is a complex mix of relations between different terms, only some of which are to be identified with individual owners.

The *!nara* harvesting system does not lend itself to be classified along the lines of idealized communal or family-based ownership. Nor is it usefully considered to be just another form of private property. Rather, the =Aoni case study can help to overcome the private/communal dichotomy and to understand the process of shifts between property regimes understood as the outcome of a multi-layered process of changing cultural values, regulations, relations and social actions. The analytic framework of institutional layers and the use of diagrams to elicit "eclipsed" social relations are merely tools which will continue to be shaped as they are being put to use for understanding diverse local cases. They are tools that allow us to do away with cumbersome and unrealistic distinction between "private property regimes" and "communal property regimes" where we encounter institutional settings that in their different aspects and layers may exhibit aspects of both.

References

Benda-Beckmann, K./F. von Benda-Beckmann (1999): A Functional Analysis of Property Rights, with Special Reference to Indonesia. In: van Meijl/von Benda-Beckmann (eds.): Property Rights and Economic Development. London; Kegan Paul

Barnard, P. (ed.) (1998): Biological Diversity in Namibia – A Country Study. Windhoek: Namibian National Biodiversity Task Force

Berry, C. (1991): Nara: Unique Melon of the Desert. In: Veld & Flora; Vol. 77; No. 1; pp. 22-3

Botelle, A./K. Kowalski (1994): Living on the Edge. Documentary Film

Botelle, A./K. Kowalski (1995): Changing Resource Use in Namibia's Lower Kuiseb River Valley: Perceptions from the Topnaar Community. Roma; Institute of Southern African Studies, University of Lesotho

Budack, K. (1977): Die =Aonin und das Meer. In: Möhlig et al. (eds.): Zur Sprachgeschichte und Ethnohistorie in Afrika. Berlin

Budack, K. (1983): A Harvesting People on the South Atlantic Coast. Ethnologie. In: South African Journal of Ethnology; Vol. 6; No. 2; pp. 1-7

Dentlinger, U. (1977): The !nara Plant in the Topnaar Hottentot Culture of Namibia: Ethnobotanical Clues to an 8,000-year-old Tradition. In: Munger Africana Library Notes; Vol. 38; pp. 3-39

Dentlinger, U. (1983): Social and Spatial Mobility along the Kuiseb River in the Namib Desert, Namibia. Unpublished M.A. Thesis. Dept. of Anthropology; University of Cape Town

Douglas, M. (1987): How Institutions Think. London; Routledge

Enviroteach (1995): Our Growing Wealth. An Introduction to the Plants We Use. Swakopmund; Enviroteach

Gell, A. (1999): Strathernograms, or the Semiotics of Mixed Metaphors. In: Hirsch (ed.): The Art of Anthropology. Essays and Diagrams. London; Athlone Press

Gordon, R. (1989): Can Namibian San Stop Dispossession of Their Land? In: Wilmsen (ed.): We Are Here: Politics of Aboriginal Land Tenure. Berkeley; University of California Press

Gregory, C. (1997): Savage Money. The Anthropology and Politics of Commodity Exchange. Amsterdam; Harwood

Grimme, C. (1910): "NARRAS", ein wichtiges Eingeborenen-Nahrungsmittel in Deutsch-Südwestafrika. In: Der Tropenpflanzer. Zeitschrift für Tropische Landwirtschaft; Vol. 14; pp. 297-302

Haacke, W./E. Eiseb/L. Namaseb (1997): Internal and External Relations in Khoekhoe Dialects: A Preliminary Survey. In: Haacke/Elderkin (eds.): Namibian Languages: Reports and Papers. Köln; Köppe

Herre, H. (1975): Die Narapflanze. In: Namib und Meer; Vol. 5-6; pp. 27-31

Hoerné, W. (1985): The Social Organization of the Nama and Other Essays. Johannesburg; University of Witwatersrand Press

Kinahan, J. (1991): Pastoral Nomads of the Central Namib Desert. The People History Forgot. Windhoek; New Namibia Books

Köhler, O. (1969): Die Topnaar-Hottentotten am unteren Kuiseb. In: The Ethnological Section, Dept. of Bantu Administration and Development (ed.): Ethnological and Linguistic Studies in Honor of N. J. van Warmelo. Pretoria

Kooitjie, C. (1997): Historic Overview of the /Aonin (Topnaar). Khoi-Khoi; Unpublished Manuscript

Moritz, W. (1992): Die Nara, das Brot in der Wüste. Aus alten Tagen in Südwest, Heft 11. Windhoek

Peristiany, J. (1939): The Social Institutions of the Kipsigis. London; Routledge

Pfeiffer, E. (1979): !Nara & Topnaar Hottentots. In: South West African Annual; pp. 158-9

Sandelowsky, B. (1977): Mirabib – An Archaeological Study in the Namib. In: Madoqua; Vol. 10; No. 4; pp. 221-283

Schapera, I. (1930): The Khoisan Peoples of South Africa: Bushmen and Hottentots. London; Routledge, Kegan Paul

Schott, R. (1956): Anfänge der Privat- und Planwirtschaft. Wirtschaftsordnung und Nahrungsverteilung bei Wildbeutervölkern. Braunschweig; Limbach

Schweizer, T. (1996): Muster sozialer Ordnung. Netzwerkanalyse als Fundament der Sozialethnologie. Berlin; Reimer

Shilomboleni, A. (1998): The !nara and Factors That Lead to Its Decline in Productivity. Unpublished Manuscript

Storad, C. (1991): Fruit of the Dunes. In: ASU Research; Winter issue

Van den Eynden, V./P. Vernemmen/P. Van Damme (eds.) (1992): The Ethnobotany of the Topnaar. Gent; University of Gent

Visser, M. (1998): Nara Fruit. The Magic Plant. In: Flamingo (Air Namibia in-flight magazine); June issue

Widlok, T. (1993): The Social Value of Water and the Explanatory Value of Ecology. Paper for the Pithecanthropus Centennial Congress; June-July. Leiden

Widlok, T. (1999): Living on Mangetti. "Bushman" Autonomy and Namibian Independence. Oxford; Oxford University Press

Widlok, T. in press. Local Experts – Expert Locals. A Comparative Perspective on Australia and Namibia. In: Casimir (ed.): Culture and the Changing Environment. Oxford; Berghahn

Part III: Institutionalising Social Learning

Anita Engels

Introduction

Part I demonstrated limitations to institutional design "from above" or "top down" when institutions are treated as black boxes. Part II put much effort in the attempt to open the black box and elucidate its internal workings and dynamics by focussing on informal institutions and social practice. The following Part III asks which conditions are necessary or conducive to integrate aspects of social practice and informal institutions into the design of formal institutions. This part of the book is about capacities for social learning and about the possibility to promote these capacities and to strengthen them. Bolstered with a broader and deeper understanding of the internal workings of the black box, we now come back to questions of institutional design and emphasise a more procedural approach. This approach allows for an appreciation of unintended effects, gradual improvements and incremental changes.

Whereas Part II sought to overcome a naive top-down approach, Part III does not simply replace this approach by a reverse and equally oversimplified bottom-up approach. Rather, it is the goal of the contributions in this part of the book to show examples where both directions become important. Formal institutions need to be confronted with social practices, and social practices likewise need to be confronted with superordinate concepts of sustainable design of formal institutions which transcend local or individual perspectives. For both analysis and practice it is important to realize that formal institutions can create better conditions for social practice, and social practice can create more appropriate formal institutions.

In this sense, Troja's contribution on negotiated rulemaking shows how cooperative conflict management often leads to a more procedural form of institutional design. The discussed examples of regulatory negotiations are attempts to make use of a communicative framework for the development of new environmental programmes and policies. This framework allows policy makers who are representatives of formal institutions to enter a discursive process with stakeholders or, in more general terms, with the addressees of policies who are guided by their everyday practices and their informal understandings and worldviews. The process is used to foster mutual recognition and, in the terms of this book, to build bridges between formal and informal institutions. Whereas several contributions so far have stressed the multiplicity and often incompatibility of different perspectives, this paper highlights ways to overcome these gaps. How can communication influence perspectives, assessments and evaluations – i.e. reality constructions – to overcome inherent antagonisms? What mechanisms and procedures can be applied to create a joint understanding of the environmental problem and of available options? Finally, the contribution asks how such communicative procedures can be integrated into the routines and formal decision-making structures of political bodies and public administrations.

Sandner's contribution changes the scene and moves the reader from negotiated rulemaking procedures in highly industrialised countries to an institution-building process in a developing country, namely to the indigenous society of the Kuna of Eastern Panama. It is an example of a successful attempt to create new institutional solutions for environmental problems such as overexploitation and the depletion of natural resources. Here, social learning takes place as a unique blend of indigenous – mostly informal – institutional settings and exogenous concepts and policy elements. Sandner discusses the crucial role of communication structures, knowledge, actor skills and power relations for this innovative combination to become institutionalised and functional. However, the differentiated analysis is not blind for weaknesses. On the contrary, the analytical tools used by the author systematically disclose weaknesses and blockages which still prevail even in this most advantageous system.

The two concluding contributions by Huber and Siebenhüner have several aspects in common. They both deal with issues related to global climate change and acid rain. Furthermore, they both apply the concept of social learning in a strict sense, defining indicators that allow for measuring the success or failure of social learning processes. Huber defines it as an increase in fairness, legitimacy, efficiency and effectiveness of policies and regulations; Siebenhüner emphasises an increase in saliency, credibility and legitimacy. Even though there is some overlap in these criteria the differences relate to a division of labour between these two contributions. Whereas Siebenhüner focuses on the aspect of scientific assessments and their potential role in policy making, Huber concentrates on the side of policy making and includes scientific assessments as only one among several factors that influence policy evolution. Each set of criteria thus reflects the specificities of the subject matter of the respective contribution. This demonstrates the usefulness of the concept of social learning in comparing different case studies and different institutional settings if it is applied in a flexible and context-sensitive way.

Huber's paper starts with the clearcut question of whether the EC Commission has learned to manage environmental issues better over time. The examples of acid rain and climate change are discussed in the broader context of environmental policy making. Huber analyses more concretely which factors fostered cross-issue fertilisations and enabled leapfrogging within the EC. However, in his conclusions Huber comes to a rather sceptical view on the potential for social learning and assumes that evolution dominates over social learning as the most visible form of institutional change. Siebenhüner comes to a different conclusion with regards to his case study on scientific assessments. He identifies important instances of social learning both in the Intergovernmental Panel on Climate Change and in the assessments that accompanied the Convention on Long-range Transboundary Air Pollution. He asks to what extent in each case social learning was helped or blocked by structural factors (e.g. hierarchies and communication structures), cultural factors (e.g. values and informal communication networks), personal factors (e.g. individual capabilities) and, finally, contextual factors (e.g. political pressures and media coverage). The two papers provide answers to the question of how to institutionalise social learning and how to improve conditions for more appropriate policy making while taking into account both formal and informal institutions. However, they also call for a careful and detailed analysis of each individual process and might be read as a warning not to become starry-eyed and overly optimistic about the chances of measurable improvements.

Markus Troja

Resolving Environmental Conflicts. Mediation and Negotiation as Institutional Capacities for Social Learning[1]

1 Introduction

This chapter presents selected results of a political science research project on mediation and negotiated rulemaking as cooperative conflict management procedures that were applied to solve environmental conflicts (Troja 2001). The project draws upon case studies from the United States and Germany to elucidate which factors contribute most importantly to success (or failure) in resolving environmental conflicts.

Decision-making processes in policy making and administration are influenced by the interplay of formal institutions, such as decision-making processes of parliamentary bodies and legal regulations, and informal institutions, such as informal agreements at the administrative level or the outcomes of political lobbying. In the fields of environmental policy and urban and regional planning, in particular, public conflicts abound, and often they are related to the decision-making processes themselves. Some of these conflicts materialise into public demonstrations and protest rallies, others even need to be solved by courtroom decisions. They are often solved in a way which is satisfying to none of the involved parties, with outcomes that have detrimental impacts on the environment. They make decision making time consuming and cost intensive and can even lead to social strife. Therefore, public conflicts can be seen as signs of deficiencies in those political and legal institutions which are supposed to lead to accepted, collectively binding decisions.

Minsch et al. (1998, pp. 179, 241-257) have developed an institutional atlas of different ways in which problems encountered in developing a policy for sustainability are addressed. They classify cooperative procedures as strategies of participation and self-organisation. Dryzek (1994, pp. 46-48) calls mediation and negotiated rulemaking exemplary institutions with which principles of discourse can be practically implemented. If social and political

---

1 The article is based on results of a research project on "Negotiation and Mediation Procedures in Environmental Policy" funded by the German Research Council (DFG) within the Priority Programme "Global Environmental Change – Social and Behavioural Dimensions".

conflicts are channelled into the form of negotiations or mediation procedures these forms become an institution as well. Compared to the more established forms of conflict resolution, such as court decisions, they constitute an institutional innovation that may compensate for some of the deficiencies of existing political and legal institutions. The broader question of this article therefore is whether and how dysfunctional institutions of conflict resolution can be replaced, reformed or supplemented by institutional innovations of cooperative conflict management procedures.[2]

Central to the effectiveness of cooperative procedures is their capacity to build an institutional framework for social learning – both internally amongst the participants and externally in the respective policy field. An internal factor is the procedures' potential to change communicative and behavioural patterns between the conflicting parties and thereby create conditions conducive to a cooperative discourse. This makes social learning in certain cases of conflict possible. Externally, the overall legitimacy of the procedures is of crucial importance. Therefore, the main concern of this paper is whether and how cooperative conflict management procedures can be embedded in the established political and administrative institutions, and how the "problem of interplay" (Young 1999, Ch. 3.2) between the new institutions (of mediation procedures and regulatory negotiations) and existing institutions can be solved (cf. chapters 6-7 below). If the implementation of such institutional innovation is successful, social learning beyond the individual case is made possible through the changes in the patterns of decision making and conflict resolution in a given policy field.

2 Cooperative Conflict Management in Environmental Policy through Mediation and Negotiated Rulemaking

The term *cooperative conflict management procedures* refers to all approaches involving governmental actors in official decision making in cooperation with private actors, such as business, associations and citizen's action groups. Not all of them are more recent approaches such as mediation and negotiated rulemaking. Instead, a wide range of other cooperative planning and decision-making procedures exist in environmental policy making. Examples include planning cells and citizen evaluations, round tables, multilevel

---

2 Alternative Dispute Resolution (ADR) describes a range of dispute resolution procedures alternative to litigation. Usually ADR is used as an umbrella term for negotiation, facilitation, mediation and arbitration (Goldberg/Sander/Rogers 1992). Instead of ADR I speak of cooperative conflict management. With this term I focus on negotiation and mediation (cf. 2).

dialogue procedures, city and traffic forums, consensus conferences, cooperative discourse, future workshops and conferences and – as often used in the Anglo-American context – focus-groups, citizen juries and community advisory panels (cf. Beckmann/Keck 1999; Hennen 1996; Minsch et al. 1998; Selle 1996).

Mediation can be defined as a process in which an impartial third party – the mediator – helps the parties in a conflict to come to an agreement. Very often such face-to-face negotiations are an alternative to litigation and public protest. Mediation is a voluntary procedure. The participants can exit the negotiations at any time. The conflicting parties set their own agenda on what issues are discussed and how the results are formulated. Contrary to arbitration or litigation, the mediator has no decision-making power and does not suggest his or her own solutions. The final agreement usually has the status of a recommendation to the political and administrative decision makers. At least for mediation procedures in environmental fields, legal contracts between private actors and official bodies are still the exception.

Mediation in public disputes is perhaps best characterised by what Meadowcroft calls a "cooperative management regime" (Meadowcroft 1998). On the one hand, it is neither a broad participatory approach of direct democracy nor a representative panel as in planning cells (Dienel 1991). Instead it brings together those actors who have a stake in the issues, whose interests are affected or who show a high degree of involvement and commitment, be it as experts or as interested citizens. Mediation is an instrument of conflict management. In contrast to forms of direct democracy the parties do not come together on the basis of representative participation, but because they are involved in a specific conflict and their approval and support is important for the implementation of solutions. On the other hand, mediation as a procedure provides a forum for information exchange and discussion concerning a specific problem, rather than representing a model of interest group pluralism. The major difference between mediation and consultative meetings is the task of finding a solution to a conflict at hand and the use of communicative techniques and facilitation tools by the mediator. Finally, in contrast to corporatism, the negotiations can be more transparent to the public. Mediation implies that the process is open for representatives of all interested parties.

Since the early 1990s, the experiences gained in the United States in environmental policy and planning (Bingham 1986; Buckle/Thomas-Buckle 1986; Susskind/Cruikshank 1987; Goldberg/Sander/Rogers 1992; Bush/Folger 1994; Folger/Jones 1994; Susskind/McKearnan/Thomas-Larmer 1999) induced many European countries to increasingly use cooperative procedures. Today the first empirical data is available documenting cooperative procedures applied mainly to controversial environment-related decision-making processes in Europe. Weidner (1998) analysed examples from twelve European countries. Another empirical survey of seventeen European countries on the state of environmental mediation shows that this cooperative procedure is being increasingly applied for both drafting plans and implementing specific projects relating to environmental policy and planning (ISTM/MEDIATOR 2000).

The same internal logic and similar procedures also apply for negotiated rulemaking, in particular the early and complementary participation of conflicting parties and independent responsibility for problem solving by voluntary participants. At times, negotiated rulemaking even includes an external mediator, too. In concerted negotiations, actors of (ministerial) administrations and from the private sector attempt to develop the substantive issues within planned programmes, laws or law-related regulations, and thereby try to improve their respective contents. The procedure particularly aims at improving the implementation of all these instruments. Negotiations are taken up precisely in the drafting phase, while the legally required participation is generally foreseen for a later period. External facilitators are often considered helpful, but they are not a prerequisite for such a procedure. Typically, an administration or a ministry will set up a committee or commission as a forum for the negotiations. In the United States the related meetings are usually open to the public (Coglianese 1997, p. 1255; Pritzker/Dalton 1995, pp. 1, 8).

The US experiences with regulatory negotiations started after the Administrative Conference made a pertinent recommendation in 1982. Subsequently, approximately 50 such procedures were carried out by federal agencies alone by mid-1995, a third of them by the Environmental Protection Agency (EPA) (Pritzker/Dalton 1995, p. 40). In Germany too, experiences have been made with such an instrument in the development of environmental policy within the framework of legal requirements. These take the shape of commissions which include a wider range of participants than negotiations within corporatist circles. In the area of law making the procedure has, however, only been applied in a handful of cases.

3 Building Institutional Capacities in Environmental Policy and Planning

The rational behind introducing cooperative conflict management procedures as institutional innovations is the hope that environmental policy can be modernised (Zillessen 1993). The connection between policy modernisation and new institutions can be elucidated by a simple concept which has been promoted by Martin Jaenicke, amongst others (Jaenicke 1996, 1997; Jaenicke/Weidner 1997). Innovation and modernisation in environmental policy in western countries result from a combination of two factors: firstly, political pressure caused by arising problems and, secondly, the level of existing capacities to address these problems. Improvements in environmental policy have never been just a direct response to the level of emissions and other ecological problems. This becomes apparent by looking both back in environmental history and across country specific variations today. For example, the ecological situation and the extent of health problems in some developing countries and parts of Eastern Europe do not automatically lead to improvements in the respective policy fields. If no adequate institutional capacities for political action exist problems may result in decline and crises. This is not only true for environmental problems but also applies to economical and other political crises.

On the other hand, if certain institutional capacities are available to cope with upcoming political problems it is also possible that the conflicts arising from these problems trigger innovations. Georg Simmel (1908) and, subsequently, Lewis Coser (1964) showed that society is in fact dependent on conflicts since they provide the basis for identity building and cohesion. Conflicts are symptoms of certain problems in a group or society that – along with these conflicts – get on the political agenda. Thus conflicts can assume a positive role for social change, and new forms of conflict management might entail institutional innovation and processes of social learning.

The initial factor in the concept of modernisation and capacity building is the political pressure which is generated by a specific problem forcing some kind of reaction in the political system. This problem-related pressure is evident in the course of environmental conflicts and in the difficulties a political system faces in dealing institutionally with the conflicts.

For a long time environmental conflicts were defined as merely distributional conflicts since at first they simply resulted in a reallocation of resources and a change of property rights. In fact, mediation as one of a whole set of alternative dispute resolution techniques first came up due to location problems. Decisions about future sites for hazardous waste facilities, waste treatment plants, streets or railway tracks are well known examples. Usually these conflicts have to be resolved within the formal institutional framework of legally required participation procedures, e.g. through public hearings. This is often unsatisfactory to all sides. For example, even though environmental groups have in the past succeeded in delaying the setting up of municipal waste incinerators they were not able to prevent their construction in the long run. Likewise, this type of conflict management is detrimental for investors because it is very time consuming and they cannot be sure if and how they will ever be able to put their plans into action. Involved citizens are also dissatisfied because they feel that they have little or no influence in the decision-making process. They are only consulted at a late stage, when much money and time have already been invested in the planning process. Usually, at this point, major decisions have already been taken. Accordingly, public administrators are reluctant to make any changes to the plans at that stage. Hence the only option of those who disapprove of the decisions is to take the case to court. In anticipation of this public administrators feel obliged to make sure that their decisions will receive the approval of the courts. Legal aspects become their main focus, although most of the parties' interests are much more complex than the adversary legal positions. Even if public authorities win the litigation there is still the dissatisfied public to deal with.

The established planning and policy-making procedures were not developed as an instrument of conflict management in the first place. This is not only true for the United States and Germany, but for western countries in general. From the point of view of effective conflict management the following weaknesses in the existing conflict regulatory institutions in public planning are noticeable:

— *Lack of information*: Mediators working in areas of public policy experience time and again that an important function of mediation prior to the phase of identifying interests is to gather information and to communicate it comprehensibly. Within the framework of the existing legal and political institutions a substantial asymmetry of information is prevalent among experts and laypersons, the administration, investors and the people affected by the decisions. The paths of decision making and opportunities to influence decisions are difficult to comprehend. People who are supposed to provide information do not take the special needs of those affected into account. This is reflected by the form in which they provide the information, and often they are considered to be biased. The high degree of obscurity leads to mistrust and to the dominance and stability of pre-existing patterns of perception, prejudices, standardised evaluations or mental models. From an expert's point of view these frames of perception and interpretation of information and situations may seem less rational, but this does not necessarily mean they are wrong. For those affected, such mental models are an efficient and relatively secure way to reduce the uncertainty and complexity of the process in order to remain capable to act and take decisions.

— *Lack of participation*: The late and limited opportunities of affected persons and citizen's action groups to participate in the planning process have repeatedly been a main criticism of legally regulated citizen participation. Both investors and administrations regard these possibilities to participate as sufficiently extensive, complicated and time-consuming. In practice, the guidelines provide for more than enough participation if the level of conflict is low. If greater conflicts of interest exist the extent of participation foreseen by the guidelines does not suffice to successfully lead to agreement and satisfaction.

— *Deficiencies of communication*: Planning and approval procedures as well as decision-making processes in general are embedded in a specific culture of communication. It tends to be hierarchical as well as adversarial in nature. As a result, it leads to further escalations rather than promoting mutual understanding and cooperation. This can be observed, for example, at discussions or forums of citizen inquiries and public hearings. Furthermore, formal procedures determined by the legal framing of a problem fall short of being able to address the complexity of environmental conflicts. A conflict in a public arena is shaped by personal, procedural and substantive dimensions which are all interconnected. The substantive dimension alone cannot be reduced to topics of (ecological, legal, technological and economic) expert knowledge. They also encompass structural, relational and value conflicts which are usually not adequately addressed in an administrative proceeding.

The three deficits of formal institutions in environmental policy mentioned above (information, participation, communication) also represent a gap between formal and informal institutions. Overcoming this gap is one of the motivations for participatory approaches like mediation and regulatory negotiations.

Capacities for a Successful Environmental Policy (Jaenicke 1996)	Specific Capacities for Spatial and Urban Planning (Healey 1998)	Capacity Building through Negotiation and Mediation (Troja 2001)
Openness of the political process for input and transparency	Local knowledge through stakeholder involvement (in combination with expertise)	— Participation and representation of affected interests
Availability of information		— Competence
Intrapolicy cooperation and interpolicy integration	Capacity to resolve conflicts	— Bargaining framework
Resources, strategies and networks of important actors involved (e.g. state officials, environment-oriented green entrepreneurs, scientists, environmental and citizen groups and the media)	Relational resources and social learning	— Level of discourse

Table 1: Approaches to building institutional capacities in policy-making processes

Having outlined some of the problems and conflicts to be tackled in environmental policy, it should now be clear how the outcome of these complex policy making processes are dependent on the already existing institutional capacities in environmental policy making and on the success of institutional innovations. These institutional capacities will determine whether a conflict leads to a crisis, for instance to an escalation of public disputes or to political impasses, or to an improvement, such as a driving force for further innovations and capacity building. Empirical case studies from 24 industrialised countries conducted by the Free University of Berlin (Jaenicke 1996) have shown some of the capacities which are important for successful environmental policy making. They are listed in the left column of Table 1. In the middle column these capacities have been attributed to three approaches which Healey (1998) developed from analysing experiences in spatial and urban planning. In the far-right column, the focus is on institutional capacities of cooperative conflict resolution procedures to further the aforementioned capacity building in environmental policy making processes (Troja 2001). The latter column draws on findings from democratic theory.

4 Case Studies

Important questions at this point are whether cooperative conflict management procedures can be applied to environmental conflicts, and whether in terms of modernisation these procedures help to activate some of the capacities for effective environmental policy and planning listed in the table above. As a first step to answer this question, this chapter presents a selection of case studies on the practice of cooperative conflict management in environmental policy making.

Due to the confines of this book the following six case studies cannot be fully documented. They serve as short illustrations of either mediation or negotiated rulemaking. The first three cases recount American experiences, the last three German ones. Methodically, the studies are based on qualitative interviews of the participants and an analysis of available documents. Three of the observed procedures dealt with moderated negotiation processes to develop policy programmes or laws (cases 1, 2 and 4); they are examples of negotiated rulemaking. The others can be considered as examples of mediation in a strictly defined sense (cases 3, 5 and 6). They all involve specific conflicts about individual projects dealing with infrastructure of some kind. All of these procedures took place from the mid to the end of the 1990s.

American Case Studies	1. Waste Tires End User Reimbursement Advisory Committee, Virginia	2. Pesticide State Management Plan of the State of Virginia	3. River Road Mediation, Goochland County, Virginia
Pressure generated by problem; prime reason for taking action	Illegal waste tire dumps in woods presented hazardous environmental and health risks. Some of them were burning for days.	Polluting of Chesapeak Bay in Virginia with hazardous materials; pesticides in drinking water	A picturesque country road with historic sites was to be widened due to several fatal driving accidents.
Political background and initiative	A legislative initiative to found a restitution fund for disposal companies brought about the need to regulate the distribution of the funds. Former attempts to regulate failed. The State Government agency had had positive experiences with moderation. The round table was supposed to recommend a programme in which companies could participate in order to receive subsidies for the recycling and disposal of waste tires.	The Environmental Protection Agency (EPA) announced that certain pesticides were to be forbidden. Further use of these or any other pesticides would be dependent on the quality of a pesticide management plan. Government agencies had had positive experiences with moderation and mediation. A committee with the representatives of various interest groups and the participant ministries was supposed to develop a pesticide management plan.	The County Government had to agree on the priorities to be assigned to state road construction monies. Granting the funding which was needed to widen River Road depended on this decision process being finalised.
Main conflict	Distribution of funds.	Controversy among several state agencies and interest groups on the use of pesticides and the validity of maximum levels	Steps of road construction such as laying of cables, forced expropriation, clearance for construction for roads running along cultural monuments, etc.

Table 2: Case Studies of cooperative conflict management procedures in the USA

| Result | Consensus was reached on the criteria for the dispensing of funds according to a prioritised classification of waste treatment strategies. This idea as part of the recommendation was however not taken over by the State Government agency. | The group came up with a plan that was the first successful plan to be approved of by the EPA within the USA. No agreement was reached on the types of limits of maximum levels due to massive lobbying efforts directed at the Virginia Department for Agriculture and the EPA. | Residents and responsible bodies agreed on a solution that included several recommendations which were supported by every member of the mediation group. Each recommendation was implemented. |

Continuation Table 2: Case Studies of cooperative conflict management procedures in the USA

German Case Studies	4. Government Commission of the State of Lower Saxony	5. Citizen dialogue on the Berlin Brandenburg International Airport	6. Round Table Detmolder Street in the city of Bielefeld
Pressure generated by problem; prime reason for taking action	Public awareness of toxic waste and a lack of treatment facilities for toxic waste created a critical situation. In addition, there was a problem of acceptance of environmental policies by businesses in Lower Saxony. Changes to the legal framework of waste disposal created further uncertainties.	The Berlin Airport had capacity problems. The aim was to avoid the level of conflict that had accompanied the construction of the West runway at Frankfurt Airport and the planning and construction of Munich Airport.	The traffic on Detmolder Street caused noise level and safety problems. There was a fatal accident on the street. Against this background, a citizens action group was initiated.

Table 3: Case Studies of cooperative conflict management procedures in Germany

Political background and initiative	Law reforms were mostly the accomplishment of the personal initiative of a minister of the environment. The Ministry for the Environment had had positive experiences with other commissions.	The Prime Minister of Brandenburg announced the construction of an airport south of Berlin which would mean the closure of the existing three airports in Berlin and creating a new one, either on a new site or by extending one of the existing airports. The initiative to mediate was taken by an undersecretary and the Brandenburg State Government.	During negotiations to build the governing coalition for the city council the idea of a mediation procedure was a concession of the Social Democratic Party (SPD) to the Green Party (Gruene) as part of a barter deal. Conflicts concerning traffic policy were transferred to mediation.
Main conflict	The main conflict arose between environmental groups, business associations, special public agencies and the Ministry for the Environment about the aims of policies affecting the disposal business.	The constellation of supporters and opponents of a new large airport was dependent on the respective location, citizen action groups, business associations and individual businesses, airport holdings, environmental groups, etc.	The question of expanding or restricting street capacity was controversial above all among citizen action groups, the city administration, individual retailers and political parties.
Result	Recommendations on the handling of toxic waste based on latest research was recognised by experts in the area. The extent to which the recommendations were implemented is controversial. Neither avoiding waste materials nor public action played an important role in the final decisions on how to resolve the problem.	The spatial planning procedure of Brandenburg was influenced. The final location decisions were however not directly influenced by the mediation procedure and were taken at another level. The dialogue was terminated prior to beginning the zoning and authorisation procedure in Berlin-Schoenefeld.	A creative and flexible solution (a variable two- and four-lane roadway) as well as immediate measures were recommended, though not in consensus. The implementation of the recommendations was largely rejected by the city administration.

Continuation Table 3: Case Studies of cooperative conflict management procedures in Germany

5 Procedural Capacities for Social Learning

Returning to the question whether mediation and negotiation procedures are a means to modernise environmental policy by activating capacities for effective environmental policy and planning, this chapter will focus on the procedural capacities of mediation and negotiation.

The key term *procedural capacities* refers to the assessment of the conflict regulation potential of the procedures themselves. Initially, this project analysed four main factors of cooperative conflict management with regard to the deficiencies in the existing institutions' conflict regulation as discussed in chapter 2: openness for participation, competence, bargaining framework (see Table 1) and the level of discourse. Since this book focuses on social learning, the chapter will concentrate on the two factors of substantial competence and of the communication modes of arguing and bargaining and, in the latter case, mostly on arguing, as most of the literature on mediation and negotiation so far is based on theories of bargaining.

5.1 Building Competence

Participation does not automatically improve the competence of the participating parties. A structured procedure, professional management of the process and the input of expert knowledge are all needed in varying degrees to build up relevant competence in cooperative conflict management procedures. Participation alone can lead to inefficient debates and dilettantism with undesired consequences for choices of action (Renn/Webler 1994, pp. 49 f). The procedural capacity is thus directed at the ability to include scientific, technical and social information which can then serve as a basis for decision making.

Competence means that existing scientific and technical knowledge will be contributed at every point in time to the decision-making process. An indicator of competence is the extent to which the procedure allows for different expert contributions and the extent to which the spectrum of varying or contradicting scientific claims is covered by the selection of expert opinions.

In all investigations of conflict management procedures ample scientific knowledge and technical expertise were contributed to the discussion and utilised for decision making. In the examples of regulatory negotiations (case studies 1, 2 and 4) expert knowledge was not sought through external experts but was exclusively represented by the participants in the procedure. Case study 4 needs to be singled out, both in comparison to the three mediation procedures and to the other American regulatory negotiations, because competence was reduced to the experts' views whereas laypersons' views and local knowledge of those affected (e.g. company employees or neighbours to the company property) were not included. The importance of scientific competence in decision-making processes might easily lead to the conclusion that expert bodies are the key to good decisions. However, this would be misleading. Risk assessments are too controversial among experts to provide a clear orientation. Scientific estimations and expert opinions reflect at first only the most current findings which for reasons of cognitive uncertainty are not free from value judgements and premises – just like the mental models of laypersons (Mayntz 1990, pp. 143 f; Beck 1986, pp. 31-35, 76 ff). Therefore, no criteria can determine a priori the quality of environmental policy independent of the value judgement of actors in environmental policy making. The quality of the solution is always dependent on how the problem is defined by the participants (Fischer 1993, p. 458). Those who live and work in a certain region and who are actors in the policy field in question possess situational, specialised, cultural and local knowledge which is also of importance for the quality of the decision (Healey 1998, pp. 1539 f). The inclusion of these diverse dimensions of rationality – in the face of the complexity and uncertainty concerning the consequences of environmental policy decisions – determines the entire rationality of a decision (Zillessen 1998a, p. 58).

Various rationalities of discourse were brought together in the American cases of regulatory negotiations: for instance, scientific and political views or views of experts in politics and administration on the one side and the perspectives of those affected by the decisions on the other.

This confrontation of different forms of knowledge, professional expertise and lay perspectives caused many difficulties and was costly and nerve-racking at the beginning of all the procedures. Participants, however, increasingly adjusted to the necessities of a discourse aimed at mutual understanding and considered this a new quality which was, through a learning process, equally achievable by all sides (see below).

In mediation procedures in which local impacts play a greater role, the necessity to consider lay perspectives and local knowledge is even more apparent. In all of the three investigated mediation procedures it is clear that the so-called laypersons contributed significantly to the competence of the procedure as a whole and the quality of the results. Inversely, in the examples of conflict management procedures it became evident that the laypersons' views changed after being confronted with expert opinion and different expertise.

"It was the information which came from the outside, the several expert opinions, the several experts who were invited, they motivated me to correct my opinion. (...) It contributed to the shaping of all participants' opinions. We developed a good competent opinion, also in terms of flight traffic avoidance." (Interviewee, case study 5)

Information source:

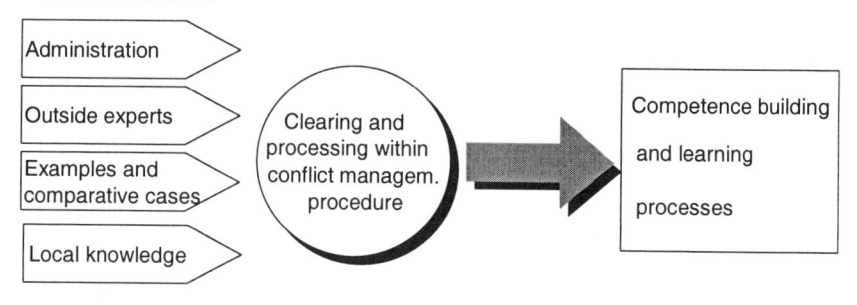

- Administration
- Outside experts
- Examples and comparative cases
- Local knowledge

→ Clearing and processing within conflict managem. procedure ⇒ Competence building and learning processes

Figure 1: Processing of information in cooperative conflict management procedures

If the factor *competence* is used as a yardstick ample proof of a fruitful connection between expert and lay knowledge needs to be taken into consideration. This leads to a rather critical evaluation of expert discourses, as in the example of case study 4, even if they might be exceedingly efficient for the processing of specialist questions. The controversial problems in environmental conflicts cannot be resolved by means of purely scientific expertise. Rather, they need diverse forms of competence. This is shown precisely by the handling of the disposal problem in case study 4. In recent years the most important problems in this area were not technical but rather social and economic. The technical development of methods of waste disposal was extremely successful and innovative on the basis of the existing specialist committees and decision-making processes. The greater challenge existed (and still exists) in creating acceptance as well as in changing production and consumption behaviour. What was missing was the systematic consideration and procedural utilisation of social competence.

Cooperative procedures have a considerable impact on the *competence* of political and administrative decision-making processes, drawing on the knowledge of public bodies, external experts and local residents. The act of communicating these different sets of knowledge between experts and laypersons constitutes an important learning process.

5.2 Level of Discourse

If decisions are to be made on the basis of the highest possible level of information and knowledge, a forum must be created as part of the decision-making process in which the different forms of local knowledge, specialist expertise and layperson assessment come together and form a consistent whole. If such a forum is to be created, cooperative conflict management has to combine different discourses and promote communication between actors: some may lead a scientific specialist discussion, others a political or public discourse and again others an ethical discourse; in each way it is a specific way to handle a conflict. Actors partaking in these discourses are guided by their own strategies, rationalities and languages. Participation and relevant competence need a third component: communicative competence.

Cooperative conflict management can help to promote communicative competence in the following ways. The goal of the procedures is to find compromises, new solutions and consensus. At the level at which specific conflicts are carried out, the conflicting parties reach acceptable agreements by way of interest-oriented bargaining and consensus-oriented argumentation. Since there is a wide range of (mainly game theory) literature on the approaches to negotiating in the framework of cooperative conflict management, it will not be dealt with here (Fisher/Ury 1981; Bacow/Wheeler 1984; Nicholson 1991, pp. 57, 59; Raiffa 1994).[3] The case studies showed that negotiation processes are not as central to conflict resolution as the literature on negotiation theory would lead us to expect. Negotiation is used for reaching compromises over details and can be effective in overcoming individual obstacles but rarely for arriving at a comprehensive agreement. The role of external mediators appears to be crucial in providing the organisational and communicative backdrop for effective negotiation.

In the following the focus is on the results on the level of discourse with respect to the possibilities of social learning processes.

The level of discourse on the micro and meso-social level of mediation or other participatory negotiation procedures contributes to the internal capacity to regulate conflict in a decision-making process in the area of environmental policy. [4] It involves questions of fairness from the perspective of the participating parties and argumentative quality. The difference between problem-

---

3 See also Troja 2001, pp. 159-176.
4 *Discourse* indicates organisational forms of communication at the macro-social level, as Engels describes in her contribution on the discourse of the mass media, the academic discourse or the parliamentary discourse. Discourses have an institutional dimension. This encompasses ideas, concepts and conceptual categories which are (re)produced and transformed and in this way ascribe a physical and social reality a certain meaning. Such practices are in the sciences, for example, the acquisition and carrying out of research projects, citing and publication in refereed journals in connection with peer review procedures, the use of scientific categories and expert terminology in each discipline, expert opinions, etc. In the media, realities are constructed through other practices, e.g. through agenda-setting according to news value which is determined by actuality, newness, dramatisation and polarisation, interviews with influential actors, staging of media events, spreading through news agencies, etc.

oriented action as understood in rational choice theory on the one hand and argumentative discourse according to Habermas on the other can be explained by a difference in one crucial assumption. Rational choice theory assumes preferences and interests to be relatively constant. Conflict behaviour, assuming that it is in principle oriented towards each actor's own benefit, can thus be explained as resulting from a change in restrictions. Such restrictions are mainly time, money, legal and social norms that can be sanctioned and similar incentive structures (Troja 1998a, pp. 9-20). Discourse theory assumes, by contrast, firstly that via communication not only self-benefit strategies determine people's behaviour but also moral arguments. Secondly, a discursively directed decision-making procedure does not only change the restrictions but may also change the preferences and interests. The strength of an argument is the driving force for that and can be seen as the basis for social learning processes. The mechanism which leads to this change and revaluation of goals and interests is the communicative utilisation of language. Communicative rationality coexists with the economic rationality of negotiations.

Conflict as a Process of Social Construction

Environmental conflicts often arise in connection with questions on the linguistic definition of a problem, on the parameters of the issues to be addressed and on which aspects of the social, ecological and economic reality are or are not to be discussed. In a site-specific conflict, for example, some participants may talk about emission levels and new jobs; others paint a picture of a threat to the landscape and their children's future. The perception of the problem and the reality of the conflict is the outcome of a process of social construction (Troja/Kessen 1999, pp. 335f.). Parties to the conflict assert their position in regard to the problem being discussed; each position represents a view which is shaped by experience as well as subjective patterns of perception and meanings (cognitive patterns). Environmental conflicts pose major problems of complexity and uncertainty over the possible consequences for the actors involved in a related decision-making situation. In such situations, individuals secure their decision-making capability above all through selection and generalisation. Cognitive patterns accomplish this *inter alia* by constructing causal relationships which have been tried and tested, through a view shaped by attitudes (and insinuations) of the other actors and finally through planning and routinised courses of action (Vowe 1994, pp. 426-441).

Ideologies, mental models, cognitive frames or patterns, meta-frames or whatever else the mechanism for constructing reality is called; parties to conflict continuously seek efficient routines for decision-making (Denzau/North 1994, Karpe 1997). These patterns are, however, rarely sensitive to changes, or to data which do not seem compatible. Since the actors partaking in the procedures come from completely different social and professional areas, and since they interact in their function as an interest representative in partly antagonistic groups, their ideological backgrounds and thus their social realities can vary in the extreme. In this case, argumentative discourse can initiate a process of social learning that is characterised by two closely interconnected mechanisms: changing perspectives and building new coalitions. The change in subjective patterns of perception and behaviour can then possibly challenge and change established structural conditions. Given this relationship of specific conflict management and societal changes the literature on "transformative mediation" speaks of "social learning through empowerment and recognition" (Bush/Folger 1994; Dukes 1996; Schwerin 1995).[5]

Making the Ideal Speech Situation Come True?

In order to activate the potential of human communication for mutual recognition and consensus, a speech situation is needed which differs from the ritualised, conflict-oriented patterns of parliamentary procedures and the mass media and which helps replace strategic actions with cooperative problem solving. Following Habermas' line of argument, the discourse must be free of hierarchical controls. This would be realised in the "ideal speech situation" (Habermas 1995, Vol. 2, p. 224). He describes conditions of communication for discourse which are not oriented towards the systemic logic of politics or of the administration of justice but of the life world of the conflicting parties. No actor imposes hierarchical control in this situation; no strategic or deceitful action occurs. Actors have communicative competence: i.e. they can bring in arguments and criticism. No restrictions are placed upon the participation of actors. It is the strength of the argument which prevails with empirical references, explanations, insight and validity of normative judgments (Dryzek 1994, p. 15).

This model of an ideal speech situation is nothing more than it appears to be – just a theoretical ideal and conceptual model. Its significance does not consist in describing the reality of conflicts in which power and strategic behaviour play an important role. Rather, it is to supply a standard for evaluation. The impossibility of realising this ideal state does not preclude using it as a criterion to evaluate real decision-making processes.

The conditions of communication in an ideal speech situation are essentially fictional. Communication requires forums which are nonetheless oriented towards these requirements as guidelines. Voluntarism, equity, responsibility for content and results, autonomy of the conflicting parties and the possibility for all affected actors to participate are all principles of cooperative conflict management as they are found, for example, in the professional

---

5   See below.

standards of mediation and in accordance with the main concept of life world-oriented conflict regulation (ABA/NIDR/SPIDR[6]). For cooperative conflict management, institutional guidelines can be derived from the ideal speech situation to approach a discourse free of controls, even though it can never be achieved entirely. These guidelines can be summarised as follows:

— All affected and highly interested groups can participate.
— Interaction takes place as face-to-face communication.
— Participants have the necessary communicative competences which may be improved under certain circumstances at the first meetings by instructing the groups about the procedure.
— Decisions are made by the rule of consensus; arguments for dissenting should at least transcend individual interests.
— Contributions are only accepted and addressed if they are comprehensible to all, appropriately suited to the topic and sincere as well as (from the perspective of each role) justifiable.
— Arguments and interests must be able to be freely voiced, as among equal partners; this requires at least temporarily a protected space with its own rules of communication.

A cooperative conflict management procedure can contribute to conflict resolution provided that space for exchange and verification of one's perspective, values and interests is available. Certain rules of organisation can be inferred from the theory of communicative action (Renn 1996, pp. 171-174). Among these are the avoidance of too limited time constraints and the acceptance by participants of the openness of the procedure for varying results. The procedure must guarantee (perhaps in the form of standing orders) equal rights and obligations of participants, even if a legitimate decision-making authority has the possibility to ignore the results outside of the discourse. The willingness to learn is given if the participants recognise in the course of the procedure that several possible types of knowledge and rationality exist, and that despite this plurality the rules are binding in order to assess the validity of statements. Parties have to maintain the willingness to translate an affective into a cognitive or normative statement. Moral condemnations of positions and parties should in general be avoided by the procedure.

---

[6] The mediation standards are found in the agreement between the American Arbitration Association (AAA), the American Bar Association (ABA) and the Society of Professionals in Dispute Resolution (SPIDR). These are the most important organisations in the area of alternative dispute resolution in the United States. The standards borrow from existing guidelines and address the problems which they have experienced; see Dispute Resolution Journal, Vol. 50, No. 1, January 1995.

Story Lines

The ideal speech situation as a framework for communicative rationality is a normative ideal. In Habermas' understanding, strategic action and communicative action remain mutually exclusive principles of rationality. However, in cases of conflicts between real persons with divergent interests and standards of moral judgements a strategy is needed to come closer to the communicative reality of political decision making. The *story lines* in Hajer's analysis of environmental policies can be interpreted as one such communicative strategy (Hajer 1997, pp. 62f.). Examples of story lines are graphically displayed curves which succinctly state "the point being made" in the research on the state of – for instance – soil, water or forests. Story lines exist if the scientific discussion on air pollution is reduced to headlines, such as "the politics of high smoke stacks", "what goes up must come down" or "end-of-pipe technologies". In particular, the debate on sustainable development is rich in effective story lines, like "efficiency revolution", "we are living in the past of future generations" or "development needs innovation". Story lines tend to use political metaphors, analogies, historical references and clichés, addressing collective fears or guilt.

Here, the strategic element of story lines becomes evident. However, they differ from blank political slogans such as "No more asylum seekers". Story lines are the outcome of a discourse between actors with very different perspectives. The discourse itself needs to follow the principles of communicative rationality. Story lines are a product of a joint communication process in contrast to different disconnected concepts of reconstructing social reality. They express social reality in terms of a formula which combines elements from different areas; this offers the participants involved in the discourse symbolic references which facilitate a common understanding. Story lines offer the possibility to change perspectives, interests and social reality through discourse and thus induce a learning process.

A story line as a product of discourse tends naturally to be interpretative. It is characterised by a loss of meaning since those uncertainties and conditions linked to the original research and expertise are lost. That is however precisely the prerequisite allowing a story line to fulfil its main functions (Hajer 1997, p. 69):

— By reducing complexity, discourses can be brought to a closure;
— With their increasing usage and assertion they become ritualised and bring stability into the debate; they rationalise with a figure of speech access to a seemingly related problem;
— The participants in the discourse can thus extend their understanding and their discursive competence beyond their own expertise and experience; the environmental activist, the politician, the scientist and the administrator can show where their work fits into the mosaic.

The power of story lines comes not least from the fact that they sound plausible and allow for identification while not contradicting the partial discourses of the actors. They rank knowledge, actors' positions and permit coalition building. According to Hajer, in their trivial and ambiguous application they are the discursive cement which holds the communicative networks together between those actors who have different or at best partially overlapping perceptions and views. Story lines shape political discourse and the political language culture. In this way they contribute to preference building. Furthermore, they change the perception of problems and the possible solutions and open up room for new discourse coalitions (Hajer 1997, p. 59). Here lies the key role of such discursively derived formulas and metaphors for processes of institutional and social change.

To summarise: in environmental conflicts the different definitions of risk, societal models and concepts of justice continue to collide with one another. These definitions, models or concepts could be exclusive but in the process of social learning they could also approach each other – this could possibly be facilitated through language in the form of story lines. Such a process can be anchored institutionally in cooperative conflict management procedures, by establishing rules which are oriented on the discourse model of Jürgen Habermas.

Results from the Case Studies

The case studies supply practical illustrations of the described discursive learning processes. The importance of story lines was very clear in the observed cases. In both American cases of regulatory negotiations and in both the German procedures of mediation such linguistic formulas of problem and solution description played an important role. The story line in case 1 (waste tyres end use) was the so-called "waste hierarchy", the disposal business' prioritised system of "reuse before raw material recycling before dumping". This hierarchy was used as the basis for the reimbursement rates. In case 2 (the pesticide management plan) the solution was discussed along the story line of "graduated response", a step-by-step response to certain measurements of the groundwater. In case study 5 (airport) one of the important story lines was "three into one" which refers to the current problem of three inner city airports which could be replaced by one. In case 6 (the Detmolder Street round table) the term "flexible solution" originated out of earlier attempts based on the principle "two-to-four-solution" or "four-to-two-solution" to lead a discussion on solutions for a reasonable and sound structure and utilisation of the driving lanes.

In these cases the story lines resulted from longer debates. The formulations could in no case be attributed to individual persons. In two cases they were explicitly highlighted as the product of the group. The loss in differen-

tiation through the reduction to a linguistic formula was described as a prerequisite for the discursive functions of story lines. Only one participant, who participated as an expert economist in case 1, criticised the loss of significance. Otherwise the depicted three central functions of story lines could be verified:
1. Closure of discourse through reduction of complexity;
2. Continuity of debates and rationalised apprehension of a problem complex;
3. The bringing together of different competences and rationalities of discourse participants.

In case study 1 complex social, ecological and economic aspects would have had to be assessed in order to evaluate the various types of usage, recycling and disposal. The scientific expertise would not have produced unambiguous results. The right rate of taxation with the corresponding steering effect could not be determined. The story line of the hierarchy of waste supplied an assessment scheme and a framework for ordering the various forms of end usage. In contrast to complicated stock taking, all could partake in the discussion on ranking the types of usages within this framework. Hence the communication became result-oriented. In addition, new and unconventional discourse coalitions emerged, e.g. between the tyre industry and the ecological interest group Sierra Club, which both approved of the waste hierarchy.

In case study 2 as well such coalitions between competing ministries (Department for Environmental Quality and Department for Conservation and Recreation) were built which were interested in getting standards for ground water into a graduated response plan. The controversy around the standards and the importance of precautionary environmental protection first took shape through the story line "graduated response". The term referred at the same time to a minimal consensus which allowed for enough openness with respect to the design and practical implementation. The detailed eco-systemic, geographical and chemical problems were dealt with at an abstract level, "broken down" and then transformed into a feasible action plan. Everybody interested was capable of participating in this discussion.

In case 5 no rapprochement in any strict sense was possible, nor was an advocacy coalition capable of establishing its position over the location of the airport. The opposing interests within the framework of a NIMBY (Not in my backyard) problem were considered to be too far apart. Here, instead of ideological obstacles rather well-defined interests stood in the way of an agreement. Beyond the question of location a new assessment of the problem resulting from the discussion during the procedure had, according to the majority of the participants, clearly led to obvious learning processes. The story line "three into one" often played an important role in this new assessment, even if it was not explicitly cited. It was the point of departure for much of the argumentation; the arguments weighed up the detrimental impacts on nature caused by an airport far away from the city against the direct human burdens and dangers in the case of a location within or near the city.

"(My position was that) we don't need such an airport. Then I learned that it is perfectly legitimate and moral if one turns "three into one". You just have to look at the people in Tegel and Pankow. If it is built somewhere where it would not be so detrimental to the residents and if the destruction of nature could be compensated for at another location, there are many possibilities. We had to learn all this." (Interviewee, case study 5)

Similar to the cases 1 and 2, in case 6 the story line "flexible solution" helped the actors to express their views on the complex questions of design and layout of the road. This represented discursive progress compared to the diffuse public and purely ideological differences which had existed until then. Confrontational labelling, such as "dreamer", "anti-business" or even "murderer" (in view of the danger of an accident on the controversial street), were replaced by a differentiated argument about a succinctly articulated solution. This occurred without the communication slipping in the other extreme of a specialist's discourse for traffic experts.

In cooperative conflict management procedures, language as a medium and result of discourse obtains the power to shape reality. Accusations and escalating confrontations are transferred through language into discourse, where they can be handled as different topics of conflict. The story lines open this discourse to different rationalities and make it possible for affected actors from the various private and public areas to contribute to the decision-making process. Common language changes the perception of the problem and hence extends the range for solutions.

In the case studies consensus by argumentation was reached only to a limited extent when it came to issues which could not be solved through bargaining. Consensus in terms of approvals which are based on conviction can be described as a common denominator or "common ground". Learning processes in the sense of a change in perspective, a reassessment of the problems and shifts in interests present at first glance an even more demanding situation and can thus be described as a search for a "higher ground". Nevertheless the case studies show that considerable potential for cooperative conflict management procedures can be found precisely in such learning processes based on mutual recognition of interests and values. This causes the level of discourse to transcend a specific problem solution.

The internal procedural discursiveness reflected in part features of the policy field in general, as many of the participants had an important role in the public debate beyond the bounds of the procedure. With a publicly controversial large project such as the construction of an airport the influence on the culture of dispute and the democratic quality of the discussion is crucial. The tenor of the interviews was: communication in a cooperative conflict management procedure does probably not lead to another opinion being approved of or even adopted; however, the conflicting parties listened to each other and began to respect each other's views. The latter statement is to be found nearly word for word in numerous interviews in all case studies.

If the results concerning the level of discourse are summarised, it becomes apparent that cooperative conflict management procedures make it possible for the most diverse actors to address the conflict in the first place. While the actors often find new win-win-solutions for a conflict, some points of controversy often remain unresolved. Contradictory interests which could not be solved through a bargaining process were usually not capable of bringing about a discursive consensus either. However, from a discursive ethical point of view conflict also means a chance to improve an existing culture of debate and a higher level of discourse in a field of policy. Through the use of case-specific cooperation procedures individual and social learning processes take place, also beyond the consensus on particular issues and the specific problem solution. The discursive ethics learned in the conflict management procedure support a civil culture of disputing in a given policy field and network of actors. The case studies clearly demonstrate evidence of this effect of cooperative conflict management on the culture of debate and the related capacities in a policy field.

The all-party commitment of the mediator is a crucial prerequisite for the perceived fairness of each procedure of conflict management through mediation. Even more important, though, is the concept of the conflicting parties' own responsibility for solving the problem. This concept of autonomy distinguishes mediation from strictly legal or administrative decision-making processes. However, mediation does not just presuppose the participants' autonomy in the procedure; a feature which would imply the level of moral justice judgements described as "transpersonal autonomous" in the typology developed by Breit, Döring and Eckensberger (this volume). By contrast, the communicative processes of a cooperative conflict management procedure promote and further an understanding of ones own responsibility for conflict management. Mediation, therefore, contributes to processes of social learning which are required for the development of a civil society based on the existence of enlightened and responsible citizens.

6 Problem of Interplay

The paper will now address the question of how this inner-procedural potential for social learning in a policy field can be institutionalised so that the respective benefits can be applied in the area of environmental conflicts. Cooperative conflict management as an innovation in public affairs does not fill an institutional vacuum. On the contrary, established institutions of conflict regulation already exist. Routines in policy making with predefined rules of the game and "well trained players" are part of these institutions. Actors in policy making, administration and interest organisations interact in a well-coordinated scheme which leads to collectively binding decisions. Procedures for planning and approval for which citizen participation is legally stipulated constitute such an established institution of decision making. In terms of the respective laws, these procedures for planning and approval also aim to weigh competing interests against each other and mediate between them. Hearings should take well-justified objections into account. Law stipulates that public hearings should lead to an agreement. The course that numerous environmental problems take indicate weaknesses in the existing institutions of conflict regulation (see chapter 2) and increasing pressure arising from the problems. However, these pressures and the institutions' capacities for cooperative conflict management described above do not automatically lead to changes in the political institutions of conflict regulation. In Germany, both in the above mentioned case studies and in comparable mediation procedures, policy and administrative decisions often remained completely unaffected by the results of mediation. This is usually possible without justification at the decision-making level. In the United States these innovative procedures are more strongly institutionalised. The right to mediation is more often taken for granted and there is much more experience supporting it. Mediation and intensive lobbying are not disconnected, as is the case in Germany. There, the aim of lobbying is to directly influence the mediation procedures or the decision makers at an early point so that a consensus among the mediation committee members has the desired results. Among the investigated cases the River Road mediation is an outstanding example of the successful embedding of mediation in the continuing decision-making processes of policy making and administration. However, even if numerous other positive examples are familar, the other case studies indicate that the successful linking of mediation procedures to existing institutions of policy-making and administrative procedures is often inadequate.

The theory of new institutional economics supplies some explanations for why the institutionalisation of mediation in the public sector is difficult. It shows that the inefficient and – from a macro-level perspective – inadequate institutions of conflict regulation may continue to exist and will not be replaced by more adequate institutions, as would be expected from the point of view of selective evolution (North 1990; Denzau/North 1994). The change in institutions for the regulation of environmental conflicts clearly depends on its history; i.e. it is dependent on its previous trajectory (path dependence). From a societal perspective, disadvantageous regulations may have resulted from a coincidental historical event and then continued to exist. Thus far, they have made it possible for actors who have over time adapted to the institutional arrangements to pursue their interests and achieve increasing returns.

The economic historian and Nobel Prize winner Douglass C. North points out that it is not the procedures themselves which compete among each other but the organisations applying the technique. In a sense, this is a similar argument to that developed by Dünckmann and Mayer (this volume) who show that not the eco-labels themselves but rather the organisations behind each label and the actors promoting them compete with each other in the coffee market. Three factors insure increasing returns for the actors, provided that the once selected course of action is maintained (Haeder 1997, pp. 200-206; North 1990, p. 113): high set-up costs, learning effects and coordination effects.

1. The introduction of differentiated laws concerning environmental issues and planning is connected with *high set-up costs*. The set of rules, including certain specifications (e.g. state-of-the-art techniques), must first be developed. In order for this system to be implemented a complex administration for environmental affairs was set up. The system based on a principle of imposing limits of permissible emissions is applied within a law-and-order approach and its traditions of police law. Numerous legal experts and engineers in the area of environmental affairs have developed a certain know-how. Investors have made decisions based on the established system of law and order. These specific state and private investments would be considered sunk costs if a basic change in the instruments of environmental policy occurred; it would mean a massive loss of value of the investments.
2. The conflicting parties achieve *learning effects* by using the formal institutions of administrative procedures. Organisations have developed in such a way as to apply the institutional procedures to their advantage. These learning effects also inhibit a change in pathway.
3. Finally, several *coordination effects* are achieved. Decision-making on infrastructure projects and planning in the public sector takes place within a complex network. The network was created in the framework of the existing administrative law with numerous formal and informal rules and contacts. Actors who are part of this network use it to secure their interests.

Those cooperative conflict management procedures which lack legal institutionalisation and formalisation may not succeed in reaching a secure, formally binding outcome and in substantially contributing to building a political will. If not even an informally binding outcome can be guaranteed, the political and social capacities to make choices and take action disperse which might have been gained for the policy-making process through efficient approaches to negotiations, a higher discursive and argumentative level of communication and competent participation. The consequences for the acceptance of policy decisions are even negative if the conflicting parties' expectations of the effectiveness of participation are disappointed.

Reliable institutional conditions for the political relevance of cooperative conflict management procedures are thus needed. In theory, two extreme forms of institutional linkage of cooperative conflict management procedures to the political-administrative decision-making process are imaginable: a close, direct coupling by which the results of cooperative conflict management are controlled and ratified by parliamentary committees; or a complete decoupling of the cooperation procedures from the parliamentary arena in the sense of a separation of functions and authority for certain issues. The cooperation procedures would thus assume the character of situational expert parliament sessions. Both poles of institutional coupling do not work, however, and would lead to problems from the point of view of democracy theory.

A close coupling is ruled out since a contradiction in the logic of action of political party competition and cooperative systems of negotiations exists (Benz 1998, pp. 208 f.). Consensus and compromise in cooperative conflict management procedures are results of a sensitive process of arguing and bargaining which are defined based on participating interests. Changes to this package through later policy decisions normally endanger the outcome as a whole and render the process worthless. If the resolutions worked out by a mediation group would have to be ratified for lack of any real alternatives, the elected representatives and democratic boards would be substantially devalued. I come back to this problem again in connection with the term *decoupling*. In addition, the direct involvement of politicians in negotiations and the granting of the right to supervise the process contradict the rules of communication in cooperative procedures which are based on equality and consensus as a mode of decision. Furthermore, the style of communication is supposed to differ precisely from the ritualised, parliamentary style. Such dimensions will possibly be brought back into the proceedings through the inclusion and prominent positioning of politicians who are at the same time publicly competing in party politics.

A complete decoupling of the procedures from the legislative arena of the respective relevant federal level is also not possible from the point of view of democratic theory. Under such circumstances, the parliamentary committees would no longer be able to fulfil their function in the policy-making system. The norms concerning representative democracy and the public character of issues would be undermined and the results of cooperative procedures would be missing from the corrective measures taken with the involvement of a public base and the generalisation of interests. Cooperative conflict management is oriented towards the participation of the actors involved in the conflict, not towards grass-root democratic, broad or representative participation. The procedures are thus dependent on being tied into the representative-parliamentary institutions. In addition, the direct transfer of decision-making competences would massively increase the pressure put upon the participants. In view of the greater public control this would limit their scope of options.

7 Institutionalisation of Cooperative Conflict Management Procedures through Loose Coupling

Actors can react from situation to situation to the dilemma between close coupling and decoupling. They can create latent structures which operate at first in the shadow of formal institutions, but which have the chance of becoming institutionalised later (Benz 1998, pp. 213-215). Looking again at practical problems of institutional interplay, some examples of such situational ways out of the dilemma between close coupling and complete decoupling can be observed.

In the United States ample enabling legislation exists. At the level of the federal-state over 2,000 single laws make mediation obligatory. Two national laws (Negotiated Rulemaking Act; Alternative Dispute Resolution Act) strongly suggest using mediation in the area of environmental affairs (Hoffmann-Riem/Schidt-Aßmann 1990, pp. 320-357; Holznagel 1994, p. 160; Zillessen/Barbian 19921, p. 20). The Dispute Resolution Act of 1998 equips the courts with decision-making authority and the financial means to utilise alternative dispute resolution procedures, above all mediation, both voluntarily and by decree (Gottwald 1999, p. 333). This is often used as an argument for formal, legal institutionalisation. Studies show, however, that the laws in administrative and in environmental law in Germany and other European countries already leave sufficient room for linking mediation to formal administrative procedures.[7] According to our studies, the resistance offered by administrators and politicians is often a much more important obstacle than legal aspects (Troja 2001, pp. 192-204, 353-380).

In the case studies, four forms of loosely institutionalised coupling of cooperative conflict management can be observed. They can be inferred from a representative-parliamentary decision-making process which hinders decoupling but also avoids close coupling: first, the participation of the decision makers in policy making and administration; second, a clearly formulated political commitment concerning the conflict management procedure; third, status reports on implementation and monitoring, combined with the obligation to justify any deviate decisions; and, fourth, improved public relations for the procedures.

7.1 Binding Commitment through Participation of Decision-Makers

"And it goes back to not having the senior level people at the table. So when a decision is made [what is important]... is that link, [i.e.] what happens between the actual Task Force

---

7   For more details, see Troja 2001, pp. 204-215, 380-385; see also the referenced literature in this publication.

members and senior staff outside of the Task Force who ultimately have veto power over what happens. So the lesson of this is that we need to pay more attention, particularly if there are interagency issues at stake, to how we get buy-in and approval from those who have veto power outside the Task Force process." (Interviewee case study 2)

Looking at the case studies, politicians who had influence over the procedures or results at higher levels only participated in the round table for the reconstruction of Detmolder Street in Bielefeld. This increased the status of the procedure. At the same time, given the decision-making competence of the committee, the demands on representativity also rose. Through a concentration of the conflicting parties representativity, however, is often a weakness in mediation, compared with other participatory procedures. A danger would also exist for participation being determined proportional to political party representation instead of according to the actual interests and those concerned. In the case studies participants sometimes voiced their opinions against this. They wanted to discuss the issues from a specialist view as well as from the point of view of those personally affected while avoiding at the same time the confrontational rituals of party politics. Practical limits to this approach also exist: policy makers at a higher decision-making level often have to act strategically. Usually they desist from or hand over participation at the operational level – in the case of the latter often because of lack of specialist knowledge or the inability to fit proceedings in their schedule.

It is still possible to clarify for individual cases which political and administrative representatives should partake in the procedures to ensure feedback from the decision-making committees. In practice, there is often a concern about whether the public administration will make any binding agreements in advance (co-optation of public administration). This can be avoided by conceding the administration an observer or auditor status with the task of feeding the necessary information into the proceedings. Through their participation policy makers are forced to observe the changed communication rules and can be put in the position of being able to reconstruct the process of clarifying interests and changing perspectives and assessment.

7.2 Mandate of the Procedure and Political Commitment

"I have also learned if at the beginning when establishing the round table there is no consensus that one is desired, then no consensus will be reached in the end that the results should be implemented (...) Therefore, its establishment must be politically desired, by the mayor, the city's administration and by the political parties in municipal government." (Interviewee case study 6)

Drawing on their experience with cooperative conflict management procedures, many interviewed participants emphasise that, from the outset of the counselling, the mandate of the procedure has to be thoroughly clarified publicly and, if possible, in writing by the responsible decision makers and the organisers of the procedures. This consists of a description of the procedural tasks, of the value of the results and how these can be used in the subsequent decision-making process. Such clarification avoids false expectations among participants who would later be disappointed. Moreover, the perceived loss of invested resources would lead to even greater political apathy and possibly to an escalation in the conflict instead of improved understanding. At the same time it is insured that policy makers themselves also have to clearly establish what exactly the purpose of the procedure is and that they are taking a first step of commitment. Furthermore, it must be clear that conflict management cannot be implemented as an alibi response to a temporary lack of decision-making capability.

The mandate beyond the participation of important actors was clear for example in the cited River Road mediation. The representatives of the local administration and the government offices for environmental affairs announced at public events that they themselves suggested the mediation procedure with the intention to implement the results later. The official government representative had made sure that her superiors supported the measure. By such a publicly declared mandate and political commitment, high-ranking decision-makers can be involved indirectly, even though their direct participation in the proceedings is not possible for the above mentioned reasons.

The criticism of the conflicting parties was based in part not on erroneous assumptions about the relative importance of the procedure but was levelled rather at the "political game" which had led to reasonable doubts about the openness of the results. In political reality the openness, which in theory is a prerequisite for mediation, can barely be observed. Most important, however, is a clear description at the outset indicating which points leave room for negotiations and what influence the procedure is supposed to have.

7.3 Implementation Reports and Required Provision of Justification

"The problem was that the committee never had a chance to discuss the recommendation that was enacted by the DEQ (Department for Environmental Quality). That never came back to us. We did our job; we made our recommendation as public input. Now as the head of the DEQ told us, [...], he says, >>You have public input, we are not bound to do what you tell us to do (...).<< They took our information and they did something else." (Interviewee case study 1)

If recommendations do not get approval by the decision-making boards and are not implemented, decision makers should be obliged to justify this publicly. In particular, the forum of participants should be presented with the reasons and ideally be given the chance to take a position in this regard. This suggestion does not mean that the goal of mediation to provide policy input should be replaced by ongoing negotiations between policy making and the forum of participants. The procedures should continue to be concluded by political and administrative decisions with a binding agreement. But an obligation to provide a report and justification can ensure that the decision makers seriously and verifiably discuss the results. Any changes in the presentation of the results would have to be backed by substantive arguments and could not be based on electoral tactics alone. Stronger institutionalisation of a required justification would give the results a more official character and higher status. Even if results are not implemented cooperative conflict management procedures could at least influence political communication. In the opinion of many participants competence acquired through the procedures, the level of discourse and the transparency of political decision making are entirely lost if no political discussions on the result follow.

A possible form of institutionalisation of required justification became apparent at the round table for pesticide management and for the River Road mediation. At those proceedings the implementation of the results became the topic of the scheduled discussions in the framework of the legally maintained formal participatory procedure. Supervision/control of implementation in this or another form, for example in the form of follow-up meetings, reports, position papers by the policy decision makers on the results, etc., should be stipulated in the framework for mediation and be part of the obligations of the political contracting authority. Organisers of cooperation procedures should work towards stipulating such clauses in the directive order.

7.4 Public Relations

"For the press it was too unspectacular, too boring. If all the people that are supposed to be fighting each other sit together and attempt to come to the point on certain topics it is not of value for the news." (Interviewee case study 5)

A further possibility to increase the status of cooperative conflict management in policy decision making is a more institutionalised and professional public relations approach, both on the part of the mediators and moderators and on the part of the political commissioners. With the exception of the round table in Bielefeld which received intensive media coverage, public relations efforts were lacking in all other procedures. Occasionally, newspaper reports were published, but they mainly referred to the conflict itself and not to the procedure taking place.

The weak presence of the media contributed to a relatively low public status of the procedures. Accordingly, the political relevance of the observed cases was not as great as it could have been with better media coverage or public relations efforts in place. The case studies revealed four approaches to bringing the procedures more into public, political and specialist debates:

1. The experience of the State of Lower Saxony Commission demonstrates possibilities which not only depend on the mass media. The results were

not only forwarded to the commissioner but also distributed to multiple users in politics, science, business and public agencies. That provided for a higher level of acquaintance with the topic and for a specialist reputation of the forum for negotiations. In the agreements to execute a cooperative conflict management procedure it was possible to determine from the outset that the results were not only to be submitted to the responsible offices in policy making and administration but were to be distributed through a larger mailing list. Besides the media, addressees could be locally and regionally active interest groups, associations, scientific organisations, etc.

2. A second approach could be to cooperate more intensively with the media during the proceedings: first, through press releases and statements to the press but, secondly, by making the mediation process partly public. All three American mediation teams contradicted the mainstream thesis that mediation needs confidentiality in the sense of excluding the public. They were of the opinion that journalists and guests from outside could take part in several meetings. However, it is then necessary that the media representatives be informed of the special circumstances of such a communication process and that they agree to the corresponding rules. This would be, for instance, that information could only be made public following the approval of all participants.

3. Currently, much is said about online mediation and the use of the internet as a forum for information and discussion for a discursive participatory procedure. The example of the mediation proceedings for Vienna airport provides insights into how the internet can be used for public relations efforts and for an extensive exchange between the mediation group and the public not directly participating in the procedure (for an overview, see the homepage of this mediation procedure at www.viemediation.at).

4. If one bears in mind that conflicting parties can find a solution for every controversial point if they understand it is a problem that they as a group share and for which a solution is being sought, the importance of some form of corporate identity for the mediation procedure becomes clear. This can be supported by a logo and whatever contributes to the building of a group: e.g. holding a public event together at which the parties to the conflict present their work to the public and, in the best case, a celebration at the end of mediation procedure.

8 Outlook

Mediation and negotiated rule making are institutions whose function of co-ordinating behaviour is supported in part by legal contracts and corresponding sanctions or, much more frequently, by informal sanctioning mechanisms. For this reason it makes sense to take a closer look at the possibilities available through informal institutionalisation. I have formulated suggestions for a loose coupling of mediation to the institutions in policy making and administration instead of advocating the legally based institutionalisation of mediation and regulatory negotiation. One reason for this is the existence of an adequate legal framework for the successful utilisation of cooperative conflict management procedures in the public sector. Improvements are always possible, but the danger accompanying the legal framing of the procedures is a loss of flexibility and a reduction in the variety of individual communication structures (Gottwald 1999).

A broader analysis of the case studies revealed considerable weaknesses with respect to the organisation and the execution of the procedures as well as to the responsibility of policy makers to include them in the overall decision-making process. Mediators and facilitators undertake too little to improve the public status of the procedures. In addition, the binding character of the procedures should be more clearly insisted upon. In particular, this should include a clear mandate for the procedure and for the relationship between decision makers and voluntary political responsibility in dealing with the procedure results. These requirements should be added to the list of professional standards of mediation, such as impartiality, openness about results and the self-responsibility of each conflicting party.

The challenges for those who are politically responsible seem, however, equally great. Politicians are even more in need of undergoing learning processes, even though this is obviously more difficult for them than for administrative officials. The latter tend to be "cooperative" since they must deal directly with the problems of implementing the decisions. When applying cooperative conflict management, politicians often come into conflict with their own understanding of their role which is founded on a "party political" view of the state. Although the political parties, according to German Basic Law (Art. 21, Par. 1), only *co-determine* the process of political opinion-forming by the people, the socialisation of party politics obviously often leads to the impression that political parties have a *monopoly* to influence this process. A self-confident and modern political system, though, would not see cooperative conflict management procedures as a competing *political* institution or as a "substitute parliament". Instead, they could be understood as a new form of policy consultation with the capacity for more open decision-making processes and a stronger source of legitimisation. Both decision makers in various policy fields and professionals in the "mediation scene" aim at creating the necessary institutional conditions to constructively utilise the results derived from such procedures.

References

Beck, Ulrich (1986): Die Risikogesellschaft. Auf dem Weg in eine andere Moderne. Frankfurt
Beckmann, Jens/Gerhard Keck (1999): Beteiligungsverfahren in Theorie und Anwendung. Akademie für Technikfolgenabschätzung in Baden-Württemberg. Stuttgart
Benz, Arthur (1998): Postparlamentarische Demokratie? Demokratische Legitimation im kooperativen Staat. In: Greven, Michael (ed.): Demokratie – eine Kultur des Westens? 20. Wissenschaftlicher Kongreß der Deutschen Vereinigung für Politische Wissenschaft. Opladen; pp. 201-222
Bingham, Gail (1986): Resolving Environmental Disputes. A Decade of Experience. Washington D.C.
Buckle, L. G./S. R. Thomas-Buckle (1986): Placing Environmental Mediation in Context: Lessons from "Failed" Mediations. In: Environmental Impact Review; No. 6; pp. 55-70
Bush, Robert A. B./Joseph P. Folger (1994): The Promise of Mediation. Responding to Conflict Through Empowerment and Recognition. San Francisco
Coglianese, Cary (1997): Assessing Consensus: The Promise and Performance of Negotiated Rulemaking. In: Duke Law Journal; No. 46; pp. 1255-1349
Coser, Lewis A. (1964): The Functions of Social Conflict: An Examination of the Concept of Social Conflict and its Use in Empirical Sociological Research. New York
Denzau, Arthur T./Douglass C. North (1994): Shared Mental Models: Ideologies and Institutions. In: Kyklos; Vol. 47; Fasc. 1; pp. 3-31
Dienel, Peter C. (1991): Die Planungszelle. Der Bürger plant seine Umwelt; eine Alternative zur Establishment-Demokratie. Opladen
Dryzek, John S. (1994): Discursive Democracy. Politics, Policy, and Political Science. Cambridge
Dukes, E. Franklin (1996): Resolving Public Conflict. Transforming Community and Governance. Manchester; New York
Fischer, Frank (1993): Bürger, Experten und Politik nach dem "Nimby"-Prinzip: Ein Pläydoyer für die partizipatorische Policy-Analyse. In: Héritier, Adrienne (ed.): Policy-Analyse. Opladen; pp. 451-470
Fisher, Roger/William Ury (1981): Getting to Yes. Negotiating Agreement without Giving in. Boston
Folger, Joseph P./Tricia S. Jones (1994): New Directions in Mediation. Communication Research and Perspectives. London; New Delhi.; Thousand Oaks
Goldberg, Stephen B./Frank E. A. Sander/Rogers, Nancy H. (1992): Dispute Resolution. Negotiation, Mediation, and Other Processes. Boston; Toronto; London
Gottwald, Walther (1999): Verrechtlichung der Mediation. Steckt eine Profession ihre Claims ab? In: KON:SENS; No. 6; pp. 331-334
Habermas, Jürgen (1995): Theorie des kommunikativen Handelns. Bd. 1: Handlungsrationalität und gesellschaftliche Rationalisierung; Bd. 2: Zur Kritik der funktionalen Vernunft. Frankfurt
Häder, Michael (1997): Umweltpolitische Instrumente und Neue Institutionenökonomik. Wiesbaden

Hajer, Maarten A. (1997): The Politics of Environmental Discourse. Ecological Modernization and the Policy Process. Oxford

Healey, Patsy (1998): Building Institutional Capacity through Collaborative Approaches to Urban Planning. In: Environment and Planning; No. 30; pp. 1531-1546

Hennen, Leonhard (1996): Das Ohr an der Basis? Konsensus Konferenzen vermitteln den Politikern die Meinung von Laien über neue Techniken. In: Politische Ökologie; No. 46; pp. 44-45

Hoffmann-Riem, Wolfgang/Eberhard Schmidt-Aßmann (1990): Konfliktbewältigung durch Verhandlungen. Baden-Baden

Holznagel, Bernd (1994): Beschleunigung von Genehmigungsverfahren durch den Einsatz von Konfliktmittlern. In: Dose, Nicolai/Bernd Holznagel/Weber, Volker (eds.): Beschleunigung von Genehmigungsverfahren. Vorschläge zur Verbesserung des Industriestandortes Deutschland. Bonn; pp. 151-169

Jänicke, Martin (1996): Erfolgsbedingungen von Umweltpolitik, in: Jänicke, M. (ed.): Umweltpolitik der Industrieländer. Entwicklung, Bilanz, Erfolgsbedingungen. Berlin; pp. 9-28

Jänicke, Martin (1997): Democracy as a Condition for Environmental Policy Success: the Importance of Non-Institutional Factors. In: Lafferty, William M./James Meadowcroft (eds.): Democracy and the Environment. Problems and Prospects. Cheltenham; Lyme; pp. 71-85

Jänicke, Martin/Helmut Weidner (Hg.) (1997): National Environmental Policies. A Comparative Study of Capacity-Building. Berlin et al.

Karpe, Jan (1997): Rationalität und mentale Modelle. Standortkonflikte um Abfallentsorgungsanlagen aus ökonomischer Sicht. Frankfurt et al.

Mayntz, Renate (1990): Entscheidungsprozesse bei der Entwicklung von Umweltstandards. In: Die Verwaltung; Vol. 23; No. 2; pp. 137-151

Meadowcroft, James (1998): Co-operative Management Regimes: A Way Forward? In: Glasbergen, Pieter (ed.): Co-operative Environmental Governance. Public-Private Agreements as a Policy Strategy. Dordrecht; Boston; London; pp. 21-42

Minsch, Jürg et al. (1998): Institutionelle Reformen für eine Politik der Nachhaltigkeit. Berlin et al.

North, Douglass C. (1990): Institutions, Institutional Change and Economic Performance. Political Economy of Institutions and Decisions. Cambridge

Pritzker, David M./Deborah S. Dalton (eds.) (1995): Negotiated Rulemaking Sourcebook. Office of the Chairman; Administrative Conference of the United States; Washington D. C.

Renn, Ortwin (1996): Möglichkeiten und Grenzen diskursiver Verfahren bei umweltrelevanten Planungen. In: Biesecker, Adelheid/Klaus Grenzdörffer (eds.): Kooperation, Netzwerk, Selbstorganisation. Elemente demokratischen Wirtschaftens. Pfaffenweiler; pp. 161-197

Renn, Ortwin/Thomas Webler (1994): Konfliktbewältigung durch Kooperation in der Umweltpolitik - Theoretische Grundlagen und Handlungsvorschläge. In: oikos (ed.): Kooperation für die Umwelt. Im Dialog zum Handeln. Chur; Zürich; pp. 11-52

Schwerin, Edward (1995): Mediation, Citizen Empowerment, and Transformational Politics. Westport; London

Selle, Klaus (Hg.) (1996): Planung und Kommunikation. Gestaltung von Planungsprozessen in Quartier, Stadt und Landschaft. Grundlagen, Methoden, Praxiserfahrungen. Wiesbaden, Berlin

Simmel, Georg (1995): Das Ende des Streits. In: Rammstedt, Otthein (ed.): Georg Simmel Gesamtausgabe. Vol. 7; Aufsätze und Abhandlungen 1901-1908; Frankfurt; pp. 333-344

Susskind, Lawrence/Jeffrey Cruikshank (1987): Breaking the Impass. Consensual Approaches to Resolving Public Disputes. New York

Susskind, Lawrence/Sarah McKearnan/Thomas-Larmer, Jennifer (eds.) (1999): The Consensus Building Handbook. A Comprehensive Guide to Reaching Agreement. London; New Delhi

Troja, Markus (1998a): Umweltpolitik und moderne Ökonomik. Der Beitrag der Neuen Politischen Ökonomie und der Neuen Institutionenökonomik zur Erklärung umweltpolitischer Entscheidungsprozesse. Münster

Troja, Markus (2001): Umweltkonfliktmanagement und Demokratie. Zur Legitimation kooperativer Konfliktregelungsverfahren in der Umweltpolitik. Köln

Troja, Markus/Stefan Kessen (1999): Mediation als Kommunikationsprozess. In: KONS:SENS; No. 6, pp. 335-340

Vowe, Gerhard (1994): Politische Kognition. Umrisse eines kognitionsorientierten Ansatzes für die Analyse politischen Handelns. In: Politische Vierteljahresschrift; Vol. 35; No. 3; pp. 423-447

Weidner, H. (ed.) (1998): Alternative Dispute Resolution in Environmental Conflicts. Experiences in 12 Countries. Berlin

Young, Oran R. (1999): Institutional Dimensions of Global Environmental Change. Science Plan; IHDP Report No. 9; Bonn

Zilleßen, Horst/Thomas Barbian (1992): Neue Formen der Konfliktregelung in der Umweltpolitik. In: Aus Politik und Zeitgeschichte; B 39-40/92; pp. 14-23

Zilleßen, Horst (1993): Die Modernisierung der Demokratie im Zeichen der Umweltpolitik: In: Zilleßen, Horst/Wendelin Strubelt/Dienel Peter C. (eds.): Modernisierung der Demokratie – Internationale Ansätze. Opladen; pp. 17-39

Zilleßen, Horst (Hg.) (1998a): Mediation. Kooperatives Konfliktmanagement in der Umweltpolitik. Opladen

Verena Sandner

Myths and Laws: Changing Institutions of Indigenous Marine Resource Management in Central America[1]

1 Introduction

There are a great number of studies about the traditional or indigenous management of marine resources. Some of these management systems have been able to prevent resource degradation over long periods of time and serve as examples for the sustainable use of common property resources. Overexploitation in these systems is avoided through a set of access rights, operational use rules and sometimes through magico-religious norms such as taboos or sacred areas. However, not all traditional institutions prove efficient for the protection of natural resources. Especially in those societies that are confronting social disruption and accelerated change, for example through the rapid integration into market economies, a breakdown of the traditional management system may take place. Often the consequence is an open-access situation in which resources are over-exploited and ecosystem degradation occurs, threatening the survival of the coastal communities depending to a high degree on marine resources as a source of income and as an important protein staple. Incentives for the creation of new institutions for effective resource management come from a variety of actor groups, for example government agencies, international conservation groups or development organisations. In some cases, it is the local indigenous population itself which tries to adapt existing institutions or create new ones to confront change and to close institutional gaps.

The indigenous Kuna of Eastern Panama, the subject of this article, serve as an example for such endogenous creation of new institutions. The Kuna are widely known internationally as an example not only for their advanced po-

---

1 The findings of this article are based on the author's research in Panama in 1994 and on the findings from a research project from 1999 to 2002. The latter was financed by the German Research Council (DFG), whom I would like to thank for the funding, and was directed by Prof. J. Bähr at the University of Kiel. During this project, entitled "Traditional Resource Management of Marine Resources in Central America: Comparing Cultural Change, Conflicting Uses and Local Solutions", research was conducted in three autoctonous populations in Central America: the Kuna of Panama, the Miskito of Eastern Nicaragua and the afro-caribbean Raizales on the Caribbean island of Providencia (Colombia).

litical autonomy which has served as a basis for the preservation of the indigenous culture and the defence of their territory against external threats. The Kuna were also the first indigenous group to create their own nature reserve in Latin America in the 1980s, based on the traditional concept of nature and managed by their own professionals (Chapin 1991; Ventocilla et al. 1995a). Despite these incentives, ecological problems in the autonomous region Kuna Yala have been increasing during the 1990s as a consequence of growing pressure on resources. Especially marine ecosystems are suffering reduced stocks and physical destruction caused by resource use through Kuna fishermen and divers.

This paper examines two perspectives on the resource problems and the related institutions. First, we will analyse the traditionally existing institutions which regulated resource use on the basis of spiritual principles, such as taboos, and the loss of effectiveness these are confronting today. The underlying driving forces for the diminishing "grip" of these institutions have to be examined, such as changing worldviews and values, as well as the processes of social forgetting associated with these changes. In a second step some of the newly emerging formal institutions will be presented which are aimed at reducing the pressure on resources and that have been created and implemented by Kuna authorities. These are designed using western scientific knowledge and institution principles on the basis of traditional administrative structures and concepts of nature. The Kuna incentives may serve as an example for the local capacity to create new institutions for environmental problems. However, there are also a lot of pitfalls and difficulties in the creation of new institutions which hamper or block the institution-building process.

2 Systems of Traditional Ecological Knowledge and Management: Some Conceptual Problems

Since Johannes' (1981; 1982) and Klee's (1980) documentations of traditional marine resource management a rich body of literature on such systems in different parts of the world has been published (e.g. Berkes 1987; Ruddle 1988; Morrison et al. 1994; Dyer/McGoodwin 1994; Hviding 1993; Durrenberger/Pálsson 1987). The terms used to describe these systems include: *traditional or indigenous resource management, folk management, community-based management, customary marine tenure sytems or local systems of resource management*, being used nearly synonymously. The basis for these systems is indigenous knowledge, defined as the "local knowledge held by indigenous peoples or local knowledge unique to a given culture or society" (Berkes et al. 1995, p. 282). Traditional ecological knowledge is regarded as a subset of indigenous knowledge, meaning a body of culturally transmitted knowledge and beliefs regarding the human-environment relationship. Following this definition, true traditional ecological knowledge (often abbreviated as TEK) is understood as the outcome of cross-generational transmission of knowledge and is a function of time (historical continuity) and space (specific local area) within a certain cultural context (Indigenous Knowledge and Development Monitor 1998). A clear definition of the term *traditional* remains difficult, however, as many scholars have stated (for an extensive discussion of the term see Berkes 1999). One question still unanswered is the necessary time span for traditional knowledge to be designated as traditional or as ancient, leaving open how many generations have to transmit practices and beliefs before these become traditional. Berkes and Folke (1994) distinguish between traditional and neo-traditional resource management systems, the latter meaning local systems which lack historical continuity but which are based on locally generated observations and knowledge. To avoid such conceptual problems, some students of resource management systems use the terms local knowledge or folk management (for example Ruddle 1994a), others prefer the term self-management in a more general sense of local wildlife management (Feit 1988). In the following the terms traditional indigenous ecological knowledge and management will be used because they seem to be the most common ones in the literature.

Definitory problems aside, traditional systems of marine ecological knowledge and management show certain characteristics that have been observed in different cultural settings around the world. Such systems have been well documented especially in Oceania as well as in fishing communities in North America and Northern Europe, and to a lesser extent in Latin America also. The findings from these studies suggest that many traditional societies manage a rich body of ecological local knowledge, which often shows similarities with scientific knowledge. Berkes' studies of North American Cree fishing management reveal that indigenous people monitor much the same information on fishing stocks as western science does (such as geographical distribution, see Berkes 1999). This specific ecological knowledge on wildlife can be considered as the first of four levels of traditional knowledge, following Berkes et al. (1995a). It exists in many societies but in itself does not guarantee resource conservation. For sustainable resource use there has to be a second level, which refers to practices and tools for resource management and which is based on the third level, the social institutions that allow for rule-making and enforcement. The fourth level, as defined by Berkes et al. (1995), comprises the world views as the underlying principles that shape environmental perception and social relations. These four levels constituting a traditional ecological knowledge system are interrelated and contribute the particular characteristics of such systems as opposed to systems of scientific knowledge and management. TEK is regarded to be holistic, intuitive and qualitative, it is based on empirical observations and the accumulation of experience by trial-and-error (Berkes 1993; Ruddle 1994b). Furthermore TEK is linked to moral and spiritual values and is deeply interwoven with indigenous cosmologies as well as with the social system including reciprocity and obligations. Thus, TEK is "an integrated system of knowledge, practice and beliefs" (Berkes 1993, p. 5) embedded in the social context.

Systems of traditional ecological knowledge may produce sustainable resource management, in which the "Tragedy of the Commons" assumed by Hardin (1968) as inevitable does not take place. In his article Hardin postulated that resources which are neither privately owned nor controlled by state authority are subject to overuse and depletion, based on the assumption that the individual resource user tries to maximise his personal gains regardless of the possible damage to the resource. This can indeed be the case with common-pool resources where neither access nor forms and levels of use are regulated and in consequence the tragedy occurs in the form of complete exhaustion of natural resources, as has been observed in many fisheries of the world. However, such a so-called open-access situation has to be clearly distinguished from managed common-property systems where a group of users defines rules and regulations for the use of commonly owned resources (see Feeny et al. 1990; Bromley 1992). In these systems users manage their resources, management being understood as the control over what resources are harvested, how much, by whom, when, how and where (Berkes 1999; cf. Schlager/Ostrom 1992). Control is established in the form of social restraints restricting resource use in a variety of ways. The most common examples for such restraints in the case of marine resource use are closed seasons for certain species, temporary or permanent closed areas, gear restrictions, limited entry to fishing grounds and specific-species prohibitions (Johannes 1982). These regulations can have a formal though unwritten character with clearly defined sanctions executed by an enforcing authority. They may also be of a more informal character such as myths and beliefs based on spiritual concepts including sanctions on a spiritual level (e.g. Anderson 1994; Ruddle 1988). The clear distinction between formal and informal regulations is not always easy to draw, especially in traditional societies with a great body of unwritten though formal rules.

Some scholars state that over-exploitation in such systems is being avoided not as a direct outcome of regulating institutions but mainly as a consequence of small population size in traditional communities and due to a lack of technology (e.g. Hames 1991; cf. Berkes 1987). A great number of studies, however, have shown that use restrictions in traditional communities may have a direct conservation effect on resources. Many of these are identical with modern management tools in fisheries (Johannes 1982), such as closed seasons and closed areas that allow for the reproduction of stocks. These have not only been in use in Oceania for centuries but are also important management tools in modern fishing science. However, the effectiveness of traditional harvest restrictions varies and societies may have some effective environmental institutions next to others which do not serve to prevent resource degradation (Ruddle 1994a).

The question whether these social regulations in fishing communities have evolved intentionally as management tools or whether the conservation effect is a by-product has been subject to intensive discussion among students of such systems. The literature suggests that this question cannot be answered in general but has to be analysed specifically for each case. Some traditional institutions may have evolved through trial-and-error in a social learning process over several generations leading to adaptive tools for the management of scarce resources. Whether perceived scarcity of resources or a crisis is a necessary precondition for such tools to be developed is another question discussed in the literature on traditional management systems which will not be further analysed here (e.g. Berkes 1999). Other traditional institutions such as magico-religious taboos which are based on cosmology may have a clear restrictive effect for resource use but may not have evolved with "conservation as their objective" (Johannes 2002, p.3; cf. Klee 1980). Thus, McGoodwin calls such practices passive means of regulation (McGoodwin 1990). Whether there is a true conservation ethic in traditional societies has been widely discussed among students. Some deny the existence of such an ethic, dismissing sustainable resource use practices as conservative by coincidence (referring to the ecologically noble savage myth). Many studies suggest, however, that there is something like a general environmental ethic in some indigenous societies (Johannes 2002). This conservation ethic about the relationship between man and nature can also be defined as the moral management of the cosmos or moral ecology (Varese 1996).

Many traditional resource systems have suffered disruption and loss of efficiency in recent times (Berkes et al. 1995). One reason for this is the shift of resource use patterns from subsistence to market-oriented use. This often means growing pressure on natural resources, rapid introduction of new technological methods and the exploitation of resources that had not been used before. The existing institutions in traditional societies are often unsuited to regulate resource use under such changed conditions and to avoid over-exploitation, resulting in institutional "vacuums" for new forms of use which are not regulated at all. This process that McNeely calls the "real tragedy of the commons" (McNeely 1992, p. 38) leads to a shift from well-managed common-property systems towards an open-access situation where quantities and methods of resource use are not limited and over-exploitation may occur. In extreme cases, resources may be irreversibly destroyed and social systems may suffer a shift to social relations being dominated by violence and distrust between community members (e.g. in the case of Mexican fishermen studied by McGoodwin 1994).

This tragedy can be seen as a product of social disruption (Hanna/Jentoft 1996). The shift from subsistence to market economy occurs in a parallel process to changing worldviews and values within traditional societies. Personal profit becomes a goal of production and replaces the formerly dominant production for daily needs. The traditional principle of reciprocity and distribution of surpluses between community members is replaced by the commercial interest to sell resources within the community and to external buyers. At the same time, traditional ecological knowledge and underlying cosmological concepts including a general respect for nature lose importance and transmission from one generation to the other is interrupted. Contrary to the shift from an economic orientation towards a sustainability approach mentioned in the introduction to this book for industrial societies, a lot of traditional communities are still in a process of growing orientation towards commercial production and a diminishing role for nature as the basis of society. The above-mentioned aspects lead to an erosion of the effectivity of traditional institutions while the creation of new ones or the adaptation of existing institutions to the changes occurs too slowly or not at all.

One possible pathway for the solution of resource problems in traditional societies which is discussed and applied internationally is the so-called cooperative management or "co-management" concept (e.g. Jentoft et al. 1998; Pinkerton 1989; Stevens 1997). This approach, also called participatory or joint management, ideally incorporates a variety of actors negotiating and sharing management functions in an equitable and democratic way (Borrini-Feyerabend et al. 2000). Being based on traditional ecological knowledge and local organisational capacities, the idea is to avoid a "top-down approach" and gain better acceptance and participation in local communities. Hanna and Jentoft (1996) describe co-management as the difficult re-embedding of responsibilities for resource management in local communities. In practice, however, truly equitable role-sharing in the institution building process does not always take place, and often participation of the local population is permitted only at an advanced stage in the planning process rather than engaging all the actors involved in the joint formulation of policies from the start (own research in Colombia and Nicaragua; see also Bryant 1997). Thus, the control of the planning process often remains in the hands of external agencies such as state ministries or NGO. Following Hanna and Jentoft, however, true co-management should mean the re-embedding of responsibilities for resource management in local communities (Hanna/Jentoft 1996). In contrast to the numerous publications about co-managment there are fewer studies on the incentives of improving resource management through the formulation of new institutions by traditional or local communities themselves. The creation of such institutions and the underlying processes of social learning have not been well studied till now (Berkes 1999).

3 The Kuna of Panama

The Kuna are an indigenous group living on the Caribbean coast of Eastern Panama (see Map 1). They belong to the Macro-Chibchan group but their origin is still the subject of discussion among scientists and has not been clearly established. There are doubts whether they are identical with the indian groups the Spaniards encountered on the Darien at the time of conquest (Howe 1998). It is held more probable that they lived in northern Colombia at that time from where they migrated or re-migrated to Panama, and this is also congruous with Kuna oral tradition (Ventocilla 1997). After centuries of conflicts with neighbouring indigenous groups and the Spanish colonisers they moved towards the Caribbean slope of the region known as San Blas, settling along the rivers on the mainland, but beginning to use the marine environment for fishing and turtling and also for trading with pirates. As recently as about 150 years ago they moved their settlements gradually onto the small coral islands close to the coast with only very few villages remaining along the mainland rivers (Howe 1974). For the analysis of resource use it is

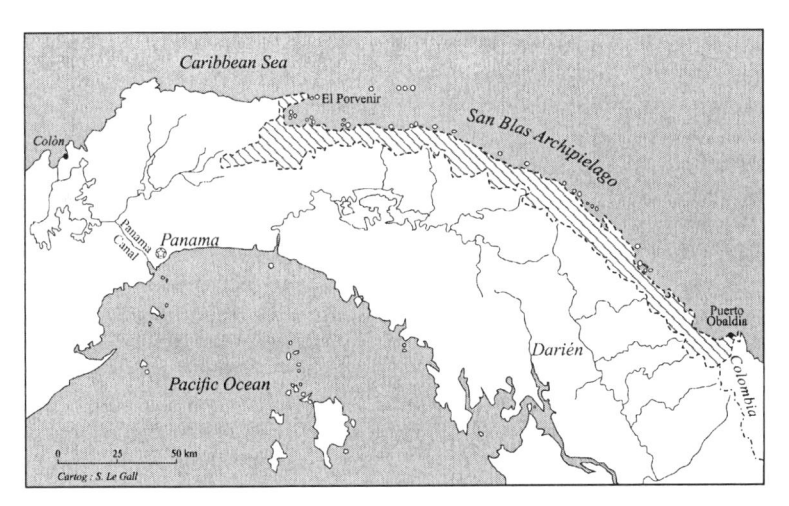

Map 1: The Comarca Kuna Yala in Eastern Panama

important to note that the Kuna people are not settled on their ancestral lands, rather they have adopted a life close to the sea fairly recently. The current population of about 32,450 inhabitants live in 51 communities on the tiny coral islands, another 20,000 or even up to 25,000 Kuna are temporarily or permanently working in Panamanian cities (Contraloria 2001; La Prensa

18.03.2002). The Kuna autonomous region "Comarca Kuna Yala", formerly known as San Blas, comprises a narrow strip of land of max. 15 km width extending for about 225 kms along the coast and the coastal waters, amounting to some 5,000 km². Adjacent to the small coastal plain with its mangroves and swamps the dense tropical forest extends up to a maximum elevation of 850 metres. Despite deforestation in some parts more than ninety percent of Kuna Yala is still covered with forest, hosting a rich fauna and flora with a high biodiversity (Ventocilla et al. 1995b). The inhabited coral islands of a few hectares each lie close to the shore with a maximum distance of 5 kms from the mainland and rise less than 1.5 metres above sea level. The marine environment is dominated by seagrass meadows and coral reef ecosystems, the latter with one of the highest number of coral species documented for the Caribbean sea (Ventocilla 1997).

The Kuna are part-time farmers and fishermen. They clear small portions of the mainland forest for the slash-and-burn cultivation of food crops, mainly plantain, bananas, manioc, yams, corn and others. The diet based on these staple foods is complemented by fruits cultivated on the islands and ocasionally with meat obtained from the hunt in the forest. The extensive cultivation of coconuts on the islands and the coastal plain serves local consumption but is mainly designated for trading with the Colombian traders who buy coconuts in exchange for a variety of goods and foodstuffs which they bring from Colombia on their small trading boats. The production of coconuts was the main commercial activity of the Kuna for decades, being of secondary importance nowadays.

The main source for animal protein in the diet of the Kuna is the sea they heavily depend on for survival. Fishing is a daily activity for most adult men and provides households with fresh fish for the daily meals. It is carried out in an artisanal fashion using dugout canoes and simple handlines with hooks. Nets are owned by some groups but can still be regarded as an exception (Sandner 2000), as is the commercialisation of fish by these groups. The prevailing handline method serves to cover subsistence needs only and fish is generally not sold on the islands. The catch of crustaceans, namely lobster and king crab, which used to be part of the daily diet up to the 1960s, is now completely designated for sale to Kuna buyers. These middlemen sell lobsters, crabs, conchs and squid to buyers from Panama city who carry the product to the city on several daily flights, destined for consumption in city restaurants and mainly for export to the United States. This commerce has attained a level representing a substantial economic activity (Ventocilla et al. 1995b). Lobster and other commerciable resources are caught by Kuna divers, who use outboard powered dugout canoes to reach the outer reefs in trips taking up to several hours. The lobster caught by freediving in small groups of men are transported alive for sale on the islands. A consequence of the growing importance of the lobster trade in Kuna Yala is the increasing specialisation of men. The multiple tasks of hunting, crop cultivation and fishing used to be alternated and a diverse diet was guaranteed. In recent decades, however, the high market prices that can be obtained for lobster led to the neglect of agriculture and subsistence fishing. Castillo and Lessios estimate the yearly harvest to reach 92.5 tons of lobster, representing a yearly income of ca. 620,000 US $ for the entire Kuna nation (referring to case studies in the year 1998; Castillo/Lessios 2001). Divers' families substitute the formerly cultivated food by purchased goods, such as canned sardines and rice because cash income has risen substantially. This leads not only to a growing dependency on one source of income but also to a lack of dietary diversity. In conjunction with the migration of men to the city who are missing as food cultivators the neglect of agriculture causes growing malnutrition, especially of children (about 70 % of children are malnourished, Castillo 1999a).

In addition to the lobster trade one of the most important commercial activities in the Comarca is the production of the "mola" which are handcrafted embroided cloths and blouses. These artful expressions of Kuna culture are part of the clothing habit of women and are increasingly crafted for sale to tourists (Tice 1997). Cruise ships visiting the islands for day-trips and small, Kuna-owned hotels bring potential clients to the region, but the greatest quantities of Molas are sold by cooperatives or individuals in Panama City, mainly for export to the U.S. and Europe. The Mola trade is one of the most important sources of income in the Comarca, next to migrant wage labor and the lobster and coconut trade. Thus the Kuna have adapted their way of life to market conditions and are integrated in national and international market networks.

Commercial relations with the outside world have been part of the Kuna way of life from the 19th century on and society has adopted the use of material goods as well as other facets of western culture (Howe 1998). However, the Kuna have successfully maintained the indigenous culture to a high degree and have not suffered acculturation and dissolution as many other indigenous groups in Latin America have (Ventocilla et al. 1995b). Elements of Kuna culture such as social structure, leadership and organisation, religion and cosmology as well as cultural identity, language and traditional medicine continue to be the foundations of Kuna society nowadays. A great number of anthropologists and other scientists have carried out studies about Kuna culture, beginning with Erland Nordenskiöld in the 1930s (Nordenskiöld 1938). One facet of Kuna culture in historical times as well as nowadays is strong unity and identification with their own cultural heritage. However, there have been processes of accelerated change taking place in recent years. Not only the growing dependence on cash income and malnutrititon are common problems but also the development of social strata formerly unknown, the emigration to Panama City, growing social problems including drug abuse, the loss of traditional ecological and mythological knowledge due to a lack of interest and transmission to the younger generation and the loss of respect for traditional authorities (cf. Chapin 1993; Ventocilla et al. 1995b). These changes in Kuna society have not only been reported by outsiders who already noted the beginnings of this process in the 1940s (Stout 1947) and its acceleration in the last few decades (Chapin 1995). It is the Kuna themselves who lament the transition from a subsistence society built on reciprocity and generosity towards a market economy, as well as cultural and sociological change. Such statements were not only made by a great number of interviewees during our fieldwork, but can also be found in a lot of Kuna publications (such as Turpana 1995).

Despite the processes of change it can be stated in the words of Chapin: "The most striking feature of Kuna society is that is has survived" (1985, p. 43). This is probably the outcome of several factors, among which two important conditions for cultural survival shall be mentioned here: the high degree of political autonomy granted by the national state and the complex internal decision-making structures in a participatory and democratic system. The latter is centered around the gathering as an arena for communication. Howe describes the functioning of the singing gathering as a means for the transmission of cosmological and mythological knowledge (Howe 1974). Several times a week community members are called to attend the gathering in the communal Congress house, the heart of every Kuna village, and listen to the chanting of the community chief, the saila. A second form of gathering is the talking gathering, an arena for the discussion of political issues, for conflict resolution and for decision-making, again presided over by the saila. This gathering serves also as the platform for reflections on their own culture. Analysing traditions and identity plays such an important role that it led Breslin and Chapin to remark that the Kuna often sound "like a convention of anthropologists" (Breslin/Chapin 1984, p. 31). Based on the local political structure there is the regional council or General Congress, consisting of delegates of each community. Its assemblies take place twice a year and are an important forum for the discussion of internal problems of the Comarca as well as external threats or cooperation with external agencies. Decisions affecting the whole region are made by the delegates and the three presiding Comarca Chiefs (Saila dummagan or Caciques) with their assistants and several commissions. What has often been remarked about Kuna society is their strong discussion culture and unity towards the external world as a coherent group which allows the Kuna to defend themselves against external threats (Moore 1984). They succeeded in defending themselves in a rebellion against the Panamanian state in 1925 after the state had tried to impose a law and measures to "civilize the indian" (Léger 1994). As a consequence of the uprising the Kuna were granted political autonomy rights in the "Comarca" territory, formally ruled by Panamanian law in 1953 (Howe 1998; Herlihy

1989). Since then they have had the right to exclude any non-Kuna from activities in the region, permitting the strong control of tourist activities as well as the exclusion of external settlers. Up to now, they have managed to reject all major projects such as mining or extensive tourist schemes, but there is growing pressure on the edge of the Comarca from landless settlers who deforest areas for cultivation as well as from heavily armed Colombian drug traffickers and gold miners. Internal laws regulate the decision-making process as well as a variety of aspects of daily life in the Comarca and postulate the traditional Kuna religion and culture as general principles.

Resource Problems and Ecological Deterioration

As mentioned above, a lot of Kuna have abandoned fishing and agricultural activities to concentrate on the commercial use of marine resources. The growing pressure on the lobster stocks has probably already resulted in declining stocks, which requires divers to search for lobster at greater depths and with increased effort. Except for a closed season of three months ("Veda") there is no control of lobster catch for example minimum sizes or quantities. But the problem of reduced abundance of a resource is not only the case for the commercialised species such as lobster, conchs, crabs and squid. The fish stocks which are only exploited for household consumption are diminishing as well and fishermen report that they are obtaining smaller numbers of fish while increasing their work load in fishing (time and distance from the islands). Fish as a daily protein source is becoming scarce and, on some islands, fish is even being imported from Panama city for several months a year. Quantitative studies of fish stocks and their state of conservation have not been conducted, nor have the reasons for the depletion of fish stocks been studied. Our own research suggests the selective pressure on some preferred species as well as the increased population are possible factors. The most important factor, however, seems to be the region-wide destruction of coral reefs by the Kuna, who are thereby removing the habitat for species of reef fish and disturbing ecosystem properties substantially (cf. Howe 1975).

The Kuna have been using coral as a construction material since the 1940s and to a growing extent in the last few decades. The reason lies in the very limited surface of the islands, which are only a few hectares in size and have to provide space for a growing population. To gain new sites for the construction of houses, families construct landfill sites adjacent to the shoreline, using coral blocks, pebble and sand from the mainland. This way, many islands have been enlarged substantially, and especially for bigger construction sites such as basketball fields or hotels, great quantities of coral have been removed from the living reefs (Sandner 2001). The amount of coral destroyed in this manner cannot be estimated, but the comparison of actual maps with historic photographs shows that the enlargement of some islands which has taken place over at least six decades must have consumed great quantities of coral reef blocks for the landfill sites. Taking into account the evidence about the destruction of coral reefs for the use as construction material in the literature and its effects on ecosystems (Hodgson 1997; Brown/Dunne 1988) it would be surprising if the extensive destruction of reefs in Kuna Yala had not damaged ecosystems and fish stocks. This is especially alarming because of the extremely slow growth rate of coral polyps and the difficulties in predicting whether coral reef damage is reversible or not (e.g. Grigg/Dollar 1990).

Further ecological problems include the growing contamination of the highly sensitive coral reefs by solid and liquid wastes produced by the Kuna on the edge of the islands. All sorts of waste, including plastic containers and cans as well as toxic substances such as acids from batteries, contribute to locally intensive pollution problems of seashore and ocean floor. Another problem is the reduction of endangered sea turtle populations which have nearly been extinguished due to local and Caribbean-wide pressure. Traditionally, the green turtle *Chelonia mydas* was hunted by the Kuna for consumption of meat and eggs. Another species, the carey turtle *Eretmochyles imbricata*, has a long history of exploitation for its shell and, despite its prohibition, trade of tortoiseshell continues to occur.

4 Traditional Institutions Regulating Resource Use

Descriptions of the resource use system in Kuna society centre mostly around the use of mainland resources. For the use of the terrestrial ecosystems such as the forest, agricultural plots and rivers, there is a set of spiritually based rules. One of them is the protection of small areas of rainforest as spiritual sanctuaries ("Kalu"), which may not be cleared of their natural vegetation (Chapin 1991; Ventocilla 1993). These traditional institutions for forest resources are still widely accepted and respected.

About the use of the marine environment there are only very few studies (Hasbrouck 1985; Charnley/de León 1986; Sandner 2000; about lobster diving: Spadafora 1999; Castillo/Lessios 2001). The traditional rules and taboos for marine resources have not been studied up to now and are rarely mentioned at all in publications about the Kuna. Hasbrouck, who studied fishing in San Blas in the 1980s denies the existence of a system of marine resource management and regulations (Hasbrouck 1985). Findings from our own research and the literature review suggest, however, that there do exist some traditional rules and regulations for the use of marine resources. In contrast to the terrestrial ones, there have been traditionally fewer regulations for the marine environment and the erosion of their effectiveness has advanced a lot further. In the following we will give some examples for such traditional regulations of marine resource use and the reasons for their failure to prevent the depletion of resources in recent times.

Consumption Taboos

There are several marine species which are traditionally excluded from consumption in Kuna culture for a variety of reasons ("specific-species" taboos as Colding and Folke call them, 1997). First, some species are considered as "unclean" because they feed in the polluted waters on the islands' edge or because their meat contains too much blood (Charnley/de León 1986). This kind of taboo is still generally respected. Second, there are consumption taboos based on a deeper spiritual meaning of the creature in question. One example is the dolphin, which, according to Kuna oral history, had been a brother of mankind in mythological times and nowadays is responsible for bringing the babies. The taboo to kill it is still widely respected as well.

For other species, however, this is not the case. Sharks, for example, have also been under a consumption taboo with two different justifications: first because of their nature as a transformed human being (Charnley/de León 1986), and secondly because their malevolent characteristics could be transmitted to the consumer. Other species such as moray eels and squid were taboo for their morphological characteristics: the slippery form of their bodies may be reproduced at birth of the consumers' children. The taboos regarding squid as well as sharks are ignored more and more often and the former taboo species find growing numbers of consumers among the Kuna. A process of social forgetting is taking place which leads to the destruction of the informal institution, the taboo. Growing pressure on edible resources which have become scarce serves as an incentive for some fishermen to experiment with the taboo. When they notice that breaking it does not lead to any spiritual sanctions for them the experience is socially transmitted and gains followers.

Another example are the two species of marine turtles which have been nearly extinguished in Kuna Yala. This fact may be partly a consequence of the transnational reduction of the migratory populations in the whole Caribbean, but the Kuna have contributed to this reduction as well despite the taboos which used to exist for the turtles. One taboo was placed on the consumption of eggs: half of the amount found on the beach had to be left there for reproduction (see interview with Cacique Guerrero in Ventocilla et al. 1995b). This taboo came to lose its effectivity in the 1970s, when people started to take the whole amount of eggs and ignore the possible spiritual sanctions. The pressure on the Carey turtle had already reached a high level in the 1920s when the world market price for its shell was high. The taboo forbids its killing as it is regarded a mythological brother of man. In order to be able to commercialise it despite the taboo, the Kuna found a method to take the shell off the animal without killing it (Nordenskiöld 1938). This was regarded as a way to respect the traditional rule and fishermen had to fear no spiritual nor social sanctions. The protective effect for the species however was not given anymore, as the animal dies quickly without its shell.

The Taboo to Commercialise Fish

Another taboo is the commercialisation of fish in general. Surpluses have not to be sold but given to other community members, otherwise a spiritual punishment, executed by Paba the Great Father, may follow. The effect of the rule is the protection of stocks against overexploitation and it serves as an "informal insurance system" as Bender et al. call it in their study about Tonga (Bender et al. 1998). This system provides the needy with fish and protects the fishermen against low revenues due to bad luck or illness. Nowadays this rule is still respected in the case of fish, as our interviews showed. For lobster and other seafood products which are heavily commercialised, however, the possible spiritual sanctions are not taken seriously enough to limit fishing and no portions of the catch are given away to other community members.

Sacred Sea Space – "Biria"

Analogous to the protected areas in the mainland forest, there are small areas of sea space that are regarded as spirit sanctuaries, called "Biria" or "Pirya" (Chapin 1991). These are whirlpools where spirits of evil creatures enter the world; at the same time they have a specific meaning for the spiritual voyages of Kuna shamans, who use it as a portal to enter other dimensions of the world. Knowledge of the location of the Biria and their complex meaning is fading and by experimenting younger fishermen find out that they do not suffer direct sanctions from evil spirits after entering the Biria area. This means for them that the concept is a "story" only and that it is not dangerous to disobey it. At the same time, some younger Kuna reinterpret the concept and use it to justify indiscriminate resource use. Elders lament that these younger fishermen have not fully understood the significance of the Biria but rather refer to it as a source where innumerable sea creatures are expulsed into the sea, meaning that their extinction is impossible.

General Respect for "Napguana" (Mother Earth) and the Sea as Part of It

Nature as an integral part of Mother Earth (Napguana) has a high value in Kuna cosmology and respect for her is one of the basic rules in Kuna society (Chapin 1993; Alvarado 1995). The sea however, has a weaker status in the cosmological worldview, and it is not of the same importance. In mythological stories of the Pab Igala (Chapin 1989) the sea is "Muu", the grandmother, and the creatures living within play only a minor role. The Kuna have probably not developed a comparable relation to the sea due to the relatively short time span of life on the islands (less than 150 years) and they are not an "originally sea-minded" people (Wassén 1949; Ventocilla 1997). This may be the explanation for the weak conservation principles for the sea in general (Hasbrouck 1985). The general guideline to protect nature has not been transmitted to marine ecosystems and thus reef destruction and pollution are not regarded as a violation of the nature conservancy principle valid for Mother Earth.

The sum of the above mentioned traditional institutions show that there are only a small number of rules and that these are far from being comparable to the complex resource management systems in the South Pacific. Rules such as limited user groups, size restrictions or closed seasons for certain species do not exist. The few existing rules, however, did probably serve to protect some species completely (such as dolphin and sharks) and others partly (turtle eggs), and the taboo over the commercialisation of fish may have prevented commercial net fishery up to now. Some of these rules are losing their "grip" nowadays as the pressure on resources grows. At the same time, cultural change leads to a loss in traditional knowledge and diminishing respect for traditional concepts and rules which come to be ignored (social forgetting), while economic profit gains importance. Regarding the traditional institutions it becomes clear, however, that even if they were still fully respected nowadays they could probably not serve as an adequate management tool to regulate marine resource use effectively. The changed forms of resource use, namely commercial exploitation of lobster and other crustaceans but also the new ecological problems such as reef destruction and pollution, are not included within the scope of the traditional institutions. This leads us to the question how these problems can be solved by the creation of new institutions.

5 The Emergence of New Institutions for Resource Use Problems: A Process of Social Learning

The Kuna have often been cited as the first indigenous group of Latin America to create their own protected area to conserve the rainforest (Chapin 1991; Ventocilla et al. 1995). This project called PEMASKY was developed by a group of young Kuna professionals in the 1980s with the assistance of several international agencies (e.g. see González 1997; Archibold 1992). Some of its goals have failed, such as experimental agriculture for the establishment of a permanent settlement to secure the limits of the autonomous region against intruding settlers (Chapin 1991). However, the general aim to protect a portion of the frontier region of the Comarca from deforestation by outside colonisers has been achieved. The project was the first attempt by a Kuna group to create a formally protected area based on Western models of conservation managed by Kunas and recognised by Kuna authorities. Since the beginnings of PEMASKY in the 1980s other incentives have followed, mainly in the form of small agricultural and forest projects designed by Kuna NGO which have worked with limited success. During the 1990s the need to protect the natural resources of Kuna Yala against destruction and depletion and the necessity to confront the growing pressure on resources for commercialisation became frequent issues on the agenda of the General Congress assemblies as well as in local Congresses and NGO. One of the most promising steps for the resolution of these problems was the creation of the Kuna Institute for Integrated Development (Idiky) in 1994, an NGO designed as an integrative part of the Kuna General Congress (Congreso General Kuna 1997a and 1998; Ventocilla et al. 1995a). One of the tasks of this organisation, which was funded by the European Union over a 4-year period, is the coordination and control of projects in the Comarca. The Institute should also serve as a pool for ideas and bring together Kuna specialists working in several NGO or research organisations. Idiky's own projects such as the Project for Sustainable Development in Kuna Yala (Desosky) started with very ambitious ideas for the resolution of a variety of resource problems, for example studies on the cultivation of lobster and certain fish species, for the improvement of coco cultivation and several other agricultural projects (Congreso General Kuna 1998). The impacts of these projects, however, remained weak. Due to a lack of administrative capacities and no continuity in funding little has been achieved overall. But despite the failure of Idiky-owned projects the institution itself plays an important role in the resolution of environmental problems, for it serves as an organisational frame for Kuna professionals who work as assessors for the General Congress and feed it with information, concepts and ideas.

Formal Regulations

Besides the creation of these projects and organisations the Kuna have developed a set of new formal regulations not only for resource use but also for a great variety of aspects of life in the autonomous region. In 1995 the "Ley Fundamental", the constitution of Kuna Yala, was passed in a democratic process by all delegates of Kuna communities and their three head caciques (Congreso General Kuna 2001). It has not been recognised by the Panamian national assembly, but is regarded as the replacement of a former national law for the internal regulation of the Comarca by the Kuna themselves. For the protection of the environment and natural resources it is of great importance as it declares their protection a specific task of the Congreso General. Biodiversity and natural resources are explicitly regarded as Kuna heritage and "traditional resource use" is defined as a necessary condition for any resource use in the Comarca. The constitution also allows for the protection of single ecosystems or areas by General Congress decree. Another important conservation tool is the obligatory assessment of environmental impact for any project with possible effects on the environment or resources under participation of General Congress members. The general framework set down in the constitution is specified in the more detailed internal Comarca Statute (Estatuto de la Comarca Kuna Yala), which is a body of regulations constantly being enlarged. The latest version of 2000 contains articles on the protection of mainland resources (trees, rivers and water sources) as well as on the use of the sea (Congreso General Kuna 2001). For marine resources the most important regulations are a closed season of 6 months for lobster fishing which has to be declared anually by the Congress and the introduction of an obligatory permit for marine resource use for commercial purposes. This also includes a tax of 0.10 US $ per pound for lobster sold in the Comarca which has to be paid to the General Congress. A fundamental condition for resource use is that only Kuna fishermen may use marine resources of the Comarca. Furthermore, there are articles forbidding pollution of the environment and obliging the Congress to develop information campaigns for pollution prevention.

Are the Formal Regulations Succesful Environmental Institutions?

In sum, it can be stated that the two new laws set down some important basic principles of resource use and environmental protection in a body of formalised, written rules. The application and enforcement of these rules however has been achieved to varying degrees to date. While some have been put into practice fairly quickly other articles have not had any effects in practice so far. One of the rules established in the Statute is the 6-month closed season for commercial lobster harvesting. The application of this rule suffered some difficulties in its first years of existence, as it had been simply ignored by resource users and no enforcement by Kuna authorities had taken place. Since 1998 the Kuna Congress has undertaken increased efforts to apply the rule in a reduced form of a 3-month closed season, during which any commercial fishing and trading of lobster is prohibited (Koskun Kalu 2002). Frequent controls of traders alongside the financial sanctioning of non-compliants helped to establish the rule. In our interviews, lobster divers and traders did not unanimously support the restriction but respected it nevertheless to avoid sanctions. Closed seasons are an effective tool for the management of lobster stocks and are regarded as a promising means for the preservation of stocks in Kuna Yala by marine biologists (Castillo/Lessios 2001). Two formal regulations had already been in existence for several decades: the prohibition of dynamite fishing and Scuba-diving techniques for lobster fishing. The latter has probably accounted for the partial protection of lobster stocks against complete depletion because it restricts harvest to the areas a free-diver can reach in repeated dives, that is to depths less than 20 metres (Castillo/Lessios 2001).

Another formal regulation that has been successfully applied in practice is the obligatory environmental impact study for projects planned in Kuna Yala. In 2001, a US-American enterprise planning the construction of a Carribbean-wide telecommunication cable had to fulfill the requirements of Kuna law and present a study about the possible environmental impacts of the cable traversing Kuna Yala. On the basis of this study, the Kuna General Congress gave permission for the project to begin (Ecology & Environment Inc. 2000; La Prensa 26.4.2001). Other articles of formal law have not been put into practice yet or fail because of the lack of practicable solutions, as in the case of the prohibition of environmental pollution. As long as there are no viable alternatives for the deposition of wastes the population on the islands can hardly avoid polluting the marine environment. For the moment, the formal prohibition of pollution remains a paper tiger without any practical consequence. However, the rule, once established in law, reflects the recognised need to solve the problem and could trigger the creation of solutions on a community level. Even if not all of the formal rules established in the new laws are put into practice in detail immediately, they can be regarded as a frame for the future design of more detailed regulations and solutions by the Kuna authorities and communities.

How Have these Formal Institutions Emerged in a Traditional Society?

The discussions about problems of resource use and management within the Kuna system of gatherings and assemblies are the basis for the creation of institutions. During the Comarca-wide assemblies the articles for the new formal laws are discussed after being prepared by the Junta Directiva, which is the presiding group of three Chiefs with their secretary and several other functionaries. During the Congress assemblies the new articles are then modified and the final version is decided upon in a democratic manner. After the assemblies the agreed articles are put into a written form by the Junta Directiva members and propagated in the communities. This process of the formulation of new regulations in Kuna society has not been studied and documented in detail to date. What seems to be an evident characteristic of this institution-building process is its social embeddedness, as it closely linked to local communities who send their delegates to the assemblies and no external agencies are involved in the process creating institutions for local problems. The high importance of communication in Kuna society and the democratic decision-making process allow for a high level of participation of the population and prevent the creation of institutions that are detached from the local realities of everyday lives.

One important factor for the creation of new institutions is the integration of new sets of knowledge and information (see Troja, this volume). New ideas and concepts are often transmitted by Kuna who are working in NGOs, among them many who hold a university degree. They contribute not only detailed scientific knowledge in their field but also concepts and ideas from international forums of discussion. They serve as agents of transmission between international arenas and organisations and the Kuna communication arenas. Examples include concepts from discussions on conservation, sustainable resource use, indigenous rights and conservation or intellectual property rights. The transmission of such concepts is possible due to the openness of Kuna culture towards innovation. Kuna culture is less closed and static as it might seem at first glance, and several authors describe the traditional openness for adaptations and innovation as a typical facet (e.g. Castillo 1999b; Archibold 1992). Elder Kuna leaders explain this openness by referring to the mythological character of "Tad Ibe" who taught the Kuna to incorporate new concepts from the outside (Chapin 1985). Thus, for many Kuna it is no contradiction to adhere to traditionally transmitted elements of culture while accepting and using new ideas. Or, as Breslin and Chapin put it, they choose new ideas from Western culture like "careful department store shoppers", taking only selected ones and adapting them to their own needs (Breslin/Chapin 1984, p. 31). Examples for this are the incorporation of the concepts sustainable development, biodiversity and environmental conservation, as the name of the General Congress's organisation "Institute for the integrated development of Kuna Yala" (IDIKY) and its "Project for sustainable development" shows. These concepts are regarded as analogous to the indigenous view of nature (e.g. Congreso General Kuna 1997b), and thus do not seem too new to the Kuna. They appear in most project proposals and programmes of Kuna NGO and could be regarded as informal institutions.

Interplay Between Traditional Institutions and Newly Emergent Formal Institutions

New institutions and projects in Kuna Yala are often labelled as a succesful mix between western scientific and traditional concepts of knowledge, as in many publications by Kuna authors (e. g. Archibold 1992). However, a closer look at these institutions reveals that sometimes modern and traditional concepts exist rather in parallel without a true integration of the two. Looking at the new laws it is obvious that their construction principles follow western examples of written rules including financial sanctions for non-compliers. These formal norms fill institutional vacuums in some cases (as in the case of the impact study), in others they replace traditional institutions. One example is the closed season for lobster fishing. Traditionally such a closed season did not exist, but another traditional institution, obligatory work on the mainland agricultural plots, had the secondary effect of protecting marine resources during the dry season. Nowadays, the local chiefs who formerly declared the season and enforced compliance have lost their authority and have no means of making people follow their decisions. One Chief, the Saila of the community of Ogobsucum where most of the population specialises in lobster diving, therefore stated that he welcomed the formal law. Due to his loss of authority he had not been able to control or restrict lobster exploitation nor declare the agricultural season as obligatory. The formal regulation represents therefore an effective tool strengthening the role of the local elected leaders in their aims to control resource exploitation.

Traditional elements of knowledge and practices are included in the Kuna constitution and the statute as well in the form of general principles, e.g. the culturally rooted respect for mother earth and the premise to protect her, as well as the high value attributed to the traditional lifestyle of the Kuna. One difficulty in the application of these norms could be, however, that it is not clearly defined what the terms traditional resource use and way of life mean for the Kuna, and thus this article could contradict some of the prevalent forms of resource use. For example it could be asked to what extent commercial activities can be termed traditional which have evolved only in the last 40 years in their current form, as in the case of lobster fishing by outboard powered boats. Another difficulty in the integration of western and indigenous knowledge sets arises in concrete projects of NGO trying to combine both knowledge systems. Despite the aims to integrate the two, practice has shown that often western scientific models, knowledge and methods dominate, as in the case of studies on flora and fauna (Chapin 1991). Traditional ecological knowledge, even though often referred to by Kuna project managers, has not been documented up to now and has not been integrated as a knowledge base in projects. Especially for the revitalisation of traditional institutions, such as sacred sea space or taboos, there have not been any incentives up to now.

Absence of Solutions for Some Environmental Problems

Considering the new formalised regulations for the use of the environment as well as the intensive efforts of Kuna NGO for the preservation of the tropical forest, it seems surprising that there are no incentives for the solution of one of the most serious ecological problems: the destruction of coral reefs. The extensive destruction of reefs by Kuna for the construction of landfill sites on the shore of the islands is probably one of the main reasons for the diminishing fish stocks and still this issue does not figure on the agenda of the Congress assemblies, nor do there exist any regulations to control reef destruction. In the constitution and the statute the issue does not appear and Kuna NGO have not developed any projects so far (with the exception of one research project of PEMASKY, see below). Our interviews with the population and local leaders revealed that this ecological problem is not perceived as such and thus is not being discussed. While the diminishing fishing yields are observed there are only very few individuals who connect the reduction in yields to reef destruction as a probable cause.

The reason for this lack of perception and discussion of the problem can be found in the traditionally stronger orientation of Kuna culture towards the mainland, reflecting the origins of the group before it migrated to the islands. The core of cosmology and mythology in Kuna culture lies on the mainland with the sacred mountain Tacarcuna (Wassén 1949). The orientation towards the mainland is reflected in a number of ways, for example in the prevalent role of the forest and its animals in mythology (see stories of the Pab Igala, Chapin 1989), or in the stronger conservation ethic valid for the forest, where sacred areas are still widely respected. Coral reefs have no comparable status in the Kuna concept of nature. In our interviews people described coral as stones and not as living organisms, and although Kuna fishermen observe the sea on their daily fishing trips, closeness to the ecosystem does not produce a realistic perception of its state of health, as Folke et al. (1998) assume for many indigenous systems. In contrast to the issues of deforestation and agriculture information about the problems of the marine environment have reached the Kuna organisations only sparsely, possibly as a consequence of a lack of information and Kuna experts (except for one Kuna marine biologist). An exception has been the fairly recent incentive of a research and mapping project of coral reefs in a joint effort by the Smithsonian Tropical Research Institute and the Kuna NGO PEMASKY with international support from the

NGO Native Lands (Asociación Ecológica Kuna PEMASKY 2001). The results of this project, which aims at mapping the state of coral reefs with sophisticated scientific methods, could give new impulse to the discussion of the issue of reef destruction in the Kuna organisations in the future.

Another reason for the absence of solutions for some environmental problems is – paradoxical as it might seem – the Kuna's self-identification as traditional stewards of nature. The Kuna are known for their strong identification with their cultural roots and traditions and constantly refer to these in their self-presentation towards outsiders, for example in the resolutions of the General Congress, in the design of projects, in cooperation with international NGO, as well as in publications of Kuna scientists (e.g. González 1993) or in their statements at international conferences (e.g. Castillo 2000). One part of their view of their own culture presented to the outside world is their respect for nature and its creatures rooted in Kuna cosmology and mythology which is seen as a central element of culture by the Kuna. However, sometimes awareness of the cultural meaning of nature and its unity with mankind leads to an idealisation of their own role as resource protectors (cf. Ventocilla et al. 1995b). It could be stated that the Kuna themselves are repeatedly creating their own ecologically noble savage myth. This myth blurs the view on some acute environmental problems which are caused within Kuna society. In our interviews, many interviewees negated such problems and described the marine environment as healthy. Some referred to the obviously stronger pollution of the capital cities' coastal waters in comparison to the presumably intact marine ecosytems of Kuna Yala and many stated that the Kuna people per se are the better conservationists.

It can be observed that the absence of new solutions for some specific environmental problems is true especially for internal problems which are not linked to the outside world, as in the case of traditional subsistence fishing, reef destruction and pollution. In these cases there are no external agents involved that could be held responsible for these problems as in the case of lobster trading. The solution of these solely internal problems, especially for the traditionally less protected marine environments, is badly addressed. Incentives that originate ouside the Comarca, like the creation of marine protected areas that had been proposed by one of the Chief Caciques in 1994 in cooperation with the Smithsonian Tropical Research Institute, have been blocked. Even though this concept could have effectively served to regenerate and preserve fish stocks and enhance the sustainbility of the resources for the Kuna it was not accepted by the General Congress delegates. The reason for this can be seen as a question of power and interest, as Kuna delegates feared a growing influence of the research institute in the Comarca and a loss of autonomy in the control of resources.

Co-Management Redefined

The widely discussed co-management concepts aimed at re-embedding control of resources in communities by integrating local user groups in management processes are being applied in the Comarca in a substantially modified way. The Kuna already have full control of resources and the institution-building process lies in their hands, within the framework of the clearly defined autonomous rights granted by the national state. Thus it is the Kuna who allow for a certain degree of participation of outside agencies such as ministries, development funding organisations or research institutes, and it is they who define the rules for the integration of these actors. The dominance of external agencies in policy design and implementation that can be observed in many co-management concepts around the world, allowing for a more or less intensive participation of local groups, is reduced to a minimum here. It is clearly the Kuna playing the stronger part in the cooperation process.

One example may illustrate this specific kind of co-management. Within the framework of a Central American-wide project (Mesoamerican Biological Corridor) the Panamanian Ministry of Natural Resources ANAM proposed the creation of a project zone in Kuna Yala (Global Environment Facility 1998). After an intensive process of discussion extending over several months the Kuna General Congress agreed to approve the project. While the ANAM documents refer to participation in a classic sense the Kuna went one step further and demanded extended mechanisms of participation and control by Kuna specialists before accepting the concept. Despite it being contradictory to the traditional concept of nature in Kuna culture the project had been accepted by the Congress in a pragmatic decision to serve as a source of funding for small development projects within the communities (Interview with the secretary of General Congress, W. Pérez, 2000). In general, the Kuna's powerful control over projects allows for the utilisation of financial sources and know-how while avoiding project colonialism in Nietschmann's sense of "colonialist conservation groups" (Nietschmann 1995). On the other hand this control of external activities may lead to the blockage of possible solutions. One example is the Smithsonian Tropical Research Institute which had been conducting research in marine biology for over 25 years in Kuna Yala but suffered the withdrawal of its research permission through the General Congress in 1994. Better cooperation, for example in the utilisation of its scientific know-how and infrastructure for local environmental protection goals, had not been considered by the Kuna delegates, although members of the institute had already created important local projects such as the children's arts workshops for the transmission of cultural and environmental values (see Ventocilla 1997). It took several years after the expulsion of the institute to create a new joint research project on coral reefs (see above). In sum, it can be stated that Kuna control of projects in development, conservation or research involving outside organisations is strong and can have positive outcomes, as in the avoidance of top-down approaches, as well as negative ones, as in the rejection of projects that could serve the Kuna's sustainable development goals.

Relation of Scales

For an analysis of the creation of institutions and their effectiveness it is important to make clear distinctions between scales with the particular actors and interest groups acting on each level and their interrelatedness. The institution-building process we have been looking at in the case of the Kuna is almost entirely taking place at a regional scale in the sense of the autonomous region (Comarca) as an administrative and cultural unit. On this level discussions take place at the Congress meetings, decisions are made by the Kuna General Congress and formal institutions for region-wide application are formulated. If we look at the local scale (meaning local in the sense of community level) the creation of new institutions hardly takes place at all. Kuna communities rarely create their own formal regulations for resource use, rather they send their delegates to the Congress assemblies and await decisions on a General Congress level which are then put into practice locally afterwards. Some NGOs or cooperatives have been founded at a community level, but most have not proven effective and disintegrated rather quickly. The reason for this concentration of the institution-building process at a regional level could be the following: resource use problems are not community-specific, rather they are fairly identical throughout the region, and capacities for their resolution rarely exist at a local level, especially access to information, administrative capacities and professionals.

On the other hand, institutions at a national level which have an operative character for the regulation of resource use have no effect in Kuna Yala due to the strong autonomy there. Existing rules and policies of national ministries are not applied in the Comarca. At the constitutional level, however, national law sets the framework for the control of development and resource use by Kuna authorities. National laws grant the Kuna autonomy in the territory defined as the Comarca and recognise the General Congress as the regional authority. The existence of specific laws as a parallel jurisdictional system to the nation-wide system is tolerated. It is only on the grounds of the self-determination granted to the Kuna that control over resources and territory remains in their hands and competing external users can be completely excluded from access to resources. The great extent of self-determination and control is probably one of the most important factors for the success of the institution-building process within the Comarca.

The next level of scale is the relation of the autonomous region with processes on an international scale. The Kuna have been connected to international trade for centuries and are dependent on international markets for the sale of their products, on tourism as an important source of income and on the import of goods from Colombia for daily needs as well. Negative impacts on an international scale include threats to the marine environment, such as pollution or the depletion of migratory species' populations (marine turtles) that cannot be solved by Kuna institutions alone. In the field of information and knowledge Kuna society shows a connectedness to international, scientific sets of knowledge, concepts and information. Access to information is held as a high goal by Kuna authorities and they have decided to allow access to the World Wide Web in several communities (Congreso General Kuna 2002). Other connections at the international level are the contacts to development agencies that are financing projects in the Comarca (e.g. the European Union) and the networks in which Kuna activists are working together with international organisations and indigenous people's organisations from other countries. The latter networks are important platforms of communication on indigenous rights and conservation (see e.g. Uraccán et al. 1998; Concultura et al. 2000), using conferences as well as the Internet as discussion arenas. The Internet is also used for international propagation of the General Congress' resolutions and decisions about current issues (e.g. electronic newsletter Boletín Kika).

6 Conclusions

The Kuna may serve as an example for a successful institution-building process within an indigenous society. A look on other groups in Central America shows that most of these confront the degradation of their resource base, lack of control over their resources and conflicts with other user groups without achieving the creation of efficient institutions for the solution of these problems. The question that remains difficult to answer is what conditions are favourable for a social learning process leading to the creation of effective institutions and which ones act against this process. One lesson that can be drawn from the Kuna example is the importance of "social capital", following Ostrom's thesis that local arrangements for the resolution of resource dilemmas can be built on high social capital in groups where actors have developed common norms and forms of cooperation over long periods of time (Ostrom 1990). The Kuna's still fairly intact system of norms and cooperation in combination with the traditional discourse culture and the democratic structures of decision-making at a regional scale allows for the creation of new institutions. Another important factor is access to specialists' knowledge and the participation of Kuna professionals in the design of new institutions as well as the traditional openness of Kuna culture towards new concepts of knowledge. Access to international pools of information facilitates the development of institutions for the prevention of resource destruction. This allows a learning process using information from cases in other parts of the world before their own resources have been depleted. In this case a crisis does not have to occur as a necessary condition for the adaptation of institutions (cf. Gunderson et al.1995). Rather the trial-and-error learning process can be cut short by learning from internationally documented examples.

The institution-building process at the Comarca scale is also dependent on power relations. It is made possible by the formally recognised autonomous status with the granted right to self-determination. A comparison with other traditional groups shows that the resolution of resource problems is more difficult to achieve for populations that have no comparable autonomous rights. Fishermen on Old Providence, Colombia, for example, have no means of controlling the highly industrialised and armed fishing fleets operating in their waters and depleting their resources rapidly for international markets, and the same occurs in the Miskito communities in Eastern Nicaragua (findings from own research). The resolution of such resource conflicts may probably lie in a different sort of solutions at a national level (state laws and enforcement of rules).

Summing up, three main important variables seem to be crucial in determining the process of social learning and institution building: social capital including communication structures, knowledge or actor skills and power relations. However, the Kuna example shows also that an indigenous group may have favourable conditions to create new rules and regulations for the solution of environmental problems but may still fail to address all of these. Whilst there are some institutional vacuums stemming from the failure of the traditional institution system to regulate resource use under changed conditions, other forms of use are not at all included in the scope of the traditional rules in Kuna Yala. Some of these vacuums are being filled by new formal regulations in the form of laws. Others are not, a consequence of blockages in the social learning process. These blockages in Kuna Yala include weak actor skills in reference to some specific environmental problems (lack of perception of these problems and lack of knowledge). Another blockage may be seen in the self-identification of the Kuna as stewards of nature which do not harm the environment in general. Finally, the question of power and indigenous autonomy also offers pitfalls where potentially useful projects and ideas are rejected for fear of a possible loss of control over resources and territory.

The study of traditional marine resource use systems and the processes of social learning and institution building in indigenous societies offers particularly interesting insights for scientists. As many researchers have stated, these processes may contribute to ecological knowledge and examples of management that can be used for the conservation of resources (e.g. Calamia 1999; Pinkerton 1989). Management of resources may be improved not only in the specific local context but also through drawing general lessons for fisheries management from traditional systems (Johannes 1994). Seen from the perspective of indigenous coastal communities, however, the question of resource management is of more direct, fundamental and vital importance, as it is directly linked to survival. Many of these communities depend to a high degree on marine resources as important sources of income and as the main staple and source of protein. Thus the solution of the environmental problems observed in many coastal communities and the protection of their resources is a very pressing issue for local people.

References

Alvarado, E. (1995): El valor del ambiente en los Kunas desde una perspectiva de género. Unión Mundial para la Naturaleza (IUCN). San José, Costa Rica
Anderson, E. (1994): Fish as Gods and Kin. In: Dyer/McGoodwin (eds.): Folk Management in the World's Fisheries: Lessons for Modern Fisheries Management. Niwot; pp. 139-160
Archibold, G. (1992): PEMASKY in Kuna Yala: Protecting Mother Earth...And Her Children. In: Barzetti/Rovinski (eds.): Toward a Green Central America: Integrating Conservation and Development. West Hartford; pp. 21-33
Asociación Ecológica Kuna PEMASKY (2001): Proyecto Arrecifes de Coral. Information Sheet, unpublished, Panamá
Bender, A./W. Kägi/E. Mohr (1998): Sustainable Open Access: Fishing and Informal Insurance in Ha'Apai, Tonga. IWÖ-Discussion Paper; No. 71. St. Gallen
Berkes, F. (1987): Common-Property Resource Management and Cree Indian Fisheries in Subarctic Canada. In: McCay/Acheson (eds.): The Question of the Commons: The Culture and Ecology of Communal Resources. Tucson; pp. 66-91
Berkes, F. (1993): Traditional Ecological Knowledge in Perspective. In: Inglis (ed.): Traditional Ecological Knowledge: Concepts and Cases. Ottawa; pp. 1-9
Berkes, F./C. Folke/M. Gadgil (1995): Traditional Ecological Knowledge, Biodiversity, Resilience and Sustainability. In: Perrings/Mäler/Folke/Holling/Jansson (eds.): Biodiversity Conservation: Problems and Policies. Dordrecht; pp. 281-300
Berkes, F. (1999): Sacred Ecology: Traditional Ecological Knowledge and Resource Management. Philadelphia
Berkes, F./C. Folke (1994): Linking Social and Ecological Systems for Resilience and Sustainability. Beijer Discussion Paper Series No. 52. Stockholm
Borrini-Feyerabend, G./M. Taghi Farvar/J.C. Nguinguiri/V.A. Ndangang (2000): Co-Management of Natural Resources: Organising, Negotiating and Learning-by-Doing. GTZ and IUCN; Heidelberg
Breslin, P./M. Chapin (1984): Conservation Kuna-Style. In: Grassroots Development; No. 8; Vol. 2; pp. 26-35

Bromley, D. (1992): The Commons, Property, and Common-Property Regimes. In: Bromley (ed.): Making the Commons Work. Theory, Practice, and Policy. San Francisco; pp. 3-15

Brown, B./R.P. Dunne (1988): The Impact of Coral Mining on Coral Reefs in the Maldives. In: Environmental Conservation; No. 15; pp. 159-165

Bryant, R.L. (1997): Beyond the Impasse: The power of Political Ecology in Third World environmental research. In: Area Vol. 29; No. 1; pp. 5-19

Calamia, M. (1999): A Methodology for Incorporating Traditional Ecological Knowledge with Geographic Information Systems for Marine Resource Management in the Pacific. In: Traditional Marine Resource Management and Knowledge Information Bulletin; No. 10; February; http://www.spc.org.nec/ coastfish/News/trad/10/1Calamia.htm

Castillo, A./H.A. Lessios (2001): Lobster Fishery by the Kuna Indians in the San Blas Region of Panama (Kuna Yala). In: Crustaceana; Vol. 74; No. 5; pp. 459-475

Castillo, G. (1999a): Manejo de Bosques y Diversidad Biológica: Propuesta de Proyecto en Kuna Yala. In: Revista Sapigarda; Vol. 5; No. 3; pp. 10-15

Castillo, G. (1999b): Proyecto de Manejo Sostenible de los Bosques del Corregimiento de Narganá – Kuna Yala. In: Taller Indígena Centroamericano: Areas Protegidas y Medio Ambiente. Memoria. Panamá

Castillo, G. (2000): Nuestra futura visión: Àreas protegidas y forestería comunitaria. In: Concultura et al. (eds.): Segunda Jornada Indígena Centroamericana sobre Tierra, Medio Ambiente y Cultura. Memoria. San Salvador; El Salvador; San José; Costa Rica; pp. 408-413

Chapin, M. (1985): Udirbi: An Indigenous Project in Environmental Conservation. In: Macdonald Jr. (ed.): Native Peoples and Economic Development. Six Case Studies from Latin America. Cultural Survival; Cambridge; pp. 39-53

Chapin, M. (1989): Pab Igala: Historias de la Tradición Kuna. Quito, Ecuador

Chapin, M. (1991): Losing the Way of the Great Father. In: New Scientist; No. 10; August; pp. 40-44

Chapin, M. (1993): Recuperación de las costumbres ancestrales: El saber tradicional y la ciencia occidental entre los Kunas de Panamá. In: Kleymeyer (ed.): La expresión cultural y el desarrollo de base. Arlington, Quito; pp. 133-160

Chapin, M. (1995): Epilogue. In: Ventocilla/Herrera/Nuñez (eds.): Plants and Animals in the Life of the Kuna. Austin (TX); pp. 115-119

Charnley, S./C. de León (1986): Uso de Recursos Silvestres en Kuna Yala Occidental. Avance de Informe Presentado al Proyecto PEMASKY, unpublished, Panamá

Colding, F./C. Folke (1997): The Relations Among Threatened Species, their Protection, and Taboos. Conservation Ecology [online]; Vol. 1; No. 1; p. 6; http://www.consecol.org/vol1/iss1/art6

Concultura; Consejo Coordinador Nacional Indígena Salvadoreño/Tierras Nativas (eds.) (2000): Segunda Jornada Indígena Centroamericana sobre Tierra, Medio Ambiente y Cultura. Memoria. San Salvador, El Salvador; San José, Costa Rica

Congreso General Kuna (1997a): El Informe Anual 1996-1997 del Proyecto de Desarrollo Sostenible en Kuna Yala, Panamá. Unpublished Document, Panamá

Congreso General Kuna (1997b): Tad Ibe. Revista bimestral, Vocero oficial del Congreso General Kuna, ed. by IDIKY (Institute for the Integrated Development of Kuna Yala). Panamá; Año 1; No. 1

Congreso General Kuna (1998): Informe Final 1994-1998. Proyecto de Desarrollo Sostenible en Kuna Yala. Unpublished Document, Panamá

Congreso General Kuna (2001): Anmar Igar. Normas Kunas. Kuna Yala, Panamá

Congreso General Kuna (2002): Boletín Kika No. 14, 22 October 2002. Official Electronic Newsletter of the Kuna General Congress, divulgated per e-mail. Panamá

Contraloria General de la República (2001): Censos Nacionales de Población y Vivienda 14 de mayo de 2000: Resultados Finales Básicos. Volumen II: Población. Panamá

Durrenberger, E.P./G. Pálsson (1987): Ownership at Sea: Fishing Territories and Access to Sea Resources. In: American Ethnologist; No. 14; pp. 508-522

Dyer, C.L./J.R. McGoodwin (eds.) (1994): Folk Management in the World's Fisheries: Lessons for Modern Fisheries Management. Niwot

Ecology & Environment Inc. (2000): Evaluación Ambiental Preliminar: Cable de Fibra Optica ARCOS-1, Ustupo, Comarca Kuna Yala. Unpublished, San Francisco

Feit, H.A. (1988): Self-Management and State-Management: Forms of Knowing and Managing Northern Wildlife. In: Freeman/Carbyn (eds.): Traditional Knowledge and Renewable Resource Management. Edmonton; pp. 72-91

Feeny, D./F. Berkes/B. McCay/J.M. Acheson (1990): The Tragedy of the Commons: Twenty-two Years Later. In: Human Ecology; Vol. 18; No. 1; pp. 1-19

Folke, C./ L. Pritchard Jr./F. Berkes/J. Colding/U. Svedin (1998): The Problem of Fit between Ecosystems and Institutions. IHDP Working Paper No. 2, Bonn. http://www.uni-bonn.de/ihdp/wp02main.htm

Global Environment Facility (1998): Panama: Atlantic Mesoamerican Biological Corridor Project. Project Document. World Bank, Washington D.C.

González, O. (1993): Kuna Yala, Panama: Sustainability for Comprehensive Development. In: Ornat (ed.): Strategies for Sustainability. Latin America. IUCN, Cambridge & Gland; pp. 53-59

Grigg, R.W./S.J. Dollar (1990): Natural and Anthropogenic Disturbance on Coral Reefs. In: Dubinsky (ed): Coral Reefs. Ecosystems of the World 25. Amsterdam; pp. 439-452

Gunderson, L.H./C.S. Holling/S.S. Light (eds.)(1995): Barriers and Bridges to the Renewal of Ecosystems and Institutions. New York

Hames, R. (1991): Wildlife Conservation in Tribal Societies. In: Oldfield/Alcorn (eds.): Biodiversity: Culture, Conservation, and Ecodevelopment. Boulder, San Francisco, Oxford; pp. 172-199

Hanna, S./S. Jentoft (1996): Human Use of the Natural Environment: An Overview of Social and Economic Dimensions. In: Hanna/Folke/Mäler (eds.): Rights to Nature: Ecological, Economic, Cultural, and Political Principles of Institutions for the Environment. Washington, D.C., Covelo (CA); pp. 35-55

Hardin, G. (1968): The Tragedy of the Commons. In: Science; No. 162; pp. 1243-1248

Hasbrouck, G.M. (1985): Subsistence Fishing Among the San Blas Kuna, Panama. MA thesis, unpublished, University of California, Berkeley

Herlihy, P. (1989): Panama's Quiet Revolution: Comarca Homelands and Indian Rights. In: Cultural Survival Quarterly; Vol. 13; No. 3; pp. 17-24

Hodgson, G. (1997): Resource Use: Conflicts and Management Solutions. In: Birkeland (ed.): Life and Death of Coral Reefs. New York; pp. 386-410

Howe, J. (1974): Village Political Organization Among the San Blas Cuna. Ph.D.diss, unpublished. University of Pennsylvania

Howe, J. (1975): Notes on the Environment and Subistence Practices of the San Blas Cuna. Working Papers on Peoples and Cultures of Central America No. 1. Unpublished manuscript

Howe, J. (1998): A People who would not kneel: Panama, the United States, and the San Blas Kuna. Washington, London

Hviding, E. (1993): Guardians of Marovo Lagoon. The Sea as Cultural and Relational Focus in New Georgia, Solomon Islands. Bergen

Indigenous Knowledge and Development Monitor (1998); Vol. 6; No. 3; http://www.nuffic.nl/ciran/ikdm/6-3/

Jentoft, S./B.J. McCay/D.C. Wilson (1998): Social Theory and Fisheries Co-Management. In: Marine Policy; Vol. 22; No. 4-5; pp. 423-436

Johannes, R.E. (1981): Words of the Lagoon: Fishing and Marine Lore in the Palau District of Micronesia. Berkeley

Johannes, R.E. (1982): Traditional Conservation Methods and Protected Marine Areas in Oceania. In: Ambio; Vol. 11; No. 5; pp. 258-261

Johannes, R.E. (1994): Pacific Island Peoples' Science and Marine Resource Management. In: Morrison/Geraghty/Crowl (eds.): Science of Pacific Island Peoples. Ocean and Coastal Studies Vol. I. Suva, Fiji; pp. 81-89

Johannes, R.E. (2002): Did Indigenous Conservation Ethics Exist? In: Traditional Marine Resource Management and Knowledge. Information Bulletin of the Secretariat of the Pacific Community; No.14; pp. 3-7

Klee, G.A. (ed.) (1980): World Systems of Traditional Resource Management. London

Koskun Kalu (2002): Boletín Informativo del Instituto de Investigaciones Koskun Kalu. Congreso General de la Cultura Kuna. Año; Vol 3; No. 2

Léger, M. (1994): L'autonomie gourvernementale des Kunas du Panama. In: Léger (ed.): Des peuples enfin reconnus. Montréal; pp. 163-199

McGoodwin, J.R. (1990): Crisis in the World's Fisheries: People, Problems, and Policies. Stanford

McGoodwin, (1994): "Nowadays, Nobody Has Any Respect": The Demise of Folk Management in a Rural Mexican Fishery. In: Dyer/McGoodwin (eds.): Folk Management in the World's Fisheries. Lessons for Modern Fisheries Management. Niwot; pp. 43-54

McNeely, J. (1992): Nature and culture: Conservation needs them both. In: Nature & Resources (UNESCO); Vol. 28; No. 3; pp. 37-43

Moore, A. (1984): From Council to Legislature: Democracy, Parliamentarianism, and the San Blas Cuna. In: American Anthropologist; Vol. 86; No. 1; pp. 28-42

Morrison, J./P. Geraghty/.L. Crowl (eds.) (1994): Ocean and Coastal Studies. Science of Pacific Island Peoples. Suva, Fiji

Nietschmann, B. (1997): Protecting Indigenous Coral Reefs and Sea Territories, Miskito Coast, RAAN, Nicaragua. In: Stevens (ed.): Conservation through Cultural Survival: Indigenous Peoples and Protected Areas. Washington D.C., Covelo; pp. 193-224

Nordenskiöld, E. (1938): An Historical and Ethnographical Survey of the Cuna Indians. Comparative Ethnological Studies 10. Göteborg

Ostrom, E. (1990): Governing the Commons: The Evolution of Institutions for Collective Action. Cambridge (MA) et al.

Pinkerton, E. (ed) (1989): Co-Operative Management of Local Fisheries: New Directions for Improved Management and Community Development. Vancouver

Ruddle, K. (1988): Social Principles Underlying Traditional Inshore Fishery Management Systems in the Pacific Basin. In: Marine Resource Economics; No. 5; pp. 351-363

Ruddle, K. (1994a): Local Knowledge in the Folk Management of Fisheries and Coastal Marine Environments. In: Dyer/McGoodwin (eds.): Folk Management in the World's Fisheries. Lessons for Modern Fisheries Management. Niwot; pp. 161-206

Ruddle, K. (1994b): Local Knowledge in the Future Management of Inshore Tropical Marine Resources and Environments. In: Nature & Resources; Vol. 30; No. 1; pp. 28-37

Sandner, V. (2000): Uso de recursos marinos en Kuna Yala, Panamá: Problemas actuales y percepción de la población indígena. Unpublished, Kiel

Sandner, V. (2001): Indigenes Management mariner Ressourcen in Zentralamerika: Das Beispiel der Kuna, Ost-Panama. In: Schellmann (ed.): Von der Nordseeküste bis Neuseeland – Beiträge zur 19. Jahrestagung des Arbeitskreises "Geographie der Meere und Küsten". In: Bamberger Geographische Schriften; Vol. 20; pp. 183-199

Schlager, E./E. Ostrom (1992): Property-Rights Regimes and Natural Resources: A Conceptual Analysis. In: Land Economics Vol. 68; No. 3; pp. 249-262

Spadafora, A. (1995): Pesquería de la Langosta *Panulirus argus* en el Archipiélago de San Blas, Kuna Yala, Panamá: Antecedentes Históricos y Diagnóstico General. Informe. Pradepesca, Panamá

Stevens, S. (ed.) (1997): Conservation through Cultural Survival: Indigenous Peoples and Protected Areas. Washington D.C., Covelo

Stout, D.B. (1947): San Blas Cuna Acculturation: An Introduction. Viking Fund Publications in Anthropology; No. 9; New York

Tice, K.E. (1995): Kuna Crafts, Gender, and the Global Economy. Austin

Turpana, A./V. Nuñez (1995): To Be or Not to Be. In: Ventocilla/Herrera/Nuñez (eds.): Plants and Animals in the Life of the Kuna. Austin; pp. 111-114

Uraccán; Centro Skoki/Iriria Tsochok/Native Lands (eds.) (1998): Memoria del Seminario Centroamericano sobre Derechos Territoriales y Legalización de Territorios Indígenas. Bilwi, Nicaragua.

Varese, S. (1996): The New Environmentalist Movement of Latin American People. In: Brush/Stabinsky (eds.): Valuing Local Knowledge: Indigenous People and Intellectual Property Rights. Washington D.C.; pp. 122-142

Ventocilla, J. (1993): Cacería y Subsistencia en Cangandi, una comunidad de los indígenas Kunas (Comarca Kuna Yala). Hombre y Ambiente 23, Año VI. Quito, Ecuador

Ventocilla, J. (1997): Baba's Creation: Flora and Fauna of Kuna Yala. In: Salvador (ed.): The Art of Being Kuna. Layers of Meaning Among the Kuna of Panama. Los Angeles; pp. 53-73

Ventocilla, J./V. Nuñez/F. Herrera/H. Herrera/M. Chapin (1995a): Los Indígenas Kunas y la Conservación Ambiental. In: Mesoamérica; Vol 16; No. 29; pp. 95-124

Ventocilla, J./H. Herrera/V. Nuñez (eds.) (1995b): Plants and Animals in the Life of the Kuna. Austin, Texas

Wassén, H. (1949): Contribution to Cuna Ethnography: Results from an Expedition to Panama and Colombia in 1947. Etnologisker Studier No. 16, Göteborg

Articles from the Newspaper La Prensa, Panamá:

26.4.2001: Kunas firman contrato con Cable & Wireless Panamá. http://mensual.prensa.com/mensual/contenido/2001/04/26/hoy/nacionales/109134.html

18.3.2002: Desafíos de una cultura. http://biblioteca.prensa.com/contenido/2002/03/18/18_6anot1.html

Michael Huber

Lessons Drawn from Burden Sharing Exercises. EC Acidification and Climate Change Policies[1]

1 Introduction

Every policy field undergoes numerous changes in the course of its development. Each change can be analysed in its own right, but only after a longer period of time does the question about learning – and the extent to which policy making has improved – make sense. This chapter analyses the evolution of European Community (EC) environmental policies and asks if policies, and policy outcome, have improved over time. Has the EC Commission learned to manage environmental issues better?

Environmental policymaking is key to modern societies. Although virtually all societies have had to manage effects of human induced environmental change, the origin of environmental policy making goes back to only little more than a hundred years. As Bert Bolin (2001, xix) puts it: "More than a hundred years have gone by since an awareness of human-induced changes of the environment emerged". It took fifty more years to translate this emerging awareness into manifest political activity. In the 1960s environmental issues emerged on the political agenda. Between the 1960s and 1990s this policy field differentiated into a comprehensive policy arena, with policies ranging from local water pollution to global climate change, covering short-term as well as long-term issues and comprising incremental, minor impacts on the health of exposed individuals as well as immediate disastrous effects on communities or societies as a whole. Today environmental policymaking covers not only a large variety of issues and features, but is also tightly intertwined with economic and social policies. Pressures to innovate technical equipment have their place in environmental policymaking along with conservation attitudes. Furthermore, environmental policymaking has established – probably more quickly and comprehensively than other policy areas – an international setting of actors and institutions to manage the trans-boundary and global aspects of environmental risks. This process of differentiation was accompanied by twenty years of intensive debate, numerous political and

---

[1] This contribution is based on material collected in the framework of the project on social learning in the management of global environmental risks (The Social Learning Group 2001a, b). Most of the data for this contribution was gathered and analysed with Angela Liberatore (see Huber/Liberatore 2001).

public conflicts and experiments. From a social science perspective numerous studies on individual aspects of this complex process have been carried out, but we know still little about the *evolution of environmental policy making*. This is because most social studies focus on single issues for a limited time horizon, while comparative views on the changes and improvements of environmental policies are constricted by small samples. In order to understand more about policy evolution it appears desirable to cover longer periods and to strengthen the comparative perspective. Only then can both general trends and the individual contributions of actor groups or single countries to environmental policies be appreciated.

A first comprehensive study to provide these desiderata has been carried out throughout the 1990s. The project on the "Social Learning in the Management of Global Environmental Risks" (The Social Learning Group 2001 a, b) covers environmental issues from their emergence to current times, i.e. in the overall frame from 1957 to 1992. It compares three environmental policies – climate change, ozone depletion and acid rain – in nine countries, i.e. Germany, the UK, the Netherlands, Soviet Union, Hungary, Japan, Mexico, Canada and the USA and in two international settings, namely the European Union and in international institutions such as the World Meteorological Organization (WMO), the United Nations Environmental Programme (UNEP) or the International Panel of Climate Change (IPCC) (the *arenas*). To be able to compare across arenas, all individual studies are based on a common "research protocol" that structures the policy process in *functions* of risk assessment, monitoring, option assessment, goal and strategy formulation, implementation and evaluation. A robust empirical basis is established on which institutional change, its attribution to individual activities and evolutionary trends can be documented and analysed in detail. Three important dimensions of policy analysis can be combined in a previously unknown way: (i) The analysis of the historical development of three issues allows us to capture not only small or accidental changes, but also the "normal" development of an issue in a systematic way. Furthermore, aspects of learning across issues become important as it might prove that institutions have been established that favour particular solutions or that favour, more generally, learning processes. (ii) The number of countries investigated, also including international and supranational settings, completes the data basis and allows us to distinguish specific routes and settings. (iii) The functional analysis established a common model for the analysis of policy processes, which sharpened the comparative studies.

In short, the project on "Social learning in the management of global environmental risks" undertook an unprecedented effort to provide a broad, solid basis for (further) analysis that generates new insights into the evolution of the environmental field in a global context. It adds another aspect when analysing environmental policies from a normative perspective as "viewing long term issue development through a "learning" lens may highlight significant processes and relationships that complement other equally partial explanations" (Clark/Jaeger/Eijndhoven 2001, p. 13). Based on the extensive data-collection of the Social Learning project, this chapter aims to highlight a single aspect of policy evolution by explaining the development of *burden-sharing mechanisms* in the European Community's (EC) climate change and the acid rain issue.

Burden sharing plays a critical role in the success of international environmental negotiations. In these negotiations situations are frequently dealt with where the unwanted impact is similar for all parties, but the levels of vulnerability as well as their ability to manage the challenge vary considerably. To obtain cooperation, the existing and expected burdens have to be allocated in a fair, efficient way by legitimate methods. This fair and efficient allocation can be obtained either by emphasising the *similarities* and therefore treating all countries in the same way (*symmetrical approach*) or by stressing the *differences*, hence differentiating policymaking according to skills, resources, interests or expectations (*differentiated approach*) (e.g. Ringius 1999). The choice of the "right" approach should be guided by estimates of the costs and benefits, whereby the main focus is on the (immediate) political costs; benefits are hardly considered systematically in the development of a tool that is tightly and inseparably coupled to policy evolution. The choice of a tool has a decisive influence on the *general institutional setting* of environmental policymaking as well. Its implicit concept of fairness and the need to establish procedures and rules to manage re-distributive aspects of policymaking organise the policy arena, decide on participation (*inclusions / exclusion*) and favour specific solutions. The development of the tool mirrors the main features of the emerging institutional setting of EC environmental policy. In the event of its success the tool might be turned into an *institution* itself, i.e. into a political rule on how to approach a specific class of environmental issues (on *institutions* see Breit and Troja, in this volume). From this perspective, the evolution of burden sharing in EC environmental policy making outlines the emergence, development and establishment of only one, albeit decisive aspect of policymaking and allows us to consider the question whether EC environmental policies and policymaking have improved over time (on *social learning*; e.g. Clark/Jäger/van Eijndhoven 2001, p. 13 ff.; Siebenhüner in this volume).

To adequately present the evolution of EC environmental policymaking three steps are suggested. *Firstly*, the main features of the tool of burden sharing are outlined. The main section of this chapter re-narrates, *secondly*, the main steps of policy making in the case of acidification and climate change, covering nearly two decades of policy making. *Thirdly*, some aspects of policy development are analysed, focusing on changes and learning processes.

2 Burden Sharing as a Tool

Burden sharing is frequently linked to the provision of a *public good* and indicates "the way in which a group of countries benefiting from a collective good agrees to share the costs of providing the collective good" (Ybema/Jansen/Ormel 2000, p. 12). It marks, however, not only the attempt to provide a public good, but also to provide it in a fair and just way. Taking this normative qualification of fairness, burden sharing most often means in the context of international studies that economically weaker countries should bear a lesser burden while wealthier actors are expected to become *leaders* in the provision of the public good.[2] The reference to *fairness* shifts the perspective on burden sharing so as to account for skills as well as political, economic or technical constraints and means "constructing asymmetrical obligations that reasonably reflect significant national dissimilarities and at the same time achieves a collective target" (Ringius 1999, p. 137). The fairness of the arrangement is not based on inner logic, beauty or other general factors, but on the practical fairness of policy outcomes, i.e. the feasibility of the tool. To evaluate feasibility, different costs and benefits surface for each actor and indicate the need for a differentiated approach to burden sharing. It has to be noticed, however, that the cost argument is discussed with a particular *political* bias as most scholars refer to the costs policies *invoke for the policy makers*. Within a differentiated concept, it is suggested that regulatory success lies beyond the borders defined by pure economic efficiency. But if complex negotiations and regulatory solutions become necessary, they substantially increase transaction costs. Here the *symmetrical approaches* appear advantageous because of the comparatively simple regulatory structure they apply: it is sufficient to set a common standard for all parties to the agreement. Although the overall outcome of such an arrangement can be expected to be sub-optimal as, for instance, a common standard tends to become the lowest common denominator (e.g. Breyer 1982) the overall costs of negotiations and policy making can be controlled and kept at a minimum. *Differentiated approaches* provide a potentially better solution as they embrace the abilities and specific constraints of the single actor, but their major flaw are their high transaction costs which can hold up the negotiation process. Policy makers are aware of these hurdles when they state – as did the German delegation to the climate negotiations under the Berlin Mandate – that

(W)e foresee enormous practical difficulties and obstacles in identifying the relevant factors affecting the emissions of different greenhouse gases, in deriving corresponding indicators, in generating reliable and comparable data needed and, last but not least, in

---

2   The notion of fairness is intentionally not defined in detail as interpretations both in the social and economic sciences as well as the political debate emphasise different criteria for balancing interests and skills.

weighting these indicators.... Parties therefore would come up with very different proposals according to their individual circumstances and capabilities. This approach would mean even more complicated and lengthy negotiations without necessarily ensuring a more equitable outcome. (after Ringius 1999, p. 138).

High transaction costs of negotiations suggest the need to choose simple forms of policymaking. If *differentiated agreements* are still implemented, three explanations for their existence have to be considered

- The assumption that the costs of establishing regulation play a decisive role for environmental regulation has to be dismissed;
- Policy makers enter the negotiations on differentiated approaches mistakenly;
- The "right" solutions change over time, depending on resources, interest constellations and public attention at specific points in time. The approaches are not mutually exclusive but rather sequential: symmetrical approaches prepare and enable differentiated approaches, and vice versa.

The third explanatory strategy seems to be the most promising one. In the course of policy evolution the conditions change, hence when observing how "good ideas" are adapted to new contexts the policy instruments should be and are adapted as well. Policy makers learn. Burden sharing might change from symmetrical to asymmetrical approaches in the course of issue evolution, depending on interest structures, resources and other factors. Policy instruments develop from standard solutions to a set of complex regulatory tools, where differentiated and symmetrical approaches of burden sharing are applied according to political (strategic) needs rather than some general cost features. To elaborate on this hypothesis some decisive events of the acid rain and climate change issue at the EC level are reconstructed to highlight the development of burden sharing and the attempts to meet distinct, partially contradictory goals.

3 EC Acid Rain and Climate Change Policies[3]

Our empirical analysis of EC environmental policymaking provide an overview of issue development from the early 1970s, when the acid rain issue emerged, to the current state of climate change policies. The issues of acid rain and climate change emerged sequentially on the EC policy agenda. Starting in the second half of the eighties, however, tight links can be observed between them with regard to emphasizing the trans-boundary nature of the issues and a specific selection of solutions, such as the setting of overall EC

---

3   The empirical basis of this section is presented in more detail in Huber/Liberatore (2001).

targets related to specific emissions. The narrative is elaborated in sections 3.1. and 3.2. and summarised in Table 3 (3.3.). The decisive turning points of environmental policy making are then analysed in detail, focusing on events where the simple burden-sharing concept is improved and refined, and taken as a basis of experience for the other issue. This analysis is presented in section 4.

3.1 The Evolution of EC Acid Rain Policy

Initially acid rain policies were concerned with the polluting contents of fuels. The regulation of sulphur dioxide reduction in the content of fuels attempted to anticipate and coordinate national regulations. Hence, acidification policy started out as *trade* policy, partly because environmental issues were not yet officially included among EC competencies. Already in the early 1970s sulphur compounds, suspended particles, nitrogen oxide and carbon monoxide were indicated in the first Environmental Action Programme (EAP) as dangerous pollutants (EC 1973). Health and local air pollution effects were of particular concern. But the rationale for EC regulation was still economic. A Directive on the *maximum* sulphur content of EC domestic fuel oils was developed as otherwise their trade across EC internal borders would be endangered by national regulations. Therefore, Directive 75/716 on the 'Approximation of the Laws of Member States relating to the sulphur content of certain liquid fuels' (EC 1975a) was adopted. After adopting this Directive the EC started to monitor activities concerning atmospheric pollution caused by sulphur compounds and suspended particulates (EC 1975b). In February 1976, an initiative aimed at harmonizing legislation related to SO_2. Instead of regulating on the level of fuels, this time the Commission suggested regulating emissions by setting an *ambient standard*. A certain level of air quality should be ensured by limit-values and guide-values for SO_2 and suspended particulates (EC 1976). Initially the UK, Germany and France opposed this attempt (see Haigh 1992a)[4], but gave up their opposition after international agreements on emission reduction were decided. The EC Commission was involved in these international negotiations on the "Convention on Long Range Transboundary Air Pollution" (LRTAP) from the beginning, while only some Member States participated. The LRTAP Convention (1979) strengthened the adoption of the air quality Directive at the EC level in 1980 (EC 1980a).

---

4   Here we find some evidence that symmetrical approaches may well generate high transaction costs as well. For this directive an egalitarian burden-sharing approach was adopted, but due to the opposition of the UK, Germany and France considerable delay was incurred.

In the early 1980s the acidification issue already played a role in the EC policy agenda although the environment was still not an EC responsibility. Environmental issues gained importance when early comprehensive results on the devastating effects of acidification were published. The Third EAP (EC 1983a) emphasized the need to combat atmospheric pollution by establishing SO_2 and NOx emission standards for large, fixed sources. In June 1983 a review of current scientific knowledge on 'Acid Rain. A review of the phenomenon in the EC' commissioned by Directorate General (DG) XI was published (ERL 1983) and a scientific symposium on 'Acid Deposition: A Challenge for Europe' was organized by DG XII (Ott/Stangl 1983; Mathy 1987). In November 1983 the main elements of the EC acid rain control policy were formulated in a Communication on 'Environmental policy in the field of combating air pollution' (EC 1983b). A month later, in December 1983, a first proposal for a Directive on the limitation of emissions from large combustion plants (Large Combustion Plant Directive, LCPD) was submitted to the Council (EC 1983c). While until now an egalitarian approach was followed, here a first step towards a differentiated approach to burden sharing was taken. Initial features of differentiation were introduced by a minor change. SO_2 emission standards for single plants were to depend on the fuels utilized. Although the directive suggested equal SO_2 percentage reductions for all Member States a certain level of fairness was introduced when the national energy policy and preferred fuel types were considered in the regulation as well. Aspects of trade and competition were still influencial, but no longer determined the acid-rain issue. This was mainly due to Germany, which changed its position on the acidification problem owing to increased national sensitivity towards forest dieback. The environmental dimension gained visibility.

After these initial changes to EC acid rain policies major developments took place at the international level. In March 1984 Denmark, France, Germany and the Netherlands participated in the establishment of the '30% Club' together with six other non EC-countries. They committed themselves to reduce their 1980-SO_2 emissions by at least 30% by 1993 and to reducing NOx emissions too. Later this year Belgium, Italy and Luxembourg also joined this '30% Club'. As far as the EC was concerned, a new situation emerged when the majority of Member States had accepted the SO_2 emissions reduction target of 30% while a minority consisting of the UK, Greece and Ireland was still unwilling to accept emission reductions. This split was also reflected in the ongoing negotiation of the LCPD at the EC level. At the Council meeting of December 1984, Germany and the Netherlands strongly supported the Commission's proposal, Belgium, Denmark and France expressed qualified support while the UK, Ireland, Greece and Luxembourg opposed it and Italy did not take a definite position (Bennett 1988). A year later, in 1985, an amended proposal was presented where tighter limit values for NOx were set and three categories of plants (according to their capacity) were identified. The split among Member States remained; only Italy joined the opposition to the proposal. However, at the same time a Directive on air quality standards for NOx was adopted (EC 1985).

In 1986 another proposal for the LCPD was advanced by the Netherlands entailing a regulatory "bubble approach" that challenged the EC approach fundamentally. Instead of regulating the performance of single plants and setting the same percentage reductions for all Member States, the 'bubble approach' focused on the different percentage reductions to be obtained by each country. To pursue their preferences in energy production and environmental policies, Member States should be free as to how they met the overall target of 45% emissions reduction by 1995. This common target was set together with diversified emissions targets for each EC Member State on the basis of its (i) total combustion plants emissions, (ii) installed generating capacity, (iii) Gross National Product (GNP) and (iv) contribution to acidification in other Member States. The Dutch attempt, however, failed to bridge the split between leaders and laggards. Curiously, it was Germany and the EC Commission which opposed the Dutch attempt as it weakened the 60% reduction by 1995 put forward in the previous proposal. EC policy making changed as far as the differentiation of goals was concerned. Distributive issues started to play a major role in negotiations. The four main categories indicated a certain acceptance to redistribute burdens from the poorer Member States to the richer ones. In addition the negotiations changed somewhat, as it became the task of EC-internal negotiations to indicate how costs and benefits could be distributed among Member States with unequal economic, social and environmental conditions. The results were not determined by the four criteria mentioned, but depended mainly on political influence and the need for a common, agreed EC policy.

Agreement on the LCPD was reached in November 1988 (EC 1988a). The final Directive included three emission reduction stages for SO_2 emissions and two stages for NOx emissions from plants of a thermal capacity equal to or greater than 50 Mw for all new plants. For plants licensed or in operation before 1.7.1987 it set different national reduction targets for each Member State and retained in this way the 'bubble approach'. As already mentioned, these percentages were decided on the basis of *political* rather than *environmental* considerations. It can be seen in the fact that the percentages of emissions reduction for large emitters such as the UK (the largest producer of SO_2 and NOx emissions in the EC) and for Italy (second largest producer of SO_2 emissions and third largest producer of NOx emissions) were significantly lower than those of Germany or France. The EC overall reduction target was not explicitly stated in the Directive, but it can be calculated on the basis of national reduction targets and data on emissions. Emission reduction of about 23% by 1993, 41% by 1998 and 57% by 2003 were decided. The first target of 23% is below the 30% target set in the LRTAP Protocol, hence the leader group was not able to persuade the laggards to adapt at least to the LRTAP results or they could not act as leaders by accepting an even larger burden.[5]

Member State	1993	1998	2003
Belgium	- 40	- 60	- 70
Denmark	- 34	- 56	- 67
FRG	- 40	- 60	- 70
France	- 40	- 60	- 70
Greece	+6	+6	+6
Ireland	+25	+25	+25
Italy	- 27	- 39	- 63
Luxembourg	- 40	- 50	- 60
Netherlands	- 40	- 60	- 70
Portugal	+102	+135	+79
Spain	0	- 24	- 37
UK	- 20	- 40	- 60
EC	- 23.39	- 41.72	- 57.38

Table 1: The LCPD-distribution of emission reductions

Once the problems related to the adoption of the LCPD had been overcome, two problems of implementation arose. One concerned the availability and comparability of the national reduction plans for existing installations that were required by the Directive; by the end of 1992 some Member Countries had not provided the Commission with their plans. The second problem concerned the feasibility of technological improvements and the related revision of limit values for emissions from new combustion plants.[6]

---

[5] In 1988 the Council adopted another Directive relevant to the acidification problem, namely the Directive on limit values for emissions of NOx, HC and CO from cars (EC 1988b; see also Arp 1993).

[6] In light of the revision of the Directive in 1994, a Working Group formed by EC officials, representatives of Member States and representatives of industry was established. Moreover, problems related to the implementation of the LRTAP Convention and its protocols were debated during the negotiation of the second sulphur protocol. In this case the issue of how and whether it was feasible to set critical loads at the European level was of particular concern.

3.2 The Evolution of EU Climate Change Policy

The EC climate change issue emerged in the late 1970s as a scientific problem. In 1979 the EC Commission adopted the Climatology R&D Programme (EC 1980b). Only in 1988 did climate change really enter the policy agenda of the Commission and the EC in general. The Commission submitted a Communication to the Council on 'The greenhouse effect and the Community' (EC 1988c) that outlined the current knowledge on climatic change and sketched the wide range of potential policy options to mitigate climate change. On the basis of the available scientific assessment, the Commission suggested a first 'screening' of possible options including preventive actions in the fields of energy and forestation, adjustment actions related to agriculture and sea level rise and, above all, research activities. The Communication envisaged a target of 20% CO_2 emission reduction in industrialized countries. It was taken from the final document of the Toronto Conference on 'The Changing Atmosphere: Implications for Global Security' (1988). The setting of a preliminary target and the discussion of policy options provided the basis of EC climate change policy. Initially the emphasis of policy making was laid on the scientific basis. In October 1990 the Energy and Environment Council stated that the CO_2-emissions should be stabilised in the year 2000 at the level of 1990 (*stabilisation goal*). This was part of a so-called *No-Regret-Policy*, which was assumed to comprise all actions to reduce CO_2 emissions at low or zero costs. The stabilisation goal comprised secure energy supply, safeguarding employment and economic growth as crucial dimensions of environmental policy making (EC 1990). In 1990 it was proposed to divide the EC into *three groups* whereby large contributors should reduce their emissions by 5%, average polluters should meet the stabilisation goal while economically weaker Member States such as Greece, Portugal and Ireland would have the possibility to increase their emissions by 15%. Climate change policy has to account not only for environmental, but also for economic and social goals. This weakened the policy as far as the stringency of the goal was concerned, but it enabled environmental issues to be taken seriously from the perspective of economic interests.

The *stabilisation goal* was considered only a first step. It was believed necessary to progressively reduce emissions after the year 2000. To ensure economic growth of all EC Member States the Environment Council emphasised the need for a *differentiated approach* that protects the economically weaker countries. At the same time the Council emphasized several times that the success of the stabilisation goal depended firstly on the willingness of *other* OECD countries, mainly the USA and Japan, to join the initiative, and secondly on the ability to find a fair system of burden sharing between the industrialized and less developed countries. Not only the differentiation among Member States, but also among sectors started to play a crucial role. A

Draft Communication (EC 1991) suggested that four sectors of industry would have to face large additional costs, i.e. they were regarded as the main 'losers' of the climate change policy. EC documents evaluated *winners* and *losers* only from the perspective of energy consumption. The rationale behind this shift in the policy perspective was based on four assumptions about climate change policy:

- A technical approach such as removal of CO_2 by filters was considered technically *not* feasible.
- It was felt that the EC has the moral, economic and political power and authority to present an example to other OECD countries for the development of climate change policy. The Commission wanted to take on a *leadership* role.
- Referring to Article 130 R of the Single European Act, environmentally sound development was envisaged, whereby rational utilisation of resources was favoured by the implementation of the *polluter pays principle* and taking into account potential *benefits* and *costs* of action or lack of it.
- The problem of policy solutions was described in terms of *market failure*. EC policy attempted to correct market failures by applying least-cost solutions and the condition that the policy leads to benefits in other policy areas.

The attempt to link environmental issues to an economic rationale was extended to different policy areas. Additional benefits of the EC climate change policy included: improving energy security, efficiency and diversification; increasing the competitiveness of EC industry; favouring a larger share of public transport in the EC and providing positive issue linkages in relation to health. In addition, industrial competitiveness started to play an increasingly important role to legitimise the greenhouse policies. Expanding the benefits of climate change policies that far into the "territory" of economic policy triggered, of course, the question of how *efficient* such policies could be. The traditional command and control type of regulation was considered unfeasible, but it was felt that a CO_2/*energy tax* would be one important step to reach the *stabilisation goal*. Taxation was meant to increase the efficiency of the differentiated approach by shifting the costs of control towards the market. It had also implications for the financial autonomy of Member States. The debate on taxation was influenced by two important problems, namely the issue of energy security and the competitiveness of energy intensive sectors within the OECD, i.e. beyond the EC borders. In particular, the matter of competitive disadvantage of industrial sectors became visible when a global perspective was taken. The economic consequences of higher energy prices inside the EC conflicted with the emphasis on the competitive advantage stated in the Commission's tax proposal resulting from the development of environmentally sound and energy efficient technologies. Such developments were expected to be a major benefiting factor of EC leadership in environmental matters that could counterbalance emerging burdens.

In June 1992 the Commission issued a Communication on a CO_2 Energy tax with a detailed proposal for taxation, which started with a $ 3 tax rate divided between an energy and a CO_2 (50/50) component. Industries with large consumption of energy could be exempted partially or totally from the tax; the extent of exemption had to be decided by the individual Member States. The strategy of the EC Commission to concentrate on the tax proved of limited success. By the end of 1992 no final political decision had been taken regarding this proposal (EC 1992), later it disappeared from the political agenda.

Again, parallel to the EC internal negotiations the EC Commission and all Member States were engaged in international negotiations. EC institutions tried to play a *leadership role* in the negotiation of the Climate Change Convention and in the Rio Conference on *Environment and Development* of 1992 (Jachtenfuchs/Huber 1993; Liberatore 1993; Huber 1997). The Environment Commissioner C. Ripa di Meana emphasised the need for the EC to take this leadership. The practical consequence of that leadership was its "negation" insofar as it was reduced to the attempt to persuade all OECD-countries, especially the US administration, to include in the Framework Convention on Climate Change a *stabilisation target* like the one decided at the EC level. The EC Commission was no leader but a follower, which perceived itself as a leader. Again, the external expectations could not be transformed into internal pressure and success. Following the Rio Conference, the Community attempted to translate into action some of the commitments by adopting – inter alias – the Council Decision on the monitoring of CO_2 emissions (EC 1993), funding research and co-ordinating national policies on climate change.

Distributive problems still played an important role in the EC internal debate on climate change. In 1990 it was proposed to divide the EC into three groups whereby large contributors should reduce their emissions of 5%, average polluters should meet the stabilisation goal while economically weaker Member States such as Greece, Portugal and Ireland would have the possibility to increase their emissions by 15%. The Commission discussed this concept of 'burden sharing' in which Structural Funds and the new Cohesion Fund of the Maastricht Treaty were to provide for a fair balance of the burden, mainly to include less wealthy Member States like Spain, Ireland, Portugal and Greece. This operationalisation of the concept of burden sharing was rejected but the need to find an equitable form of burden sharing remains high in the EC and on the international agenda for climate change. Between 1992 and 1996 climate change policies disappeared from the EC policy stage. In 1996, the issue was taken up at a workshop in Dublin again, where DG XI presented delegates and negotiators with a proposal on burden sharing that focused on energy efficiency and differences across sectors. This internal negotiation exercise was – at least from the side of the Commission – motivated again by leadership aspirations and fear of the loss of political credibility. Political credibility was under pressure as the Commission continued its leadership strategy at international negotiations but failed to establish a common policy within the EC. At the Dublin meeting a common target of 10 percent emission reduction by 2005 was suggested. The debate on how it should be shared by all Member States failed to generate a feasible result and had serious implications for the desire for external leadership. In 1997 the so-called *Triptique Approach* to share emission reductions was launched under the Dutch Presidency. The main difference to the previous attempts was the explicit link between national and sectoral emission reduction schemes, with the marked differences in CO_2 emission reduction adapted to sector potential and constraints.

Country	Stabilisation Goal	Emission reduction 8%
Belgium	-5	-10
Denmark	-5	-25
Germany	-?	-25
Greece	+25	+30
Spain	+25	+17
France	+13	0
Ireland	+20	+15
Italy	0	-7
Luxembourg	0	-30
Netherlands	-5	-10
Austria	--	-25
Portugal	+30 +40	+40
Finland	--	0
Sweden	--	+5
UK	0	-10

Table 2: The CO_2 emission reduction at 2010.

In Zeist (NL) four burden sharing schemes resulting from such a new perspective were presented; different levels of commitments and implementation skills were modelled. Although the approach had flaws at the technical level the conceptual innovation was well received by negotiators and later implemented by a Directive (Ringius 1999, p. 145). This *Triptique Approach* with its double burden sharing across sectors and nations shaped the further discussion. Still, the size of emission reduction was disputed as the large contributors wanted to reduce their commitments and the other Member States were unwilling to increase their efforts. The actual outcome of this discussion is summarised in Table 2. Although the results are lower than the estimated "natural emission reduction", the success of the burden sharing scheme was to include laggards into this policy and keep it open for conceptual improvement. The effects of these improvements will come to bear when further reductions are discussed. Again, it is less the issue of *effectiveness* but of *legitimacy* (internal and external) that decided on the success of the burden-sharing scheme.

3.3 Overview

	73-78	79-82	83-85	86-87	88 - 92
Causes					
Acid rain	SO$_2$ Emissions from fuels	Household emissions, SO$_2$, NOx, VOC	SO$_2$, NOx, VOC from all sources		
Climate change		Human and natural emissions		CO$_2$ emissions of energy sector	All greenhouse gases, mainly from energy and traffic
Effects					
Acid rain	Trade, health, city	Local and transboundary effects	Forests, eco-systems, transboundary effects		
Climate change		First vague idea		First findings	All greenhouse gases
Solutions					
Acid rain	Regulations of SO$_2$ contents of fuels, research, monitoring	Air quality standards. Research, international agreements LRTAP	LCDP, regulation of car exhaustion, international agreements		
Climate change		Research		Research on energy efficiency	Energy efficiency, taxation, research
Main Frame					
Acid rain	Trade issue	From trade to environmental issue	Environmental issue. Since 1995: Sustainability		
Climate change		Scientific issue		Environmental issue / energy	Sustainability issue to trade issue

Tale 3: Timescale of EU environmental policies from 1970 until 2000

4 Policy Evolution, Burden Sharing and Social Learning

Burden sharing has evolved with the field of EC environmental policies. Initially it was an answer to the question of how to start an EC environmental policy when the Community lacks legal competency and has to face considerable internal opposition. Once established, the idea of successful burden sharing shifted from *legitimacy* towards *fairness* and, later on, *efficiency*. In both issues at stake burden sharing started from a simple symmetrical concept, as any other solution would have marked pronounced differences between Member States. Such an approach was chosen to keep the costs of negotiation low but also because the environmental laggards were initially reluctant to negotiate. When the need for coordinating efforts between Member States emerged, differentiated approaches were preferred as they persuaded laggards to cooperate, if only reluctantly in the beginning. This general development is now reviewed briefly at the level of general policy evolution and at the level of the specific burden-sharing tools applied. This review provides the necessary background for some concluding remarks on social learning.

4.1 Policy Evolution

Until the late 1980s EC environmental policy was not meant to exist. However, the EC Commission was active in this policy field from the outset of the LTRAP negotiations in the 1970s. Hence, the main problem for the EC was to legitimise the emergence of an EC environmental policy – against the expressed will of some Member States. The specific "novelty" of environmental issues shaped the course of policymaking, whereby the tool of burden sharing helped to manage some aspects of this apparent legitimacy deficit. Focusing on legitimacy alone, crucial aspects of policy making might be overlooked. Ideally, policies ought to be equally *fair*, *legitimate*, *effective* and *efficient*. Up to a certain point it seems possible to increase *fairness*, *legitimacy*, *efficiency* and *effectiveness*, but after this "point", these criteria can be expected to be conflicting. For example, the initial burden sharing arrangements in the acidification issue increased legitimacy by including all Member States, but they were not effective as far as the emission reduction of single countries and the EC overall was concerned. The main task of policy makers is to establish the *best possible combination*, a combination that might change over time. Apart from the problems of identifying this best possible combination, it may also be subject to *political strategies*. The criteria and their combination can be utilised by all political actors with astonishing results that can be illustrated with the example of *efficiency*. A traditional (still relevant) view on environmental policies says that they inflict additional costs on society. Hence, it appears difficult to link the success of a new policy to *efficiency;* additional costs always decrease efficiency, society would appear to be better off without or at least with fewer environmental policies. An alternative use of the *efficiency* criterion can be illustrated when it was introduced to the self-understanding of EC climate change policies in the 1990s (Jachtenfuchs/Huber 1993; Huber 1997). Interpreting environmental policies as pivotal momentum for technology development strategies implies a different use of the *efficiency* criteria as – suddenly – economic benefits can be gained and accounted for. Reference to *efficiency* can be used to de-legitimise a policy as well as it to increase its competitiveness among policies, hence its legitimacy. To identify the main facets of this policy evolution and to highlight the role of burden sharing, the emergence and development of the two issues at stake are re-narrated briefly using these four criteria – *legitimacy, fairness, efficiency* and *effectiveness* – as guidelines for policy development.[7]

EC acidification policy started applying a *symmetrical approach* to legitimise this new policy arrangement. It depended on international negotiations. The LRTAP negotiations were initiated by "receiver countries" like Sweden (no EC Member) and ignored by "sender countries" like the UK or Germany. In most EC internal reports, the motivation to embark on a new and conflictual policy among Member States is marked by an *enlightening* attitude, promoting environmental protection and increasing awareness about the transboundary nature of acidification. As not all EC Member States joined the LRTAP negotiations initially, rather than providing the basis for cooperation these negotiations created an EC-internal split among Member States that implicated the Commission, restricted mainly by the fact that formally this task could not be dealt with by the EC Commission. Consequently, the policy process was less concerned with, for instance, the *efficiency* of measures than with the establishment of a perspective that focused on *inclusion* and *communality*. *Legitimacy*, both formally and informally, was at the centre of political attention; *formally* as only with the Single European Act (1987) was the legal basis for the EU Commission to act on environmental issues established, *informally* as it appeared problematical to represent the evident lack of internal agreement among Member States as a common, coordinated and environmentally progressive EC position. Still, the EC Commission agreed to emission reductions, although initially a qualified majority of Member States opposed such a policy. One main EC internal aspect for ensuring the emergence of this novelty was to introduce a *differentiated burden-sharing*

---

[7] In Huber/Liberatore (2001, p. 304 f.) the reference was made more widely to the notions of *trade, environment* and *sustainability* indicating the formal reference used in EC documentation. *Trade* was used until 1987 to cover for the lack of formal competence from 1987 to the beginning of the 1990s, *environment* as an independent policy area and *sustainability* refers to environment as a cross cutting policy. Fairness, efficiency, effectiveness and legitimacy are more general and at the same time more adequate to highlight the major adaptations of the burden-sharing tool.

scheme; a novelty for environmental policy making in general. In a first phase of international negotiations, at both the international and the EC-level a *symmetrical approach* was adopted although both the *skills* to manage acidification but also the *impacts* differed considerably. The 30% Club can be seen as an attempt to unite the environmentally friendly, receiving countries in such a symmetrical approach. The minimal success indicates that the main *problem of including* all exporting countries could not be resolved. *Apparently, inclusion can be managed by symmetrical approaches only under very restricted conditions.*

The lack of inclusiveness triggered the need to embark on differentiated approaches. When West Germany changed its position from being a reluctant to an eager participant as *forest dieback* was recognised as an urgent problem in several German regions, strong momentum for international negotiations was created. It also changed the EC orientation in internal negotiations. With Germany one important exporting country realised that it was a receiving country too. For a successful EC acidification policy, *all* Member States had to participate in negotiations. A *differentiated approach* to burden sharing appeared therefore to be the only promising way to achieve this objective. It could provide incentives also for the laggards to join the agreement and so improve the *potential* (not necessarily the factual politics) for emission reduction. EC climate change policy could be interpreted in the same vein: the leadership aspiration of the EC Commission established pressure on the discordant Member States to agree to place the issue high on the agenda. An initially suggested 20% emission reduction for all Member States (and all OECD countries) was announced to be a feasible first goal. Later the more conservative, but already differentiated *stabilisation goal* was decided. The *symmetrical approach* could not be used as a starting point for successful emission reductions as what appeared to be too little for the environmentally friendly, economically strong countries such as Denmark, Germany and the Netherlands, was considered too much burden for the industrially less developed, laggard countries such as Ireland, Portugal, Greece and Spain. To find a common policy platform a differentiated approach was introduced. There is, however, one major difference to acidification: climate change could be dealt with in an accelerated way as *burden sharing* was already a tested, well established policy tool. The EC Commission had learned. In the climate change issue the reference to burden sharing defines indicators for similarities and differences among Member States (e.g. economic productivity, population, political atmosphere, ambitions of leadership) that have been used and discussed before.

Acidification and climate change were successful policies as far as their emergence is concerned. Evaluating the initial success of the policies from a *legitimacy* perspective, i.e. how far policy makers included laggards and reluctant actors, does not imply that *legitimacy* considerations determine the entire policy process. Once the policy process was set in motion, *legitimacy* did not need to be discussed further. Now *fairness* started to play an increasingly important role as policy making was concerned with the adequate, fair distribution of emission reduction, considering the skills and impact of all actors, but also solidarity. In the LCP Directive four "objective" criteria of emission reduction were taken as the basis for political negotiations. In the climate change case, this structure was adopted in the first step of establishing the *stabilisation goal*. *Fairness* reflected the distribution of emissions, skills, damages and power among Member States, but in the climate change case came the additional insight that *within* countries the burden had to be shared between sectors. Hence, the burden-sharing concept evolved further, when for example the idea of *losers* and *winners* came to bear on the climate change policy. The outcome of these negotiations failed to improve the state of the environment in the short and medium term but improved the conditions for participation and, in particular, the environmental commitment of Member States.

Fairness was not the only point of reference to emerge. Once a burden-sharing scheme was established in principle, issues of *efficiency* became apparent. Particularly in the context of climate change *efficiency* plays a strategic role, which became evident in the discussion about the CO_2-energy tax. This tax implies a fundamental policy change, as it is no longer politically pre-established distribution that should guide burden sharing. The tool became more dynamic and market-driven, political control is restricted. Again, aspects of *legitimacy* emerged as introducing a CO_2 tax would have been a breakthrough in the area of financial policies for the EC Commission – unwanted by most Member States. The CO_2 tax has also other consequences as for example the expected effects could invalidate the previously negotiated burden-sharing scheme. It is important that by introducing a CO_2 tax, it would no longer be the political actors to define environmental policies, but the market would establish a *fair* distribution of burdens and benefits. This loss of control may be taken as a good reason for the EC Commission to carefully contain such instruments even if they might increase *efficiency*. Parallel to *efficiency* considerations the implementation of SO_2 emission reductions was taken up for revision. It was intended to verify the *effectiveness* of the regulatory strategies. Some discontent with implementation – in particular of the SO_2 emission reductions – has been mentioned, but rarely gained sufficient attention to reflect back on the policy process. *Effectiveness* has not played a crucial role in environmental policymaking until now, which can be interpreted as both a shortfall and a political strategy. The establishment of the European Environment Agency (1992) enables the EC Commission to control the effects of policy decisions in a more systematic way, but direct effects on the issues at stake cannot be reported yet.

A simple sequence of issue evolutions could be hypothesised. The sequence of foci reflects the policy process from emergence (*legitimacy*), problems to find a simple solution (*fairness*) and towards a more elaborate self-understanding of the policy (*efficiency*). The first round does not conclude the policy process, but is the starting point for new problems and solutions of a new cycle. Parallel to this development institutional features evolve and this common institutional context binds issues together as the new climate change issue did not start from scratch but was based upon the experience previously made in the EC acidification policy. Policymaking is speeded up and allows for further differentiations of the tool.

4.2 Development of Burden Sharing

This generalised structure of policy evolution can be reconstructed at the level of instruments too. The first tool applied to the acid rain issue was – as was assumed – simple. No considerations of differentiation in terms of costs, economic growth or other more general political concerns were made explicit. Faced with the problem of *inclusion/exclusion*, first steps towards differentiations were made. The different stages of developing a "bubble approach" focused on the different percentage reductions to be obtained by each country, calculated from a complex set of variables including the total combustion plant emissions of a country, its installed generating capacity, the Gross National Product (GNP) and its contribution to acidification in other Member States. These "objective" measures represent the ability to manage emission reduction while an important fifth factor of *political influence* was never made explicit. Still, it was assumed that laggards could reduce their contribution to the emission reduction while leaders were more inclined to take on an extra burden. Although several more attempts to re-adjust the weights given to the single factors were discussed before the final burden-sharing model for LCPD was decided upon, a *basic mechanism* was established already with the first draft. Climate change policy could profit from this *learning process*. Having taken the first step from the *symmetrical* to the *differentiated approach*, the assumption was that the concept itself would evolve, would become more complex and provide a more adequate solution to distributive issues. Looking at EC climate change policy we can detect some important steps into this direction. When the EC established the so-called *stabilisation goal* in October 1990 the Environmental Council emphasised the need for a *differentiated approach* that protected the economically weaker countries. Parallel to economic concerns the concept of *sustainability* has opened the environmental debate to *efficiency* concerns (Jachtenfuchs/Huber 1993; Huber/Liberatore 2001). The issue was described less in terms of *fairness* and more in terms of *efficiency*. This led to a focus on economic measures. In the period up to the Rio Conference and soon after, a *CO_2/energy tax* was the central strategic issue at the EU level. A competing method of *tradable emission permits* was already applied in the ozone layer depletion issue and discussed in expert groups. Only recently, tradable permits were adopted for the EC climate change policy. Although the actual decision cannot be discussed in detail, the basic considerations can be outlined.

Emission permits provide even more flexibility and efficiency than other economic burden-sharing instruments. Wealthier countries can *buy* emissions from developing countries and thus organise the emission reduction in a more efficient way. The highly efficient energy systems are not improved further but simpler and cheaper technology is applied elsewhere with the effect of emission reductions at considerably lower costs. Emission permits may be interpreted as a refinement of the economic tool but they addressed the *fairness* issue not so much in terms of skills or impacts of environmental challenges but in a new and more complex form, namely *the efficient use of fairness*.

The EC level experienced difficulties when the potential efficiency increase challenged the *fairness* and *legitimacy* gains of the policy already achieved. With the focus on market tools, the EC entered a new stage of burden sharing, in which the traditional burden-sharing scheme represented a *static* view on the parties of an agreement not providing any incentives to improve emission reduction *after* the burden-sharing scheme was established. Fiscal instruments such as permits overcame the *leader / laggard* divide by incentives, and challenged the initial distribution of the burden-sharing scheme. Environmental policies became more flexible and dynamic. Reservations about permits have focused – rightly – on the unfair, powerful position of the industrialised countries vis-à-vis developing countries. The industrialised states are losing control; the weaker parties cannot gain influence.

5 Concluding Remarks on Social Learning

The hypothesis that costs of negotiation about burden sharing determine the policy strategy could be rejected here; approaches to burden sharing are influenced by other factors. The cases of acidification and climate change indicated that conditions of *inclusion/exclusion* played a central role. At an institutional level the increase of EC competencies and, as a consequence, the related boost of power played an equally important role in shifting the burden, and also responsibility, among Member States. The role of individual countries to delay or accelerate decisions or in favouring specific tools has to be accounted for as well. Additional mention should be made of the strategy to present the EC Commission as a *leader* in an emerging policy field for which it had no competence and hardly any experience. In other words, this chapter shows that *efficiency* is only one reference point for policymaking and in many circumstances not even an important one.

The multitude of factors that influenced the policy process and changed over time complicates statements on *social learning*. Improvement cannot be measured in terms of better cost estimates that make it easier to determine if symmetrical or asymmetrical approaches should be chosen. The empirical case indicates that learning is more complicated and difficult to distinguish from evolutionary processes than expected. Improvement can take place at two distinct levels:

– *A policy is more efficient, fairer, more legitimate and/or effective.* From this perspective, the arrangements of linking environment and trade to legitimate the Commission's interventions are resolved in the Single European Act (1987) where environmental issues are among the competencies of the Commission. There are numerous local learning processes to be identified, not all of which have a direct relation to environmental policy making.
– A new institutional setting is established that shifts attention onto the second level of improvement. Here the issue is no longer if the policy outcome has been improved, but if the institutional setting is able to better accommodate changes and expectations about (combined) fairness, efficiency, effectiveness and legitimacy (on *institutional learning*, see Jachtenfuchs/Huber 1993; Siebenhüner in this volume).

This chapter seems to suggest that evolution dominates the policy process and learning plays only a minor, if any, role. The outcome of policies seems to depend on intrinsic motivations, chance, uncontrollable external interests and generalised legal institutions. Nobody intended to learn, improvement just happened. However, linking the acidification and the climate change issue, a learning effect can be detected as the development was seemingly *accelerated* in the case of climate change; the potential of adaptation was increased. The experience with the burden sharing of SO_2 emissions – and to some extent the successful conclusions of the Montreal Protocol concerning ozone depletion in 1988 (Huber/Liberatore 2001) – made it clear that a *symmetrical approach* to CO_2 emission reduction is bound to fail. In the climate case it was always assumed that the burden needed to be differentiated. The quicker start and wider experience, plus the fact that environmental policies were established as an EC responsibility in 1987, allowed the political negotiations to concentrate on a more sophisticated, fairer burden-sharing scheme. The reduction of choice led to differentiation. We might state that the EC Commission learned from experience and this learning process contributed to the differentiation of burden sharing towards a more dynamic model.

Another learning process can be hypothesised when the advocates of the environment accepted aggressively promoting *efficiency* as a guiding principle of environmental policies and succeeded in persuading economic actors to follow this line of argumentation (Jachtenfuchs/Huber 1993). Suddenly new possibilities for policy making were disclosed, not all of which remained under the firm control of policy makers. The unwillingness to accept the CO_2 tax and – for more than a decade – an emission permit scheme indicated that altering the reference point of environmental policy making was not a well thought through strategy and hardly any of its consequences could be controlled by individual policy makers. The institutional setting in environmental policy making can be said to have improved, not because of the single solutions suggested but because a broader set of possibilities is acceptable for the overall process.

The "economic" approach to negotiations interpreted the emergence of differentiated approaches to burden sharing a failure. High transaction costs, large uncertainties and only sub-optimal results (in terms of emission reduction) could be expected. For an approach focusing on long-term issue developments, also across issues, the emergence of differentiated approaches reflect learning processes as they may improve substantially the political potential of environmental policies. The EC Commission learns, and is able to promote the issue and itself. Identifying these processes requires an evolutionary approach that goes beyond the focus on single decisions, interests and resource distribution and so unveils other features of policy making, described by legitimacy and fairness. Taking up these additional and often conflicting reference points, the narrow framing of policies in terms of costs (and sometimes also benefits) is challenged. It is somewhat ironic that the focus on evolutionary processes highlights learning processes, for the policy makers as well as for the social scientists observing policy making.

References

Arp, H. (1993): Technical Regulation and Politics: The Interplay Between Economic Interests and Environmental Policy Goals in EC Car Emission Legislation. In: Liefferink/Lowe/Mol (eds.): European Integration and Environmental Policy. London; Belhaven Press

Bennett, G. (1988): The EC Large Combustion Plants Directive. Paper to the Workshop EnvRisk '88. Energy and Environment: The European Perspective on Risk. Como

Bolin, B. (2001): Preface. In: The Social Learning Group: Learning to Manage Global Environmental Risks. A Comparative History of Social Responses to Climate Change, Ozone Depletion and Acid Rain. Volume 1. Cambridge (MA); MIT Press

Breyer, S. G. (1982): Regulation and Its Reform. Cambridge (MA); Harvard University Press
Clark, W.C./J. Jäger/J. van Eijndhoven (2001): Managing Global Environmental Change: An Introduction to the Volume. In: The Social Learning Group, Learning to Manage Global Environmental Risks. A Comparative History of Social Responses to Climate Change, Ozone Depletion and Acid Rain. Volume 1. Cambridge (MA); MIT Press
EC (1973): First Environmental Action Programme. O.J. C 112. 20.12.1973
EC (1975a): Directive on the Approximation of the Laws of the Member States Relating to the Sulphur Content of Certain Liquid Fuels. 75/716
EC (1975b): Decision on a Common Procedure for the Exchange of Information Between the Surveillance and Monitoring Networks on Data Concerning Atmospheric Pollution Caused by Certain Sulphur Compounds and Suspended Particulates. 75/441
EC (1976): Proposal for a Directive on Air Quality Limit Values and Guide Values for Sulphur Dioxide and Suspended Particulates. COM (76) 48. 25.2.1976
EC (1980a): Directive on Air Quality Limit Values and Guide Values for Sulphur Dioxide and Suspended Particulates. 80/779
EC (1980b): Council Decision of 18 December 1979 Adopting a Multi-Annual Research Programme of the EC in the Field of Climatology. O.J. L 12. 17.1.1980
EC (1983a): Directive on Measures Aimed at Combating Air Pollution Due to Motor Vehicles Emissions. 83/351
EC (1983b): Communication of the Commission to the Council Concerning Environmental Policy in the Field of Combating Air Pollution. COM (83) 721 Final
EC (1983c): Proposal for a Directive on the Limitation of Emissions of Pollutants into the Air from Large Combustion Plants. COM (83) 704 Final
EC (1985): Directive on Air Quality Standards for Nitrogen Dioxide. 85/203
EC (1988a): Directive on the Limitation of Emissions of Pollutants into the Air from Large Combustion Plants. 88/609
EC (1988b): Directive Amending Directive 70/220/EEC on the Approximation of the Laws of the Member States Relating to Measures to Be Taken Against Air Pollution by Gases from the Engines of Motor Vehicles: 88/76
EC (1988c): The Greenhouse Effect and the Community. Commission Work Programme Concerning the Evaluation of Policy Options to Deal with the Greenhouse Effect. COM (88) 656. 16.11.1988
EC (1990): Policy Options in View of the Community's CO2 Emission Stabilization Target. Working Paper Proposed by the Commission. SN/538/90
EC (1991): Community Strategy to Limit Carbon Dioxide Emissions and to Improve Energy Efficiency. Council Conclusions. SN/283/91. 13.12.1991
EC (1992): Proposal for a Council Directive Introducing a Tax on Carbon Dioxide Emissions and Energy. COM (92) 226. 30.6.1992
EC (1993): Council Decision 93/389 Establishing a Monitoring Mechanism for CO2 Emissions. O.J.L 167. 9.7.1993
ERL (1983): Acid Rain. A Review of the Phenomenon in the EEC and Europe. London; Graham and Trotman
Haigh, N. (1995): Climate Change Policies and Politics in the European Community. In: O'Riordan/Jaeger (eds.): Politics of Climate Change. A European Perspective. London

Haigh, N. (1992): Manual of Environmental Policy: The EC and Britain. Harlow; Longman

Huber, M. (1997): Leadership in the EU Climate Policy: Innovative Policy Making in Policy Networks. In: Andersen/Liefferink (eds.): The Innovation of European Environmental Policy. Copenhagen; Scandinavian University Press

Huber, M./A. Liberatore (2001): A Regional Approach to the Management of Global Environmental Risks. The Case of the European Community. In: The Social Learning Group, Learning to Manage Global Environmental Risks. A Comparative History of Social Responses to Climate Change, Ozone Depletion and Acid Rain. Volume 1. Cambridge (MA); MIT Press

Jachtenfuchs M./M. Huber. (1993): Institutional Learning in the European Community: The Case of the Greenhouse Issue. In: Liefferinck/Lowe/Mol (eds.): European Integration and Environmental Policy. London; Belhaven Press

Mathy, P. (ed.) (1987): Air Pollution and Ecosystems. Dordrecht; Reidel Publishing Company

Ott, H./H. Stangl. (eds.) (1983): Acid Deposition: A Challenge for Europe. Brussels; European Commission G XII

Ringius, L. (1999): Differentiation, Leader and Fairness: Negotiating Climate Commitments in the European Community. In: International Negotiation Vol. 4; No. 2

The Social Learning Group (2001a): Learning to Manage Global Environmental Risks. A Functional Analysis of Social Responses to Climate Change, Ozone Depletion and Acid Rain. Volume 1. Cambridge (MA); MIT Press

The Social Learning Group (2001b): Learning to Manage Global Environmental Risks. A Functional Analysis of Social Responses to Climate Change, Ozone Depletion and Acid Rain. Volume 2. Cambridge (MA); MIT Press

Ybema, J.R./J.C. Jansen/F.T. Ormel (2000): Project Definition and Some Key Concepts and Issues. The Joint CICERO-ECN Project on Sharing the Burden of Greenhouse Gas Reduction Among Countries. Oslo; (CICERO-WP 1999:12)

Bernd Siebenhüner

Social Learning at the Science-Policy Interface - A Comparison of the IPCC and the Scientific Assessments under the LRTAP Convention[1]

1 Introduction

Social learning in environmental contexts requires a strong knowledge base to allow societies to properly tackle environmental problems. Science can be seen as one of the crucial producers of this kind of knowledge and, therefore, the interface between science and political decision making is a crucial bottleneck for the exchange of scientific knowledge and informational needs on the side of political actors. It is not only the need to feed scientific knowledge into societal decision-making processes but also the feedback from the political realm to the scientific community that has to be designed accordingly.

In areas such as climate change, ozone depletion and transboundary air pollution, decision-makers as well as scientists are confronted with a new and unknown quality of complexity, uncertainty and dynamics given the worldwide scope, the large number of relevant factors and the long time horizons to be considered. To cope with these problems, societies, groups and individuals have to develop new institutions on the basis of social learning (Breit/Troja in this volume; Lee 1993; Parson/Clark 1995; The Social Learning Group 2001).

In these learning endeavours at the interface between science and policy, scientific assessments play an increasingly important role (Biermann 2002). They help to organise, evaluate and present the relevant knowledge for the needs of decision making and thereby facilitate knowledge transfer from scientific and expert communities to political arenas. Scientific assessments can be found on several levels of political decision making from local advisors to national expert committees and international assessment bodies. In this chapter, I will concentrate on two assessments on the international level addressing the problems of climate change and transboundary air pollution.

---

1   This chapter builds on research findings that have been laid down in more detail in Siebenhüner 2002a and 2002b. The study was part of the Global Environment Assessment Project (GEA) hosted by the Belfer Center for Science and International Affairs at the Kennedy School of Government, Harvard University. Funding was provided by Deutscher Akademischer Austauschdienst and National Science Foundation; it is gratefully acknowledged.

These international assessments have been carried out over a significant period of time which allows for an analysis of the developments they went through. In the terminology of this book, they themselves can be understood as institutions with a certain potential for social learning in the sense of institutional change. Over the time being, they changed in scale, participation schemes, basic rules and their organisational components. These changes should be examined in the following chapter on the basis of a specific conceptual framework that applies the concept of social learning to the specific conditions of scientific assessments (Clark et al. 2002).

In this context, the paper will address the following questions: How did the assessments at hand learn over the years and in the different phases of the assessment process? What internal structural, cultural, personal and contextual factors can facilitate learning in assessments? What conclusions can be drawn to improve learning processes in assessments in general?

To answer these questions, I will first develop a conceptual framework for social learning in scientific assessments drawing particularly on literature on organisational learning (section 2). Second, two case studies will be presented and analysed on the basis of the above mentioned questions. These are the Intergovernmental Panel on Climate Change (IPCC) (section 3) and the assessments under the Convention on Long-Range Transboundary Air Pollution (LRTAP) (section 4). Both cases are iterative processes with significant changes of the assessment institutions over time. Nevertheless, they differ in some of their basic structures and in their role in political decision-making processes which renders them interesting for a comparison. Whereas the IPCC is a global scientific assessment body in large part detached from the political negotiation processes, the LRTAP assessments have been conducted in close conjunction with the negotiation processes and respective information needs. Finally, comparative conclusions will be drawn from the results of the two case studies in section 5.

2 Conceptualising Social Learning in Assessments

In the context of scientific assessments, a specific approach is called for to allow for a successful description and analysis of the social learning processes involved. Drawing principally on concepts of learning from political science and organisational studies, this section attempts to develop a conceptual framework for the analysis of learning processes in international assessments addressing environmental problems.

2.1 Assessments as Learning Processes

As opposed to the traditional view of assessments being centred around the final product such as written reports and documentation, more recent definitions regard assessments as "the entire social process by which expert knowledge related to a policy problem is organized, evaluated, integrated, and presented in documents to inform policy or decision-making" (GEA 1997, p. 53). This definition focuses on the numerous and overlapping social processes within the production of a document, which seems to be crucial for the understanding of the final outcome.

What could count as learning in assessments? Building on the general definition of social learning as processes of institutional change that "cause a *successful* readjustment of the relations of human beings and their environment" (Breit/Troja in this volume; p. 18), further specification seems necessary to properly distinguish progress from backlash in learning processes in assessments. Therefore, a closer examination of the types of knowledge that can be learned is required. In other words, we need to take a look at the institutions that can be changed in assessments in order to make assessments successful in the attempt to solve environmental problems.

Learning takes place in any kind of institution at nearly any time; the fundamental question, however, is whether it is heading in the right and productive direction. In previous studies (GEA 1997, p. 70), two major fields of knowledge have been identified as desirable in assessment processes: substantive and procedural knowledge. The former refers to the actual problems addressed, the details, the integration and the general level of research. In the case of environmental assessments it will be the precise knowledge, for instance, about climatic changes, their causes, impacts and possible solutions or about the causes and abatement strategies for soil and water acidification. The latter field of knowledge is concerned with how the assessment is designed, referring to questions like who participates in it, which decision-making procedures are adapted, on which scale and scope of the problem at hand it will focus, and how uncertainty is dealt with. For the purposes of feasibility of the subsequent case studies, it seems necessary to concentrate on the category of procedural knowledge in order to generate some kind of transferable and general conclusions.

With this specific focus, the question as to what learning could mean in respect to scientific assessments can be addressed much better. Research conducted within the Global Environmental Assessment Project revealed insights into what an effective assessment might look like and which requirements have to be fulfilled for it to be influential in decision-making processes. On the basis of the findings of the project it can be assumed that assessments have most influence when they attain to be salient to the potential users, credible in regard to the scientific methods and legitimate in the way the assessment is designed (Clark/Dickson 1999; Clark et al. 2002). Thus, the following three criteria indicate the direction in which learning in a qualified sense could take place:

- *Saliency:* Learning in assessments takes place when the assessment process or its products are made better known to participants in a certain area of policy making so that they will perceive the assessment as relevant to them and their decision-making situations.
- *Credibility:* Assessment or its participants are learning to become more credible when the facts, causal beliefs and options outlined in the assessment are regarded as "true" or, at least, worth using instead of other, competing information.
- *Legitimacy:* Learning in an assessment takes place when it is increasingly able to convince a participant that the goals pursued in the assessment correspond to those that the recipient would have kept in mind had he/she conducted the assessment.

We can summarise that scientific assessments learn when they change the way the assessment is conducted in order to become more salient, credible and legitimate or when participants acquire general abilities to conduct more salient, credible and legitimate assessments which are founded on changes in knowledge and beliefs. This concept follows the notion that learning is not necessarily an absolute increase in knowledge because there are always losses of knowledge that allow for the acceptance and memorisation of new knowledge.

2.2 A Conceptual Framework

For the purposes of this study, a conceptual framework is required that helps to generate hypotheses about possible influences on learning in assessments. This concept as depicted in Figure 1 draws particularly on the literature on organisational learning. Concepts of organisational learning – also named as "the learning organization" (Senge 1990) – have been developed in management studies to describe processes of organisational change that take place at a collective level.[2] Scientific assessments could also be considered as collective efforts by a number of individuals bound together in a collective body. In this sense, they are comparable to commercial organisations which also act as collective bodies consisting of numerous individuals. Therefore, applying concepts from management studies and from organisational learning in particular might generate useful insights about learning processes in scientific assessments.

---

2   For related studies see Argote (1999); Argyris/Schön (1996); Carnall (1999); Probst/Büchel (1997); Schwandt/Marquard (2000); Schreyögg (1999, 2000); Senge (1990)

Structural factors
- Storage of knowledge
- Hierarchy/leadership
- Density of the network
- Communication structures
- Reflective mechanisms

Contextual factors
- Political pressure
- New scientific findings
- Media coverage
- Other assessments

Cultural factors
- Values, norms and beliefs
- Informal communication networks

Social Learning in the Assessment

Personal factors
- Individual capabilities
- Dissatisfaction, conflicts

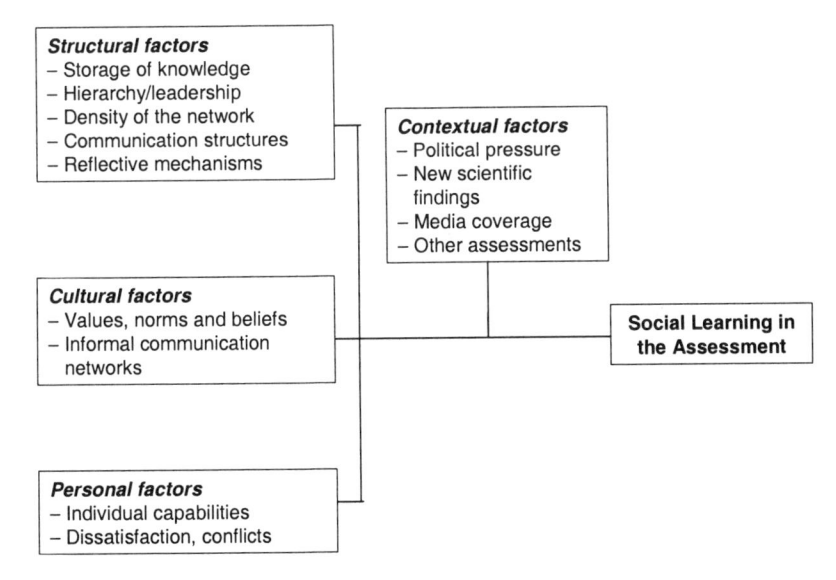

Figure 1: Conceptual framework

In management studies, significant attention has been paid to the *formal structures* of organisations and the impact they have on the behaviour of the individuals and on processes of change and development. In regard to collective learning the following factors have been identified as being influential:

- *storage of knowledge* from past learning experiences concerning technical and cultural knowledge such as norms and values,
- clear *hierarchy and leadership structures* that provide enough flexibility and individual freedom for learning at the individual level as well as at the collective level,
- intense, open and transparent *communication structures* for information diffusion,
- the introduction of *reflective mechanisms* which should help to make use of past experiences by reflecting on them and to turn them into action of any kind.[3]

Apart from the formal organisational structure, *informal and cultural aspects* of the organisation have gained increasing attention by scholars of management processes in recent years. These so-called "soft factors" refer to the

---

[3] Reflective mechanisms are the formally or informally installed means by which an organisation learns. They could be either largely informal like focused personal communication among participants or highly formalised and sophisticated in the form of institutionalised committees with a distinct set of rules of procedure.

human relations inside the organisation. In relation to learning within assessments, I will concentrate on the following factors:

- commonly shared set *values and norms* committed to creativity, flexibility and the solution of actual problems,
- existence of *informal communication networks* committed to learning and change.

Since individuals are crucial to any form of collective processes, *personal factors* have to be taken into consideration as well. It is, after all, people that organisations consists of and that have to carry out the learning processes. Therefore, the subsequent case studies will concentrate on the following factors:

- *personal capabilities* such as proficiency in reflecting on past learning experiences, abilities to generate, collect and accumulate new knowledge,
- attitudes of *dissatisfaction* and *conflict* which foster the demand for change and might spark off learning processes.

Many of the observable learning processes in organisations are triggered by *contextual factors* rather than by more internal organisational ones. For the study of learning processes in organisations as well as in assessments, these contextual influences could be highly significant. Changes in the general framework conditions of an assessment could trigger changes in the assessment process itself or in the internal factors as described so far. These factors include political pressures, new scientific findings, criticisms from NGOs, industry or from the media and experiences with other assessments.

3 The Case of the IPCC

The Intergovernmental Panel on Climate Change (IPCC) was established in 1988 as a scientific advisory body to the United Nations Environmental Programme (UNEP) and the World Meteorological Organization (WMO). It has been designed as an intergovernmental organisation that is basically scientific in its membership but involves governmental participation in the process of approval of the major conclusions. Since its beginning, the IPCC has produced three major assessment reports (concluded in 1990, 1995 and 2001) and a sizeable number of special reports and technical papers as well as supporting materials such as guidelines and documentary material. Over the years the IPCC has undergone several changes in regard to the internal structures and procedures which renders the case interesting from a learning perspective.⁴ Therefore, this analysis will focus on the procedures used in the IPCC processes as dependent variables and it will subsequently examine the organisational and contextual factors as laid out in the conceptual framework that might have had an influence on the organisation's ability to learn and on its original learning processes.⁵

3.1 Procedural Learning

What crucial learning events can be observed in the IPCC assessments that reflected past experiences and fed into changes towards more salient, credible and legitimate assessment designs? The key processes will be described in chronological order along the sequence of assessment reports.

First Assessment and Supplementary Reports (1988-1992)

When the IPCC was founded in 1988, it exhibited a unique and innovative structure and design. Whereas its precursor in the international arena, the Advisory Group on Greenhouse Gases (AGGG), established in 1986, consisted of a handful of scientists almost exclusively from Northern industrialised countries (Agrawala 1999), the IPCC was based on an intergovernmental approval mechanism being open to governments from all over the world. The centrepiece of this intergovernmental mechanism was the involvement of numerous governments in the formulation of the questions addressed and in the approval of the final reports (Bolin 1994a).

In the beginning, the IPCC had to learn from other, previous environmental assessments. Here, the example of the ozone assessments was perceived to provide important lessons. Having resulted in strict and effective political regulation, the international ozone assessment concluded in 1985 was regarded as a success story that should provide a blueprint for the climate assessments in IPCC. However, there was only a handful of people who participated in both assessments and who were able to bring in their experiences. In addition, most of the scientists involved were hardly familiar with the UN consensus processes due to their almost exclusively scientific career paths.

---

4   The IPCC has been described in its structure and evolution over time by Agrawala (1998a, 1998b); Alfsen/Skodvin (1998); Boehmer-Christiansen (1994a, 1994b); Franz (1998). An overview can also be obtained on the internet at *http://www.ipcc.ch*.

5   This case study is based on an analysis of written documents and on personal and telephone interviews with the following experts: Bert Bolin (former IPCC chairman), John Houghton (IPCC, Head of Working Group I), Martin Parry (University of East Anglia), James McCarthy (Harvard University), Neil Leary (Technical Support Unit, Working Group II), Richard Moss (US-Global Change Research Programme), Narasimhan Sundararaman (IPCC Secretariat), Steven H. Schneider (Stanford University), Robert T. Watson (IPCC chairman).

The mechanism was new to most of the participants and they had to learn how to use it effectively and how to develop it further given the little formalisation it had in the beginning.[6]

When examining the first phase of the IPCC in the light of learning, one can identify the organisational set up of the IPCC as a unique invention when compared to previous attempts to design the science-policy interface in the climate field. The IPCC provided a new and advanced way to facilitate science-policy communication by ensuring saliency and credibility. The governments' ownership of the whole process and the final documents lead to a significant increase in saliency when compared with the loosely connected AGGG assessment. Credibility was granted through the design of the IPCC as a scientific body with no political decision makers being involved as authors. Moreover, even the First Assessment Report had a review procedure that was deemed to ensure high scientific standards. Even legitimacy had been increased through the establishment of the IPCC when compared to previous climate assessments. The attempt to include scientists from all parts of the world was a significant progress in this respect, even though scientists from developing countries were highly underrepresented in the preparation of the First Assessment Report.

The completion of the First Assessment Report in 1990 provided the opportunity to reflect on the experiences of the IPCC processes themselves and what could be learned for future assessments. This reflection took place in the form of discussions in the Bureau and the plenary sessions but there was no formal document prepared. One of the main lessons learned by the participants of the first assessment was clearly the political aspects of the IPCC process, which was new to most of the scientists. When they had to adapt to the fact that the agenda of the assessment was set mostly by political needs, major discussions emerged and significant scepticism was expressed by some of the scientists involved. Nevertheless, acknowledging the political function of the whole endeavour, a supplementary report was prepared that – together with the first assessment report – was said to be highly influential on the negotiations of and final agreement on the framework convention in 1992 (Agrawala 1998b; Bolin 1994b). Therefore, this reflection process can be seen as helpful in increasing the effectiveness of the IPCC assessment by raising saliency for political decision-makers.

---

6   Initially, the IPCC took over the general rules of procedure from the WMO. The first set of rules of procedure that were specific to the IPCC were formally approved in 1991 and filled only one page. At the end of the third assessment the document was 16 narrowly printed pages in length (IPCC 1999).

Second Assessment Report (1992-1995)

The Second Assessment Report was completed in 1995. At the time of its preparation, one significant incidence of learning in the sense of reflection of past experiences can be detected. At its sixth session, the Panel established a special Task Force on the IPCC Structure that reported to the eighth session of the IPCC in 1992. Its purpose was on the one hand to comply with the requirements of the framework convention introducing several new bodies like the Conference of the Parties et cetera. On the other hand, the Task Force was asked to outline the Working Group structure of the second assessment and to suggest ways to allow for the participation of NGOs in the IPCC process, as demanded by several environmental NGOs. The Task Force was open to all the members of the IPCC including government representatives, authors and the Bureau members. The Task force convened three times and prepared a report that led to the adoption of a 4-page document about new rules of procedure of the IPCC at its ninth plenary session (IPCC 1992).

The core of these new rules dealt with the specific and highly sophisticated type of review procedure that was imposed to ensure scientific quality and credibility to both the scientific and the political community. Now, the review process took place in two subsequent rounds involving first a review by scientific experts and then by governmental officials. This formalisation of the peer-review process aimed at increasing credibility, but the suggestions made by the Task Force implied few actual changes to the processes already in place. However, they led to a tremendous increase in the number of reviews each author had to take into account.

The report of the Task Force and the resulting decisions by the plenary reacted to critical comments from the political world, whereas only a few criticisms from the scientific community were addressed in the report and in the revision of the rules of procedure. Nevertheless, the Task Force could be seen as a first institutionalised effort to reflect on the experiences of the first period of the IPCC's existence and it was fairly successful in promoting changes to its procedures. Moreover, due to its organisational structure it was open to all the members of the IPCC and provided a high degree of legitimacy to the outcome.

In the period of the preparation of the Second Assessment Report, significant organisational innovations were introduced that aimed at clarifying the relationship between politics and science in the field of climate change. When the First Assessment Report was under preparation, the political nature of their work became obvious to the participants through the high level of contestation they had been confronted with. In order to maintain credibility to the scientific community, the science-policy interface had been filled with a number of committees (see Figure 2). In 1993, a Joint Working Group (JWG) located between the IPCC and the negotiating bodies for the framework convention on climate change was established to facilitate direct communication among the scientific and political committees. Apart from this Group, the Framework Convention on Climate Change (FCCC) established two standing bodies consisting of government delegates: the Subsidiary Body for Scientific and Technological Advice (SBSTA) and the Subsidiary Body for Implementation (SBI). Through these bodies communication between political decision makers and IPCC scientists has been significantly formalised.

From a learning perspective the introduction of these new bodies can be seen as a response to criticisms concerning unclear boundaries between scientific and political aspects of the assessment. They certainly led to a clarification of the roles at the science-policy interface but they were mere additions and their introduction did not imply changes to the assessment itself.

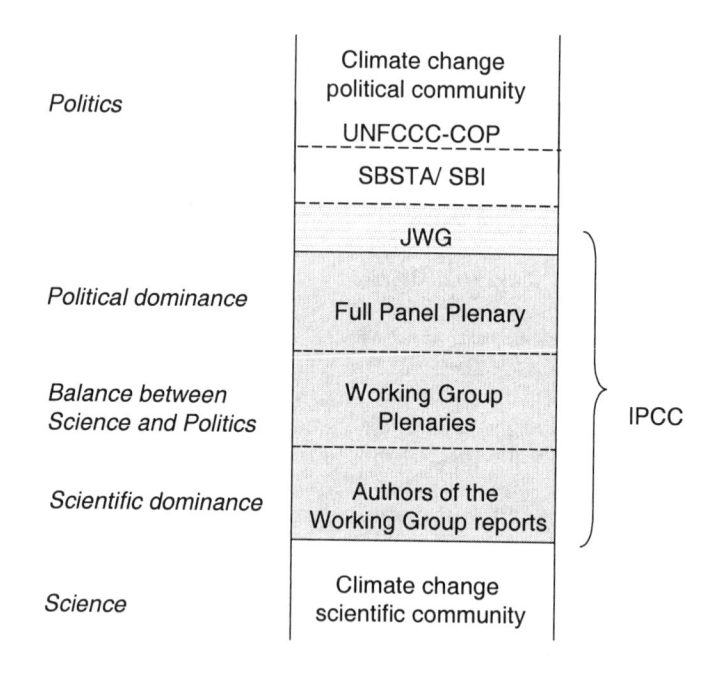

Politics	Climate change political community
	UNFCCC-COP
	SBSTA/ SBI
	JWG
Political dominance	Full Panel Plenary
Balance between Science and Politics	Working Group Plenaries	IPCC
Scientific dominance	Authors of the Working Group reports
Science	Climate change scientific community

Figure 2: The Intergovernmental Panel on Climate Change

Third Assessment Report (1995-2001)

A somewhat different approach has been taken to facilitate learning from the second assessment and to feed the results of these reflections into the design of the Third Assessment Report starting in 1996. At that time, the first chairman of the IPCC was about to step down and his successor had been elected. In a one-year transition period both were working closely together to ensure continuation of the work and to allow for a transfer of knowledge from the predecessor to the successor.

The new chairman started out by attempting to consider what was the right structure for the IPCC. Instead of establishing a specific task force, he himself prepared a White Paper addressing a number of key questions and suggesting a new structure and procedural improvements for the third assessment (Watson 1997). The draft was based on critical articles in the scientific literature, on government statements and on a number of workshops on specific substantial matters such as mitigation technologies, regional projections of impacts and uncertainty (Moss 2000). The chairman received over 90 responses from governments, NGOs and scientific experts and he attempted to consider them in the preparation of the final decision paper on the design of the Third Assessment Report, which was then adopted by the plenary session. Altogether, this iterative process took a little over a year and it was certainly a larger effort than the design of the second assessment when measured in comments considered and in rounds of iteration.

One of the main challenges for the design of the third assessment report was how to deal with the criticisms raised in the so-called chapter-8 debate.[7] In the aftermath of the release of the second assessment report, a number of US-based scientists backed by the Global Climate Coalition (GCC) launched a massive assault against the final version of chapter 8 of Working Group I which concluded that "the balance of evidence suggests a discernible human influence on global climate" (Houghton et al. 1996, p. 4). The accusations published in widely read magazines such as the Wall Street Journal were serious; they charged the lead authors of the chapter of having changed the text of the final version after it had already been officially approved by the Working Group plenary. Thereby, they claimed, the chapter authors violated the IPCC's rules of procedure and the fundamental standards of peer review. However, the accused authors and Bureau members of the IPCC could successfully prove these accusations wrong and no IPCC-member state government joined in the criticism (Edwards/Schneider 2001). Yet, the debate brought some deficits to the surface that had to be addressed in future assessments.

---

7   An extensive analysis of the chapter-8 debate can be found in Lahsen (1998). An in-depth study of the arguments concerning peer-review put forward in this discussion is included in Edwards/Schneider (2001).

The awareness of these deficits on the part of the IPCC leaders led to another institutional innovation in the preparation of the third assessment. The incoming chairman suggested in his White Paper the introduction of so-called "review-editors" whose function was to oversee the review process, i.e. to ensure that authors appropriately dealt with the comments from the expert and government reviewers (IPCC 1999). Because sceptics were afraid of delays in the timing of the assessment, the number of review editors was limited to two and they were invited to the author meetings to witness the processes and to give timely comments and suggestions. Thereby, their work was not a blind (i.e. anonymous) review process. Not all authors regarded the installation of review editors a completely helpful improvement of the process since not all of the review editors were similarly diligent in fulfilling their job – a task that required reading and consideration of the various versions of the chapter drafts and up to 200 comments.

The introduction of the review editors demonstrated a considerable degree of reflection of the ongoing processes going beyond the framework of previous conceptions of the IPCC process. These changes accompanied a shift in the general perception of the IPCC process. When the IPCC scientists were confronted with legalistic arguments in the debate about their scientific statement and the procedures that led to it, they had to realise that the form of scientific discourse they were used to was not appropriate under these circumstances. They encountered procedural arguments from lawyers that could not be dealt with on the basis of scientific arguments based on a common notion of truth and credibility. Therefore, they had to adapt to the conditions of legal discourse, which resulted in more precise formulations of existing rules of procedure and in procedural innovations. It seems hardly exaggerated to state that the IPCC had to incorporate a new rationale that originated in the political realm. Nevertheless, the outcome of this reflection was the introduction of another refinement of the scientific procedures that were certainly able to increase credibility at the expense of further bureaucratisation and extension of the assessment process. In so doing, saliency of the assessment has been put in jeopardy because the processes were extended and the IPCC had even more problems in delivering timely policy relevant information.

3.2 Influences on Learning

What factors have proven important for learning in an organisation like the IPCC? Following the conceptual framework, some key factors will be highlighted that can be regarded influential in the learning processes of IPCC as described above. Nevertheless, due to the complexity of the social processes involved, causal relationships can be traced back to these factors only with great difficulty.

Looking at ways to *save existing knowledge* at the IPCC, one can identify a fairly simple system in place. It is maintained in the first instance by the secretariat in Geneva where all the official documents are stored. Given the heavy work load of the secretariat, its responsiveness to requests for certain materials is limited. Most of the procedural information and specific information about the individual Working Groups is held by the Technical Support Units (TSU) of each Working Group. They provide the necessary basic information for new participants in the process, be they authors, reviewers or even review editors. Except for the TSU of Working Group I which always remained in the UK, the location and the staff of the TSU kept changing over the three assessment rounds due to revolving host countries. The continuity of the work and the ongoing processing of information have suffered from these shifts.

In terms of *hierarchy,* at first glance the organisational structure of the IPCC seems fairly complex with its various functions, bodies and decision-making procedures. The chairperson presides over the IPCC Bureau consisting of five vice-chairs plus the co-chairs and vice-chairs of the Working Groups. Each Working Group has two co-chairs and six vice-chair positions that are usually shared equally between representatives from industrialised and developing countries. The work of the Working Groups is coordinated and administered by individual TSUs that are mostly located in industrialised countries from which they obtain their funding. The Bureau prepares the decisions to be taken at the plenary sessions, which are attended by government officials from the member countries of UNEP and WMO. At these regular annual meetings, the Panel accepts and approves IPCC reports and decides on work plans, the structure and outlines of reports, the IPCC rules of procedure and the budget; it also elects the chairperson and the Bureau. It is the responsibility of the co-chairs of the Working Groups to select the lead authors of the chapters based on government nominations and to coordinate their work. The number of authors has risen to nearly 1500 leading and contributing authors over all three Working Groups in the Third Assessment Report.

Concerning the *communication processes* between the scientific and the political communities, it has frequently been stressed by interviewees that – apart from keynote addresses – scientists involved in the IPCC process usually refrain from participating in the negotiation process in order to ensure their scientific neutrality. Although no documented rules exist on this issue, direct official interaction between both spheres is limited to the more formalised fora and processes. While policy makers can influence the structure of each assessment process, the whole process of preparing the chapters and the first round of peer review remains exclusively in the scientific realm. Governments come into play in the second round of review when their comments are being solicited and they have a major role in the approval of the Summary for Policymakers and the Synthesis Report. There are only a few settings where both groups come together for direct communication. The most important one is certainly the Joint Working Group (JWG). It has been emphasised by interviewees that the introduction of highly specialised reports in 1994 and so-called 'rapid response' Technical Papers in 1996 emerged from intense discussions in the JWG. Since then, these reports have significantly facilitated the transfer of scientific and technical information into the political process (Agrawala 1998b). However, formal communication structures still have room for improvement as far as the internal interaction between the working groups is concerned. Moreover, external communication with the negotiating bodies and the general public is far from being perfectly designed to optimally facilitate mutual learning. In particular, dialogue with the general public is scant in the preparation of the IPCC reports. Communication remains in a one-way mode where scientists try to explain their findings to the public. The procedures are still barely oriented towards fostering a more open dialogue to include so-called lay knowledge or the general concerns, thoughts and attitudes of the public in different parts of the world which might trigger significant learning processes within the IPCC. By taking this kind of knowledge more seriously, the IPCC might gain more saliency to users within the general public and more legitimacy since a broader range of perspectives could be encompassed in the process.

The IPCC employed different *reflective mechanisms* to learn from past experiences. In the Second Assessment, a Task Force was formed for this purpose which was open to all the members of the IPCC and could therefore be labelled as highly participatory. From the Third Assessment Report onwards there has been a tendency to design the learning efforts more centrally and to keep them under the closer control of the chairman. It was the chairman himself who prepared the White Papers about the future structure of the IPCC and who collected comments on it and fed them into a final suggestion to the IPCC panel.

What were the underlying *cultural values and norms* that the people inside the IPCC shared and how did these values contribute to learning in the IPCC? It was a shared general belief among the participants that science could lead to better decisions in the problem area at hand. Because the IPCC assessments have been prepared by scientists, basic rules and principles of science also govern most of their discussions, arguments and ways of interaction. For example, a commonly shared notion of truth which could be found through repeated testing and empirical research could provide an avenue for bringing discussions to a conclusion. In the case of the chapter-8 debate, the basic beliefs of most of the participants clashed with the legalistic rationale brought forward by the critics. IPCC scientists had to adapt to this kind of thinking which in the end led to the adoption of new rules of procedures.

Informal communication structures are regarded as crucial for organisational learning. The most important form of communication was informal communication among a core group of IPCC officials. These individuals were members of the IPCC Bureau who met regularly to discuss and decide about most procedural issues and also about the future design of the IPCC. This holds especially for the learning endeavours in the period from 1988 until 1997. It changed slightly when the second chairman took over and kept the reflection mechanisms more under his personal supervision.

In general, the whole IPCC process relies heavily on the *individual personalities* involved and their personal contacts with one another. It is their constant contribution to and engagement in the IPCC procedures that kept the process running especially since the IPCC does not provide any financial compensation for them (which again hinders Southern participation especially in the core group). Although the whole organisation has gone through a process of bureaucratisation, it is still a small group of people well known to each other that prepares the important decisions. Nevertheless, the rules of procedures in place and the bureaucracy behind it are strong enough to keep individuals from dominating the process. Fundamental decisions can only be made by the panel itself and not by the chairperson or other Bureau members. However, the chairperson is powerful enough to keep certain ideas or concepts out of the process by executing his power as chair of many sessions.

One crucial initiator for learning processes in the IPCC has been the *conflict* about chapter 8 in the Second Assessment Report where several individuals from outside the IPCC felt dissatisfied with the final outcome and the procedures that led to them. Their criticism sparked off a major conflict and lead to significant adjustments and changes in the IPCC rules of procedure.

What *contextual factors* influenced learning within the IPCC? One of the main influences in the first phase of the IPCC was the success of the international ozone assessment. Participants in the IPCC either took part in this assessment or knew about it from diverse sources. Its design as an international assessment and close linkage to the negotiation processes with strict regulation over the outcome caused many people to regard the ozone assessment a success. Over the years, however, it became clear to many of the participants in the IPCC and in the climate change negotiations that the climate case was not entirely similar to the ozone case given the different structures of the problems (Benedick 1999).

The *media coverage* of the IPCC and its reports grew enormously over the years and certainly led to some adjustments in the IPCC procedures. Thus, Bureau members became rather cautious about releasing information to the press without having it double-checked. One reason for the careful interaction with the media was the fact that the criticism of chapter 8 in the Second Assessment Report was first published in the daily press, drawing public attention to the internal procedures of the IPCC. IPCC members realised at that time that incorrect or poorly phrased press releases or interviews could harm the IPCC's reputation. On the other hand, through these incidents most of the IPCC members developed some kind of a fortress mentality as far as external relations were concerned. From a learning perspective, this mentality has to be seen rather critically since it inhibits the opportunities to bring in new knowledge into the organisation and to foster dialogue and open exchange. Thus, by and large, the intense media coverage seems that it had a slightly negative effect on learning in the IPCC over the years although it certainly led to high public awareness of the problems of climate change.

4 The Assessments under the LRTAP Convention

The Convention on Long-Range Transboundary Air Pollution is one of the main international efforts to combat acidification and other damages to ecosystems, buildings and human health in Europe and North America. Since 1979, eight protocols on different pollutants and procedural matters of the convention have been signed under the auspices of the United Nations Economic Commission for Europe (UNECE). The Convention has set up a multi-layer organisation to include scientific assessments on the numerous technical and scientific questions of air pollution.[8] Scientific assessments of the effects of air pollution have been carried out under the Working Group on Effects whereas assessments on methodological questions, like modelling, and the monitoring have been organised in the form of Task Forces that directly reported to the Executive Body of the Convention. Generally, the assessment bodies were more closely linked to the negotiation process than in the climate change area. However, the whole organisational structure and the institutions of scientific assessment evolved over the period of more than two decades since the signing of the convention.[9] In these scientific bodies some changes over time and some reflexive learning took place.[10]

---

[8] For an overview of the different bodies and organisational connections under the convention see the internet under: http://www.unece.org/env/lrtap/welcome.html.

[9] The evolution of the political processes under the LRTAP-convention, the protocols and their effectiveness have been analysed by Levy (1993); McCormick (1997, 1998); Primo (1998); Swanson/Johnston (1999); Haas/McCabe (2001).

[10] This case study is based on an analysis of written documents and on personal interviews with the following experts: Keith Bull (UNECE-Secretariat), Henning Wüster (UNECE-Secretariat), Leen Hordijk (Wageningen University, formerly IIASA), Stacy VanDeveer (University of New Hampshire), Noelle Eckley (European Environment Agency).

4.1 Procedural Learning

What kind of procedural learning processes could be detected in the course of these events? Concentrating on the way the scientific assessments developed in regard to their organisational set up, their design and the interaction with the negotiating bodies, a distinction will be made between three overlapping phases. These are not focused on the advancements in the negotiations and the different protocols established under the convention since these largely remain in the political realm.

Setting up the Organisational Structure (1979-1988)

After the signing of the convention in 1979 it took a while until the organisational structure including the assessment bodies with the two main working groups and various task forces had been established. As a first important step towards implementation and towards setting up an effective organisational structure for the assessments, the first protocol under the convention ensured the funding for EMEP, the "Cooperative programme for the monitoring and evaluation of the long-range transmission of air pollutants in Europe". By collecting, processing and analysing air-pollution data, EMEP was the precondition for both the political negotiations and scientific advice. Also at a very early stage in the convention process, the Working Group on Effects came into being to provide the scientific information on which the negotiations of further protocols were based. It collected its information from a number of special international programmes focusing on the different effects of air pollution such as soil degradation and damages to forests. The last working group to be established was the Working Group on Abatement Technologies. It was focused on technologies and industrial processes to reduce emissions. All these organisational units were dedicated to providing information for the political negotiation process and they were seen as necessary to convince policy makers to take action. Although the convention considered scientific information pivotal to its processes, the first negotiations and the resulting protocols were hardly based on scientific information. The first three technical protocols were based on a flat-rate approach that pursued fixed rates of emission reductions without clear links to effects which did not require substantive scientific inputs.

For this phase no instance of deeper reflection on the process of scientific assessment as a whole was reported by the interviewees. The learning effects focused on the establishment of a functioning organisational structure for the negotiation and effective implementation of the convention and its protocols. The general tasks were already described in the convention itself so there was little room for fundamental experimentation about how to conduct scientific assessments under the convention and how to feed scientific information into the process. Moreover, the newly established institutions for the provision of scientific information for the political processes remained rather marginalised since the first protocols were predominantly political. This is not to say that the assessment bodies were useless and ineffective. They managed to establish a scientifically credible and politically legitimate assessment process, which was still lacking some salience to the policy makers.

Introduction of the Critical Loads Concept and the RAINS Model (1988-1999)

It was already in the 1988 protocol on nitrogen oxides that the innovative critical loads concept was mentioned as a possible conceptual framework for future protocols under the convention and it was through this concept that science was fed into the process. Whereas the flat-rate approach used a fixed percentage of emission reductions, the "second generation" of protocols starting with the sulphur protocol of 1994 was effects-based and adhered to the critical-loads approach. According to Haas/McCabe (2001, p. 327), "the concept was virtually revolutionary in diplomacy because it assigned differential national obligations based on the carrying capacity of vulnerable ecosystems rather than a politically equitable (and arbitrary) emission cut." In regard to the evolution of the scientific assessments under the convention, the introduction of the critical loads concept was equally revolutionary even though the resulting changes were based on a deep reflection not of the assessment processes but of the concept itself.

What was the critical loads concept about? As phrased in the Nitrogen-Oxides protocol, "critical load means a quantitative estimate of the exposure to one or more pollutants below which significant harmful effects on specified sensitive elements of the environment do not occur according to present knowledge" (Article 1). The 1991 VOC protocol also included damaging effects on human beings in this definition. In essence, this concept focused on regional damages and approached pollution control from this aspect in order to effectively protect ecosystems and human health (Bull 1992, 1995). By contrast, previous pollution abatement strategies concentrated on overall emission reductions at all sources largely irrespective of the actual damages of specific emissions in certain regions. Whereas here it was mostly a matter of political negotiation over how far emissions had to be reduced, in the critical-loads approach different emission-reduction requirements could be deduced for different regions. This allowed for more cost effectiveness. However, effective pollution control under the critical-loads approach required reliable scientific input in order to get some indication about the regional effects and emission reduction requirements.

In the LRTAP convention the crucial means to link scientific data on actual damages and environmental stress with the political processes under the critical-loads approach was the RAINS model – an integrated assessment model developed by the International Institute for Applied Systems Analysis (IIASA).[11] It allowed for the analysis of alternative strategies to reduce acidification and other damaging impacts on a regional scale and in this respect it served as a "scenario-generating device" (Alcamo et al. 1990, p. 1).

The introduction of the RAINS model can be seen as an approach to integrate the scientific and technical information generated by the various task forces and working groups under the convention in order to provide highly policy-relevant information. Since the critical-loads approach required significant scientific input to the political negotiation processes to determine the relevant emission reduction targets and to decide about the best abatement strategies to reach these targets, the RAINS model quickly gained great prominence.

In terms of saliency, the use of the RAINS model in the negotiations on further emission reductions, in particular in the preparation of the second sulphur protocol signed in 1994, gave a boost to the applicability of scientific information in political processes. In addition, the model was accepted by negotiators as scientifically credible and politically legitimate in the way it has been developed (Patt 1998). Its introduction resulted in significant structural changes to the whole assessment process and its connection to the negotiation processes which led to an increase in saliency, credibility and legitimacy.

On the level of the individual working groups, two external reviews of the Working Group on Effects took place. One was carried out in 1992/93 when government delegates to the Executive Body questioned the need for two additional groups, the ICP on Integrated Monitoring and the Task Force on Mapping. The Executive Body decided to request an external review from an expert in the field of acid rain research who had not been involved in the LRTAP-processes so far. The report concluded that there was a need for better communication among the ICPs working under the Working Group on Effects. Up to that point the different ICPs were working rather independently and hardly communicated with each other. After the evaluation had highlighted this deficiency, the ICPs started to cooperate more closely and to develop work patterns that were more specifically tailored to the convention.

In sum, there is a tendency to increase saliency of the work of the various assessment bodies through intensified and more focused communication among the sub-units and through the integration of their results in the work of the Bureau, which tailored the outcomes to the political decision needs. Following this successful outcome, another review was requested from the same external reviewer four years later.

---

11   The model and its sub-models are described by Hordijk (1988) and Alcamo et al. (1990). The integration of the model in political processes is discussed by Tuinstra et al. (1999).

Restructuring after the Gothenburg Protocol (1999-2001)

The Gothenburg protocol signed in 1999 is perceived as a "third generation" of pollution control protocols as it takes into account the interdependencies of environmental effects such as acidification, eutrophication and ground ozone accumulation and the related pollutants based on the critical-loads approach to achieve effective reductions of environmental damages at least cost (Jagusiewicz 1999). Given the current state of knowledge on the causes and damaging effects of air pollution, the Executive Body decided that no further protocols will be negotiated under the LRTAP-convention. Consequently, some major restructuring took place in order to redirect the organisational set up towards the reversed focus on implementation and review issues which also had significant implications for the scientific assessment bodies under the convention (Executive Body 1999).

The Working Group on Abatement Techniques was dissolved since its main task was the preparation of technical annexes to the protocols. The Working Group on Strategies had been renamed in order to add its responsibility for the review of the current protocols and for possible revisions and initiatives. In addition, the focus on health effects was introduced in collaboration with the World Health Organization (WHO). Moreover, integrated assessment modelling was moved away from the political processes resulting in possible decreases in the saliency of its work for the political decision makers. In general, the political influence of integrated assessment modelling in the LRTAP process decreased after the conclusion of the 1994 sulphur protocol while the scientific orientation of the modelling has been strengthened. Nevertheless, it is generally expected that communication between the modelling community and the political bodies will continue given the history of their links in past negotiation processes.

However, the restructuring did not put an end to the processes of reflection over the future strategies and pathways to combat transboundary air pollution. The topic was discussed at a specific workshop in 2000 which was deliberately intended to facilitate further learning – in particular since it covered topics central to the development of scientific assessments such as sector integration, linkages between global models and regional or national scales, the role of economic models and advancements in integrated assessment modelling (Nordic Council of Ministers 2000). New directions of scientific assessment under the convention as described in the workshop documents include the integration of health aspects and the narrowing of the monitoring grids from 150 km^2 to 50 km^2. These efforts might lead to greater saliency to regional users as well as to users from other communities like the public health community. Moreover, the development and use of dynamic rather than static models and the close examination of uncertainties involved could serve to improve scientific credibility of the assessment (Bull 2000).

4.2 Influences on Learning

What factors could be held accountable for the learning processes within the scientific assessments of the LRTAP-convention? As with the IPCC case study, this question will be addressed on the basis of the conceptual framework as developed in section 2.

One of the main success factors for the LRTAP convention and its assessments was certainly the continuity of a large proportion of its personnel especially in the first decade of its existence. Thereby, newly acquired technical and procedural *knowledge* could be kept inside the organisation and passed on through individuals. However, in the beginning of the 1990s, a number of people, in particular political officials, left the convention and turned to the newly emerging hot topic of climate change. Nevertheless, those individuals that were key to the advancements of the political processes and most of the scientists remained active within the framework of the convention contributing to the successful input of scientific and technical information into the political processes. In addition, the secretariat remained at the same location and had a fairly constant staff, which allowed for the uninterrupted continuation of processes and for the accumulation of valuable procedural knowledge.

The *hierarchy* in the LRTAP organisation can be characterised as rather flat since the main decision-making body is the Executive Body which received informational inputs from the subordinated Working Groups. The Working Groups meanwhile supervised the Task Forces and the ICPs that were affiliated with them. Moreover, there were no specific rules of procedure for the LRTAP processes as in the IPCC case. The convention simply used the general UN rules of procedure which are based on the consensus principle. Due to the organisational structure of the diverse ICPs and Task Forces, there could be no domination of the whole process by one individual. Decision making is highly participatory in terms of the involvement of the parties to the convention – at least as far as the Executive Body and the Working Groups are concerned. In comparison with the IPCC, the heterogeneity of participants in the LRTAP process was significantly lower as there were no developing countries participating. Jagusiewicz (1999, p. 17) points out that the Executive Body "has always been sensitive to new scientific evidence, to innovative approaches to solving the problem and to the need to protect human health and ecosystems effectively and cost-effectively." Given the body of evidence presented above, there seems to be some justification for this position. Thus, the Executive Body could be seen as a supporting factor for learning processes in the LRTAP-convention in general.

Most of the scholars examining the LRTAP assessments highlight the continuous, iterative communication between scientists and negotiators as one of the crucial preconditions for the successful transfer of scientific knowledge into the political negotiation processes (Eckley 1999; VanDeveer 1998). However, it has to be questioned to what extent this has to be credited to formal *communication structures* or to informal communication networks. Formal communication relationships exist mainly between the Working Groups and their subordinate Task Forces and ICPs and between the Working Groups and the Executive Body – mostly mediated through the Working Group on Strategies and Review. Since the working groups and task forces had a constant exchange of staff members who attended meetings of other groups or of the Executive Body, intense interaction was possible. This structure granted the flow of scientific and technical information into the negotiation processes. Since many personal relationships were existent between the individuals of this core group, informal communication played an important role in the interaction between negotiators and scientists as well as among the two groups.

In terms of *reflective mechanisms*, the assessment bodies utilised mainly three means to facilitate learning: international workshops, critical discussions within the Executive Body and external reviews. The workshops were organised around various specific questions that came out of the task forces and working groups and included scientific expertise from outside of the convention process. Thus the set of participating external scientists varied from one workshop to the other. In the workshops external scientists from the participating countries brought in their often detailed and highly specific knowledge and were asked to make it more accessible for policy makers and integrative modelling approaches. Thereby, they helped to develop the integrated assessment models that became crucial in the second phase. Moreover, the workshops were a means to ensure scientific credibility by including high-ranking scientists. Since participation was international, legitimacy was ensured as well. However, organising a workshop is a lengthy process. From the initial idea to the actual event, it usually took a year or even longer. Since the workshops – especially in the initial phase of the convention – were mostly centred around scientific issues, there was little room for reflection on general procedural questions like how the whole assessments process works and how it might be designed better.

Whereas the workshops provided rather indirect opportunities for reflection on procedural issues, occasional evaluation and discussion in the Executive Body were more focused on the development of the organisational structure, its functioning, its effectiveness and the assessment process. However, these discussions took place more on an ad-hoc basis and have mostly not been based on thorough evaluations. In most cases, they were raised by certain country representatives with the aim of reducing the costs of the LRTAP process.

External review was another means to install reflective elements in the assessment process which proved to be successful in identifying problem areas and in triggering the required changes. It seems crucial that these reviews are conducted by highly respected individuals or bodies from outside the process in order to maintain their independence and their credibility.

As far as shared *values, norms and beliefs* among the participants in the LRTAP process are concerned, it can be said that the standards of technical knowledge even among the negotiators were high when compared to other international negotiations since most of the individuals involved are – or have been – scientists. In this way, a common framework existed among them in the field of (natural) scientific methods and norms. In addition, interviewees pointed out that they also had a commonly held commitment to reduce air pollution and to improve the environmental situation in Europe and North America. Learning processes with regard to improvements of the assessment certainly profited from these commonalities.

The LRTAP process has been driven by a small number of *individuals* from both sides, the political and the scientific realm. On the political side it was in particular the Swedish delegation leader who managed to energise the process. In the scientific area, scientists involved in the negotiations were important for the progress of the process since they learned to think strategically in their interaction with the policy makers. They became cautious in the provision of certain information and in the timing of the release of information as their insights into the dynamics of the political processes improved. In this way, the scientists adapted to the rules of the assessment processes and proved to be able to learn about the political functions of their engagement in the assessment.

What influence did *external factors* have on learning in the LRTAP assessments? In the first phase until the beginning of the 1990s political pressures from the East-West confrontation permeated through the whole process and forced participants to follow the general rules of political interaction between the different systems. On the other hand, the LRTAP convention was one of the few fields of East-West cooperation at that time and thus it was given priority among policy makers who were interested in this kind of bilateral communication and collaboration. However, there were certain limits to the development of the convention and to the learning possible in the process, in particular with respect to the political functions of the assessment.

5 Comparison and Conclusions

The two case studies presented in this chapter allow for a comparison on several grounds. First, both assessments under consideration have significant structural differences in their organisational structures and in the general preconditions under which they work. While the IPCC is a large-scale and truly global endeavour that has to address North-South relationships, the LRTAP assessments are exclusively concerned with Northern industrialised countries. The links to the political negotiation and decision-making processes in the LRTAP case are much stronger than the links between the IPCC and the climate negotiations. Being a large and highly bureaucratised undertaking, the IPCC can hardly be as flexible as the LRTAP assessments with their small groups in close contact with policy makers.

Second, the problems at hand are different. Climate change is a long-term and large-scale problem with high uncertainties and comparatively little account of actual damages so far. Transboundary air pollution, by contrast, has caused sizeable and palpable damages in the participating countries. In addition, scientific evidence is much larger in this case.

Third, both cases differ in certain features of their ability to learn. Generally speaking, the LRTAP assessments were more flexible and able to change radically whereas the IPCC showed more incremental improvements. Although we also find accounts of far-reaching learning processes in the IPCC case, the analysed changes in the overall structure and the rules of procedure of the IPCC adhered to a mode of adaptation and incremental improvements. However, the initial structure of the IPCC in 1988 was clearly revolutionary in comparison to all other assessment endeavours as yet. By contrast, the LRTAP assessments demonstrated somewhat higher flexibility, exhibited a capacity for thorough institutional changes and can be expected to continue this learning path in the current situation of restructuring.

In conclusion, a comparison of the learning processes in the two assessments shows some variation which might be explained through the differences in the structural, cultural, personal and contextual factors as shown in Table 1.

What are the conclusions to be drawn from these findings and what are the facilitators of learning that should be given greater attention in future assessments? Summarising the findings of this study, we can distinguish between indirect and direct facilitators of learning processes. Among the indirect factors that have to be present in order to make learning possible or more likely to occur we have to consider the following:

- Provision of *continuity in the basic administrative and organisational functions* through constant offices or a constant stock of people in charge with these tasks,
- Establishment of a *small but dense network of active people* who run the core activities of the assessment and who are in constant communication with each other,
- Clear *commitment to learning* and the installation of reflective mechanisms,

- Establishment of *intensive informal communication relationships* especially between scientists and decision makers,
- Existence of *energetic change agents* in key positions in the assessment organisation.

Influences on Learning	IPCC	LRTAP assessments
Storage of knowledge	Changing location of the TSUs, stable secretariat	Stable basic administrative structures
Hierarchy and leadership	Central role of the chairmen; large number of scientists, governmental and other representatives involved	Highly participatory decision making; small number of active people in the assessment process
Formal and informal communication	Clear boundaries between scientists and government representatives	Open and intense interaction between the scientists and the negotiators
Reflective mechanisms	Specific Task Force and revision of white papers	Workshops, reviews by the Executive Body, external review
Values and norms	Belief in scientific truth	Environmentalist goals
Personal factors	Integrative chairpersons	Highly committed core group of negotiators and scientists
Dissatisfaction and conflict	Dissatisfaction with certain cross-cutting issues	Little conflicts within the assessment bodies
Media coverage and external criticism	Severe external criticism in one case, high exposure to public debate	Little public attention

Table 1: Differences between the IPCC and the LRTAP assessments

On the side of the direct facilitators, the cases demonstrate the importance of conflicts or external criticism in sparking off learning processes in both assessments. In the IPCC case it was the chapter-8 debate that led to a revision of the rules of procedure and a partial rethinking of the whole assessment endeavour. In the LRTAP assessments it was the external evaluation that initiated learning processes in the Working Group on Effects. However, the cases also demonstrate that some learning processes have been initiated through interruptions or pauses in the assessment processes, for instance after the finalisation of a major assessment report.

References

Alfsen, Knut/Tora Skodvin (1998): The Intergovernmental Panel on Climate Change (IPCC) and Scientific Consensus. How Scientists Come to Say what They Say about Climate Change. In: CICERO Policy Note; No. 3; Center for International Climate and Environmental Research, Oslo

Agrawala, Shardul (1999): Early Science-Policy Interaction in Climate Change: Lessons from the Advisory Group on Greenhouse Gases. In: Global Environmental Change; No. 9; pp. 157-169

Agrawala, Shardul (1998a): Context and Early Origins of the Intergovernmental Panel on Climate Change. In: Climatic Change; No. 39; pp. 605-620

Agrawala, Shardul (1998b): Structural and Process History of the Intergovernmental Panel on Climate Change. In: Climatic Change; No. 39; pp. 621-642

Alcamo, Joseph/Roderick Shaw/Leen Hordijk (1990): The RAINS Model of Acidification. Science and Strategies in Europe. Dordrecht; Kluwer

Argyris, Chris/Donald A. Schön (1996): Organizational Learning II. Theory, Method, and Practice. Reading (MA): Addison-Wesley

Argote, Linda (1999): Organizational Learning. Creating, Retaining, and Transferring Knowledge. Boston; Kluwer

Benedick, Richard E. (1999): Contrasting Approaches: The Ozone Layer, Climate Change, and Resolving the Kyoto Dilemma. In: WZB-discussion paper; No. FS II 99-404; Berlin; Wissenschaftszentrum Berlin

Biermann, Frank (2002): Institutions for Scientific Advice: Global Environmental Assessments and their Influence in Developing Countries. In: Global Governance; Vol. 8; No. 2; pp. 195-219

Boehmer-Christiansen, Sonja (1994a): Global Climate Protection Policy: The Limits of Scientific Advice. Part 1. In: Global Environmental Change; Vol. 4; No. 2; pp. 140-159

Boehmer-Christiansen, Sonja (1994b): Global Climate Protection Policy: The Limits of Scientific Advice. Part 2. In: Global Environmental Change; Vol. 4; No. 2; pp. 185-200

Bolin, Bert (1994a): Science and Policy Making. In: Ambio; Vol. 23; No. 4; pp. 25-29

Bolin, Bert (1994b): Next Step for Climate-Change Analysis. In: Nature; No. 368; p. 94

Bull, Keith (2000): What Are the Needs for the Revisions of the Protocols and Strategies on Transboundary Air Pollution? In: Nordic Council of Ministers. Workshop on Future Needs for Regional Air Pollution Strategies. Copenhagen; Nordic Council of Ministers; pp. 59-64

Bull, Keith (1995): Critical Loads – Possibilities and Constraints. In: Water, Air, and Soil Pollution; No. 85; pp. 201-212

Bull, Keith (1992): An Introduction to Critical Loads. In: Environmental Pollution; No. 77; pp. 173-176

Carnall, Colin A. (1999): Managing Change in Organizations. 3rd ed.; Harlow; Prentice Hall

Clark, William C./R. Mitchell/D. W. Cash/F. Alcock (2002): Information as Influence: How Institutions Mediate the Impact of Scientific Assesessments on International Environmental Affairs. In: Clark/Mitchell/Cash/Alcock (eds.): Global Environmental Assessments: Information, Institutions, and Influence. Cambridge (MA); MIT Press; in review

Clark, William C./Nancy M. Dickson (1999): The Global Environmental Assessment Project: Learning from Efforts to Link Science and Policy in an Interdependent World. In: Acclimations; No. 8; pp. 6-7

Eckley, Noelle (1999): Drawing Lessons About Science-Policy Institutions: Persistent Organic Pollutants (POPs) under the LRTAP Convention. ENRP Discussion Paper E-99-11; Cambridge (MA); Kennedy School of Government, Harvard University

Edwards, Paul N./Stephen H. Schneider (2001): Self-Governance and Peer Review in Science-for-Policy: The Case of the IPCC Second Assessment Report. In: Clark/Edwards (eds.): Changing the Atmosphere: Expert Knowledge and Environmental Governance. Cambridge (MA); MIT Press

Executive Body of the Convention on LRTAP (1999): Report of the Seventeenth Session. Geneva; United Nations; (available at: http://www.unece.org/env/lrtap/conv/report/ebair68.htm)

Franz, Wendy (1998): Science, Skeptics, and Non-State Actors in the Greenhouse. ENRP Discussion Paper E-98-18; Kennedy School of Government, Harvard University

GEA (The Global Environmental Assessment Project) (1997): A Critical Evaluation of Global Environmental Assessments: The Climate Experience. Calverton; CARE

Haas, Ernst B. (1990): When Knowledge is Power. Three Models of Change in International Organizations. Berkeley; University of California Press

Haas, Ernst B. (1991): Collective Learning: Some Theoretical Speculations. In: Breslauer/Tetlock (eds.): Learning in U.S. and Soviet Foreign Policy. Boulder; Westview Press

Haas, Peter/McCabe (2001): Amplifiers or Dampeners: International Institutions and Social Learning in the Management of Global Environmental Risks. In: The Social Learning Group. Learning to Manage Global Environmental Risks: A Comparative History of Social Responses to Climate Change, Ozone Depletion and Acid Rain. Cambridge (MA); MIT Press

Hordijk, Leen (1988): A Model Approach to Acid Rain. In: Environment; Vol. 30; No. 2; pp. 17-42

Houghton, J./L.G. Meira Filho/B.A. Callandar/N. Harris/A. Kattenberg/K. Maskell (eds.) (1996): Climate Change 1995. The Science of Climate Change. Contribution of Working Group I to the Second Assessment Report of the Intergovernmental Panel on Climate Change. Cambridge (NY); Cambridge University Press

IPCC (1992): Report of the 8th Session of the IPCC, Harare, 11-13 November 1992. Geneva; IPCC Secretariat

IPCC (1999): Procedures for the Preparation, Review, Acceptance, Adoption, Approval and Publication of IPCC Reports. Annex to the Report on the 15th Session of the IPCC, San José, 15-18 April 1999; (available at: http://www.ipcc.ch/meet/meet.htm)

Jagusiewicz, Andrzej (1999): The History of the Convention on Long-range Transboundary Air Pollution. In: Pollution Atmosphérique; December; pp. 13-21

Lahsen, Myanna (1998): The Detection and Attribution of Conspiracies: The Controversy over Chapter 8. In: Marcus (ed.): Paranoia within Reason. A Casebook on Conspiracy as Explanation. Chicago; The University of Chicago Press

Lee, Kai (1993): Compass and Gyroscope. Integrating Science and Politics for the Environment. Washington DC; Island Press

Levy, Marc (1993): European Acid Rain: The Power of Tote-Board Diplomacy. In: Haas/Keohane/Levy (eds.): Institutions for the Earth: Sources of Effective International Environmental Protection. Cambridge (MA); MIT Press; pp. 75-132

McCormick, John (1998): Acid Pollution. The International Community's Continuing Struggle. In: Environment; Vol. 40; No. 3; pp. 17-45

McCormick, John (1997): Acid Earth. The Politics of Acid Pollution. London; Earthscan

Moss, Richard (2000): Ready for IPCC-2001: Innovation and Change in Plans for the IPCC Third Assessment Report. In: Climatic Change; No. 45; pp. 459-468

Nordic Council of Ministers (2000): Workshop on Future Needs for Regional Air Pollution Strategies. Copenhagen; Nordic Council of Ministers

NRC (National Research Council – Board on Sustainable Development) (1999): Our Common Journey. A Transition toward Sustainability. Washington DC; National Academy Press

Parson, Edward/William C. Clark (1995): Sustainable Development as Social Learning: Theoretical Perspectives and Practical Challenges for the Design of a Research Program. In: Gunderson/Holling/Light (eds.): Barriers and Bridges to the Renewal of Ecosystems and Institutions. New York; Columbia University Press

Patt, Anthony (1998): Analytic Frameworks and Politics: The Case of Acid Rain in Europe. ENRP Discussion Paper E-98-20. Cambridge (MA); Kennedy School of Government, Harvard University

Primo, Juan Carlos di (1998): Data Quality and Compliance Control in the European Air Pollution Regime. In: Victor/Raulstiala/Skolnikoff (eds.): The Implementation and Effectiveness of International Environmental Commitments: Theory and Practice. Cambridge (MA); MIT Press; pp. 283-303

Probst, Gilbert/Bettina Büchel (1997): Organizational Learning. The Competitive Advantage of the Future. London, New York; Prentice Hall

Schreyögg, Georg (ed.) (2000): Organisatorischer Wandel und Transformation. Wiesbaden; Gabler

Schreyögg, Georg (1999): Organisation. Grundlagen moderner Organisationsgestaltung. 3rd ed.; Wiesbaden; Gabler

Schwandt, David R./Michael J. Marquard (2000). Organizational Learning. From World-Class Theories to Global Best Practices. Boca Raton; St. Lucie Press

Senge, Peter (1990): The Fifth Discipline. The Art and Practice of the Learning Organization. New York; Doubleday

Siebenhüner, Bernd (2002a): How do Scientific Assessments Learn? Part 1. Conceptual framework and case study of the IPCC. In: Environmental Science & Policy; Vol. 5; pp. 411–420

Siebenhüner, Bernd (2002b): How do scientific assessments learn? Part 2. Case study of the LRTAP assessments and comparative conclusions. In: Environmental Science & Policy; Vol. 5; pp. 421–427

Swanson, Timothy/Sam Johnston (1999): Global Environmental Problems and International Environmental Agreements. Cheltenham; Edward Elgar

The Social Learning Group (2001): Learning to Manage Global Environmental Risks: A Comparative History of Social Responses to Climate Change, Ozone Depletion and Acid Rain. Cambridge (MA); MIT Press

Tuinstra, Willemijn/Leen Hordijk/Markus Amann (1999): Using Computer Models in International Negotiations. The Case of Acidification in Europe. In: Environment; Vol. 41; No. 9; pp. 33-42

UNECE (1999): Future Priorities. Note by the Bureau. Geneva: Executive Body for the Convention on Long-range Transboundary Air Pollution; EB.AIR/1997/3

UNECE (1979): Convention on Long-range Transboundary Air Pollution. Geneva; United Nations

VanDeveer, Stacy D. (1998): European Politics with a Scientific Face: Transition Countries, International Environmental Assessment, and Long-Range Transboundary Air Pollution. ENRP Discussion Paper E-98-09. Cambridge (MA); Kennedy School of Government, Harvard University

Watson, Robert T/Ian R. Noble/Bert Bolin/N.H. Ravindranath/David J. Verardo/David J. Dokken (2000): Land Use, Land-Use Change, and Forestry. Cambridge, New York; Cambridge University Press

Watson, Robert T. (1997): White Paper on the Third Assessment Report and the IPCC Bureau, Annex to the Report of the 12th Session of the IPCC Bureau, Geneva, 3-5 February 1997

Anita Engels and Timothy Moss

Institutional Change in Environmental Contexts[1]

1 Introduction

To come a full circle we return, in this concluding chapter, to the title of the book: "How Institutions Change – Perspectives on Social Learning in Global and Local Environmental Contexts". It is now time to summarise our responses to the central questions: How *do* institutions change? How *can* we induce dynamics of social learning? What *have* we learned about institutional change in global and local environmental contexts? Drawing on the conclusions from the various case studies and disciplinary perspectives presented in this book we bring together some broad lines of argument and suggest research and policy implications.

This book has focussed on institutions through which human beings interact with their natural environment. Some institutions are specialised in regulating these interactions, other institutions do not particularly address environmental concerns but heavily influence the way resources are used or pollution is generated. As Mitchell mentions in his paper, while far from all of the specialised "environmental institutions" actually affect and improve environmental quality, processes such as technological development and economic globalisation affect environmental quality on a much broader scale, and often in a detrimental way. Environmental problems or environmental institutions thus cannot be treated in isolation; they are bound up with other policy fields and realms of social practice. Environmental problems require us to seek wide-ranging, complex institutional arrangements, and frequently they raise issues of fairness, equity and legitimacy central to institutions in general. However, environmental research is particularly instructive on the interdependency of global and local policy fields. The environmental problems we address require policy solutions not just at the international or national levels but in particular at regional and local levels. It is at the sub-national level that the need for guidance in resolving conflicts of interest over resource use is often very great. The institutional arrangements we analyse are correspondingly wide-ranging and include multi-level arrangements and the vertical interplay between institutions at different policy levels and different "layers" of social practice. In this sense, our book deals with a group of (environ-

---

1 These conclusions are the outcome of group discussions in the task force and inputs from individual authors. For all their help we are very grateful.

mental) institutions in (environmental) contexts that share some common aspects which make them special to a certain degree. Nevertheless, many of the lessons on institutional change – its major impacts, limitations, driving forces etc. – can be applied more generally to institutions and institutional change in other contexts as well.

Our conclusions will be organised around two ways of reading the book. The first follows the chronological order of the book and identifies lessons which can be learned in each of the three main sections. The second will provide cross-cutting analysis and follow questions of general concern which were raised in the book's introduction. In this way we hope to generate research and policy implications which transcend the contributions by individual authors.

2 Institutional Change, Social Practice and Social Learning – Findings from the Research

Part I: Reshaping Institutions

All the papers in the first section of the book refer to policy-driven forms of institutional change. They discuss examples which were deliberately designed to alter behaviour of individual and collective actors: international environmental regimes, specific national and international programmes of forest management, the spatial reorganisation of water management regimes in the EU and attempts to introduce sustainability criteria into regular market institutions in the case of coffee production standards. They all involve changes to formal institutions such as laws, market regulations and intergovernmental agreements. Each of these institutional solutions provides *innovative* attempts to redesign institutions. That is, they are already expressions of *earlier* learning processes, such as new governance forms, more holistic instruments, more far-reaching goals, new spatial units, new actor constellations, new forms of intergovernmental cooperation, market instruments etc. International solutions to environmental problems are not new, but more recent international environmental institutions represent innovative forms of institutional design, showing greater sensibility towards national institutions and reliance on scientific assessments for instance (Young 1998; Heinelt et al. 2001). The EU Water Framework Directive has been celebrated by many as an outstanding new approach because it strengthens the river basin as the appropriate territorial unit of water management, following an ecosystem logic of spatial organisation. Likewise, the introduction of environmental production standards seeks to overcome the perceived antagonism between economic and environmental goals and to create a new synthesis. Yet, all examples also show specific problems that occur even in the most innovative attempts to design formal institutions. We group the most important ones together as problems of fit and problems of interplay (cf. IDGEC Science Plan in Young 1999).

Problems of fit concern the relationship between institutions and the spatial, geographic or political extension or distribution of the respective environmental problem. One of the most obvious problems of fit is a transboundary pollution problem which states or regions seek to address individually, without taking into account the sources of the problem external to their national or regional boundaries. International environmental regimes usually respond to this problem. However, as Mitchell shows, it is often very difficult to include all responsible parties into one regime or to enforce compliance by all parties. Even if these institutions effectively influence state behaviour, it is in no way guaranteed that this also affects environmental quality. Addressing the right environmental unit is thus of crucial importance for the *environmental* effectiveness of an institution. In the case of coffee productions standards (Dünckmann and Mayer), the unit which is expected to adapt to the standards is the single farm. However, ecological problems of coffee production are felt at a regional level, a much broader geographical unit not encompassed by most production standards. Extending the geographical remit of the market institution to fit that of coffee production – for instance linking ecological farms with each other in order to identify and develop ecologically healthy regions instead of creating eco-islands – is crucial to ensuring environmental effectiveness.

The example shows a second type of problem of fit: Institutions should not only fit with the physical or material environment, but also with the socio-economic system with which they interact. In this sense, characteristics of the coffee market, i.e. consumption and production patterns, have to be considered when establishing environmental production standards. Ecological production standards are introduced to help protecting the environment. But participants in the coffee trade adopt these standards only if they see advantages in competition, e.g. a new way to achieve higher prices or new marketing channels. If a standard fails to offer these market advantages to every part of the coffee commodity chain, it will not be successful.

The example of the EU Water Framework Directive demonstrates this even more dramatically (Moss). Even though the Framework Directive can be seen as a successful outcome of the search for a better spatial fit between an ecosystem and an institutional regime, river basin management runs the risk of overlooking problems of wider socio-political fit. Incompatibilities between different territorial units of governance need to be acknowledged which can give rise to problems of legitimisation and accountability, and fresh mismatches with other policy fields relevant to water management. The example shows the need to consider the territorial unit of the river basin in a broader context of overlapping social, economic, political and physical spaces.

Institutional arrangements need to reflect the complexity of the interdependencies of biophysical and socio-economic systems. This seems to be a clear and simple lesson. However, the discussion of the Water Framework Directive takes us further in problematising the search for the 'right' solution in general, which implies there is one to be 'found'. The apparent simplicity of the ecosystem logic of river basin management is suggestive of a comparatively simple organisational 'fix', but the paper reveals limitations of transposing ecosystem logics to institutional arrangements. As was shown, the focus on ecosystem logics can also distract attention from socio-economic and cultural dimensions which are of equal importance for the effectiveness of institutions. Rather than searching for 'the' (evasive) solution – or applying a blueprint – it makes more sense to comprehend institutional change as a framing process in which different frames of reference or logics assert themselves against or in conjunction with one another (cf. Häder/Niebaum 1997).

Problems of interplay concern more directly the relationship between different institutions or different institutional levels. We have distinguished between problems of vertical and horizontal interplay. Both concern boundary problems, as with problems of fit. However, instead of addressing the boundary between an institution and the environmental resource it seeks to regulate or to protect, this type of boundary problem centres around boundaries between an institution and other institutions, i.e. jurisdictional or administrative boundaries. The examples highlight the importance of emerging boundary problems in attempts to design and implement institutional change from above because it is often along these fault-lines that institutional arrangements can come unstuck. We need to be able to identify – preferably in advance – where areas of overlap and interdependency exist, what issues are contentious and what steps might be taken to improve the relational links.

Problems of horizontal interplay often relate to cross-sectoral policy integration, as is important for many of the more complex environmental problems. A straightforward example would be the difficult integration and harmonisation of water management and agricultural policies, where efforts undertaken in one domain often counteract efforts in the other (Newson 1997; Lowe et al. 1997). The example of coffee production standards reveals more fundamental interplay between state and market networks, illustrating the importance of government for market institutions. The concept of interplay should thus not only be viewed as a potential problem. In the case of market based standards, the market is not able to establish effective environmental institutions on its own because of its internal logic which lacks incentives to avoid free-riding. In this case we need effective interplay with legislation. Interestingly, proponents of the ecological sector of the coffee market actively called for government intervention to regulate the eco-market.

Problems of vertical interplay abound in the case studies discussed in this section. They address the general question of institutional change 'from above', which is often fraught with problems (cf. Ostrom 1990). Sensitivity is needed for the applicability of new policy styles to existing institutional arrangements at subordinate levels. The EU Water Framework Directive serves as an example for institutional change induced 'from above' and shows how high expectations of changes initiated by a peak regime can be problematic. Yet, the attempt by the Water Framework Directive to induce institutional change and to harmonise European water policy was widely welcomed by the 'institution bearers', even in Germany where required adaptation was particularly great. The Framework Directive was seen as having an innovative effect, arguably owing to the emphasis placed on procedural mechanisms for greater cross-sectoral and trans-boundary cooperation and for offering new leverage for water managers over other policy fields. This indicates a hidden adaptability of even well entrenched formal institutions where the interests of the key players can be protected or furthered within an altered policy framework. Forest management has become a pioneering field in the creation of policy networks designed to overcome problems of vertical interplay (Obser). The emergence and development of a number of international and national policy initiatives and instruments since the mid-1980s have contributed some innovative forms of multi-level and multi-stakeholder environmental governance. Despite scepticism at the prospects for major changes emerging from international collaboration, efforts to transcend the divide between national and international forest policies are showing some positive effects. Recent initiatives by an informal forum of advisors from the major international organisations (IFAG) and two groups of pro-active governments have made a significant impact in influencing the attitudes and habits of the relevant states in the absence of a legally-binding forestry convention. An important key to their relative success in achieving innovative and credible policy commitments can be attributed to building up a network of expert communities at both international and national levels beyond the immediate remit of UN organisations. The crucial question of acceptance and its influence on the environmental effectiveness of institutions was also raised in the example of coffee production standards. Very strict (high impact) standards for coffee production were only adopted in some isolated farms that form eco-islands without any real ecological impact. Weaker standards – with seemingly less direct ecological impact – have a greater potential of contributing to sustainability on a broader scale, as more farms are able to adopt these standards.

If we try to link problems of (spatial) fit to problems of horizontal and vertical interplay, we are able to generate a more complete picture of problems of induced changes. Solving problems of fit at the local or regional levels is complicated by hierarchical dependencies (problems of vertical interplay) and the 'messiness' of interdependency with practices of other policy fields at the operational level (problems of horizontal interplay). Coping with multiple institutional layers is the most obvious form of complexity which makes it difficult to isolate individual dimensions for redesign. Existing institutions at all levels show a remarkable variance in their degree of adaptability to changes.

Understanding these problems and anticipating typical barriers and faultlines in redesigning formal institutions is a necessary step to improving our institutional capacities for solving environmental problems. However, it is only a first step which leaves many questions unanswered. The analysis of formal institutions is subject to inherent limitations. Policy-driven efforts to change existing institutional arrangements embody particular assumptions about how institutions change and how the bearers and addressees of institutions are likely to respond to pressures for change. Yet the institutional designers themselves are often unable to predict responses or offer explanations for success or failure of institutional reform. They are often surprised about the unintended consequences of induced institutional changes. These explanatory factors constitute for many a black box, the internal dynamics and workings of which remain hidden. Both practitioners and analysts of formal institutions often overlook the importance of processes inside this black box. To researchers of informal institutions, however, understanding what goes on within this black box takes centre stage. In the second part of this book the authors have tried to reveal some of the internal workings in order to broaden our conceptual understanding of how institutions change.

Part II: Linking Institutional Change to Social Practice

Whereas Part I analyses policy-driven institutional change and the problems often encountered in this endeavour Part II widens the perspective and explores the root causes of such problems in order to explain the reasons for unintended negative effects and for successful intended effects of deliberate institutional change (for a conceptual overview see Clemens/Cook 1999). The focus shifts onto informal institutions and the interactions between formal and informal institutions at different social, political and cultural levels. The aim was to provide building blocks for a better understanding of problems associated with institutional change and to highlight the value of informal institutions. The papers in Part II can all be readily ascribed to social-practice models of institutional analysis, as defined by Young (2002:29-51). In contrast to collective-action models, which treat actors as decision makers basing their choices on utilitarian calculations, social-practice models emphasise the role of culture, norms and habits as sources of behaviour. This is reflected in assumptions made about the identity and character of relevant actors, the sources of actor behaviour and the extent to which actors are affected by social constraints (Young 2002:32). Thus social-practice models look beyond policy makers to nongovernmental organisations, corporations and individuals, they highlight the importance of discourses and role definitions in shaping behaviour and explain social action as a factor of forces which transcend the maximisation of net benefits (see also Douglas/Ney 1999).

A leading hypothesis of Part II was that problems of implementation and lack of institutional effectiveness often lie in the incompatibility (misfit) between formal and informal institutions, or between rules and social practice. That presupposes the concept of embeddedness of formal institutions in informal ones. The idea of institutional embeddedness in more general terms has been advanced most prominently by Granovetter who demonstrated the influence of various institutional factors on the seemingly straight-forward and unambiguous organisation of capitalist economies (Granovetter 1985). Multiple forms of embeddedness are discussed in the literature, often referring to the relationship between rather technical or instrumental organisational structures and their institutional context (Dacin, Ventresca and Beal 1999). In the context of this book, we apply the concept rather to the embeddedness of formal institutions in norms, value systems, ideas and worldviews. One way to reformulate this, and to establish a link between institutions and social practice, is to say that informal institutions generate particular "ways of seeing" and "ways of speaking", which themselves broadly shape our established "ways of doing", another term for social practice. This is explored with studies of social practice, informal institutions and their interaction with formal institutions at three different levels of social organisation, each one analysed from a different disciplinary perspective.

Societal discourses are at the centre of the contribution by Engels on the institutionalisation of risk perceptions. The analysis starts with ways of speaking (discourses) and their dependence on ways of seeing (world views and risk perceptions). Both can be seen as framing options for ways of doing, in this case for developing societal responses to the global threat of man-made climate change. Risk perceptions are defined here as informal institutions in which both formal institutions and social practice need to be embedded in order to be accepted as legitimate options. The study of climate change discourses illustrates how the stabilisation of a common risk perception in one country supported the successful development of a national policy on climate change based on this dominant risk perception. However, the attempt to transfer the successful national solution to the level of international environmental regimes failed or proved difficult because of competing risk perceptions in other countries. The paper shows how national differences in the informal institutional foundations of formal institutions and social practice can be used to explain why, in the international arena, conflicts over the right way to deal with climate change emerged and prevailed. The paper thus highlights the need for mechanisms of mutual recognition and exchange to overcome deadlock constellations.

Breit et al. pursue the question of how actors come to act on behalf of environmental protection. They focus on ways of doing (social practice) and reconstruct the embeddedness of these ways of doing in ways of seeing (justice judgements). All this takes place at the level of individual actorhood. A typology of justice judgements is used to differentiate between heteronomous and autonomous moral orientations on the one hand, and between an interpersonal and transpersonal way of interpreting social reality. They come to the conclusion that differences in justice judgements result in variations in the willingness to take personal responsibility for ecological remedial action. Thus the interpersonal-heteronomous type gladly delegates responsibility to politicians and those in authority. The interpersonal-autonomous type, by contrast, distrusts formal institutions and relies instead on solidarity and cooperation between local actors to solve common problems jointly. The transpersonal-heteronomous type attributes responsibility rather to experts, relying on the rationality of formal institutions. The fourth type – transpersonal-autonomous – stresses the need for interaction between the political arena of formal institutions and the informal norms played out in civil society. The central argument of Breit et al. is that personal responsibility is required at every institutional level possible, whether it is the expert working in a regulatory institution or the citizen or the consumer. Moreover, their typology transcends the level of individual actorhood and elucidates formulas and patterns of argumentation used in discourses at the level of civil society. In this sense, the authors show how formal democratic institutions need to be understood as being rooted in informal institutions.

The article by Widlok provides a third perspective in which a particular institution in a local setting is dissected and the different societal and individual layers as well as social practice are reconstructed in interaction with each other. It uses a case study of a property regime of the Topnaar in Namibia to critically appraise the strict differentiation between institutional regimes – in this case of private and public property – that is frequently taken for granted by policy makers, demonstrating how this fails to capture the complexities of locally instituted practices. The Topnaar harvest and trade a wild cucurbit and have increasingly been under ecological, political and economic pressures which have contributed to changes in their property institutions. The argument is made that more generally our assumptions about how institutions work and change only inadequately capture the institutional dynamics encountered locally, in particular outside highly bureaucratic settings. The article suggests that local institutional dynamics become more visible when institutions are analysed as consisting of a number of interacting layers. Instead of categorising institutions as amorphous wholes or packages this approach helps to identify various formal and informal aspects that make up all institutions at work in a particular place. Dissecting an institution into these aspects, here understood as layers of values, regulations, relations and actions, also helps to reconceptualise institutional change. It is suggested that conceptualising institutional change in terms of interacting layers is more productive than to think of it in terms of competition between two (or more) institutional packages. The layered model allows us to trace institutional changes that originate either from changes in cultural values and regulations or from changes in social relations and actions. It also allows us to see that there can be inbuilt contradictions in institutional arrangements that undergo different changes at the various layers. This is true for the property regime of the Topnaar where strong group-centred identification with the local natural resources is maintained while relations between owners, harvesters and traders have undergone irreversible changes and actions by individuals have adapted markedly in response to changing environmental conditions.

To summarise, the contributions in this section analysed conditions of institutional stabilisation and destabilisation as a basis for new and innovative forms of social practice. They did not directly intend to provide solutions, but to shed light on where answers to questions of social learning might be found. Following on from this, the task of part III of the book has been to explore ways of improving these conditions systematically and demonstrating how social learning can contribute to more effective environmental institutions.

Part III: Institutionalising Social Learning

Part III returns to the issue of managing institutional change, but focuses on ways of embedding social learning into institution-building processes. The examples reflect both cases of successful social learning and cases where learning has not taken place in any important way. The absence of learning is of equal importance for the purpose of this section. It seeks to identify conditions under which social learning can occur (or is unlikely to occur) and how these can be promoted or strengthened; that is, finding ways of building institutional capacity which reflect an understanding of the importance of social practice to institutional effectiveness. What procedures and mechanisms can create favourable conditions for effective institutions to develop? How can they contribute to institutional capacity-building? The papers contributing to this part of the book address certain actor skills as the most basic enabling conditions. The capacities of individual actors to identify environmental problems, shoulder responsibility for acting, take decisions, deal with conflicts etc. are a necessary precondition for successfully managing institutional change. However, individual actors can more successfully make use of their capacities if the surrounding communicative structures allow them to do so. An enabling institutional setting is needed for environmentally sound social practice to emerge. Yet this, as well, can be inadequate if actors lack political influence or if their initiatives are at odds with political objectives, structures or procedures. Suitable institutional settings therefore also depend on issues of power and influence. Actor skills, communicative structures and power structures are thus central concepts in this part of the book.

Several papers stress the importance of *actor skills*, referring specifically to openness towards other perspectives, reflective capacities and specific communicative skills. Sandner addresses a case of institution-building where actor skills are central: a local resource management system in an indigenous group in Central America. The Kuna people of Panama serve as an example of a traditional society responding to increasing pressure on resources by creating their own formal institutions following western examples such as closed fishing seasons. The specific combination of respect and appreciation of ones own traditional culture and openness to innovations such as international paradigms of resource protection (sustainability) and certain examples of formal institutions (formal laws including financial sanctions) allow for new institutional designs. In such cases, the social capital (Ostrom 1990) in an indigenous society can be substantial enough for local institutions to be created even without outside help, contrary to the assumptions of so-called co-management approaches.

Siebenhüner shows how learning processes by individuals helped improve the quality of scientific assessments for addressing both climate change and transboundary air pollution. The example of the Intergovernmental Panel on Climate Change (IPCC) revealed in particular how an assessment procedure can rely heavily on the individual personalities involved and thus how, in addition to all the contextual and structural factors, the personal commitment and motivation of scientists can be important in keeping the assessment process alive. In the second example on the Convention on Long-Range Transboundary Air Pollution (LRTAP) Convention, scientists learned to think strategically in their interactions with policy-makers and, more generally, adapted to the rules of decision-making in the context of controversial (environmental) policies. In spite of these findings Siebenhüner leaves no room for doubt that communicative and power structures clearly determine the chances of success and failure of scientific assessments, however capable individual researchers or policy-makers involved in the process prove to be. Rather than an absolute increase in knowledge (which can be known and applied by individuals), social learning would in this instance mean changes in the communication structure of assessments in order to render them more salient, more credible and more legitimate.

The paper by Troja, exploring social learning in a very different arena of localised environmental conflicts, similarly observes the importance of communication skills and the structures which support them. He observes how, on the one hand, communication skills become a relevant factor in face-to-face-situations and, on the other, where *communication structures* help channel emerging conflicts and deal with them constructively. Discursive designs and professionally facilitated communication processes enhance negotiated solutions between policy makers, different sectors of administration (cross-sectoral policy integration) and addressees with different interests. The communication structures in mediation processes support competence-building for all these actors by bringing together relevant expert and local knowledge. It is shown that the power of language and argumentation can change interests, as well as how environmental issues are defined and perceived. Actors establish new forms of communication in a specific field of political and social life and a new culture of conflict.

To return to the Kuna example (Sandner), it is important to note that a culture of discourse and openness are traditionally important features of Kuna society which allow the discussion and resolution of environmental problems on a local scale. However, the example also demonstrates that more fundamental *power structures* often account for the effectiveness of institutional change. In this case, rule enforcement as part of the resource management regime is possible due to strong social control in a traditional society. One of the most important conditions is the strong political autonomy of the Kuna and the recognition of their exclusive rights to territory and resources by the Panamanian state. This autonomous status allows the complete exclusion of competing outside users. This poses a major threat to resources in other indigenous groups such as the Miskito of Eastern Nicaragua where local decision-makers have no means to control the excessive resource use by national and transnational companies. The evolution of local self-determination and control over resources allows for the creation of solutions on a local scale, independent of national policies.

In Troja's account of negotiated rulemaking the embeddedness of mediation procedures in the wider political-administrative framework is an important precondition for social learning to take place at a level beyond individual mediation. Wherever it is possible to implement the results of negotiated solutions, individual cases can be part of broader policy-learning at the macro level. This requires, however, strong links between the level of face-to-face negotiations and the level of formal decision-making in relevant policy fields. Such links are not widely evident, though, as decision makers – that is, the key-players in the context of formal legal, administrative and political institutions – often fear the de-stabilisation of these institutions and related informal procedures like lobbying. Some aspects of power structures even vary in a systematic way, as the example of cross-national variations in the legal and administrative status of negotiated rulemaking in Troja's paper shows. These specific features hinder or strengthen capacities for conflict resolution. In the USA, some positive experiences were gained with the formal institutionalisation of mediation laws to establish cooperative procedures as a form of social learning. The EU is also discussing regulations supporting alternative dispute resolution procedures in the field of civil and commercial rights. In Germany, by contrast, such laws are not yet in sight. The results of this paper show that a loose coupling between formal and informal institutions can have very favourable results. Formal institutionalisation, however, undermines those capacities for social learning that are based on the informal and case-specific communication process.

Huber's contribution on EU environmental policy making reveals yet another limiting or restricting aspect of power structures. His case study takes into account decade-long time spans for the analysis of issue development at the EU. The central question of his paper is to what extent learning processes can be observed from one policy issue to another. His results warn us to be sceptical of the learning potential in the EU. Surprisingly little learning was observed: cross-issue fertilisations occurred in rare cases but did not change the overall evolutionary patterns of the policy process. Environmental policy making slowly improved over time, but no leapfrogging could be achieved. Most importantly, it was not possible to institutionalise the incremental improvements at a more formalised level. Huber explains how the specific power structures within the European Union enforce a perspective of equity and fairness. As a consequence, environmental policy making at the EU is not evaluated for its environmental effectiveness, and policy development is to some extent an end in itself.

All the examples in this section call for a discursive and reflexive design of institutions. Crucial for the success of institutionalising social learning are, among others, the existence and promotion of certain actor skills, the creation of enabling communication structures and an acknowledgement of existing power structures which can be both restrictive (as in the EU example) and constructive (in the case of the Kunas' political autonomy). It is therefore important to, first, identify – and respond to – barriers at all levels of social organisation. Secondly, it is crucial to identify strengths of existing institutions, formal and informal alike, and to build on them and regard them as useful resources. These two strategies imply, thirdly, that blueprints for institutional design should be avoided. The idea of the perfect institutional fit should be substituted by a more process-oriented understanding of context-specific institution building.

3   Research and Policy Implications – a Cross-Cutting Analysis

The purpose of this section is to draw from across all three parts of the book general lessons for both policy and research communities. We shed more light on two central distinctions which have been made in many of the individual contributions throughout the book: first, the analytical distinction between formal and informal institutions, and second, the more process-oriented distinction between intended and unintended change. We then aim at a reflection on the relationship between institutions and social practice, followed by a more systematic view of different scales of institutionalisation. Finally, we try to define pathways of social learning, bringing together the lessons on relevant conditions for, and mechanisms of, social learning which are provided by the range of case studies in this book.

Formal/informal institutions: A central conclusion of this book is that the embeddedness of formal in informal institutions is a fact of utmost relevance for (environmental) policy making and institutional design. In Moss' case study on the EU Water Framework Directive the positive response of water managers to the institutionalisation of river basin management even in those countries with little administrative experience of it indicates the prevalence of the concept as an informal institution in professional circles. Resistance to far-reaching reform of existing organisational structures in Germany demonstrates also, though, the strength of other informal institutions, such as the sense of identity of water authorities with their political-administrative territories. Conversely, informal institutions function in the shadow of formal institutions. The issue at stake is not more or less embeddedness but striving for a better or more appropriate form of embeddedness. This implies the need for policy makers to recognise the limits to the effectiveness of institutional design on the one hand, and for civil society to acknowledge the dependency of informal arrangements on formal structures and procedures on the other.

The political acceptability of legal control, technological innovation or price control largely depends on whether they are agreed upon or acknowledged by citizens. Breit et al. demonstrate how the willingness of individuals to act and to take responsibility depends on informal institutions, in particular on justice judgements. Instead of trying to minimise the influence of informal institutions it would, therefore, be wise to use them as a resource. From this perspective, the existence of informal institutions does not only explain why policy-driven institutional change often fails to produce the intended outcomes, but it can also explain why in some cases processes of intentional change succeed, as informal institutions provide the normative basis from which formal institutions can unfold their strength. Informal institutions shape risk definitions and processes of discourse and communication, and thus set the framework within which individual acceptance of responsibility and individual commitment can emerge. The contribution by Troja on alternative dispute resolution shows how mediation and negotiation processes combine informal and formal institutions in a new and fruitful way. Expert knowledge and professional capacities of conflict resolution are transferred from an abstract and formal level of political regulation to the level of concrete and face-to-face activities. It also emphasises that specific individual and collective preconditions are needed, such as an openness for communicative and discursive processes. This type of openness is represented in the typology of Breit, Döring and Eckensberger by the so-called autonomous justice perspective.

The distinction between formal and informal institutions is, however, an analytical construct which is useful in some contexts but not valid in all. In practice, formal and informal institutions are interwoven parts of a whole. Furthermore, we can observe how informal procedures can become formalised over time and how an institution may be regarded as informal in one context but have the authority of a formal institution in another, for instance in developing countries. The distinction, therefore, is not rigid over time and space. The EU Water Framework Directive offers an interesting example of how an informal institution – the guiding principle of river basin management – is currently being stabilised into more formal structures and procedures. What originated as a concept in the minds of aquatic ecologists and hydrologists and was subsequently adopted as a basic principle for river basin management in a small number of European countries is now being elevated to a formal institution applicable across the EU.

The distinction between formal and informal institutions is not new, but in political arenas it is often overlooked. We have observed, for instance, how informal institutions are not taken into consideration in the design of formal institutions (see Troja); as a result the formal institutions do not function effectively. Conversely, we have also observed how informal institutions can become sidelined if the actors involved fail to appreciate how the framework of formal institutions can affect their scope for action. Consequently, actors need to learn how to 'play' the formal rules as well as rely on good communication (Breit et al.).

Part of the problem is the tendency – in research and practice – to address formal institutions in certain (political) arenas and informal institutions in other (social) arenas at a 'lower' level of hierarchy. In our research, by contrast, we have noted the operation of informal institutions (e.g. risk perceptions) at national and international levels and the relevance of formal institutions over community disputes. It would be useful to focus less attention on the strict distinction between formal and informal and rather concentrate on how they shape each other. A bottom up-approach which observes and describes the kinds of formal institutions evolving from social practice is but one perspective within the social sciences. Other perspectives are also available. From the perspective of political science, for instance, institutional change needs capacities for managing the interplay between formal institutions, rules, regimes, programmes, policies and regulations on the one hand and the respective informal institutions, social practice, perceptions and perspectives of individual adressees on the other hand. The interplay of formal and informal institutions can be observed very clearly when it comes to open conflict over the introduction of new formal institutions like environmental rules and regulations or the planning and authorisation processes for projects with adverse environmental impacts.

Intended/unintended change: This distinction builds on the notion of the limitations to deliberate institutional design. Institution designers need to reckon with unintended effects and consider them when designing (formal) institutions. The latency of informal institutions often results in unintended changes; likewise, the complexities and interdependencies of multilayer institutional arrangements create a favourable environment for evolutionary or adaptive modes of change rather than revolutionary or strategic changes.

By looking at a particularly long time frame of two decades, the contribution by Engels shows how the inertia and complexity of societal discourses generates unintentional change. Several examples demonstrate the limitations to deliberate institutional change. Scientists had warned of man-made climate change for many years before they could eventually attract the media's and public's attention. Their attempt to wilfully establish a new risk perception on which a public policy to prevent climate change could be based did not automatically yield the planned outcome. It took a long time to become established and even then it developed an unforeseen dynamic. The contribution demonstrates the limitations to attempts to successfully steer media attention or the policy process given the high degree of dependence on too many different factors and contingencies of historic paths. This does of course not mean, however, that intentional action is in vain. In particular it should be recognised that, once a new risk perception is stabilised, it defines legitimate ways of acting. It is then often easy to create issue linkages or to frame newly emerging problems in line with, or in analogy to, existing risk perceptions and problem definitions. Political activists often use this kind of knowledge, tailoring their campaigns to the specific ways of seeing in a given country at a given time.

Procedures need to be installed into institutional arrangements which enable actors to allow for, and respond to, unintended effects; this places greater emphasis on procedural aspects to institutional design. The EU Water Framework Directive deliberately avoids specifying how the environmental objectives should be achieved in each River Basin District. It is up to the authorities within the River Basin District to reach agreement on the measures and procedures required for the task. This has had the interesting effect at an early stage in the implementation process of encouraging these authorities to negotiate closely with colleagues from other states and, in some cases, with representatives from other affected policy fields. An unintended effect of the Framework Directive, it thus appears, has been to promote new forms of governance for water resources, regardless of their ultimate success or failure.

The example of market based institutions raised in the article by Dünckmann and Mayer shows that there are different ways of designing and adapting institutions and of influencing the success or failure of new institutions. On one hand there are institutions of the political sphere, e.g. environmental legislation, that are established in a hierarchical top down procedure. Institutions succeed if they are put into practice and show the intended positive effects. For these cases, participative procedures during the design process and feedback cycles for evaluating the intended and unintended effects of the institutions are of vital importance. On the other hand, institutions such as production standards and environmental labels are subject to the different logic of competition and markets. There are always a number of different but similar standards on the market, and new ones can be introduced to the market at any time. But only those standards that are accepted by producers, traders and consumers are able to survive in a competitive environment and this is not always the best standard (in terms of environmental impact) but the most competitive one.

Here, two lessons deserve a mention. First, unintended consequences of intended change should be taken into account by institution designers. Second, both analysts and institution designers should be open to the potential benefits of unintended changes, as they need not be detrimental to the aim of improving environmental quality.

Institutions and social practice: Institutions are an important source of new forms of social practice and vice versa. Institutions often allow for new "ways of doing" which combine in innovative ways divergent, and sometimes hitherto contradictory, goals or strategies. Positive examples of this enabling role of institutions can be observed in many of the case studies of this book, the creation of a new niche market for sustainable coffee production being one of them. In traditional societies, however, the opposite process can also be observed in institution-building. The traditional holistic view of man's relationship with the environment as it is reflected in traditional institutions such as taboos or sacred space (being a mix of social, spiritual and nature-related values deeply rooted in culture) is increasingly being fragmented into separate fields of interest. New formal institutions developed in traditional societies often address single resource problems. In the case of the Kuna (Sandner), a separate field of environmental policy has never existed, because the "environment" is traditionally regarded as one component of the inseparable unity of man with his cosmological and spiritual worldview. There, the earth is seen not only as the provider of resources for survival but as the basis of culture and existence of man. In recent responses to environmental problems, however, the "environment" is coming to exist as a separate field of discourse, action and policy, being dealt with by specialists and being regulated by isolated formal institutions.

These examples show how institutions open up opportunities for social practice while closing down others. In her contribution on environmental discourses Engels argues that risk perceptions are necessarily selective, i.e. each positive selection of certain risks addressed by society necessarily produces blind spots. However, a social learning perspective helps to identify some types of blind spots as weaknesses in the attempt to regulate man-environment interactions in a more sustainable way. Huber, for instance, shows that the evolution of the climate change and acid rain issue in the EU follows a pattern that is systematically blind to the criteria of efficiency and effectiveness. Likewise, the Kuna in Sandner's contribution lack awareness for pollution, even though they are an indigenous society which sees itself as the source and guardian of a highly sophisticated environmental protection regime. Some environmental problems are simply not perceived by the Kuna. This is due to a lack of information on the possible consequences and to their self-identification as guardians of "mother nature" which can blind them to locally produced environmental degradation.

The importance of institutions for social practice is, however, not a one-way relationship. Social practice can equally inspire the creation of new institutions. Sometimes social practice can turn into routinised behaviour and therefore achieve the status of a stabilised institution, or it can be important in the sense of keeping institutions alive. The case of labelled coffee (Dünckmann and Mayer) shows how closely institutions depend on social practice. Obviously the success of a coffee production standard depends on consumer choices to buy labelled coffee. Institutional effectiveness depends on corresponding social practice. Participatory forms of social practice have a specific potential to trigger institutional change, as is argued in several contributions (Troja; Breit et al.). However, not all social practice is of course the source of change towards more sustainable environmental institutions. Other examples also reveal how social practice can turn detrimental, causing considerable environmental damage and thus creating a need for institutional change. The overuse of natural resources as demonstrated in the contributions by Sandner and by Widlok can serve as examples for this kind of interaction.

Different scales of institutionalisation: This book discusses institutions on different spatial scales, ranging from a global or international scale via the national and regional down to the local scale. There are several systematic differences between the local and global scales. The papers in this volume have drawn particular attention to the issue of political representation and legitimisation. At the local level the affected actors are more likely to be able to develop effective communication within the group, but often fail to integrate key players or to embed their own arrangements within broader formalised – and politically or administratively recognised – procedures and structures. At the international level decision-makers are more frequently included;

here the problem is rather one of lack of acceptance of the results. This simple observation serves to highlight the importance of recognising the suitability of different kinds of institutional arrangements at different scales of social practice. The differences apply not just to institutions as static rule systems but also to processes of institutional change. The papers in this volume have demonstrated how the driving forces for institutional change vary across different scales and also how the responsiveness of institutions to change varies in speed and intensity at different spatial and organisational levels. Scale-specific approaches to institutional change could help target better arenas where improvements are needed most and assist the encouragement of more suitable institutions.

A closer look at the local scale allows additional insights on environmental institutions. In many concrete local contexts it is difficult to identify institutions as "environmental institutions". Even where this identification is possible, there is still partial overlap with other institutions that may, at first sight, have nothing to do with human-environment interactions. Taking an approach based on analytical layers (Widlok) it is easy to envisage how a clear environmental connection with regard to one layer (e.g. that of cultural values or regulations) can go together with apparently non-environmental aspects dominating the other layers (e.g. that of social relations over trade). Consequently, changes can be triggered through aspects that may – initially – have nothing to do with human-environment interactions. Similarly, institutional changes may be prevented or skewed in non-intended directions because there are bridges at some layer between an environmental institution and other institutions. Again with regard to the Namibian case study, traditional leadership is an example of an institution where at the layer of cultural regulations a strong bridge with the institutional practices of resource use and allocation exists.

Many environmental problems cannot be understood if they are analysed at one isolated scale only. Accordingly, searching for institutional innovations to address these problems mostly involves the complex interplay of different scales. The identification of effective environmental institutions on one scale leads to the question of up-scaling or down-scaling this particular institutional arrangement. In institutional analysis the focus of attention commonly lies on the difficulties of implementing institutional innovation top-down. Several examples in this book show, conversely, how the stabilisation of locally effective institutions can jeopardise the stabilisation of institutions at 'higher' scales which are nevertheless essential for coping with transboundary or crossboundary external effects. An important result of the book is that the interactions between different institutional scales should be seen as a dynamic process in which mutual stabilisations and destabilisations emerge. This dynamic offers windows of opportunity for making institutions more environmentally effective.

Pathways of social learning: One of the principal purposes of this book has been to use the concept of social learning in order to elucidate a broader picture of how institutions change (see also The Social Learning Group 2001a, 2001b; Mann 1990). The aim was to avoid a deterministic understanding of institutional change, as a series of rationalist responses to performance deficiencies, and to include reflections on the reasons for institutional failure and on possible options for improvements in the equation. Social learning entails a feedback process in which the bearers and/or addressees of institutions assess the past impact of institutional arrangements and adapt their own actions accordingly. This learning process can occur at all levels of social organisation, as the variety of settings covered by the papers demonstrates. Social learning can be deliberately nurtured to improve capacities for conflict resolution. Equally, it can develop unintended with unpredictable results. As several papers have stressed, social learning can have a detrimental, as well as a beneficial, impact on the way people use environmental resources, for instance as a way of circumventing compliance. For this reason its value for improving environmental institutions should not be idealised. The prospects and problems of social learning as a form of institutional change have been analysed for a range of environmental contexts. This has resulted in an array of diverse forms and settings of social learning suitable to improving institutions pertinent to environmental protection. But have we been able to identify particular patterns of social learning which are more favourable than others? Can we recommend particular pathways of social learning? It has not been the purpose of this book to be prescriptive. The premature state of knowledge and the complexity of processes of institutional change prohibit recommendations of this kind. We can observe, however, certain key characteristics to the examples of social learning covered in the book.

The first and most pertinent characteristic of the observed social learning processes is a general openness to change. Examples have discussed this openness at the level of individual actors and their willingness to accept innovations, to cooperate and to communicate with others who differ in fundamental ways from one's own position or from one's own way of seeing environmental problems. Likewise, openness and flexibility at more aggregate levels of social organisation are important facilitators. As Siebenhüner mentions, in-built flexibility in the institutional arrangement allows for more revolutionary changes, whereas less flexibility more often leads to adaptation and incrementalism as the dominant pattern of change. Several contributions have demonstrated the importance of this point in international negotiations and the design of international environmental regimes.

The second characteristic is the overarching role of conflicts, over the use of natural resources as well as over divergent or even contradictory institutional solutions and alternative development paths. We cannot hope to have one harmonised understanding of the world which is valid for every social and cultural scale – nature is irreducibly contested (Macnaghten/Urry 1998). The book has illustrated this with many contributions. Some have highlighted conflicts between institutions typical of highly industrialised OECD countries and those of their low-income developing country counterparts. Others have emphasised conflicts between different institutional levels, between nation-states or between groups of individuals. The important question is thus how to make use of conflicts in processes of issue evolution, political decision making and institutional change in general or, in other words, how to establish institutional procedures and mechanisms to make social learning possible. Participation, representation and political autonomy have been discussed as crucial elements to channel conflicts, negotiate (partial) solutions and develop constructive ways of dealing with conflicts in order to avoid deadlock situations.

These arguments have, thirdly, led to a broader understanding of institutional effectiveness and performance. Processes of social learning are often defined as a gain in institutional effectiveness, and induced institutional change is expected to yield the desired outcome or impact on the environment (see examples in Haas et al. 1993). However, many contributions have taught us also to take into account indirect or secondary effects, unintended outcomes and more fundamental changes at the level of informal institutions. Many learning processes are accompanied by costly experiments, delays and detours and might look slow and ambiguous in their results. However, in the long run, they may still prove more efficacious than seemingly straightforward efforts of induced institutional change.

4 Concluding Remarks

Much institutional change is needed to achieve a more sustainable future in local and global environmental contexts. This book has discussed evolutionary and adaptive patterns of change as well as revolutionary or more disruptive ones. The perspective on processes of social learning has prompted us to look systematically for mechanisms and root causes of changes and to strive for a broader and deeper understanding of institutional dynamics. Using a common language ("institutionalese") has helped us to achieve cross-disciplinary synergies and to develop a set of questions to which we generated at least some answers. Even though we cannot provide blueprint solutions and fireproof design knowledge we hope that the common language also facilitates the communication of our results beyond the realm of social science research in academia – both to natural scientists and to practitioners in the field.

References

Clemens, Elisabeth S./James M. Cook (1999): Politics and Institutionalism: Explaining Durability and Change. In: Annual Review of Sociology, Vol. 25; pp. 441-463

Dacin, M. Tina/Marc J. Ventresca/Brent D. Beal (1999): The Embeddedness of Organizations: Dialogue & Directions. In: Journal of Management; Vol. 25; No. 3; pp. 317-356

Douglas, Mary/Steven Ney (1999): Missing Persons: A Critique of Personhood in the Social Sciences. Berkeley; University of California Press

Granovetter, Marc (1985): Economic Action and Social Structure: The Problem of Embeddedness. In: American Journal of Sociology; No. 91; pp. 481-510

Haas, Peter M./Robert O. Keohane/Marc A. Levy (eds.) (1993): Institutions for the Earth. Sources of Effective International Environmental Protection. Cambridge (MA); MIT Press

Häder, Michael/ Hendrik Niebaum (1997): Pfadabhängigkeit in der Umweltpolitik. In: Lutz Metz/Helmut Weidner (eds.): Umweltpolitik und Staatsversagen. Perspektiven und Grenzen der Umweltpolitikanalyse. Festschrift für Martin Jänicke zum 60. Geburtstag. Berlin; Edition sigma; pp. 463-472

Heinelt, Hubert/Tanja Malek/Randall Smith/Annette E. Töller (eds.) (2001): European Union Environment Policy and New Forms of Governance. Aldershot; Ashgate

Lowe, Philip/Judy Clark/Susanne Seymour/Neil Ward (1997): Moralizing the Environment. Countryside change, farming and pollution. London; UCL Press

Macnaghten, Phil/John Urry (1998): Contested Natures. London, Thousand Oaks, New Delhi; Sage

Mann, Dean E. (1991): Environmental Learning in a Decentralized Political World. In: Journal of International Affairs; Vol. 44; No. 2; pp. 301-337

Newson, Malcolm (1997): Land, Water and Development. Sustainable management of river basin systems. 2nd ed.. London/New York; Routledge

Ostrom, Elinor (1990): Governing the Commons: The Evolution of Institutions for Collective Action. Cambridge et al.; Cambridge University Press

The Social Learning Group (2001a): Learning to Manage Global Environmental Risks. A Functional Analysis of Social Responses to Climate Change, Ozone Depletion and Acid Rain. Volume 1. Cambridge (MA); MIT Press

The Social Learning Group (2001b): Learning to Manage Global Environmental Risks. A Functional Analysis of Social Responses to Climate Change, Ozone Depletion and Acid Rain. Volume 2. Cambridge (MA); MIT Press

Young, Oran (1998): The effectiveness of international environmental regimes: a midterm report. In: International Environmental Affairs; No.10, Vol.4, pp.267-289

Young, Oran et al. (1999): Institutional Dimensions of Global Environmental Change. Science Plan; IHDP Report No.9; Bonn

Young, Oran R. (2002): The Institutional Dimensions of Environmental Change. Fit, Interplay, and Scale. Cambridge (MA), London; MIT Press

About the Authors

Heiko Breit (PhD) studied sociology, philosophy and psychology and works at the German Institute for International Educational Research in Frankfurt/Main. His main research interests are the development of justice judgements, responsibility and democratic skills.

Thomas Döring (PhD) studied psychology and worked at the German Institute for International Educational Research in Frankurt/Main, where he conducted research on moral judgments and control beliefs in risk management strategies of everyday conflicts. Now he works at the Adolf-Bender-Centre in St. Wendel, Saarland, Germany.

Florian Dünckmann (PhD) is a Lecturer at the Department of Geography, University of Kiel, Germany. He has written extensively on smallholders and environmental conservation, social conflicts in rural areas and on the implications of international trade for developing countries. He has mainly carried out his research in Latin America, particularly in Brazil.

Lutz H. Eckensberger is Professor of Psychology at the Johann Wolfgang Goethe-University and Director of the German Institute for International Educational Research in Frankfurt/Main. His main fields of research are the role of justice judgements and risk constructions in societal contexts, e.g. environmental conflicts. His wide research interests cover methodological issues, action theory, moral development, cultural and cross-cultural psychology. He has published extensively in the fields of cultural psychology and the development of moral judgement.

Anita Engels received her PhD in Sociology at the University of Bielefeld, Germany. She has worked on global environmental change, both in the context of industrialised and developing countries. Her fields of interest are environmental sociology, social studies of science and technology, globalisation theory, and more recently economic sociology. She is currently involved in research on science globalisation and in a cross-country comparison of the emergence of green markets. From 1999-2001 she was granted a postdoc fellowship at the Center for Environmental Science and Policy at the Institute for International Studies, Stanford University, California. She works at the Institute for Global Society Studies, University of Bielefeld.

Michael Huber is AON Senior Research Fellow at the Centre for Analysis of Risk and Regulation, London School of Economics. He earned his MA at the University of Vienna and his PhD at the European University Institute, Florence. His main research interests include organisational theories, financial risk management - specifically in the insurance sector, risk regulation, EU environmental policies and university issues.

Claudia Mayer holds a doctorate in geography. Her PhD was on "Eco-Label in the world-coffee market - an institutional analysis on the global commodity chain of coffee". She is working currently in the Office for Social and Ecological Standards at the GTZ (Deutsche Gesellschaft für Entwicklungszusammenarbeit GmbH). She has published, among others, on trade policies and social and ecological standards.

Ronald B. Mitchell is an Associate Professor with tenure in the Department of Political Science at the University of Oregon. He earned his PhD in Public Policy at Harvard University in 1992 and was a Visiting Associate Professor at the Center for Environmental Science and Policy from June 1999 through December 2001. He has published a book with MIT Press as well as numerous articles in scholarly journals. His research focuses on the effectiveness of international institutions at influencing the behaviour of states and non-state actors. He teaches courses on international relations theory, international environmental politics, and international regimes.

Timothy Moss read European Studies (BA) at Sussex University before going on to St. Antony's College, Oxford, to complete an MPhil in European History and a DPhil thesis on local politics in Weimar Germany. Since 1993 he has worked as a research associate at the Institute for Regional Development and Structural Planning (IRS) in Erkner, near Berlin, becoming head of the research department "Regional institutional change to protect public goods" in 2003. His research focuses on the current socio-spatial reconfiguration of urban infrastructure systems (for water, sewage, electricity) in response to liberalisation/privatisation and the spatial reorganisation of water management around river basins.

Andreas Obser is assistant professor of international relations and public administration at the University of Potsdam (Germany), associate director of the Master of Global Public Policy (MGPP) Program, executive member of the global public policy institute (gppi), and advisory board member of the International Forest Policy Dialogue (IWRP/GTZ). He received his doctorate from the University of Leipzig (Germany) and studied international politics and public administration at the Universities of Constance (Germany), Stockholm (Sweden) and York (Canada). On behalf of the Federal Ministry of

Economic Cooperation and Development (BMZ) and a number of international organisations, he directed various strategic long-term evaluations on the reform of international development cooperation and strategic management of international programmes. Andreas Obser is head of a research project on "Public Governance in International Multilevel Arrangements" which is funded by the German Research Foundation (DFG), Bonn, Germany.

Verena Sandner is a geographer at the Department of Geography of Kiel University, Germany. She is currently studying for a PhD in social geography with a thesis on the traditional management of marine resources in Central America. For this project she has conducted research in the indigenous regions of Eastern Panama (Kuna) and Caribbean Nicaragua (Miskito) as well as on the Colombian island Providencia with its Afro-Caribbean population. Her fields of research and interest include sustainable development, social geography, indigenous peoples and coastal management.

Bernd Siebenhüner is junior professor for ecological economics and head of the GELENA-research group on social learning and sustainability at Carl von Ossietzky University of Oldenburg. He is also deputy leader of the Global Governance Project at the Potsdam-Institute for Climate Impact Research (PIK). Bernd Siebenhüner holds a Ph.D. from Martin-Luther University Halle-Wittenberg (2000) and Master's degrees in Economics (1994) and Political Science (1995), both at the Free University Berlin. He has been a post-doctoral research fellow at John F. Kennedy School of Government, Harvard University, USA. His research interests include social learning, ecological and environmental economics, environmental policy, corporate environmental management, sustainable development and ecological ethics.

Markus Troja studied political science and communication science at the University of Muenster, Germany. He worked at the Institute for Public Policy and Planning at the Carl von Ossietzky University of Oldenburg, Germany. There he received his Ph.D. in political science. He has been a visiting associate at the Institute for Environmental Negotiation at the University of Virginia, Charlottesville, U.S.A. Currently Markus Troja is senior partner at MEDIATOR, Center for Conflict Management and Research, Oldenburg. He works as a professional mediator in public and business disputes and as a trainer and consultant for business companies and public administrations.

Thomas Widlok received his MSc and PhD in anthropology at the London School of Economics and Political Science where he has also taught. He has been a researcher with the Max Planck Institute for Psycholinguistics, the University of Cologne, the Center for African Areas Studies (Kyoto University) and the Max Planck Institute for Social Anthropology in Halle. Currently he is lecturer in anthropology at the University of Heidelberg. His special fields of interest are comparative hunter-gatherer studies and anthropological theory. He has carried out field research in northern and central Namibia and in north-western Australia and is author of *Living on Mangetti. 'Bushman' autonomy and Namibian independence* (Oxford University Press 1999). His other publications include work in cognitive and linguistic anthropology, on the theory of corporate bodies and numerous articles on southern African and Australian ethnography.